THE CONCERTO

ABRAHAM VEINUS

DOVER PUBLICATIONS, INC.

NEW YORK

Published in Canada by General Publishing Company, Ltd., 30 Lesmill Road, Don Mills, Toronto, Ontario.
Published in the United Kingdom by Constable and Company, Ltd., 10 Orange Street, London WC 2.

This Dover edition, first published in 1963, is a revised republication of the work originally published by Doubleday, Doran and Company in 1945 and by Cassell and Company Limited in 1948.

International Standard Book Number: 0-486-21178-9
Library of Congress Catalog Card Number: 63-19503

Manufactured in the United States of America
Dover Publications, Inc.
180 Varick Street
New York, N. Y. 10014

When this book first appeared it was dedicated to my father. I offer it again to him now with the names of his affectionate grandchildren, Peter and Roger.

Contents

Preface to Dover Edition

IT is generally held, and with reason, that an author is hardly the most reliable person to appeal to for a disinterested appraisal of his own work. Yet the proposal to prepare for republication a book written under difficulties two decades ago is, in effect, just such an appeal. Upon rereading, one discovers much that one would no longer care to say, and perhaps a few things that one is no longer capable of saying quite so well. Neither discovery is conducive to comfort; nor is it any great satisfaction to note either the respects in which one must look askance at one's 'former self, or the respects in which early convictions have in the course of twenty years merely hardened into habit.

To attempt the sort of revision in which one seeks for a continuing contemporaneity with oneself would now entail a new book, and that, for obvious reasons, is best provided by someone else. For one thing, one cannot hope to be both the person one was and the person one now is. (The soldier in Stravinsky's story who tried it came understandably to a bad end.) For another, an alternative and more impersonal notion of how this history ought to be written is best provided by an alternative and more impersonal mind. Taste and judgment have had obviously much to do with the making of this book. However much I may now wish to have once possessed more of clarity and less of expansiveness of expression, and however much I may now regret a certain unbecoming intolerance towards composers and works that did not interest me overly much, it is not at all apparent that the remedy for these deficiencies lies in that remarkable mysticism known as absolute history. For a history along these lines, the usual specialized (and invaluable) literature is available. More so perhaps than when this book was first written, it seems to me that scholarship is neither a retreat from the exercise of taste nor a refuge from the making of a judgment, but the responsible authorization for both the one and the other. A musicologist, one hopes, can be something other than a dreary janitor of music history tidying a magnificent cathedral where none living come to pray.

In the practical business of putting a book together, taste and judgment necessarily express themselves in the overall layout of chapters, and in the character of one's prose. In regard to the former, it still seems sensible to have dealt with the early concerto somewhat sketchily, to have weighted the book heavily towards Mozart, and to have allocated to Beethoven a separate chapter. For the purple prose, I make no apology. One can see such colours as one pleases while reading; and if there are passages which should once have been reconsidered, it does not appear obvious that revising them now into soiled grey or pale lilac would be an improvement.

As for metaphors and reifications, I would use fewer of them now than apparently I once found acceptable. But music is in essence non-verbal, and in an effort to verbalize I would think metaphor is still largely unavoidable. Style of metaphor is essentially a matter of taste and convenience with regard to relative accuracy and relative vividness of description. One's taste may change, but the convenience of metaphor is liable to remain a fixed principle of language. Metaphor as a substitute for precise reasoning in the exact sciences is obviously indefensible. But there is something of common sense lacking in the wholesale decrying of metaphor in descriptive and in historical writing. It is, one hopes, generally understood that in discussing electric currents one is not charting the flow of the Mississippi River, that in analyzing social strata one is not reporting on the superimpositions of igneous on sedimentary rock, that one can look up to someone five inches shorter than we are, and that one can read of concentrates of counterpoint deployed in a sonata design without supposing that this must have happened during the Civil War. Those who profess to be misled by metaphors of this type had best give up reading. There are, after all, for the simple in soul less confusing ways (like a blow on the head) for acquiring a knowledge of relationships.

Clarity is another matter entirely. Such limited alterations as have seemed unavoidable are, in the main, of two kinds: the deletion of phrases and sentences whose meaning now escapes me, and the addition of phrases and sentences to paragraphs that now seem otherwise obscure. The Bibliography of recorded performances through 1947 has been omitted from this edition; any attempt to keep such a list current under present circumstances would be an undertaking far beyond the scope of this revision.

A. V.

Florence
July, 1963

CHAPTER I

The Early Concerto

THE species of music called concerto has a long and richly varied history. Compositions bearing the name, or some recognizable derivative of it, are met with occasionally in the sixteenth century, and abundantly all through the seventeenth. Perhaps nothing is so startling as the wide variety of musical forms—string quartets, ballets, motets, madrigals, masses, and cantatas—which, at one time or another, have been titled concertos. It is more than a linguistic curiosity that a Beethoven violin concerto, a Handel concerto grosso, a Viadana motet, a Monteverdi madrigal, and a Bach cantata, should all have been described by their composers as concertos. The word has manifestly changed in its meaning from one century to another; yet in its most generalized and literal connotation—two or more instruments or voices performing together, i.e. in concert with each other—it has remained unaltered, and in this broad sense has served as a proper description of each of the above-mentioned compositions. By way of illustration, a mid-sixteenth-century fantasia for two lutes by Francesco da Milano refers to the second lute as the concerted or concerto lute (*liuto in concerto*). In its most elementary sense, concerto simply means to play in concert.

Only in a most general sense can the concerto music, so called, of the sixteenth and seventeenth centuries be reckoned the forerunner or even ancestor of the modern instrumental concerto. There is no logically rigid sequence of cause and effect, no inexorable evolution of nerve system and bone structure bridging the three and a half centuries of concerto music from Gabrieli and Viadana to Stravinsky and Schön-berg. Chronology and causality are necessarily secondary considera-tions, for while a family tree can in a general way be established, the line of descent from Viadana to Schönberg unfortunately unfolds itself as the furthest distance and most devious direction between two points. It is more to the point to examine the concerted (concerto) music of the earlier centuries with a view toward isolating certain specific principles and practices, examining the forms in which they flourished, and tracing their maturation to the point where they were able to sustain the ample proportions and the numerous complexities of the modern instrumental concerto. Thus, as a musical form, the madrigal does not lead to the violin concerto; but the principle of composition embodied by Mon-teverdi in those of his madrigals which he titled concertos does reach fulfilment, after proper elaboration and transplantation, in the solo instrumental concerto.

While the word "concerto" means simply to play in concert, in actual musical practice it soon developed the more specific connotation of music designed for concerted performance by contrasted or dis-similar bodies of tone. Thus a collection of motets and madrigals by the Venetian masters Andrea and Giovanni Gabrieli, published in 1587 under the title of *Concerti . . . per voci e stromenti . . .*, comprised com-positions for double chorus and instrumental accompaniment; and in 1595 a similar volume of eight-part motets for double chorus with instrumental accompaniment by Adriano Banchieri was published, en-titled *Ecclesiastical Concertos (Concerti ecclesiastici)*. With Gabrieli the notion of contrast, of dissimilar tonal bodies pitted against each other, was established as the essence of a concerto relationship. Not only the polarity of voice and instrument—sufficient in itself to establish a concerto relationship—but the possibilities of two sharply differentiated choral bodies were also investigated. In the Gabrieli *Concerti* of 1587 there is, for example, a twelve-part motet, *Angelus ad Pastores*, in which a six-part chorus of low voices alternates with, and sings in concert against, a six-part chorus of high voices. This differentiation in registers and the massing of a powerful body of sound in each proved a fruitful tech-nique. Earlier than the Gabrieli *Concerti* there is an eight-part *Te Deum Laudamus* (1571) by Leonhart Schroeter similarly divided between a high and a low chorus of four voices each, and in the *Cantiones Sacrae*

Octo Vocum (*Sacred Songs for Eight Voices*) by Samuel Scheidt (1620) there are several examples of the same procedure.[1]

The differentiation of tonal bodies or tone colour was basically sufficient to define a concerto relationship for the seventeenth century. Thus in a motet or a mass the simple addition of one or more instruments to the vocal forces was reason enough for the appearance of such terms as *concerto*, *concertare*, *concertato* in the title of a composition. The mingling of voice and instrument was by no means a seventeenth-century discovery. It was practised as far back as the Greeks, flourished among the troubadours, and was well entrenched in sixteenth- and seventeenth-century practice outside the narrow confines of compositions specifically called concertos. Simple contrast of tone colour, as a definition of a musical form, is too generalized to have much meaning. However, as a basic musical procedure it provided a mine from which enterprising composers could extract the manifold possibilities of concerted music, a rich natural resource which sustained a century of music makers. The acceptance of this principle of contrast, rivalry, opposition, was like the acceptance of a ground theme upon which composers for a century built ever more specific and carefully defined variations.

One of the first important steps toward enriching the meaning of contrast or rivalry between tonal bodies appears in the *Ecclesiastical Concertos* (*Concerti ecclesiastici*) of Ludovico Viadana, the first volume of which was published in 1602. In contrast to the earlier concertos of Gabrieli and Banchieri (works for massive double chorus with instrumental accompaniment), Viadana pared the concerto principle down to one, two, three, four voices singing to an instrument (the organ); and in so doing cleared the field for the monodic, rather than the polyphonic, style, introducing the possibilities of pitting a solo voice (rather than a massed chorus) against an instrumental tutti. However, if Viadana opened a new avenue for concerted music, he was loath to exploit its advantages. The handling of the solo voice is technically timid. Running scale passages, demanding a modicum of virtuoso ability, are all but completely absent. As befits an ecclesiastical motet,

[1] Praetorius in his *Syntagma musicum* (Vol. III, 1619), the famous compendium of contemporary musical practice, declares that a *Concert* (concerto) exists precisely when a low chorus and a high chorus oppose, or sound together with, each other.

voice and organ move in beautiful and dignified concert with, rather than against, each other.

This effort not to aggravate the differences between the concerted forces has been the hall-mark of many a composer contributing a new direction to the evolution of the concerto. Later in the century Corelli's prodigious accomplishment in establishing the concerto grosso as a vital instrumental concept also took shape as an effort to equate the solo group of instruments (concertino) with the tutti mass of the orchestra (concerto grosso), and to assure each group equal and undifferentiated participation in the development of the same musical material. A like timidity is manifest in the introduction of the concerto principle into the madrigal and the mass. The first thought in both cases was to instruct that instruments could replace some of the vocal parts at the discretion, or in accordance with the desires, of the performers. No especial account was taken of the specific technical endowments of the instruments, which simply substituted for, or re-enforced, the voice parts verbatim.

In the case of the mass this seems to have been, at the outset at least, more a matter of practical necessity than of deliberate choice. It has been conjectured that in some vocal choirs, where unfortunately one of the voice parts was either wholly missing or only weakly represented, replacement or re-enforcement by instruments was a simple expedient for securing the proper number and strength of voice parts called for by the composer. The use of instruments to support the voices was therefore a matter of choice. Thus in a group of masses for eight voices published in 1596, the composer, Ippolito Baccusi, instructed that instruments might be so joined to the voices; and several decades later (1631) Merula likewise gave performers the option of rendering his two- to twelve-part masses and psalms either with or without instruments (*con istromenti e senza se piace*). In the mass, as in other vocal forms, the union of voices and instruments was sufficient reason for such a phrase as *Messa concertati* which appears throughout the seventeenth century in the titles of masses by Banchieri, Grandi, Rovetta, and others.

The focusing of attention on the solo voice supported by an instrument and the transition from a polyphonic to a monodic style soon made their way into the august domain of the poly-voiced, unaccompanied mass. Here too, Viadana helped prepare the groundwork with his *Missa Dominicalis* for solo voice (soprano or tenor) and organ, published in the second volume (1607) of his *Ecclesiastical Concertos*. As in the motet concertos in this compilation, the solo makes little compromise with its ecclesiastical dignity. It is a solo only by virtue of the fact that it stands alone, not by any assumption of the virtuoso embellishments which adorn or disfigure the solo concerto of a later century. A bolder awareness of the potentialities of a solo voice even within a form so dignified as a mass is evident in a *Kyrie* (1597) of Giovanni Gabrieli, in which the upper voice is drawn sharply away from the remaining body and permitted to indulge in extensive and eminently unecclesiastical coloratura.

The development of the solo part in a virtuoso fashion is obviously, from the viewpoint of the instrumental concerto, a matter of some importance. The secular madrigal will serve as a more pointed illustration than music for the church, for once the liberation of the solo voice is accomplished there are no ecclesiastical inhibitions restricting its freedom of movement. Significantly the liberation of the solo voices was accomplished via the introduction of instruments into the unaccompanied, poly-voiced madrigal, and the consequent establishment of a concerto relationship between two contrasted bodies.[1] With characteristic clarity, Monteverdi, in his sixth book of madrigals (1614) made the necessary distinction between the traditional five-part unaccompanied madrigals and those with instrumental accompaniment. The latter he specifically marked to be sung in concert to a clavicembalo (*concertato nel clavicembalo*), and carefully differentiated in style from the unaccompanied compositions. The concerted madrigals contain extensive passages for solo voice with instrumental accompaniment. The element of contrast is no longer, as with Viadana, a matter of the simple polarity of voice and instrument. The solo voice is well supplied with rapid scale runs and figurations, and otherwise enabled to acquit itself in a thoroughly soloistic and virtuoso fashion. In addition these extensive virtuoso solo passages alternate with relatively more staid

[1] The introduction of instruments into the unaccompanied, poly-voiced madrigal was attended with the same halfhearted option which characterized their appearance in the mass. Thus Quagliati in the preface to his first madrigal book (1608) and Rontani in his *Gli Affetuosi* (1610) placed the question of using instruments at the discretion of the performers.

sections for full vocal choir, in a manner quite analogous in principle to the later instrumental concerto with its alternation between restless solo figurations and a restful, sonorous orchestral tutti. The procedure is carried still further in the seventh book of madrigals (1619) which Monteverdi frankly titles *Concerto*. The coloratura for the solo voice is even more elaborate and is set against a greatly enriched instrumental tutti (as many as nine instruments). The generalized definition of a concerto as a contrast between dissimilar elements here approaches (as nearly as possible within the confines of music still basically vocal) a specifically modern meaning. The seventh madrigal book casts a spotlight upon the rivalry between a virtuoso solo (voice) and a relatively full-scored orchestral tutti. It is this comparatively modern practice which Monteverdi designates, in the title of his work, as a *Concerto*.

There is little point, so far as history of the instrumental concerto is concerned, in pursuing in further detail the ramifications of the seventeenth-century vocal concerto. It is sufficient to note that the concerto principle evolved from a mere playing together (Francesco da Milano) to a motet for double chorus with instrumental accompaniment (Gabrieli, Banchieri) embodying the essential element of contrasted bodies of tone.[1] Viadana pared this down to a solo voice with instru-

---

[1] Our own word "concert" (French *concert;* German *konzert;* Italian *concerto*) shows a similar duality in meaning between agreement (playing together) and contention (rivalry of dissimilar elements). To act in concert, meaning to act together, is a familiar phrase. However, concert, in a now obsolete sense, has been used as a synonym of dispute or contest, e.g. "concert the Truth of those Passages," meaning to contradict them. (See *New English Dictionary:* Concert, 1689, Apol. Failures Walker's Acc. 11.) Likewise concertation (obsolete) meaning contention or disputation, e.g. "A concertation or striving between virtue and voluptuositie." (See *New English Dictionary:* Concertation.)

The musical uses of the word "consort" show the same difference in meaning. (Originally consort was an erroneous representation of the French *concert* and the Italian *concerto*, and was gradually replaced during the eighteenth century by the modern form concert.) A group of similar instruments playing together was called a consort, e.g. a consort of viols. An ensemble composed of contrasted instruments (winds and strings, recorders and viols) was called a "mixed consort." The title of one of Thomas Morley's publications will serve to illustrate the use of the word: "The First Booke of Consort Lessons, made by divers exquisite Authors, for sixe Instruments to play together . . . ." (1599).

Both concert and consort were also used in the modern sense of a gathering for the performance of music. Modern English usage is unique in that we now distinguish between a concert (public musical performance) and a concerto (the musical form). One word is used for both concepts in French, German, and Italian.

ment, and Monteverdi brought the meaning of the word still closer to later instrumental practice by liberating the solo voice as a virtuoso part alternating with a relatively full orchestral tutti. The remaining vocal concertos of the seventeenth century are variations on this line of development. It remains simply to remark that among the Heinrich Schütz *Kleine geistliche Konzerte* (1636) and the Johann Hermann Schein *Opella nova, geistliche Konzerte* (1618, 1627) there are already tokens of the range and subtlety of expression which the most elementary applications of a concerto idea can yield in the work of men of evident genius. In the little Schütz concertos (solo songs and vocal ensembles with organ) the solo voice hardly achieves virtuoso status, while the organ is treated only occasionally to a solo interlude (symphonia). Yet this limitation suggests nothing of the sheer drama which Schütz realizes through such a brief burst of massive organ sound as, for example, in his setting of the Psalm *Eile mich Gott zu erretten*. The extent to which concerto principles provided the groundwork for church composition in more massive forms is evident in Schütz's oratorio *Historia der Geburt Jesu Christi*, his *Psalm XXIV*, his *Magnificat*, and such sacred pieces as the *Gesang der drei Männer im feurigen Ofen*, and *Es erhub sich ein Streit in Himmel*: magnificent tapestries of tone, sonorously coloured by wind and string choirs, richly woven with solo voices and massed choruses, all alternating with, or thrust head on against, each other.

Yet if the principles of concerto music—contrasted tonal bodies, solo-tutti rivalry, virtuoso display—were, in substance, outlined in the vocal concertos of the seventeenth century, before these general concepts could function as the basis of large instrumental structures like the concerto grosso or the violin concerto, transplantation to the soil of pure instrumental music was essential. Experience in the particularized problems of instrumental writing is a prerequisite for the maturing of large-scale instrumental forms. Thus a violin concerto might, in principle, look back to the coloratura solos in a Monteverdi madrigal, but as a matter of practical composition its specific instrumental technique would rest necessarily upon the achievements of solo violin music, rather than upon vocal coloratura.

As elaborated by Gabrieli, the instrumental canzon and sonata displayed a division of the ensemble into contrasted instrumental groupings. In effect, the continual playing off of one against the other, as in Gabrieli's *Sonata piano e forte*, produced a kind of concerto for two instrumental choirs which alternated with each other and then merged together in massive orchestral tuttis. (The sort of concerto technique, adapted from the motet for double chorus, appeared anew, after a period of quiescence, in the concerto grosso.) Individual solos also appeared occasionally. The soprano instrument in each choir stepped forward embellished with runs and figurations, converting the canzon momentarily into a double concerto for two solo instruments and orchestra. Or else, a few solo instruments would engage in a brief fugal passage, answered by a massive homophonic passage for all instruments together.

As might be expected, the instrumental soloist eventually made his way into the opera orchestra. For centuries the opera has been the favourite market-place for the virtuoso to display his wares. During the opera, the prima donnas would brook little competition from their compatriots in the pit, but in the overture the solo instruments might safely indulge themselves to their hearts' content. Thus, in the Venetian opera symphony (overture) in the latter half of the seventeenth century, trumpeters flourished forth in brilliant solos and duets against the more thickly massed, more slowly paced, orchestral body. Sacred music as well as secular felt the virtuoso's presence, and in the church sonatas and symphonies, no less than in the operatic overtures, trumpet solos and duets were by no means uncommon. Even more than the Venetian opera, the French opera under Lully contributed significantly to the maturing of a concerto orchestration. In the Lully overtures, chaconnes, and ballet movements the alternation of a woodwind trio (two flutes, or two oboes, and bassoon) with a large string orchestra offered an instrumentation pattern significant for the concerto grosso.

While orchestral music elaborated the manifold problems of scoring for massed choirs of instruments and established certain orchestral procedures upon which the eighteenth-century concerto could safely rest, the solo literature of the seventeenth century accomplished the essential task of exploring and expanding the technical possibilities of the individual instruments. The story of its accomplishment need not be followed in detail. Suffice it to say that in Carlo Farina's *Capriccio stravagante* (1627) such items in the violinist's stock in trade as pizzicato, tremolo, double and triple stopping, col legno and sul ponticello are all exploited; while in the matter of range Marco Uccellini's fourth solo violin sonata (1649) already achieves a high F ′ ′ ′. In this general connection the activities of the world famous seventeenth-century instrument makers—the Amati, Guarneri, and Stradivari—prove a factor of considerable importance.

It is interesting to note in passing that in the music for the organ, once the instrument was freed from the trammels of vocal part writing, an elementary concerto style made itself immediately evident. The peculiar characteristic of the instrument is that it can perform with equal ease either as a monumental tutti or as a brilliant solo. Thus in the Gabrieli *Intonations for Organ* (*Intonazioni d'organo*), published in 1593, and in the organ tablature book of Leonhard Kleber (1524) we find compositions in which the solo-tutti concerto relationship is expressed in a continual interplay of heavy, sustained chords (tutti) and lively running scale passages (solo). Solo lute music likewise offers many similar examples.

Set between orchestral and solo instrumental music, the chamber music of the seventeenth century (concerted sonatas for several instruments) appears as a middle ground for a kind of uneasy compromise between the two. A sonata for three or four instruments was not massive enough as a concerted unit to take over bodily the principles of orchestral scoring, nor could it, without incurring self-destruction, freely indulge the individual instruments in soloistic distractions. It vacillated between concerted and solo music and out of its dilemma brought forward a curious and charming little concerto form. Concerted movements in which all instruments, submerging their virtuoso proclivities, participated jointly were relieved by solo movements dominated by each instrument in turn. It must have seemed an effective compromise, for examples are found throughout the century. Thus in a Valentini sonata for violin, cornettino, bassoon, and trombone (1639) each instrument steps forward with a solo movement of its own; and as late as 1694-96 (well past the appearance of the concerto grosso) a Buxtehude sonata for two violins and viola da gamba begins and ends with concerted movements enclosing between them a group of solo movements, one each for each of the instruments supported by the cembalo. The form of the work as a whole is necessarily loose and episodic, even more so than analogous modern jazz pieces in which each instrument comes forward in turn for its lick. A further contribution of the chamber music of the seventeenth century lay in the rich trio sonata literature for two violins and continuo. Proven to be an eminently stable instrumental unit, it was assimilated bodily as the concertino choir in the Italian concerto grosso.

It remains then to note briefly the various types of instrumental music which during the sixteenth and seventeenth centuries went by the name of concerto. The description of the second lute in a fantasia for two lutes (*c.* 1550) by Francesco da Milano as *liuto in concerto* has already been mentioned. In much the same elementary sense—concerted performance by undifferentiated tonal bodies—Diego Ortiz, the eminent sixteenth-century theorist, speaks of a *Concierto de* (4, 5) *vihuelas,* 1553; and early in the seventeenth century there appears in Melii's *Intavolatura di Liuto* (published 1616) three canzons and a corrente *concertate a due Liuti* (concerted for two lutes). Shortly thereafter, in the seventh sonata for violin and bassoon contained in Dario Castello's *Sonate concertate* (1621) the word *"concertate"* appears in the sense of a concert of dissimilar instruments.

Toward the close of the seventeenth century the word "concerto" appears in a series of compositions by Torelli, Taglietti, Felice dall' Abaco, and others which are perhaps best described as orchestral sonatas. They show no differentiation in instrumental tone colour and are restricted to a very occasional use of solo interludes. In the *concerti a quattro* contained in Torelli's Op. 5 (1692) there are no solo episodes whatever. The first violin is given more prominence than the remaining strings, which act simply as an accompaniment. The preface to Torelli's *Concerti musicali,* Op. 6 (1698), indicates the rarity of solo interludes in this kind of composition, as well as the orchestral fashion in which these string quartets were probably performed. "Note, that wherever in the Concerto you find the word *solo* written," he writes, "it is to be played by one violin alone. For the remainder, the parts may be doubled, or even re-enforced by three or four instruments apiece." Few of the twelve concertos in this collection have solo episodes at all, and when they do occur they cover no more than four to twenty measures at a stretch. Since most of the concertos are content with straight four-part writing throughout, and since the parts may be taken by as many as four instruments apiece, we have in effect a sonata for string orchestra in which the word "concerto" applies principally to the concerted manner of performance. Likewise in Taglietti's *Concerti a quattro*, Op. 4 (1699), the division into solo and tutti occurs only once in the entire collection; while in Abaco's *Concerti da chiesa*, Op. 2 (published *c.* 1712-14), only two of the concertos show explicitly defined solo interludes.[1]

The title of Abaco's collection, *Concerti da chiesa* (*Church Concertos*), indicates the distinction which prevailed between church and chamber style. The church concerto, as might be expected, was rather severe, with a predilection for fugue writing and little patience with soloistic display. The chamber concerto indulged itself in charming dance movements and was, indeed, little more than a sophisticated dance suite. Most of the works just discussed are of the pure church variety, although the Taglietti opus shows the mixture of both elements which soon replaced this duality in style. The distinction was, however, carried over into the mature concerto grosso and we shall meet with it again in the next chapter.

[1] See A. Schering: *Geschichte des Instrumentalkonzerts*, page 37.

CHAPTER II

The Concerto Grosso

IN Alessandro Scarlatti's opera *Telemaco* (produced in 1718) Minerva is accompanied by a small body of strings seated in the chariot in which supposedly she makes her descent from heaven. This small string group, acting as a unit apart from the main body of strings in the orchestra, is in consequence called the "concerto" of Minerva (*concerto di Minerva*). Similarly, the *concerto di oubuoè*, which makes its appearance in several Scarlatti scores, is a unit of two oboes and bassoon "regarded as a single mass of sound" (Dent).[1] The scoring of Scarlatti's *Tigrane*, for example, divides the orchestra into a string group, two horns, and a *concerto di oubuoè*. In this usage, the word *concerto* refers simply to a group of instruments concerted together and operating as a unit.

In a concerto grosso, the orchestra is divided into two such concerted units unequal in size and strength, one called the *concerto grosso*[2] or large concerted unit (*grosso* for short), the other the *concertino* or small concerted unit. In each unit, the bass complex is called the *continuo* (*basso continuo*), comprising at a minimum a keyboard instrument (harpsi-

---

[1] The examples from the Scarlatti operas are drawn from E. J. Dent's *Alessandro Scarlatti*.

[2] The term "concerto grosso" occurs as early as 1591 in the preface to Malvezzi's *Intermedii et Concerti*, where it denotes the body of instruments accompanying the voices. The term "ripieno" is used as early as 1602 by Viadana in his *Concerti ecclesiastici* to indicate the full tutti tone of the organ accompanying the solo voice.

chord) for the realization of the figured or unfigured bass, and a melody instrument ('cello) for the support of the bass line. Other instruments may be added to the continuo complex, either by specification or optionally as the occasion warrants. The *grosso*, or large concerted unit, is in effect the main orchestral mass. Customarily it comprises the two violin sections, the viola section and the 'cello-continuo complex, with several performers per string part. The *concertino* is in effect a solo unit (one performer per part) comprising customarily two violin parts and a continuo ('cello and harpsichord). These are normative descriptions: as matters stand, for example, in a concerto grosso by Corelli. But wide variations from the norm in the composition of both *grosso* and *concertino* are not only possible, but commonly encountered. The concerto grosso rests then upon such strategies of composition as may be called into play by such a division of tonal forces.

The juxtaposition of two such unequal choirs brought into play a whole category of orchestral effects. The grosso was necessarily a heavier, louder, more deliberate body of tone; the concertino, lighter, softer, and more agile. The continual shifting from choir to choir produced a fascinating chiaroscuro of dynamics, weight, and movement; and when the concertino was taken over by the wind trio against a grosso of strings, a rich and easy source of colour contrast was instantly brought to hand. Clearly this was too fruitful a technique to remain the exclusive property of one instrumental form; and so we find the concerto grosso as a principle of orchestration applied in such diverse fields as the opera, the sacred cantata and the oratorio.

The first great figure to dominate concerto grosso composition was Arcangelo Corelli (1653-1713). As his dates indicate, Corelli lived through an era which saw the development of vital instrumental techniques, forms, and styles. The extension of the boundaries of instrumental technique, the foundation of a new concerto design, and the necessary creation of a new instrumental style were the dominant problems of his lifetime, and to each of these closely interwoven developments Corelli contributed in a manner highly individual and at the same time sufficiently generalized to serve as an historical contribution of the first importance.

In the field of instrumental technique Corelli's twelve solo sonatas for violin and continuo, Op. 5, maintained their reputation even to-

ward the close of the eighteenth century as the basis "on which all good
schools for the violin have since been founded" (Burney). Corelli's
treatment of the violin, however, was not marked by any concession
to virtuoso showmanship. The concerti grossi, Op. 6, for example,
show a rather conservative approach to intricate passage work and to
the exploitation of the higher reaches of the instrument. His contemporary Gasparini hailed him as the "supreme virtuoso of the violin,"
yet from his music one would conjecture that Corelli was much more
the conscientious musician to whom proportion and restraint were
qualities more basic than brilliance and display. It would seem that even
as a performer he was unaccustomed to dealing with difficulties, for the
story goes that in the performance of a Scarlatti masque Corelli dis-
graced himself by failing to sight-read an awkward violin part which
called for a high F.[1] Corelli's contribution to violin technique rested,
therefore, not so much on the discovery of new effects as in establishing
a reasonable, typical, and in this sense fundamental treatment of the
instrument upon which later composers were able to expand.

In the crystallization of the concerto grosso Corelli participated more
vitally than any of his contemporaries. His own work—not published
until 1712—appeared later than the concerto grosso publications of
A. Scarlatti, Lorenzo Gregori, Torelli, and Valentini. Yet it would seem
from Georg Muffat's eyewitness account that Corelli's concerti grossi
were heard in Rome at least as early as 1682, a date considerably prior
to the concerto grosso publications of his contemporaries.[2] However,
regardless of priority, the essential importance of his work lies in the

[1] The story has come down to us from the famous eighteenth-century historian, Charles Burney, to whom it was recounted by "a very particular and
intelligent friend," who in turn heard it from Geminiani.

[2] The publication date of Corelli's Op. 6 is usually given as 1712. Dr. Alfred
Einstein finds reason to believe that the opus could not have been issued earlier
than the autumn of 1713. He is further of the opinion that the concertos are a
posthumous publication, issued by Roger of Amsterdam in 1714, a year after
Corelli's death. We have no certain evidence to guide us in establishing the
date of composition, apart from Muffat's report that he heard Corelli conduct
concerti grossi in Rome in 1682. The publication dates of the earliest concerti
grossi are: Lorenzo Gregori 1698, Torelli 1709, Valentini 1710, and Alessandro
Scarlatti's English publication which appeared probably in the first decade of
the eighteenth century. Schering reports two works by Alessandro Stradella
entitled *Sinfonie a più Instrumenti* composed throughout in concerto grosso
style and technique. The Stradella works date most probably from the 1670's.

ease with which he handled the imbalances of the new concerto technique. His procedures may seem a shade safe: he limited himself to string scoring, relied heavily upon an alternation pattern of concertino and grosso, and rarely considered the venturesome possibilities that might arise from disrupting the self-contained unity of the concertino group and releasing its components as individual solos. Yet his work had the singular and most vital merit of establishing, more effectively than the work of any predecessor, the sense for what was natural and hence normative in concerto grosso writing. An accomplishment of this kind bespeaks an exceptional order of creativity, for the rectification of imbalances implicit in the juxtaposition of unequal tonal forces, is hardly to be accomplished by rule. In the last analysis, it is a matter made to seem natural by refinement of ear, and normative by the judgment of genius. The old sixteenth-century rivalry of contrasted choirs wore its new instrumental dress with natural dignity and a well-tailored ease. The numerous details of form, style, and technique fell into place with a self-evident logic which profoundly impressed his contemporaries. The German composer, Georg Muffat, bore witness, in the preface to his own *Concerti grossi*, to the "great pleasure and wonder" of hearing a Corelli concerto grosso for the first time. It was Corelli's models which helped establish the new concerto practice throughout Italy and Europe. Moreover, once norms are well understood, as they are in Corelli's concerti grossi, the possibilities for experimental deviation are almost automatically indicated. In subsequent examples by other composers, one finds expected variations in the size of the concertino unit, in the kind of instruments comprising both the concertino and the grosso (wind and string mixtures, for example) and a freer approach towards disassembling the concertino unit into its individual solo components.

Biographically speaking, there is not much to relate concerning Corelli. Of the earlier part of his life there is little known. It is reported that he travelled in Germany (Munich, Hanover, Heidelberg), although the accuracy of this report is doubtful. Likewise it is reported that he visited Paris in 1672, and this report also cannot be given much credence. We do know that he established a prodigious reputation for himself both as a performer upon the violin and as a composer; and that his talents won him the patronage of Cardinal Pietro Ottoboni, in whose palace Corelli lived (with certain intermissions) until his death. We know that he worked on several occasions with Alessandro Scarlatti, and with Handel; and that the latter is said to have remarked of him that "He [Corelli] likes nothing better than seeing pictures without paying for it, and saving money." As a matter of fact Corelli did leave, after his death, a sizable collection of paintings and a very considerable sum of money.

His music retained its popularity for many decades after his death, and as Hawkins tells us in his *History of Music* (1777), "all that heard it became sensible of its effects; of this there is no better proof than that, amidst all the innovations which the love of change had introduced, it continued to be performed and was heard with delight in churches, in theatres, at public solemnities and festivities in all the cities of Europe for near forty years." The fact that the popularity of Corelli's music has extended from "near forty years" to near two hundred and fifty is the simplest and profoundest testament to his simple and profound genius.

The first eight of Corelli's concerti grossi, Op. 6, are church concertos, the last four chamber concertos. The stylistic distinction between the two which has already been noted points further to the interesting fact that a form which we have come to regard as pure concert music should have had, at one time, a place of importance in the church ceremonial. Organ preludes and interludes had long been essential elements in the church service. With the growth of pure instrumental music and with the decline of Italian organ art after the death of Frescobaldi, chamber ensembles and larger orchestral formations pre-empted the position of the organ. Limited at first to canzonas and church sonatas, the high mass in time admitted the most varied kind of instrumental fare. At the high mass for the coronation of Karl VI in Frankfort (1711), for example, in addition to four motets with instrumental accompaniment, three instrumental concertos were allotted a place in the ceremonial: a 'cello concerto after the Te Deum, a violin concerto after the communion, and a concerted symphony (orchestral sonata) with trumpets as a finale. In all probability the Corelli church concertos not only were performed in church but were intended as music proper for specific occasions. The eighth concerto, for example, bears the explicit designation "concerto composed for the night of the nativity" (the famous *Christmas* concerto).

In our present-day concert-hall renditions there has been a tendency to think of the concerto grosso either as an orchestral miniature or as an enlarged chamber music. We hear the concerto grosso literature sometimes in modernized arrangements and transcriptions which rest on the assumption that the instinctive nobility of the music, its rolling and sonorous harmonies, are in need of more substantial orchestral embodiment than the composers of the period were able to provide. In part the assumption is correct, for this music should be rendered with a sense for structural magnificence and tonal splendour. It is worth noting, however, that the composers of the period were not as ill-equipped as we might imagine. Corelli, for example, is reported on one occasion to have led a string orchestra of one hundred and fifty performers.

In style and in musical structure the Corelli concertos are models of quiet dignity and sober repose. His harmonies are sonorous and full, applied like warm flesh tones over a perceptible framework of well-joined bone and muscle. His melodic units are usually simple and brief. Clarity and proportion are his guiding principles, and concertino and grosso are meticulously equalized as factors in the formal structure. With rare exceptions, the concertino acts as a single unit, putting forward the melodic thesis of the movement, while every few measures the grosso joins in adding deliberation and weight to the dissertation. Only in the chamber concertos do individual instruments step forward to an appreciable degree. In the twelfth concerto grosso the first violin steps out of the concertino unit and dominates the music as a virtuoso solo. This tentative and exceptional incursion into the domain of the solo concerto was heavily exploited by later composers, notably Vivaldi. However, even in the church concertos there is an occasional concession to chamber style. The final allegro of the first concerto grosso, for example, is really a concerto for two violins and string orchestra. The 'cello is dropped from the concertino group and is used only to re-enforce the periodic re-entry of the grosso, while the abbreviated concertino enjoys in consequence a greater measure of soloistic freedom. The modification is worth mentioning, for it is in essence the principle of Giuseppe Torelli's concerto grosso style. The posthumously published concerti grossi of Torelli (1709) are in reality double concertos. Within the concertino unit the two violins hold an aloof and independent discourse between themselves, while the 'cello provides a perfunctory continuo accompaniment. With Torelli, the concertino is no longer a democratic unit in which all three instruments are levied and rewarded alike, but assumes the character of an accompanied solo duet. No longer as in Corelli do concertino and grosso necessarily share the same melodic material. The just proportion and thematic unity, which in Corelli bind concertino and grosso together, are relinquished by Torelli in favour of a more pronounced solo-tutti relationship and a greater freedom in form.

With Corelli's work as a foundation, the concerto grosso spread rapidly to other countries. Muffat, impressed with the music he had heard in Rome, carried the new gospel back with him to Germany; while two of Corelli's pupils, Geminiani and Locatelli, expounded their master's principles, each in his own highly individual fashion, in England and Holland respectively.

Geminiani (c. 1674-1762) is one of the singularly unfortunate composers whose restless and original music was blessed neither by the wholehearted approbation of his contemporaries nor by the vindication of posterity. Little is known of his early life beyond the fact that he was born in Lucca about 1674, that he studied the violin in Milan with Carlo Ambrogio Lunati, the hunchback ("Il gobbo"), and subsequently appeared in Rome as a pupil of Corelli and possibly also of Alessandro Scarlatti. Prior to his appearance in London in 1714 he conducted the orchestra at Naples (1711) where his failure was supposedly due—the story is again one of Burney's secondhand accounts—to his wild and erratic beat, "his tempo rubato, and other unexpected accelerations and relaxations of measure" which threw the orchestra into confusion. His first reputation on English soil was made by a collection of twelve violin sonatas with harpsichord and bass (Op. 1, 1716) whose difficulties few violinists in England were able to master. Thus from the very first there is a distinct cleavage between master and pupil. Corelli, in his violin sonatas, had been content to standardize his violin technique on a rather conservative basis. Geminiani, by far the greater virtuoso of the two, emphasized the setting and the solution of new technical problems. Similarly, with respect to the concerto grosso, the Corellian ideal expressed itself in symmetry of form, proportion between unequal choirs, and a modest approach to melodic and harmonic invention. After paying tribute to his master by publishing the Corelli violin sonatas as concerti grossi in an arrangement of his own,

Geminiani moved forward in a new and, to his way of thinking, a more significant direction. He enlarged the concertino trio into a string quartet by adding a solo viola; not so much for the sake of a new sonority as to secure ample room in which to work out his elaborate polyphonic ideas. His melodies are characterized by a restless chromaticism, his harmonic structure by an experimental and progressive interest in modulation. There is in his music that curious and compelling mixture of austerity and passion which arises whenever a bold imagination labours within the confines of a rigorous polyphonic technique. His constant interest in extending the boundaries of instrumental music led him to publish revised editions of his work in which further intricacies of counterpoint and ornamentation were added to an already complex score. He had a frank interest in experimentation and sought to codify his findings in such theoretical works as his *Guida Armonica* (*Guide to Harmony*), his *Art of Playing the Violin*, and his *Treatise on Good Taste*.

While Geminiani enjoyed considerable reputation during his lifetime as a composer, teacher, violin virtuoso, and, incidentally, as a collector of paintings, his music was unfortunately measured by Corellian standards and found wanting in proportion, refinement, and repose. Critics from his day to our own, with a few notable exceptions, have been content with variations upon Dr. Burney's original dictum. "As a musician," wrote the eighteenth-century historian, "he was certainly a great master of harmony, and very useful to our country in his day; but though he had more variety of modulation, and more skill in diversifying his parts than Corelli, his melody was even inferior, and there is frequently an irregularity in his measures and phraseology, and a confusion in the effect of the *whole*, from the too great business and dissimilitude of the several parts, which gives to each of his compositions the effect of a rhapsody or extemporaneous flight, rather than a polished and regular production." Burney was perhaps too close a contemporary of Geminiani and too obsessed with a veneration for the honourable dead, to do justice to the vibrant experimental spirit that enlivens Geminiani's music.

Pietro Locatelli (1693-1764), another pupil of Corelli, carried the concerto grosso to Holland and in his very first publication (*Concerti grossi*, Op. 1, 1721) revealed, like Geminiani, a thoroughly individual approach. Not only had Corelli's two pupils wandered far from the precepts of their master, but each struck out in a different direction

and emerged as polar opposites of one another. Both pupils expanded
the framework of the form by extending the concertino group from a
trio to a string quartet. (Locatelli even made use of a concertino quintet with two violas, against a five-part string orchestra.) But their
motivations were apparently quite different. Geminiani found the
extra viola essential in working out a four-part fugue, while Locatelli
sought a richer tonal surface upon which to project his sweet and delicately figurated violin solos. Both, likewise, were violin virtuosi of the
first water, and both were sound enough as composers to forego bravura display in their concerti grossi. Each was a romantic after his own
fashion; Geminiani in his search for new harmonic resources, Locatelli
in his elaboration of a discreetly decorative melancholy. Geminiani was
one of the last masters of the rigorous instrumental fugue; while
Locatelli, who was certainly no tyro at the art of fugue-making, emerged
as one of the first masters of what the nineteenth century subsequently
celebrated as "poetic expression."

With Vivaldi, Handel, and Bach the concerto grosso reached the
peak of its development, for not only did their creations contain the
most enduring music produced in this form, but in their hands the form
itself yielded virtually every last resource inherent in it. Vivaldi, the
first of the three to publish concerti grossi, concerned himself with a
variety of techniques not in themselves new. The concertino was alternately expanded to four solo violins and contracted to two. A richer
and more expressive tone colouring was achieved by using winds as
well as strings. The concertino unit was disrupted and the several
instruments released as individual solos, while in the ripieno the separate
parts (violas or 'cellos) were likewise occasionally brought forward as
solo voices. He regarded the concerto grosso not only as a medium for
absolute music but made an interesting attempt to transform it into a
vehicle for the most explicit kind of programmatism. The net result is
usually music of great beauty and always music bearing the indelible
imprint of a keen and powerful imagination.

Vivaldi was no innovator in the use of any of these techniques. Like
Corelli, he sought, in a sense, to codify the instrumental resources
already at hand; but the range of his inquiry was wider, and the variety
of techniques which he incorporated into the concerto grosso produced
inevitable dislocations which he solved by boldly adapting the form to

the individual requirements of each technique. In consequence there is no composer, with the exception of Bach, who exhibits a wider variety of form in the concerto grosso and, since his solutions were successful, so unified and personal a style.

In his use of a concertino of four violins, for example, Vivaldi had before him precedents established in a comparatively limited fashion by Fontana, Legrenzi, Domenico Gabrielli, Torelli, and many others. However, in his concerto grosso for four violins, Op. 3, No. 10 (the same concerto which Bach subsequently arranged for four claviers and string orchestra), Vivaldi's treatment of this unusual concertino group marked an important advance in the direction of the future solo concerto. In the opening allegro each of the violins steps forward in turn as a solo instrument, quite after the fashion of the Valentini and Buxtehude sonatas mentioned in the preceding chapter. The episodic character of these earlier pre-concerto efforts is, however, eliminated in Vivaldi by a closer structural unity which obtains among the solo episodes themselves and between each of these episodes and the tutti passages for concertino and grosso combined. The solo episodes grow out of the context of the music and are not detachable movements as was the case in earlier compositions of this kind. In this sense the Vivaldi concerto grosso form emerges as a halfway house on the road to the solo concerto.

Similarly variety in instrumental tone colour had been known before Vivaldi, yet no concerto composer of the period so assiduously explored the nuances of varying instrumental combinations. The collection of approximately two hundred and fifty concertos in Turin attributed to Vivaldi contains double, triple, and quadruple concertos for the most diverse assortment of wind and string solos (concertinos of oboe and 'cello, or two 'cellos, or three violins, or two violins and two 'cellos, etc., with the usual ripieno of strings frequently replaced by a full orchestra of wind and strings); as well as a host of solo concertos for violin, viola d'amore, 'cello, flute, oboe, bassoon, and even mandolin. On the evidence, Vivaldi must be regarded as one of the first great orchestral experimenters.

In the Christmas concertos of Corelli and Torelli we have two notable instances of the concerto grosso used as programme music in a general sense. However, the four concerti grossi which Vivaldi entitled

The Four Seasons and included in his *Il Cimento dell'Armonia e dell'-
Inventione* (*The Strife between Harmony and Invention*), Op. 8, are the
most explicit examples of programmatic naturalism the concerto grosso
has to offer. Each concerto is set to a sonnet describing one of the
seasons of the year, and the individual movements, as well as passages
within each movement, are collated to specific lines of poetry which
they are intended to illustrate. Geminiani had also sought, in a work
entitled *The Enchanted Forest*, to render the events of the thirteenth
book of Tasso's *Jerusalem;* but if the preface to his violin method is a
safe guide to his programmatic theories, Geminiani was concerned to
deal, as Beethoven did later, more with expression of emotions than
with naturalistic tone painting. "The Intention of Musick," wrote
Geminiani, "is not only to please the Ear, but to express Sentiments,
strike the Imagination, affect the Mind, and command the Passions. . . .
But as the imitating the Cock, Cuckoo, Owl and other Birds . . . and
all other such Tricks rather belong to the Professors of Legerdemain
and Posture-masters than to the Art of Musick, the Lovers of that Art
are not to expect to find anything of that Sort in this Book." Only an
artist with considerable confidence in the intrinsic merit of his music
would dare contradict so obviously sensible a doctrine. Yet it is precisely this kind of imitative naturalism which Vivaldi employed in his
Seasons. In all truth the value of the music does not rest in Vivaldi's
gift for an aptly descriptive phrase but rather in the rollicking peasant
melodies and in the deeply emotional slow movements which are contained in the four concertos. It is indicative of his daring that while,
unlike Geminiani, Vivaldi had no specialized interest in advancing contemporary knowledge of harmony and modulation, yet when the
text called for it—as in the slow movement of the *Autumn* concerto—
he showed himself a master of strange and arresting harmony.

There is no better tribute to the provocative vitality of Vivaldi's
music than the fact that it found such especial favour with Johann
Sebastian Bach. Six of the concerti grossi published by Vivaldi as *L'Estro
Armonico*, Op. 3 (a title which may be translated as *Harmonious Rapture*),
were arranged by Bach for other instrumental combinations. The
third, ninth, and twelfth concerti grossi in this series were arranged by
Bach as clavier concertos; the tenth concerto grosso was rewritten as

a concerto for four claviers; and the eighth and eleventh transcribed as concertos for the organ.

Only an incomparable composer like Bach could regard Vivaldi's splendid creations as raw material for his own finished work. Only Bach could surpass Vivaldi in the handling of his own material, and it is only when we compare the original with the arrangement that we realize the Italian master's comparatively limited imagination. In the Bach transcriptions the harmony is fuller and occasionally the melodic line altered. Perhaps the most revealing difference is Bach's manner of developing a beautiful inner voice figuration which Vivaldi is content to leave in outline. That Bach could improve upon Vivaldi is no reflection upon the Italian master, for Bach—as his reworkings of his own music indicate—was capable of the even more prodigious task of improving upon himself. It is worth noting that in some instances, as in the organ transcription of Vivaldi's concerto grosso in A minor, Op. 3, No. 8, Bach found very little to improve upon and was more or less content to adapt the Vivaldi work to the instrument for which he was transcribing.

Vivaldi's career is known to us chiefly in its general outlines. He was born in Venice and received his first musical instruction from his father, who was apparently one of the city's distinguished violinists. The *Visitor's Guide to Venice* (1713) indicates that the playing of both father and son was one of the worth-while tourist attractions, for it notes "among the best who play the violin are Gian-Battista Vivaldi and his son, priest." Vivaldi subsequently studied with the famous operatic composer Giovanni Legrenzi (1626-90), whose music likewise stimulated Bach, although in a more limited and altogether different fashion. Vivaldi's nickname, "*Il prete rosso*" (the Red Priest), referred to his beard and profession, although in 1737 one of the ecclesiastical authorities of Ferrara forbade his appearance in the city on the grounds that he was a priest "who did not say mass." Vivaldi, incidentally, admitted the charge and justified it on the basis of an illness suffered since birth which interfered with his ecclesiastical obligations. Thus disappears regretfully the legend of how Vivaldi was suspended by the Inquisition for leaving mass in order to jot down some music which had just entered his head. There is no record of any such suspension of office, and according to Vivaldi the interruption was prompted by biological rather than aesthetic motivations.

It is a curious fact that the four great musical conservatories in Venice were attached to pious hospital foundations which, in origin, were not intended as schools for music. The Ospedale della Pietà (Hospital of the Pietà) where Vivaldi was appointed professor of violin in 1709 and *maestro dei concerti* in 1716, was a foundling hospital for girls. The children, brought up at the state's expense, were given expert musical instruction upon all instruments, and a music school developed with a girls' choir and a girls' orchestra reputed to have been the finest in Venice.

Certain it is that the quantity and character of Vivaldi's concerto output was an outgrowth of his duties at the Pietà. The excellence of the Pietà orchestra, which a French visitor, Charles de Brosses, praised for "the perfection of its symphonies," for its string attack, and for its "well-drilled execution," provided Vivaldi with a first-rate proving ground for his orchestral experiments; while a steady flow of compositions in this form was ensured, as a record of 1723 notes, by the stipulation that Vivaldi should furnish the Pietà with two concertos a month. The concerto, it would seem, implemented Vivaldi's service at the Pietà, just as the cantata did Bach's position at the Thomasschule at Leipzig, and the symphony Haydn's duties at the Esterhazy court. Apart from his travels as a violin virtuoso and as an opera composer, and a few years in Mantua as *maestro di cappella* in the service of the landgrave of Hesse-Darmstadt, Vivaldi's most constant association was with the Pietà. Toward the end of his life Vivaldi left both the Pietà and Venice, and according to a contemporary account died in poverty in Vienna.

We turn back now to England, where the German-born George Frideric Handel lived and worked during the largest portion of his life. The bulk of Handel's concerti grossi are contained in two sets, the first (Op. 3) consisting of six orchestral concertos for winds and strings (also called Oboe concertos), the second (Op. 6) comprising twelve concertos for strings only. The latter collection, composed incredibly enough in one month (September 29 to October 30, 1739), is scored for a concertino of two violins and continuo ('cello and harpsichord) against a grosso of strings. This is the traditional Corellian precept of concerto grosso orchestration, and Handel does not, in essence, step beyond it.

One can, of course, find a miniature violin concerto movement, such as the penultimate allegro in the sixth concerto, in which the concertino is reduced to one solo violin; or even movements scored only for string orchestra with the concertino discarded entirely, e.g. the last two movements of the fifth and the final allegro of the sixth concertos. Such movements are exceptions and serve to underline the rule. These concertos are, in an important sense, typical of Handel's activity, for just as he devoted a lifetime to preserving for the English stage the tradition of Italian opera, so in this series of concertos (Op. 6) he presented the English concert hall with an enduring monument to Italian instrumental art. In these twelve concertos Handel's personal style acts like a musical magnifying glass, projecting the music of his predecessors in broader and more noble proportions. The surface technique derives from Corelli, but in the effortless dignity of its slow movements, the broad-backed joviality of its dance measures, in the brilliant and uncomplicated counterpoint of its fugue movements, the Op. 6 series is unmistakably Handelian.

The concerti grossi for winds and strings (Op. 3) are better known as the Oboe concertos, although the oboe is by no means as consistently dominating as such a title might suggest. These concertos were performed apparently in 1733 at the wedding celebration for the Prince of Orange and Princess Anne, Handel's pupil. Individual movements, however, date considerably prior to this event, for some are orchestral adaptations of movements from the clavier suites, while others had been heard earlier in his operas. The fourth concerto, for example, dates from 1716 and served as the second overture to Handel's opera *Amadigi*. Likewise in the sixth concerto both movements are drawn from previously composed music: the first movement from the opera *Ottone*, and the second from the finale of the first clavier suite in D minor which, incidentally, also reappears in Handel's fourth organ concerto.

Apart from the use of winds in the Op. 3 series, the progress of the concerto grosso form with Handel is largely a matter of the varying number of movements and styles in which the concertos are cast. Taking both sets together, Handel alternates the solemn gestures of the French overture, with vigorous double fugues and elegantly idealized dances, spaced out in concertos varying from two to six movements. To secure instrumental variety Handel utilizes in both sets the curious device of varying the concertino-ripieno relationship from movement to movement within the concerto itself. In the B-flat major concerto, Op. 3, No. 2, for example, the concertino for the first and fourth movements consists of two oboes and two violins against a ripieno for string orchestra. The second movement, however, is scored for solo oboe and string orchestra; the third movement for first violin and first oboe in unison, second violin and second oboe in unison, viola and cembalo with bass support; while the final movement utilizes a concertino of two oboes and 'cello against the ripieno of strings. The G minor concerto, Op. 6, No. 6, exhibits a similar, though less extensive, variety, for in addition to the regular concertino trio (two violins and 'cello), there is a movement for solo violin and string orchestra, and one for string orchestra alone with the concertino eliminated entirely.

Like the cantata, passion, toccata, chorale, and fugue, the concerto grosso reached the peak of its development with the greatest master of the age, Johann Sebastian Bach. Bach had no occasion to be as extensively interested in the form as Vivaldi. Yet if Bach's survey of the field was concentrated, it was none the less complete. The six Brandenburg concertos date from Bach's Cöthen period (1717-23) when his duties as conductor of an eighteen-piece orchestra no doubt prompted him to give some thought to chamber music for small orchestra. From Bach's dedication, written in French as was proper in German court circles, and with fulsome flattery as was proper in addressing a patron with favours to dispense, one gathers that he had had the opportunity of performing for the Markgraf of Brandenburg some years earlier; and from the nature of the compilation it would appear that Bach put his best foot forward in the hope of attracting the interest of a prospective patron. The individual concertos are designed not merely to please the ear, but to delight a connoisseur assumed to be knowledgeable in the ramifications of the art of concerto grosso composition. In any case they were received by the Markgraf of Brandenburg with a dedication (dated March 24, 1721) in which His Royal Highness was reminded of the "condescending interest" he had expressed in Bach's "small talent," and was humbly enjoined by the composer not to judge the imperfections of the concertos by the severity of his "fine and delicate taste." There is no record of an acknowledgment or reward to the composer for his labour, nor any certain evidence that the Markgraf had the con-

certos performed. It is certain that they were not considered worthy to
be classed with the concertos of Vivaldi, Valentini, Venturini, Bres-
cianello, and others, for, in the inventory of the Markgraf's library
undertaken after his death, Bach's music was not accorded the honour
of being mentioned by name. The six concertos were included in two
job lots totalling 177 concertos and were put up for sale at four
groschen apiece.

The Brandenburg concertos are valuable primarily for their intrinsic
merit, but they are of interest also as an exemplification in miniature
of the character of Bach's creative thinking. Like his cantatas, chorales,
and fugues, they are, in a sénse, definitive summaries of all that has
gone before in the field; and while the models of certain of his predecessors undoubtedly carried more weight with him than others, the
guiding influence in his music remained above all the clarity with
which he himself diagnosed the problems of a form, and the completeness with which he accomplished their solution. Certainly in no single
group of concertos is there such variety in instrumentation and inner
structure. The range of Bach's thought in these concertos is worth examining even at the risk of a tedious enumeration of detail.

It has already been noted that Vivaldi was not the first Italian to
exploit occasionally the sonorities of wind and string combination;
while with the Germans, who possessed an early master of this art in
Heinrich Schütz, it became the identification tag of a national concerto
grosso style.[1]

In the first Brandenburg concerto, scored for winds and strings with
the addition of a violino piccolo, Bach tends to minimize a formal predetermined concerto polarity and to write in effect an orchestral composition in which concerto techniques are a constantly available resource.
In the first movement, there are short phrases punctuating the overall
orchestral texture in which one hears fleetingly a concertino unit formed
of two horns and continuo (comprising 'cellos, basses, bassoon and

---

[1] A rather extreme example of the German passion for wind and string combination is the concerto grosso for four choirs by Gottfried Heinrich Stölzel.
The first two choirs are each scored for three trumpets and two tympani; the
third choir for three oboes and a bassoon, and the fourth for four violins, viola,
'cello, and bass. Two cembalos are added to the whole. (See Denkmäler deutscher
Tonkunst, Erste Folge, Bd. xxix-xxx.)

harpsichord) or two oboes and continuo, or two violins and continuo. In the third movement, the violino piccolo appears as a soloist, but it also unites with a horn, or with an oboe, or with the first violin line to form a variety of concertino groupings. In the second movement, at the outset, individual instruments take the main melody in turn, not as concerto soloists, but much in the manner in which such a melody would be shifted from instrument to instrument in a symphonic slow movement. This, however, is followed by an extended concertino interplay of oboe, violino piccolo and continuo. The freedom with which Bach manipulates concertino groupings as alleviations of mass and variations of texture is carried somewhat further in this first concerto than elsewhere in this set. But it is symptomatic of the general freedom of procedure that essentially characterizes all six of the Brandenburg concertos.

Appended to this three-movement concerto is a fourth movement designed as a little suite (a menuetto with two trios and a polacca). In itself, it forms a small treatise on instrumentation, a colourist's study in the art of symmetrical dissimilitude. The menuetto itself is scored in symphonic rather than concerto style, for the wind choir (three oboes and a bassoon) doubles the string choir voice for voice, while the two horns provide the necessary rhythmic accent. The first trio is entirely for winds: two oboes and bassoon. The menuetto returns with the full complement of winds and strings, and is now succeeded by a polacca for string orchestra alone. Once again the full-choired menuetto returns and once again is followed by a second wind trio, this time for two horn parts and the three oboes in unison. The recapitulation of the menuetto for full orchestra concludes the movement. The instrumental design of the movement is based, therefore, on the following symmetrical succession: full orchestra, wind choir, full orchestra, string choir, full orchestra, wind choir (varied), full orchestra. Handel's practice of varying his instrumentation from movement to movement has already been noticed. It is characteristic of Bach that in this single effort he should have canvassed the territory with so much greater clarity and thoroughness.

In the second Brandenburg concerto, Bach stipulates a concertino quartet comprising a flute, an oboe, a violin and a trumpet. Upon occasion we hear the concertino as a unit, but more often than not it breaks up into various combinations of its components (trios and duets) and further, each instrument emerges as a soloist in its own right. The winds are also employed as an addition to the main body of strings, endowing the orchestral mass with an appreciable accretion of colour and force. A certain festive character pervades the two outside movements. By way of contrast, the orchestral mass is eliminated entirely from the slow movement, and the trumpet is banished from the remaining concertino. (The trumpet, rather obviously, contributes an exhilarating instability to the concertino. Clearly its presence would contribute a most unwelcome distraction to the close-knit intimacy of the slow movement.) The movement becomes then the purest chamber music, an intimate and singularly close conversation of flute, oboe and violin over a steady continuo bass. The interpolation of such intimate chamber pieces to serve as slow movements occurs also in the fifth and sixth concertos in this set.

In the fourth Brandenburg concerto, a concertino of two flutes and violin provides a less startling contrast to the string orchestra. It has sometimes been maintained, with rather unnecessary emphasis, that the fourth concerto is not a concerto grosso at all, but really a solo violin concerto. Actually, the two flutes are frequently appended to the grosso, and the violin is released as a full concerto soloist. In so far as this happens, for that stretch of the composition we are listening no doubt to a solo violin concerto. However, in point of fact, sometimes the two flutes are joined to the violin and the three perform as a unit. And in so far as this is the case, we are listening to a concerto grosso. The mixing of concerto types is a clearly possible procedure and actually not an especially risky one. Bach avails himself of it and, within any given movement, shifts his emphasis from concerto grosso to solo concerto as his judgment dictates.

In the fifth concerto, the concertino unit is a violin, a flute and a harpsichord—entirely too standardized a trio ensemble to be taken at face value. Actually, as is soon evident, the harpsichord is released from the routines of its continuo obligations, and treated as a solo instrument: an intimation of the fact that the early development of the solo clavier concerto is intimately bound up with Bach. The extended cadenza for solo harpsichord in this fifth Brandenburg concerto is still perhaps the most stunning piece of harpsichord writing in the literature for the instrument. (The use of a modern concert grand in place of a harpsichord, while of course possible, is usually regrettable. One can offer sympathy, but hardly encouragement, to the pianist who would like to have the use of this concerto.)

The two remaining Brandenburg concertos, Nos. 3 and 6, are scored entirely for strings, and once again Bach goes far beyond the practice of his predecessors. Neither concerto shows the conventional concerto grosso division into a concertino trio and a ripieno quartet. The third concerto is scored for three string choirs composed of three instruments apiece: three violins for the first choir, three violas for the second, and three 'cellos for the third, the entire ensemble supported by a double bass and a cembalo. In the tutti passages the instruments in each choir perform in unison, so that each choir becomes one voice in a three-part harmony. In the solo passages the instruments split up so that each choir becomes in itself a unit of three-part harmony. Thus there are nine potential solo instruments, opposed to a tutti of three choirs. Fundamentally the character of this concerto derives from the continual breaking up and re-forming of choirs, from the continual interplay of the massing and dispersion of instruments. This process in one choir never quite coincides with its occurrence in another, so that as one choir breaks up into a trio of solo instruments another re-forms to oppose it as a solid tutti unit. After two hundred years this concerto is still the epitome of fluid instrumental writing. Music is in essence a mobile art, and this concerto is above all a study in the art of instrumental mobility, organized with the most intense concentration and carried off with the most astonishing fluency.

The sixth Brandenburg concerto is scored for two viole da braccio, two viole da gamba, and 'cello, with the customary double bass and cembalo support. The violins are excluded and the concerto takes on, in consequence, a deep, sober colouring. In the second and third movements, and in fleeting moments during the first, the two viole da braccio and a 'cello form the concertino group. Here again Bach has taken a conventional pattern of orchestration and given it an uncommon application.

It has been customary to characterize Bach as the peak of a tradition, to contrast him with an innovator like Wagner, to see in him a composer whose historical contribution consisted in summarizing the styles, forms, and techniques of his predecessors. As a generalization it is, in the main, correct. Yet, apart from the important fact that Bach did break new ground in the creation of the clavier concerto, such a word as "summarize" is open to possible misinterpretation. The task of summarizing the practice of a period is primarily the task of a theoretician. The creative composer—and Bach certainly possessed one of the most inexhaustible creative imaginations known in the history of the several arts—if he chooses to build upon the total experience of the past, must necessarily, by virtue of his creative instinct, do more than simply summarize this experience. He will expand it, realize to the full its hitherto unsuspected possibilities, and in so doing offer an occasional model significant for the future. After Bach there was a decisive reorientation in a new direction motivated by social and musical factors alike. It is important to assess Bach primarily as the climax of a tradition; it is also important to note those elements in Bach (secondary, it is true, in the total body of his music) which emerge in a kind of half-light out of the tradition in which he is working, and point in the direction of the future. Deep cleavages are the obvious and primary manifestations of growth or change; yet the abyss which divides one generation from another is negotiated via a subterranean continuity of tradition, by a casual and unseen passing of the torch, by the firm and unspoken insistence of the tremendous experience of the past to which even the boldest innovator falls secret heir.

Bach treated the concerto grosso, at least from the point of view of instrumentation, with more systematic variety than his predecessors, and realized out of the principle of contrasted choirs instrumental combinations unique in the history of the form. With respect to the structural relation between the concertino and ripieno choirs it has been said that Bach adopted Vivaldi's precept of competition between solo instruments rather than Corelli's treatment of each choir as an indivisible unit. This is especially evident in the second Brandenburg concerto where each instrument in the concertino is given ample soloistic encouragement. In many of his slow movements Bach carries this emphasis on the special tone colouring of the concertino group to the point of dispensing with the string orchestra ripieno entirely. Thus the slow movements of the second, fifth, and sixth Brandenburg concertos, and the slow movements of the triple concerto in A minor and the two-clavier concerto in C major are scored exclusively for the solo instruments, contrary to Handel's practice of discarding the concertino and relying solely upon the ripieno.

The opening movements of the first, third, and sixth Brandenburg concertos are, however, organized from a fundamentally untraditional point of view. The customary division between the two choirs obtains only in a limited fashion, for the solo interludes are rare and unusually brief, and the customary distinction in thematic material (which helps clarify the functions of concertino and grosso in the second Brandenburg concerto) is entirely lacking. They are more nearly symphonic movements than pure concerto movements. As in the symphonies of the next generation, the orchestra acts as a single entity, balancing and juxtaposing diverse combinations of sound mass and tone colour in the interests of symphonic variety. Since the partisan interests of each choir are largely surrendered and since the movements proceed chiefly on the basis of one unit only—the orchestra as a whole—they represent a highly advanced stage in the evolution from the concerto grosso to the symphony. This evolution is likewise evident in the second movement of the first Brandenburg concerto, but with the modifications incidental to an elegiac adagio. The main theme of the movement is alternately taken up by the solo oboe, the solo violin, and the 'cellos doubled by the bassoon. Here, too, contrary to traditional concerto grosso practice, the opening section (eleven measures) of the movement is not organized around these instruments as around a concertino unit. Bach's viewpoint is again closer to later symphonic practice in which a solo instrument will emerge from the orchestral complex whenever the music calls for its particular tone colour. These movements are significant as crossing-points over the seemingly impassable abyss between two forms and two generations.

It is interesting that several of the movements in the Brandenburg concertos appear as choral movements in his sacred cantatas. The Bach cantata still went under the title of concerto, and since the cantata was a form which he explored with the most thoroughgoing care—he left nearly three hundred examples—it is not surprising that his scoring in this field recapitulates nearly the entire foregoing history of the concerto principle. In his cantatas scored in conservative motet style, the instruments double the voice parts, reviving, in effect, the old motet concerto in which two equal choirs, one vocal and one instrumental, are contrasted to each other. In a large number of the cantatas individual instrumental solos, carefully selected with regard to their tone colour and the meaning of the text, are joined to the solo voices, and the principle of competition between contrasted solos is added to the rivalry between choirs. It is a short step from here to combine vocal and instrumental solos, vocal and instrumental choirs, multiply the variety of dissimilar sound masses and tone colours, and adapt for such a movement an already existing instrumental concerto in which these principles are a matter of course. Thus, to cite just one example, the opening movement of the third Brandenburg concerto, which served us a while back as a high point in pure instrumental technique, was absorbed by Bach into the opening movement of the 174th church cantata *Ich liebe den Höchsten*. While this concerto movement is now called a symphonia, the cantata itself is appropriately enough titled a concerto.

The concerto grosso, in its broadest definition, includes any composition written for a group of solo instruments contrasted with a larger mass of tutti instruments. The Bach concertos for two, three, and four claviers with orchestra, the double violin concerto, and the triple concerto in A minor, may conceivably be regarded as concerti grossi. Where these works belong is entirely a matter of definition, a question of fixing more or less arbitrarily the point through which a line will be drawn separating the concerto grosso from the solo concerto for more than one solo instrument. The decision would no doubt have been relatively simple for Corelli, for his concerto grosso is strictly defined as a division between choirs. The concertino is simply the smaller choir, not an assemblage of individual solos. If the concertino were to dissipate into individual solo instruments, Corelli, if we may infer his ideas from his music, would probably have considered this contrary to the strict principle of the concerto grosso. This is precisely what happens in the works that Vivaldi called concerti grossi, which proves nothing more than that the concerto grosso may be narrowly defined in more than one way. The merits of the matter will not be argued here. Suffice it to say that for reasons which have no close bearing on the question it seems relatively simpler to discuss Bach's double, triple, and quadruple concertos in connection with his solo violin and solo clavier concertos.

CHAPTER III

The Early Solo Concerto

THE solo concerto is based upon one of the most ancient, fundamental, and ever-recurring principles of artistic creation. It has been compared in principle to a Greek tragedy in which the drama of an individual's fate achieves meaningful context against a backdrop of solemn commentary by the chorus; to which one might add a further comparison with the soliloquies of the Shakespearean drama in which the soloist, so to speak, meditates upon the social complex from which he has momentarily detached himself. In the solo concerto musical interest is aroused and sustained on the basis of an opposition between one instrument and many. In this sense it has been described as a musical reflection of the everyday and ever-engrossing human drama of the, individual lost in, emerging from, and pitted against the multitude.

Translated into musical terms, the crux of the composer's problem in a solo concerto is simply this. One single element, a solo instrument drawn out of the orchestral complex, becomes the object of sustained and concentrated attention. Initially there is a sharp dislocation in tonal balance, in relative mobility, between solo and orchestra. The essential drama of the solo concerto is posited upon this dislocation, while the essential artistry of the composer consists in absorbing it into a well-rounded and strongly-unified musical organism with no sacrifice of inner drama for the sake of outer form. Every concerto composer is a Tintoretto at heart bent upon the coherent projection of an off-balance design. The problems implied in this technique are the common concern of the several arts. One thinks almost instantly, for example, of the spotlight technique of Caravaggio, early Rembrandt, and the minor Dutch painters, where the disproportionate concentration of light upon one figure is intended to dramatize, yet not destroy the compositional unity of the painting.

While the existence of the solo concerto as an independent instrumental form dates back only some two and a half centuries, its ultimate ancestry lies in the ground source of music itself. The innocent virtuosity of folk music, the polarity of leader and chorus in communal folk singing is its long-forgotten foundation. The principle survived in medieval church music and was comfortably ensconced with appropriate modifications in the sacred and secular vocal music of the sixteenth and seventeenth centuries.

The solo concerto involves a fairly complex strategy of musical composition, and its immediate derivation lies not so much in a direct and simple evolution from some prior instrumental form as in the more general process of absorbing and redirecting those relevant currents of musical thought which flowed toward it from many different directions. It took its materials where it could find them and from the blueprints of rival musical forms fashioned a structure distinctively its own. Two of the most obvious (and opposite) sources for the solo concerto were the opera and the concerto grosso.

The solo concerto turns on the fundamental fact that, in its fullest extension, it is incompatible with a close polyphonic technique. While one instrument reigns supreme, the remainder must relax for the while into a background accompaniment, thus destroying the essential equality of all participants postulated in the working out of a fugue. This correlation between the ascendancy of the virtuoso and the elaboration of a monodic style had long been established in the opera house. Approximately a century before the appearance of the solo instrumental concerto the Florentine camerata had founded their opera upon a conscious negation of counterpoint. With the growth of the opera, the accent on the prima donna, on a monodic style, and on a solo-tutti rivalry expressed in the orchestral ritornels which punctuated the operatic aria, had become the accepted fundamentals of operatic style. They were publicly known and widely applauded, for the opera, earlier than other musical forms, had transferred its base of operations from the limited confines of the aristocratic court to the public opera house. Thus the opera offered pertinent models from which the solo concerto could benefit. It is interesting that Albinoni and Vivaldi, two of the most significant figures in the development of the solo concerto, should have been so strongly interested in operatic creation; while the character of many Tartini adagios caused Burney to remark that they "want nothing but words to be excellent pathetic opera songs." In a later day, Spohr's *Gesangsszene* concerto was openly patterned after an Italian opera scene, while the slow movement of the Mozart piano concerto in E-flat (K. 271) provides a deeply moving example of how well the operatic aria and recitative can be absorbed into a concerto movement. The trumpet symphonies of the late seventeenth-century Venetian opera have already been cited as evidence of the instrumental virtuoso's presence in the opera orchestra. The violin virtuoso was like-wise a powerful drawing card. In the London opera Veracini enter-tained between the acts with demonstrations of violin virtuosity; while the level of instrumental technique demanded of the solo violinist in the ritornels in some Scarlatti operas was on a par with the standards of a violin concerto.

The preceding chapter has already indicated the extent to which the concerto grosso served as a testing ground for the solo concerto. The line of development from one concerto form to another may be traced in the disintegration of the concertino unit (rare in Corelli, usual in Vivaldi) and the emergence of each instrument as an individual solo. In those compositions where each concertino instrument takes a solo in turn, or where the first violin dominates to the extent that the remain-ing concertino instruments simply form a light background accom-paniment, it is a moot point whether we have a concerto grosso or a solo concerto. The solo concerto was encouraged by, but was by no means entirely a product of, this process of concertino disintegration. Although the solo concerto appeared later than the concerto grosso, it did not wait until after the concerto grosso was dead. The two con-certo forms existed side by side, and the process of breaking up the concertino unit into its constituent solos was perhaps as much a result of the presence of the solo concerto as it was a cause for the further encouragement of the solo concerto. Music history rarely follows a line of simple evolution. Cause and effect have been known to exchange places freely with each other. Both concerto forms were in large measure created by composer-performers like Torelli, Vivaldi, and Locatelli. As violin virtuosi they manifested a natural interest in their instrument in concerto grosso and solo concerto alike; and as intelligent composers they did not fail to put their experience in one concerto form to use in another.

The first significant impetus toward the creation of the modern solo concerto came from Italy. In its most rudimentary form, as exemplified by Tomasso Albinoni (1674-1745), episodes for the solo violin were simply momentary interruptions of the dominant orchestral texture, a brief variation in tone colour and tone mass. Since Albinoni has been so thoroughly overshadowed by his contemporaries, it is worth recalling that J. S. Bach found several of his themes worthy of fugal treatment. Albinoni's main interest, however, was the opera (he has some fifty to his credit) rather than the solo concerto. The violin concertos of Torelli (the last six in his Op. 8, published in 1709) are a more vital starting-point, for solo and orchestra confront each other here for the first time on an equal footing. The incidental character of the solo interlude no longer obtains, yet the mutual suspicion with which solo and orchestra regard each other still points to an early and experimental effort. Starting from scratch, Torelli's first concern was to make clear the distinction between solo and orchestra, and since the weak and strong points of the two equal contenders had not been probed with respect to each other, Torelli took the elementary precaution of protecting them from, rather than combining them with, one another. The orchestral portions and the solo episodes tend to be closed off from each other. The solo does not intrude while the orchestra is on stage, while the orchestra in turn respects the soloist's right to undistracted and unabbreviated utterance. Thus for the most part the solo violin is accompanied only by the çembalo. Solo and orchestra do not usually share the same melodic material and have, to all intents and purposes, very little to do with each other. From the viewpoint of later practice where the drama of the concerto conflict lies in the willingness of solo and orchestra to tangle with each other, this standoffish sparring, this timid avoidance of jurisdictional dispute, appears unenterprising and structurally immature. Torelli, however, did clarify the boundary line between solo and orchestra, and for the edification of future concerto composers he did establish, for better or for worse, the precedent of entrusting the leading musical ideas to the orchestra while the solo entertained with virtuoso display.

Like many a composer of the period, Torelli was a church musician. He performed on the violin or viola in the orchestra at S. Petronio in Bologna where the earliest solo literature for the violoncello also developed. Domenico Gabrielli and Giuseppe Jacchini were both 'cellists at S. Petronio. Gabrielli's ricercari are among the first contributions to the solo 'cellist's repertoire, while Jacchini's *Concerti per camera* (*Chamber Concertos*), Op. 4, 1701, are accounted the earliest efforts in the field of the 'cello concerto. Jacchini's stipulations for chamber rather than church performance is also one of the first of its kind, and points once again to the probable church setting for many of the solo concertos of the period. It is significant that the first three generations of violin concerto composition in Italy were dominated by churchmen or church musicians. Torelli and Tartini were church musicians, while Vivaldi, who stands between them, was a priest. The Bach clavier concerto transcriptions are a momentous landmark in this respect, for, as we shall see, they bear the imprint of a church musician composing directly for an early equivalent of our modern concert hall.

The favourable conditions under which Vivaldi pursued his interest in the concerto have already been outlined. As in the concerto grosso, so in the solo concerto Vivaldi's music is characterized by an inexhaustible variety, a constant experimentation, a sure sense of construction, and a gift for warm, vibrant melody. Vivaldi's virtues are worth celebrating. His slow movements are often romantic though never sentimental; his finales frequently gay and athletic, yet never slick and self-consciously muscle-bound; his opening allegro movements passionate and noble, yet devoid of the mock heroics which have clogged so much of the music of the last hundred years. His programmatic bent is evident in those of his solo concertos which bear such titles as *The Tempest, Night, The Goldfinch, Pleasure, Inquietude, Repose;* and his gift for instrumental variety in the number of solo instruments (violin, viola d'amore, violoncello, flute, oboe, bassoon) for which he composed a veritable host of concertos. He used the *scordatura*, or deliberate mistuning of the violin, which had been known in Italy as early as 1629 in a violin sonata, Op. 7, No. 2, by Biagio Marini, and had subsequently become a favourite device with such German virtuosi as Biber and Strungk. He was, with A. F. Bonporti (d. *c*. 1740), among the first to write a variation movement in a solo concerto (e.g. the second movement of his flute concerto, Op. 10, No. 6) an example which few among his contemporaries and immediate successors followed. Bonporti, incidentally, is worth mention, for his concertos (Op. 11, 12) show a mature use of a recitative style in pure instrumental music. Bach, in his D major toccata, his chromatic fantasy and fugue, and in his third organ concerto, had a worthy predecessor in Bonporti.

Vivaldi's solo concertos enjoyed the highest respect throughout Europe; they were applauded in Paris and widely studied and imitated in Germany. Just as Muffat had earlier paid tribute to Corelli's models, so now Quantz spoke in praise of Vivaldi; and just as Bach had found fruitful study in Vivaldi's concerti grossi, so likewise did he put the Vivaldi solo concertos to use in transcription.

While Vivaldi's interest ranged far beyond the violin concerto, the violin, above all other instruments, most consistently engaged his attention. It is probable, judging from the varying degrees of technical difficulty exhibited by the violin concertos, that many of them were used by Vivaldi for teaching purposes. Indeed, it has been suggested that, if properly classified, they might constitute a useful instruction book for the violin. The students at the Pietà were singularly fortunate in having such a violin method available, and one thinks with regret of the unstimulating mediocrity of the school concertos through which the modern intermediate student must for years labour in an effort to achieve mastery of his instrument.

The violin concerto was created by professional violinists and intended mainly for their own use and also for performance by other virtuosi. The element of personal display was bound to loom large, controlled, to be sure, in the body of the concerto by that inevitable sense of artistry which characterizes the entire music of the period. Almost with the birth of the form the cadenza appended to the end of a movement emerged as the principal vehicle for uninhibited showmanship. The cadenza found a modest haven with Torelli, and more ample room for display in some which Vivaldi wrote for several of his violin concertos. However, it was Pietro Locatelli, reputed to have had "more hand, caprice, and fancy, than any violinist of his time" (Burney), who in his *L'Arte del Violino*, Op. 3 (1733), accorded the cadenza

its most consistent and elaborate expression in violin literature prior
to the demon virtuoso productions of the nineteenth century. Each of
the twelve concertos in this collection comes equipped with two
caprices appended to slow and fast movements alike. The caprices
distinguish themselves from other such cadenza interpolations in the
concertos of the period by the exorbitant demands they made upon
the performer and by the fact that, contrary to the usual practice of
indicating where the performer might improvise, they were explicitly
written out by the composer. The concertos themselves are not, as one
might expect, mere vehicles for virtuosity. The violin writing is
relatively modest, reflecting Locatelli's penchant for expressive,
cantabile melody. In the caprices, however, the virtuoso reigns
supreme.

It is hardly necessary to show that the practice of improvising, or
even writing out, cadenzas can be noted in instrumental music immediately prior to the appearance of the solo concerto. The habit of
expanding a cadence into a brief coloratura cadenza can be traced back
to folk sources (e.g. the cadence of the well-known English folk song
Westron Wynde); while improvisation, which is the heart of the cadenza, is a medium natural not only to folk expression, but a creative
technique practised more or less widely in every age from the Greeks to
modern times. The stock melodies of the Greeks (*nomoi*) were most
likely formulas guiding improvisation. Certain portions of the liturgical plain chant (e.g. the alleluia) expanded as early as the eighth or
ninth century into elaborate coloraturas; while the writings of medieval
English theorists indicate that English discant was in origin a method
of improvisation applicable to any cantus firmus. The figured bass
technique which dominated the seventeenth and eighteenth centuries
was in essence an improvisation upon a given bass with notation for
proper harmonic sequence as a guide. Realizing a figured bass at sight
was part of the equipment of any performer who hoped to earn a living
from his profession. Textbooks in the art of extempore variation, such
as Christopher Simpson's *The Division Violist* (1659), were available
to musicians; while eighteenth-century audiences were regaled with the
fabulous improvisations of a Handel or a Mozart.

With such composer-performers as Mozart and Beethoven, the
cadenza reached its height as a medium for spontaneous improvisation.

The fame of their extempore renditions has come down to us from more than one wonder-struck observer, and one needs only to remember the profound sincerity of their music to conjecture with reasonable certainty that their cadenza improvisations were aflame with creative fire and controlled by a stupendous knowledge of the craft of composition. Few of their cadenzas have come down to us in written form, and while these few are vastly superior to the stereotyped and tasteless showpieces appended by later virtuosi, as cadenzas written down coldly after the fact one can hardly suppose that they reflect completely the living excitement of the extempore creation. Furthermore, the cadenzas which Mozart did write out were intended less for himself than for friends and pupils. There are no written cadenzas for the majority of his maturest piano concertos; a clear indication that for his own performance Mozart confidently relied upon his ever-present ability to make worth-while music.

With the cleavage between composer and performer and the increasing emphasis on specialization of function (of which more will be said in another chapter) the cadenza became what it is today—a showpiece pure and simple with little pretence to artistic value. It is now a composed piece, a solo étude comprising a number of routine difficulties, the successful rendition of which is taken by less critical members of the audience as proof that the performer is worth the price of admission. The composition of cadenzas for Mozart and Beethoven concertos has been entrusted, in consequence, to virtuosi or distinguished pedagogues who understand how to write brilliantly for their special instrument, but who do not necessarily understand, as the composer did, how to write music. According to modern concert-hall practice, the cadenza may now be defined as that part of the concerto where the orchestra stops playing and the listener, to all intents and purposes, stops listening, so that all and sundry may concentrate upon the bag of tricks which the performer as wizard-virtuoso (not as a maker of music) is to trot out for inspection. The cadenza usually bears only a fragmentary relation to the remainder of the movement. It is the display counter of the concerto, wherein the soloist exhibits not the profundity of his musicianship but the agility of his fingers. It is worth noting that a few composers since Beethoven have attempted to absorb the cadenza into the body of the concerto and to give it musical mean-

ing, e.g. Schumann in his piano concerto, Mendelssohn in his violin
concerto, and Rachmaninoff in his first and third piano concertos.
The solution, it would seem, is either for the composer to write the
cadenza himself (which most composers do today) so that at least a
certain amount of stylistic unity will obtain, or else to dispense with it
entirely (which many composers have done). It is perhaps too much to
expect that our modern performers will bother to learn enough music
to master the art and science of effective improvisation. It is a lost and
wholly unlamented art so far as the respectable musical world is concerned. Our jazz musicians are alone in their understanding of the more
creative aspects of virtuosity, and to their jam sessions we are indebted
for the preservation of the exciting art of extempore creation.

It is not feasible to render here a detailed account of the early violin
concerto, for practitioners of the art were numerous and their work
neither entirely available nor entirely interesting. Musicians in those
days were more thoroughly trained than they are now in music as an
art, rather than solely in the violin as a profession. Narrow specialization had not yet been forced upon the performer either by economic
pressure or by social dogma, so that any virtuoso worth his salt would
as soon compose a concerto for his own use as adopt the work of
another. Thus, violin concertos by Alberti, Tessarini, Somis, Veracini,
etc., many of them well thought of in their day, are of secondary
interest historically and intrinsically when measured against the accomplishments of a Vivaldi, Tartini, or Bach; yet the standards of the
period with respect to craftsmanship were sufficiently high to ensure
that their music will always stimulate our natural enjoyment in a
commodity soundly made and flawlessly polished.

The dominating position which the Vivaldi concertos enjoyed for
several decades were in time successfully challenged by Giuseppe Tartini, a younger contemporary and one of the most arresting personalities of the period. Celebrated as the "Master of Nations," Tartini drew
around him in Padua an international circle of admiring students who
garnished the impassioned appeal of his music with a liberal dose of
strange anecdote. With the passing of the centuries the romantic
personality of the master merged imperceptibly into a background of
attractive fable, so that at this late date fact is distinguished from fiction
only with difficulty. We know little of his early life except that he was

a student in theology and law at the University of Padua (1709), and that his chief interest even then was fencing and violin playing. The revelation of his secret marriage to a protégée of Cardinal Cornaro provoked extreme parental displeasure, for the marriage put an end to their plans for the priesthood as his profession. He was cut off financially and forced to flee the city by a charge of abduction which the Cardinal levied against him. The record of the vital formative years between his flight from Padua and his reappearance there in 1721 is confused. It is variously reported that he fled into the provinces, earning his livelihood as an itinerant musician and that he took refuge in the Franciscan monastery at Assisi. Fragmentary records show him in Ancona as a member of an opera orchestra, and later in Assisi, his last stopping-place before Padua. It is impossible to know with certainty who his teachers were (if indeed he had any) and to what musical and ideological influences he was subjected during this formative period. It has been conjectured that he studied with an organist, Padre Boemo (Bohuslav Czernohorsky), although other names, equally obscure, have been offered. The tradition has come down to us that at some point in his wanderings Tartini heard the violin-playing of Veracini and was sufficiently impressed with his own comparative lack of technique to return to Ancona for a period of concentrated study. During his early exile Tartini is credited with having discovered the acoustical phenomena of the "third tone" (called also the "resultant" or "differential" or "Tartini" tone) produced when two sustained sounds are vibrated simultaneously. Tartini was hardly equipped to explain scientifically the generation of this differential tone (so called because the number of its vibrations is equal to the difference between the vibrations of the two generating tones); but it did serve him as an excellent guide to correct intonation in double-stopping and was later incorporated into his poorly-received theoretical work, *Trattato di musica* (*Treatise on Music*).

Concerning Tartini's return to Padua, the story goes that he was recognized in Assisi when the curtain behind which he was playing was accidentally pushed aside. A reconciliation with the Cardinal having been effected, Tartini returned safely to Padua. In any case his appointment in 1721 as solo violinist at Sant' Antonio in Padua had all the earmarks of a triumphant recall. As a mark of singular favour, the customary audition for the post was dispensed with and other inducements, such as the right to perform also in the theatre, added to his contract; all of which would indicate that at the age of twenty-nine he had already won for himself the reputation of an outstanding virtuoso. He travelled outside of Italy for a while and ultimately returned to Padua, where he founded his famous "School of Nations."

Tartini has been described as a child of his age; a rather pat evaluation which will serve for any composer since no man lives wholly apart from his period. Tartini's violin concertos fall between 1720 and 1770, a strategic half-century encompassing the last thirty years of Bach's creative life and the first twenty years of Haydn's. While chronologically he serves as a comfortable bridge between Bach and Haydn, his artistic personality stands fundamentally apart from either. The naïve sophistication, the unassuming elegance of early Haydn, as well as the characteristic intellectual rigour with which Bach controlled his most impassioned personal devotions, are secondary characteristics of Tartini's art. He is more limited than either, not only because his effort was concentrated largely in the violin, but because of the narrow and intense subjectivism which prevails in his music.

Tartini was one of the most troubled and contradictory spirits of his age, a brilliant secular virtuoso who willingly embraced the dogmas of a church musician. Religious-secular raiment was accepted wearing apparel for an early eighteenth-century composer. A churchman like Vivaldi wrote and published secular programme music and, for the purpose, turned to secular poetry with no sense of strain; but Vivaldi was perhaps the last of the great Italian virtuosi to wear this coat of many colours with conspicuous ease. Tartini's sober religious nature, touched by an obscure and deeply embedded mysticism, sought uneasy delight in secular romantic poetry. The literary fragments which he identified with his music he inscribed in a long indecipherable code over the movements of his concertos. They were mnemonic devices intended for his own edification (and also possibly to ward off the censure of the Church); scraps of verse sufficient for him to recall the entire poem, culled largely, not from Petrarch as has been stated so often, but from minor lyric poets. Some are banal love lyrics, others sober moral precepts pointed directly at himself. In the latter case a concerto movement became for him a kind of inner ethical meditation. Unlike Bach's musical sermons, delivered to the crowds at large gathered for a Sunday or holiday service, the intent of Tartini's sermon-izing was coded carefully for private use.

Whatever sentiment Tartini may have concealed in his ciphers lies openly revealed in his music, for Tartini was a complete romantic long before romanticism had become the main stream of musical expression. Even his story of how his famous sonata *The Devil's Trill* came to him in a dream reads like Coleridge's later account of the inspiration for *Kubla Khan*. It is odd that a man who in his music lived so com-pletely on a level of subjective emotion, who spoke the language of passion with such directness and authority, should have longed so earnestly and with such bitter disappointment to be acclaimed a theoretician, a man of reason, a leading intellect pre-eminent in the cold science as well as in the living art of music. Janus-faced, his tem-perament pointed in one direction, his ambition in another; and yet temperament ruled even in his struggle to have his treatise published and recognized. With typical conviction of the worth of what he had to say, he humbly renounced all right to his theoretical discoveries, declaring it the work of God alone and fanatically castigating himself as an ass and a sinner. The obstacles which this "man of reason" found in his path to publication he denounced categorically as the work of the devil, crying out that "the Lord would walk among the infirm of the earth and choose among them one to confound the mighty."

The music left by his engrossing personality includes a large number of violin sonatas, some, like *The Devil's Trill*, still justly celebrated, as well as a minimum of one hundred and twenty-five authenticated violin concertos, a few of which fortunately still occupy a place of distinction in the modern concert repertoire. The significance of his contribution to violin technique can hardly be overestimated. Quantz, a German contemporary and a composer and theoretician of note, reported on the excellence of Tartini's double-stopping, his ability to execute trills and double trills equally well with all fingers (a notable addition to left-hand technique), the ease of his playing in the highest positions, and his rare gift for tossing off the greatest difficulties with-out apparent effort. He brought the violin bow closer to modern specifications and wrote a short treatise on the art of bowing which even to-day violinists may read with profit. The technical difficulties of one century are frequently child's play for the virtuosi of the next, yet the fingering and bowing technique requisite for a clean performance of Tartini's *The Devil's Trill* still imposes hours of careful practice upon our most skilful violinists. Above all, Tartini's contribution to violin playing lay in his use of the instrument as a vehicle for an intensely emotional lyricism.

The early violin concerto reached its peak in Italy with Tartini, in France with Leclair, and in Germany with J. S. Bach. The development of the violin concerto in France was retarded by a variety of national peculiarities. France has been the traditional battleground for aesthetic controversy in music. Gluck and Piccinni, neither of them Frenchmen, settled the merits of their respective theories and practices in Paris, with Parisian audiences and critics cast in the role of partisan electioneers marshalling support for their favourites. The deluge of pamphleteering and article-writing which covered Paris during the earlier controversy between Italian comic opera (Pergolesi) and serious French opera (Rameau)—a dispute in which even the august encyclopedists (Diderot, D'Alembert, Rousseau) were involved—placed aesthetic discussion in Paris on a level with an election campaign. To a much milder degree, the concerto also became in France something to theorize over, especially since it was an Italian importation and raised, therefore, the dearly beloved question of the rapprochement between French and Italian style which French composers and critics deliberated for nearly a century. A substantial body of musical opinion in France during the first third of the eighteenth century considered that the instrumental concerto as practised by the Italians was antithetical to the essential nature of French music. In addition (or perhaps this was part of what was being justified) France, unlike Italy, possessed no long line of violin virtuosi. French instrumental music was addressed to the amateur, the courtly dilettante, the competent student, rather than to the professional performer; and French instrumental technique remained sufficiently backward for a composer like Rameau to specify as late as 1741 that one part of an instrumental trio might be performed either on a violin or a flute, and another by a viola or a second violin.

The preface to Jacques Aubert's (1678-1753) *Concerts de symphonies,* which dates as late as 1730, is interesting in this connection. After noting that Italian concertos have had some success in France, and that just tribute has been rendered "to all who like Corelli, Vivaldi, and several others have done excellent work in this form," Aubert goes on to observe "of that sort of music, that notwithstanding the competence of some of the performers, the taste for it was not universal, especially among those ladies whose judgment has always determined the pleasures of the nation." Aubert was especially aggrieved at the young folk who were attempting to sharpen their technique on the difficulties "with which nearly all these works have of late been encumbered," and in so doing were "losing the elegance, the clarity, the beautiful simplicity of the French style." He found as damaging evidence against the Italian concerto the fact that it was a virtuoso piece and could be performed "only by a small number of illustrious people." As an early apostle of *Gebrauchsmusik*, Aubert argued for music which could be performed by the more or less competent pupil, as well as by the master, and which could be rendered equally well on all sorts of instruments.

So long as the demands of the amateur remained paramount, the solo concerto with its extensive technical requirements was bound to make slow progress. Moreover, the opera and the suite were the two forms which exhaustively engaged French musical thought. The suite, which functioned in France as a kind of national art form, was a sequence of short dances which emphasized simplicity of line, elegance of articulation, and intimacy of feeling; characteristics which Aubert feared would be coarsened and violated by the virtuoso pageantry of the Italian concerto. The opinion was by no means unanimous. A much greater composer than Aubert, François Couperin, dedicated several of his efforts to a union of French and Italian style. One such effort is clearly titled *The Reunion of Taste or New Concertos* (*Les goûts réunis ou nouveaux concerts*) (1724), augmented by an "apotheosis of Corelli." Another effort, the *Instrumental Concerto* (*Concert instrumental*) of 1725, in which Lully is now apotheosized, contains an overture with the programmatic inscription: "Apollo persuading Lulli and Corelli that the reunion of French and Italian styles will make for perfection in music." Possibly Couperin was right—an analogous attempt was made on a more extensive scale in Germany to amalgamate the suite and the concerto; but the historical development of the two forms lay in opposite directions, and both Couperin and the Germans failed. While his intentions were no doubt honourable, Couperin's compromise was written in the kind of musical French no Italian concerto composer of the period could read. His works are too essentially French in form and feeling for any outside influence to find a successful foothold.

The early French concerto is in reality simply a dance suite scored principally for a trio of instruments, with the word "concerto" used chiefly in its rudimentary sense to indicate a concerted manner of performance. For example, an early trio (1697) by Montéclair is frankly titled *Serenade or Concerto . . . suitable for dancing (propre à danser)*. The so-called concertos of Couperin, Rameau and Aubert may likewise be described essentially as suites rather than as concertos. The early sense of the word "concerto" survives in French music as late as 1741 in a Rameau trio titled *Pieces for Clavecin in concert with a Violin or a Flute, and a Viola or a Second Violin*.

While the French preoccupation with the suite retarded the development of the solo concerto, the French opera offered its instrumentalists no practical encouragement in that direction. Though the Lullian opera overture contributed one of the instrumentation patterns upon which the concerto grosso was developed, and though the operatic aria in France offered as serviceable a model for the solo concerto as did the operatic aria in Italy, the standard of instrumental technique in the French opera orchestra was far below that of Scarlatti's Neapolitan opera orchestra. The violinist in the French opera orchestra was called upon to render difficulties by no means commensurate with those which Scarlatti set for his instrumentalists. There is a vital difference between illustrating a general formal principle and offering the concerto composer a practical technical foundation upon which to work. Unlike Italy, neither the church nor the opera house in France afforded the virtuoso much opportunity to develop. Consequently in France the source of the solo concerto lies neither in the church nor in the theatre, but in the public concert hall. Also, since the solo concerto had so little opportunity to evolve out of a native French background, it was forced to look abroad, principally to Italy, for its models. A public concert organization, the Concerts spirituels, as it was called, was founded in Paris in 1725 and exerted an important influence to this end, for it facilitated the appearance of many Italian violin virtuosi who brought with them the concertos of their native land. The influence of this organization expanded, attracting the virtuosi of all Europe and stimulating the growth of the solo concerto in France to the point where, in Mozart's and Beethoven's time, Paris had already become the home of a French concerto style boasting such distinguished violinists as Viotti, Rode, and Kreutzer. The first great master of the French violin concerto was, however, Jean Marie Leclair (1697–1764), who learned the art from an Italian, G. B. Somis, an excellent violinist and a sound composer. Leclair composed two volumes of violin concertos (Op. 7, 10).

In Germany the progress of the solo concerto was relatively smooth, for the reception accorded foreign models was generous to the point of simple imitation, and both Italian and French practice were woven into the fabric of German art. The habit of learning from Italy was ingrained in German music, for all through the seventeenth century Germany had sent her finest musicians across the Alps to study the latest developments of a continually progressing art at its source. The line of German concerto composers is long. We note here only Johann Georg Pisendel (1687–1755) the doyen of German violinists; Georg Philipp Telemann (1681–1767), one of the most gifted and prolific composers of the period; and Johann Sebastian Bach (1685–1750) toward whom all streams of musical thought flowed as so many rivers toward a mighty sea.

Pisendel studied with the best masters Italy had to offer, Torelli and Vivaldi, and brought back with him to Dresden, where he served as leader of the Electoral orchestra, an excellent violin technique and a sound knowledge of the Italian craft of concerto composition. His violin concertos belong to the earliest German efforts in the form and show, at best, a definable individuality of style, a respectable gift for melody, and an occasional moment of inspiration. His compositions are few, for he was something of a perfectionist, given to recasting and repolishing the same work several times over. In his lifetime his reputation was principally that of a virtuoso, and the regard in which he was held is indicated by a violin concerto which Vivaldi composed for his use.

Georg Philipp Telemann was Bach's senior by four years. Musical opinion in eighteenth-century Germany rated him above Bach, and while history has justly revised this verdict, it serves nevertheless to indicate Telemann's formidable qualities as a composer. Upon two occasions Telemann was given preference over Bach in the consideration for a vacant post. At Weimar, Bach served only as court organist and chamber musician to Duke Wilhelm Ernst, for the more desirable position of Kapellmeister was already occupied. Upon the death of the incumbent (a musician named Drese) Bach, who was in line for the post, was passed over entirely and the first offer went to Telemann. Telemann declined, for he was then engaged in Frankfort, and the vacancy was filled by Drese's son. Again in 1722, when the important post of cantor at St. Thomas's church in Leipzig was made vacant by Kuhnau's death, Telemann was the first to be approached. This offer Telemann also rejected, for he had only recently accepted a position in Hamburg as director of the town music. Only when negotiations with Telemann, and with the second candidate, Graupner (the author, incidentally, of several beautiful concerti grossi), had fallen through was the post offered to Bach.

Despite an unavoidable rivalry for available positions, the relationship between Telemann and Bach seems to have been absolutely cordial. Telemann respected his rival, and Bach, with his unfailing appreciation for another man's merit, copied out whole cantatas by Telemann for study and use. Telemann was indeed an amazingly gifted composer. His facility as contrapuntalist, in an era of the greatest masters of polyphony the world has known, drew praise from Handel, who, it is said, declared that Telemann could write an eight-part motet as easily as anyone else could write a letter. Telemann's facility is perhaps the secret of the tremendous popularity he enjoyed with his contemporaries. His music is immaculately made and as delightful to listen to as anything one would hope to find even among the greatest masters. He lacks (as who does not) the immensities of musical intellect and human emotion which the friendship of time has revealed in the Bach scores; immensities which the limitation of a single performance could scarcely have revealed to Bach's contemporaries.

Telemann's fertility in all musical forms is breath-taking. His concerto production alone totals over a hundred and seventy compositions and is too varied in form and function to be characterized in a single sentence. It will suffice here to deal with one of the most interesting aspects of his secular concertos: his interest in the suite, which points to the influence of French music. Telemann himself, in an autobiographical notice published by Mattheson in his *Ehrenpforte*, tells us of the origin of this national-stylistic orientation. In 1704 he was appointed Kapellmeister to Count Erdmann von Promnitz at Soreau. There he was stimulated to compose suites in the manner of the French overture, for, as he tells us, the Count "was newly returned from France and liked these forms. I secured the works of Lulli, Campra, and other good

masters, and set myself to work in the same style, to such good purpose
that in two years the overtures numbered two hundred."

The suite was an older musical form than the concerto, and one
dearly beloved by the amateur musician. For a while, it made itself
felt in the concerto and in turn sought to take over from the newer
form some of its most characteristic elements. This interpenetration
of influences produced a short-lived mutation, a concerto-suite of
which Telemann left many, and Bach a few, examples. Many of the
Telemann suites are scored for string orchestra plus a solo instrument.
The Telemann suite in A minor, for example, is scored for solo flute
and strings, and is, in effect, a real virtuoso flute concerto in suite form.
The second Bach suite in B minor is similarly an authentic flute concerto composed in a series of short dance movements, rather than in the
traditional three-movement concerto form. The influence of the virtuoso concerto upon the suite is apparent in these compositions. The
reverse relationship—the influence of the suite upon the concerto—has
an older history and goes back to the early distinction between the
church and the chamber concerto. The early chamber concerto, it will
be remembered, was chiefly distinguished from its sacred counterpart
by its use of short dance movements taken over from the suite. With
the disappearance of this dual concerto style, the three-movement
form (as in the Bach Brandenburg concertos) emerged as the permanent
type characteristic even of the present-day concerto. In the first Brandenburg concerto, Bach succumbed momentarily to the old influence of
the suite, appending, as an afterthought to a complete three-movement
concerto, a group of short dances. The solo concerto, apart from
exceptional instances, remained free of the influence of the suite. One
of the exceptional cases occurs, as we may expect, in Telemann. His
violin concerto in D major contains such suite movements as a corsicana, a polacca, and a menuetto. It is, in essence, a three-movement
violin concerto with the menuetto functioning (as it does occasionally
in Mozart, for example) as the final movement. Between the first and
second movements a corsicana is interpolated, and between the second
and third a polacca, making five movements in all. In German clavier
music a similar attempt was made to combine the suite and the concerto. The clavier suite had become the special province of the amateur
performer, and the concertos designed for his use made the necessary
concession to amateur taste. In his clavier concertos Bach remained

aloof from this confusion of styles. However, his minor contemporaries (Kunzen, Petzold, Leffloth, Tischer) obliged with an assortment of gavottes, minuets, sarabands, bourrées, and rondos. This crossbreeding failed to produce a hardy offspring. The solo concerto was primarily a virtuoso piece, and both the amateur and the composer who sought to humour him were soon compelled to recognize the fact. The only surviving element of the suite is the rondo, which retained its hold on the last movement of the concerto. (In many of his concertos Mozart writes the word "rondeau," emphasizing his derivation from the French suite.)

Only three of the Bach violin concertos have come down to us in a form which we may hold to be authentic. Two are solo concertos (A minor and E major); the other is the famous concerto for two violins in D minor. All three also appear as clavier concertos, and it has been supposed that several other violin concertos now lost survive in transcriptions for the clavier. There is nothing "historical" or dated about the three concertos. They live completely in a timeless world of their own. The slow movement of the E major concerto, for example, stands quite apart from anything that has gone before in the form. There are many slow movements in concerto literature reflecting the profounder levels of human emotion, but it is only in the andante of the fourth Beethoven piano concerto, and in an occasional slow movement in a Mozart piano concerto, that we are given concerto music so thoroughly drained of every vestige of virtuosity, music which penetrates so completely through the intense heart of sound into the very sounding centre of human experience. The slow movement of the E major concerto is outwardly a free chaconne. The basic subject of the movement is, except for a brief intermission, continually present, usually in the bass, outlining as it were the ultimate bedrock of human emotion upon which the solo instrument offers its simple and affecting commentary. Like Beethoven in the andante of his fourth piano concerto, Bach understood how simple is the anatomy of a great emotion. If Bach's slow movements lie beyond the emotional horizon of previous concerto composers, they live likewise in remote seclusion from the atmospheric tone poems which are found in abundance in the slow movements of the romantic concerto. The adagio of the E major concerto—and this may be said of the slow movements of the two other violin concertos—because of its directness of expression, and because of the simple polyphonic rigour with which this expression is controlled, is not music which we can forcibly lay hands on, from which we can compel service to our own particular personalities, adding to it the coloration of our momentary moods. We can make no private bargains with Bach, for, with the selflessness of the truly great, he has endowed this movement with an existence of its own. We are frankly compelled out of ourselves and, with great emotion, become aware of every ounce of our apperceptive power ironbound to the inexorable movement of the music.

The concertos of Johann Sebastian Bach for solo clavier and orchestra are noteworthy apart from the intrinsic merit of the music. For one thing, they are among the first specimens of their kind. For another, stimulated by Bach's needs during the period of his conductorship of Telemann's musical society, the seven concertos for solo clavier and orchestra bear witness to a vital musical revolution in Germany, the pivotal point of which was the slow decline of the church as the centre of musical life and the emergence of the independent public concerto hall in its stead. Telemann's society, founded in 1704 and directed by Bach from 1729-36, was one of the earliest and most influential of the eighteenth-century societies of musicians who assembled weekly for the practice and extension of their art. At an earlier period these Collegia Musica, as they were called, were confined exclusively to the participating musicians themselves. In time the concerts were broadened out to include listeners as well, and by 1741 an attempt was made by Zehmisch in Leipzig to involve the general citizenry in a plan for the formation of a new society for giving concerts. The gradual displacement of the church by the concert hall raised a number of important problems for secular instrumental music, not the least of which was the development of the keyboard concerto in German music.

During the period that Bach directed the Telemann Musical Society the weekly programmes were composed mainly of his own music and that of his most talented pupils. Prodigious demands were made upon him for the creation of requisite music; and while these concerts have been recognized as the motivation for his seven clavier concertos, the specific manner in which they determined the structure, style, and content of these concertos has been a matter for considerable disagreement.

The varying interpretations are all founded on the fact that these clavier concertos are not original creations, but arrangements or transcriptions of other works, principally of violin concertos. The simplest explanation, and one frequently offered, is that Bach lacked sufficient time to write new music and so hurriedly converted what he already had on hand. The following from Schweitzer is typical of this opinion: "Bach needed clavier concertos, when he directed the Telemann society. The arrangements are often made with quite incredible haste and carelessness; either time was pressing, or he felt no interest in what he was doing."

There are, of course, other and more searching explanations based upon a closer analysis of the problems Bach most probably was confronted with in the writing of a clavier concerto. It is worth recalling that the instrumental concerto was, as we have seen, the product of a great succession of Italian composer-violinists (Corelli, Torelli, Vivaldi, etc.). Bach's youth and his early development as a composer coincide with the early expansion of the instrumental concerto via a heavy emphasis on the violin. The clavier concerto had yet to be created. The clavier, up to this point, had been used as a solo instrument only in sonatas, suites, and smaller forms. As a member of the orchestra its role was subsidiary, serving to accompany the solo episodes for the violin or to outline and strengthen the massed harmony of the orchestra. The fifth Brandenburg concerto of Bach is quite exceptional in this respect, for the cembalo is admitted into the solo concertino unit and provided with an extended solo cadenza. The clavier lacked an amplified concerto technique of its own, for there had been no general widespread attempt to requisition the particular resources of the instrument for the virtuoso work which a concerto demanded. It has, therefore, been suggested (Schering) that Bach turned logically to violin concertos already composed, and brought the clavier concerto into being by the simple process of altering the violin solos in a manner more or less appropriate to the clavier. This explanation assumes the priority of a violin style even in the clavier transcriptions, and much has been written to show that in the process of translation from one instrument to another Bach did not wholly eliminate the essentially violinistic figurations of the original. Quite another explanation argues, on the contrary, that clavier style was, at all times, uppermost in Bach's mind. Spitta, for example, finds that in the violin sonatas and suites which were subsequently arranged either wholly or in part for clavier, or organ, as well as in the violin concertos transcribed for the clavier, a comparison of the arrangement with the original shows the root to have been clavier rather than violin style. The germ of the idea of making the clavier predominant Spitta finds in the concertos even in their original stage as violin works. He argues that Bach no doubt "felt that the style of his violin concertos was so much moulded by his clavier style that their true nature could only be fully brought out in the shape of clavier concertos." The difference in viewpoint is not easily resolved, for stylistic analysis is still as much a matter of personal opinion as it is a matter of fact, learned critical dogma notwithstanding. On historical grounds—and on such a basis only—it is necessarily more logical for Bach to have turned to violin music as a source for his clavier concerto style, rather than vice versa. However, regardless of the merits of either argument, it is reasonably certain that considerations more vital for music history than an accidental lack of time or (for Bach) a mysterious lack of interest motivated the creation of these clavier concertos out of previously existing compositions.

The seven concertos for solo clavier and orchestra represent only part of the general problem of Bach's activities as a transcriber of his own and other composers' music. To the romantic and modern mind this is one of the most singular aspects of Bach's all-encompassing genius, for composers since Beethoven have been nourished upon a consistent diet of "self-expression," upon the consolations of an "it may be a poor thing but it's my own" philosophy, which looks with deep suspicion upon one composer openly imitating, or appropriating for his own use, the work of another. The typical romantic mind is reflected, for example, in the over-eager denial of a Dvořák or a Sibelius that any actual folk tune had ever been quoted in their music. After Beethoven it is rare to hear of a calm acknowledgment of indebtedness such as Brahms expressed when the similarity between the last movement of his first symphony and the last movement of Beethoven's ninth was pointed out. The habit of borrowing freely has been revived since the turn of our century, particularly in the work of some poets who have ransacked the whole of the world's literature for an apt image or an acute analogy. However, since he lived in no waste land, Bach found healthy sustenance in the music of his immediate contemporaries, recasting for his own purposes the scores of such a variety of composers as Vivaldi, Legrenzi, Albinoni, Marcello, Telemann, and Prince Ernst of Weimar.

Before we turn to the possible reasons for this phase of Bach's activity, a review of how it affected his work in the concerto is in order. The definitive word has not yet been said concerning the origins of each of the clavier concertos, for the originals from which some are conjectured to have been transcribed are still not discovered. Of the seven solo clavier concertos, the third in D major and the seventh in G minor are transcriptions, one whole tone lower, of the violin concertos in E major and A minor respectively. The sixth clavier concerto in F major is likewise a transcription, one whole tone lower, of the fourth Brandenburg concerto. In the original the concertino unit is composed of a violin and two flutes. In the transcription the flutes remain, but the violin is replaced by the clavier. Since the clavier has a wider keyboard range, it absorbs both the solo violin part from the concertino and the bass continuo from the ripieno. Even in transcription the work retains something of the character of a concerto grosso. The second concerto in E major is the last of the seven with definitely established sources. It has its counterpart in movements from three Bach cantatas, *Gott soll allein mein Herze haben, Ich geh und suche mit Verlangen,* and *Stirb in mir, Welt.* However, it is not certain that the cantatas were the direct sources from which Bach worked, and a clavier work has been conjectured to be the immediate model for the transcription. The sources of the remaining concertos, Nos. 1, 4, and 5 in D minor, A major, and F minor respectively, are in doubt. Internal evidence is the basis for the belief that the fourth concerto in A major is probably founded upon a clavier or organ original, although a violin model has not been entirely discounted, and even an oboe d'amore has been suggested. It has also been supposed that the original was a work by Bach. It has long been the general consensus of opinion that the first concerto in D minor is a reworking of a lost violin concerto. However, on the basis of double-stopping and general technique, a case has been made for a seven-stringed viola d'amore as the original instrument. It has also been argued, on stylistic grounds, that Bach's original model was not a work of his own, but possibly a concerto by Vivaldi. This particular aspect of the question is complicated by an obvious resemblance the concerto bears to two of the Bach cantatas,

Ich habe meine Zuversicht and *Wir müssen durch viel Trübsal*.[1] In the latter cantata, the opening movement, scored for organ and orchestra, is a direct analogue of the opening movement of the concerto. Organists who know this work are aware that they possess in its tremendous opening movement an organ concerto superior to any since conceived for the instrument. The second movement of the concerto and the first chorus of the cantata are likewise analogues of each other, and together constitute perhaps the most subtle and profoundly sensitive example in Bach of the relationship between cantata writing and concerto writing. It has been suggested that the original for the fifth concerto in F minor was also an unknown violin concerto, although once again it has been conjectured (largely on the basis of the fragmentary pizzicati accompaniment in the slow movement) that the model was not Bach's own, but possibly a work by Vivaldi.

The concerto for four claviers and orchestra is clearly a transcription of Vivaldi's concerto for four violins, Op. 3, No. 10. Of the three concertos for two claviers and orchestra, the third in C minor is an arrangement of Bach's famous concerto for two violins and orchestra in D minor. The first, also in C minor, had been assumed to be a transcription of an unknown violin work but has been reconstructed as a double concerto for violin and oboe. The second concerto in C major is an original work. Similarly the two concertos for three claviers and orchestra are generally regarded as original works rather than as transcriptions.

The four organ concertos (all without orchestra) are transcriptions. The first and the fourth are based upon violin concertos by Prince Johann Ernst of Weimar, Bach's patron and pupil, who possessed a fair talent heavily influenced by the Italians. In some measure the Bach concertos reflect the worth of the originals upon which he worked. These two are noticeably the weakest of Bach's entire concerto production. The Prince died at the age of nineteen, and a number of his

---

[1] Tovey professes to "see red" over the notion of a non-Bach original, which is a totally irrelevant thing to be seeing, although it is very hard not to sympathize with him. The D minor concerto is a prodigious and impassioned creation representing Bach at his greatest in the clavier concertos. This alone does not preclude the possibility of a Vivaldi original, although the respectable erudition devoted by Aber to suggesting a Vivaldi model still adds up, in the strictest sense, to nothing more than a suggestion.

violin concertos were subsequently edited by Telemann. The two remaining organ concertos, Nos. 2 and 3, are modelled after works by Vivaldi. The second, based upon Vivaldi's concerto grosso for two violins and orchestra, Op. 3, No. 8, is the finest of the group and stays, interestingly enough, remarkably close to Vivaldi's original. The third is notable chiefly for an arresting recitative slow movement.

Bach's interest in transcription is one of the conventional talking-points in Bach scholarship. In any close consideration of his concertos, it is indeed a difficult subject to avoid. It has already been suggested that the process of transcribing violin concertos for the clavier was founded on the historical development of the concerto by the Italian composer-violinists and that Bach's procedure was to learn from available models by adapting them to the new clavier requirements. In large measure Bach's general interest in the work of other composers was a matter of learning from accessible examples. As a young man his study of Buxtehude gave him command of the finest tradition in German art. He also studied the idiom of the French school at Celle; and during his nine-year stay at Weimar, where musical culture under the leadership of Prince Johann Ernst was orientated toward Italy, Bach undertook a careful study of Italian music with particular application to the scores of Vivaldi, Corelli, Legrenzi, and Albinoni.

It has also been argued, with rather unnecessary emphasis, that Bach's transcriptions are wholly an expression of a personal idiosyncrasy. Schweitzer, for example, alleges that Bach "liked other people's music in the most uncritical way, simply because it stimulated his own creative activity . . . . Bach transcribed the Vivaldi and other concertos not to make them more accessible to the public at large, nor to learn from them, but simply because this was his way, and it gave him pleasure." From Magister Pitschel, a contemporary of Bach, we hear something along the same line, for in a letter to a friend he reports that Bach "cannot, they say, ravish people with his own combinations of tones, until he has played something from a score to set his imagination in motion." Whatever truth there may be in this report does not preclude the strong probability that Bach also profited from the scores he was transcribing. Nor is the argument for psychological idiosyncrasy especially compelling when one considers that such transcription was a fairly common practice in Bach's time. For example Mattheson, the foremost critic of the period, tells us in his *Das beschützte Orchester* (1717) that "Compositions of this order (*concerti grossi, sinfonie in specie,* overtures) may also be played upon a polyphonic instrument, for instance upon the organ or harpsichord; a few years ago the celebrated S. de Graue, the blind organist of the new Dunes Church in Amsterdam, played from memory and with remarkable clearness in my presence, upon the excellent organ in his church, the latest Italian sonatas and concertos in three and four parts."

Any of the above theories, or better still, all taken together, offer a reasonable insight into Bach's preoccupation with the music of other composers. However, a similar process of expansion and refinement obtains in Bach's attitude toward his own scores. He had as little compunction in reworking his own music as in appropriating the music of his contemporaries for the purpose. For example, the first and third movements of the magnificent triple concerto in A minor for clavier, flute, violin, and orchestra are founded upon an earlier prelude and fugue for clavier in the same key. If we were to place the first movement of the concerto alongside the clavier prelude we would have, in effect, a miniature musical laboratory wherein we might retrace the musical chemistry (one might almost say alchemy, were it not that the little prelude is in its own way as pure gold as the concerto) involved in precipitating out of a simple clavier prelude a sonorous and complex concerto movement. The same procedure can be duplicated on a smaller scale and in a less dramatic fashion by comparing almost any of the originals with the Bach transcriptions. The essential point is that Bach operated, almost in a literal sense, as a creative logician, uncovering, realizing, and expanding hitherto unsuspected conclusions from the barest of musical premises. From this point of view the transcriptions become one more instance of Bach's tremendous gifts for musical engineering; a gift which served as a prerequisite for a principle of creation so basic with him that it may be taken as a definition of his place in the history of music. Unlike a composer such as Berlioz, who was primarily a frontier fighter, a settler in unexploited and unprotected territory, Bach tilled traditional soil and, on the rare occasions when he embarked on new ventures, sought relevant examples to guide the freedom of his effort. Basically Bach's musical personality was that of a surveyor or "spectator of all musical time and existence" (Terry), one who knew how to select a rough path for which others had broken ground, and take leave of it only when, under his hands, it had become a broad and magnificent highway already arrived at its ultimate musical destination. This he did not only for the originals which he amplified in transcription, but in a broader sense for the cantata, passion, toccata, for organ music, and indeed for the whole of the art of polyphony.

To return to the clavier[1] concertos of Bach, there is a caution to be observed in the relation between the solo instrument and the orchestra. Unlike the later piano concertos of Mozart and Beethoven, the balance of forces in the Bach clavier concertos is not an outgrowth of a head-on clash and rivalry between the two. In the piano concertos from Mozart onward, the dominance of the solo instrument is a direct consequence of its frank opposition to the orchestra. Two evenly matched forces are contrasted to, and thrust against, each other. No matter how finely balanced the two may be, the contrast which derives from this duality has become the basic musical fact toward which the composer's and the listener's attention is directed. In his clavier concertos the premise upon which Bach proceeds stands so thoroughly apart from the premises of a Mozart or Beethoven piano concerto that a marked difference must be observed in one's orientation toward these works. In Bach's time the clavier, as the instrument to which the figured bass was entrusted, formed an essential part of every concerto. It served to support the solo instrument and operated as a unifying force in the orchestral tutti. Even in the clavier concertos of Bach an accompanying clavier was employed. Since besides the solo clavier, another clavier figured as part of the orchestral ensemble, and since the tutti passages were as a rule rather thinly orchestrated, it followed that there would be a reduction in the marked opposition between solo and orchestra and in the element of contrast derived from this opposition. Furthermore, the solo instrument is kept at work all through the orchestral tuttis, so that Bach's main point, which was to achieve an overall predominance of clavier tone, was certainly carried. The clavier is not so much the solo instrument as it is the predominant instrument. The clavier concertos are thus aptly described by Spitta as "clavier compositions cast in concerto forms, which have gained, through the co-

---

[1] "Clavier" is the general term used at this time to include all keyboard instruments with strings. However, there is no doubt that the large harpsichord with two manuals was always used in concertos such as these.

operation of the stringed instruments, in tone, parts, and colour." The case is even more pronounced in the concertos for two, three, and four solo claviers. Here again it is the dominant mass of clavier tone, rather than an opposition of equal forces, which is the key to the concerto. The orchestra is even regarded by Bach as a dispensable element. In the slow movement of the C major concerto for two claviers the orchestra is dropped entirely.

The ultimate expression of this approach is a concerto for solo clavier without orchestra. Bach's *Italian* concerto is not a solitary example, for similar works were composed by his contemporaries; nor is it a *reductio ad absurdum* as one might at first suspect, for the clavicembalo (or harpsichord) with two manual keyboards, for which the *Italian* concerto was composed, is a polyphonic instrument capable of carrying many voices at once and of contrasting them dynamically, *forte* and *piano*, by means of a proper juxtaposition of the two keyboards. In the *Italian* concerto, the concerto contrast is carried dynamically by the *forte-piano* indications which Bach wrote into the score, while in place of tone-colour rivalry a single clavier tone reigns unchallenged. Bach's designation of the work as "a Concerto in the Italian taste" ("*einem Concerto nach Italienischem Gusto*") refers chiefly to the singing, cantabile style of the Italian violin concertos. This is most evident in the slow movement where the flowing right-hand melody soars over a discreet left-hand accompaniment with a grace of line and a profundity of feeling modelled after, yet unmatched by, any of his Italian contemporaries.

In a measure, Bach's evasion of the crucial concerto problem, which is to draw the solo instrument away from the mass and to treat it in a virtuoso fashion, is a reflection of his conservative allegiance to the old polyphonic church forms. The basis of his entire art is polyphony, the careful juxtaposition of voices or instruments so that all contribute equally in the development of a single subject. Each voice in a fugue carries on with no subservience to, or domination over, the remaining voices. Indeed, the organic cohesiveness, the sense of oneness instantly evident in Bach's polyphony, depends upon the clearest projection of each of the simultaneously sounded and apparently self-contained lines of musical thought. The unity of a polyphonic work rests upon a contradiction, i.e. the ability of several equal parts to fuse together into a single impression despite emphasis on their equality and on the lack of subservience of one part to another. In the early portion of this chapter it was indicated that the solo concerto, in its fullest extension, is anti-thetical to a rigorous polyphonic design, for if one instrument is regarded as a virtuoso solo, the other instruments cannot at the same moment be on a par with it. The solo concerto is more at home in the opera house than in the church, yet in Leipzig where Bach worked it was the church that was being slowly replaced by the concert hall, and it was from the church and from a long preoccupation with poly-phonic forms that Bach stepped into his new surroundings. A carry-over from church to concert hall is not surprising, especially since in his clavier concertos Bach could resolve the contradiction by dealing with an instrument which he could treat soloistically and polyphonic-ally at the same time. Furthermore, the presence of another clavier in the orchestra dulled the contrast in tone colour between solo and tutti which might have disturbed the evenness of his contrapuntal texture. Thus Bach's clavier concertos are not solo concertos in the modern sense of the word. They are defined by the precise historical moment of their evolution. They were created by a church musician adapting himself to the conditions of the new concert hall, and they retain, in consequence, much of the conservative polyphony of the church with comparatively few concessions to straight homophonic writing and to the soloistic display so pronounced in the later piano concerto.

This survey of the early solo concerto can hardly conclude without mention of the Handel organ concertos, among the first important efforts in this rarely practised form. The four Bach concertos for solo organ are the least vital part of his contribution to the concerto, and for once Handel surpasses Bach in a form in which both worked. For Bach the organ was principally a liturgical instrument tied body and soul to the church service, while for Handel it was a vehicle for dramatic extemporization in the concert hall. The largest portion of Bach's organ music is bound up closely with the chorale, in the treatment of which Bach acknowledged no master. Only a smaller portion is dedicated to the virtuoso capacities of the instrument. Bach and Handel were, if contemporary accounts be trusted, probably the two greatest organists the world has known, and the virtuosity of both performers carried over, with a different emphasis in each case, to the music they composed for their favourite instrument. The great virtuoso organ music of Bach, the toccatas and fugues, lies outside the province of the concerto, Handel's virtuoso music within it.

The entire orientation of Handel's art was in the direction of the concert hall, in keeping with a tradition which, for reasons of political and social history, was more firmly established in England than on the continent. The Handel oratorio, for example, is in essence a dramatic, non-liturgical choral piece heard more appropriately in the concert hall, where Handel originally presented it, than in the church. Handel presided over the concert performances of his choral music from his place at the organ, extemporizing at intervals upon the instrument, and introducing the organ concertos as part of the evening's entertainment. The advertisement of a dramatic piece by Handel sometimes lured the prospective customer with the offer of an additional organ concerto. For example, the advertisement of a Handel opera issued in late April 1739 read: "At the King's theatre in the Haymarket, Tuesday, May 1st, will be represented a dramatic composition called Jupiter in Arcos; intermixed with choruses, and two concertos on the organ." In November 1739 the performance of Handel's setting of Dryden's *Alexander's Feast* and of another ode by Dryden was accompanied, so Burney tells us, by two concertos for several instruments, and a concerto on the organ.

There are four volumes of organ concertos by Handel, two issued during his lifetime, and two after his death. The first set of six was published in 1738, the second in 1740. Both sets were published with the specification "for the Harpsichord or Organ." The two posthumous publications appeared in 1760 and 1797. It is frequently the case in these organ concertos that Handel adapted sometimes freely, sometimes literally, movements from earlier compositions originally scored for different combinations of instruments. The F major concerto, known as *The Cuckoo and the Nightingale* because of a bit of imitative naturalism in the second movement, is an example of such a transcription. Every movement is derived from music already composed in another form. The first movement is adapted from the first movement of the trio-sonata, Op. 5, No. 6, for two violins, or two flutes and bass. The second and third movements are based upon the second and third movements of the F major concerto grosso, Op. 6, No. 9. The final movement is derived from the second allegro from the Op. 5, No. 6, trio-sonata.

Sir John Hawkins in his *A General History of the Science and Practice of Music*, published in 1776, has left us an interesting account of Handel's manner of performance in his organ concertos. It is worth quoting not only for its historical value, but because the characteristics of his technique in performance are also the essential characteristics of the concertos he performed.

"As to his performance on the organ, the powers of speech are so limited, that it is almost a vain attempt to describe it otherwise than by its effects. A fine and delicate touch, a volant finger, and a ready delivery of passages the most difficult, are the praise of inferior artists: they were not noticed in Handel, whose excellencies were of a far superior kind; and his amazing command of the instrument, the fullness of his harmony, the grandeur and dignity of his style, the copiousness of his imagination, and the fertility of his invention were qualities that absorbed every inferior attainment. When he gave a concerto, his method in general was to introduce it with a voluntary movement on the diapasons, which stole on the ear in a slow and solemn progression; the harmony close wrought, and as full as could possibly be expressed; the passages concatenated with stupendous art, the whole at the same time being perfectly intelligible, and carrying the appearance of great simplicity. This kind of prelude was succeeded by the concerto itself, which he executed with a degree of spirit and firmness that no one ever pretended to equal.

"Such in general was the manner of his performance   Silence, the truest applause, succeeded the instant that he addressed himself to the instrument, and that so profound, that it checked respiration, and seemed to control the functions of nature. . . ."

Handel's organ concertos stimulated widespread interest in the form among minor English composers. For the most part English organ concerto composers such as Avison and Felton worked in the shadow of Handel's dominating presence. While their work is derivative, it is not wholly without merit. If Handel is the model and one is a capable imitator, the result is bound to be music probably lacking in inspiration, but certainly not deficient in a fundamental solidity of construction and in a pleasant if not especially important, elegance of style.

CHAPTER IV

The Classical Concerto

JOHANN SEBASTIAN BACH died in 1750. Possibly the same year, and certainly no later than 1755, Haydn was engaged in the composition of his first string quartet series. One need only compare Bach's *Art of Fugue* with Haydn's first quartets to gauge the depth of the abyss which lies between them. The principle of change is axiomatic in human history; this comparison serves to illustrate how, at the very moment the old achieves its crowning architectural glory, the new is already emerging on a secure foundation. Long before 1750 the architects of the new music (Bach's sons among them) were working side by side with a master like Bach whose musical edifices were to be the last and the most imperishable of the splendours of the past.

The issues at stake in the conflict between the old and the new went deep into the fundamentals of the art. Style, form, and temperament, the basic elements of which identify the music of an age, were passed in review and basic reorientations effected in each. Polyphony gave way to a homophonic idiom, the fugue to the sonata form, and the sober church spirit to the gallantries of the aristocratic salon. Stylistically the change from a polyphonic to a homophonic idiom was neither sudden nor complete, but the emphasis had shifted unmistakably. Bach often wrote harmonically, but almost always from an implied contrapuntal standpoint. His sons helped to reverse the procedure; and by the time

Haydn was ready to tackle his Op. 20 series of string quartets he was compelled into a deliberate effort to recover the ancient art of polyphony for its potential use in a sonata movement. Polyphony was never lost sight of in Haydn or Mozart, but its use was now reserved for specific occasions within the body of a dominantly homophonic texture.

Both fugue and sonata are formal processes rather than formal molds; in both cases the processes are, each in its separate way, developmental; and, moreover, elements of the one are not excluded from appearing in the other. Yet the differences between the two are considerable. Fugue process is based on counterpoint, i.e. on the interweaving of several lines of music simultaneously. The main subject of a fugue must necessarily be one capable of development in terms of linear combinations. The harmonic mass (the vertical aspect, so-called) is by no means negligible in a Bach fugue; yet we are mainly aware of it as dispersed into a simultaneity of horizontal lines whose interweaving is established as the prime focus of attention.

In a sonata structure, one customarily encounters a multiplicity of subjects, initially set forth (in what a textbook will call the "exposition" section) one after the other, and disposed, to begin with, in an ordering of simply contrasted tonalities, e.g. the first subject, or subject group, in the tonic (or "home") key, a second subject, or subject group, in the dominant key (or if the first subject is in minor, the second may well occur in the relative major). A transition, as eventful in new material as in any given instance the composer finds desirable, serves to carry us from one key to another, and hence from one main subject group to another. A group of closing formulas will close off the exposition and serve to announce that the materials of the movement have now been set forth.

Then follows a "development" of the materials just stipulated. With composers like Mozart and Beethoven, the sense of development is usually conveyed by a process of breaking up the subjects into smaller component units, by modulations into tonal territory remote from the tonic key, and by the unfolding of contrapuntal combinations. In brief, one will find here such resources as seem best calculated to lay bare those ramifications of the original material as are, in the composer's judgment, most significant. The vital sense of what is important cannot be stipulated by rule. In part what distinguishes Beethoven from a conscientious mediocrity is just this ability to see into the potentialities for development of a musical subject, and, moreover (since there are always far more possibilities than can be used), just this ability to make enduring judgments in the selection of these ramifications and compelling revelations concerning their relationship to one another. The development section is the heart of the sonata movement, imposing a maximum levy upon imagination, judgment and knowledge.

Eventually the development section winds its way homeward via such devious or direct paths as seem best suited to the particular movement. The tonic key again achieved—and this tends necessarily to be a heralded moment in the strategy of the movement—the material is then reviewed (not merely repeated, as the term "recapitulation section" might erroneously suggest) in the light of what now remains to be said and summarized through it. A coda to complete the movement forms the closing portion of the recapitulation, although it may upon occasion be enlarged to the point where one may choose to construe it as a separate section.

This is necessarily a somewhat schematic and simplified textbook description; yet it will serve our purpose as an approximate guide to the complex happenings within a concerto movement cast in sonata form. At the moment, the point to be noted is that with the growth of sonata-form construction, harmonic writing clearly displaced polyphony as the dominant idiom in instrumental music. The change in musical style had its counterpart in a change in the principles of formal construction.

Because of its sharp contrast in melodies and tonalities, the sonata form has sometimes been thought to be essentially more dramatic than the fugue. The difference, however, is not one of degree but of kind. The fugue can be as dramatic or as lyrical as the sonata, but it will be so in its own specialized way. The sonata composer will rely upon the open conflict of themes and of major and minor tonalities; the fugue composer, if he is so minded, upon dissonant strettos and thick chromaticisms which, as in many Bach fugues, impart a monumental and concentrated intensity to the music. The greatest masters of the sonata form—Haydn, Mozart, and Beethoven—understood the dramatic values of polyphony and continually deployed concentrates of counterpoint to buttress the open arraignment of conflicting melodic forces.

The point is worth attention, for Mozart in his concertos made much of it.

In temperament the younger composers shifted away from the severe intellectual concentrations and the aloof monumental passions of J. S. Bach, to the cultivation of an easy and gracious melodic line, a cool and limpid harmonic background and, above all, an air of elegance, refinement, and well-bred gallantry. Music had, by and large, moved from the church ceremonial to the aristocratic salon. The patronage of the nobility was more eagerly sought after than the discipline of the church, and the amusement of titled dilettanti deemed more profitable than the service of the Lord. The concert hall was also slowly but surely developing into a powerful attraction, and composers were bending a willing ear toward public taste. Haydn and Mozart, the two greatest composers to inherit the new tradition, absorbed its most worth-while elements and, as complete artists, responded as well to the deeper currents which stirred below the surface of the new ideals. With immense human insight, both composers realized that refinement was not incompatible with profundity, gaiety with pathos, and a precise and clipped utterance with a broad and swelling passion. Great minds and great hearts of all ages have much in common; it is usually among mediocrities that the differences in temperament between one period and another are marked as irreconcilable alternatives. The alternatives of the mediocre mind are scarcely edifying to contemplate, but they do illustrate, if only in reverse, the temperamental limitations of an age. Thus the polyphonic mediocrity who aped Bach's idiom was at worst dull, while the empty-headed gallant who mimicked Mozart's speech was at best insipid. The small minds of Bach's age took themselves seriously both in private and in public. If they were not inspired, they were at least ponderous and learned. The small hearts of Mozart's age, like the literary wits in eighteenth-century England, were concerned to be pat rather than profound. Small talk was studied and witticisms prepared in advance, for a composer could afford to be shallow provided he showed poise. One's musical manners were always on display, and to be thought dull was a cardinal social disgrace. Small wonder that Mozart, whose music, however uneven, never degenerated into small talk, should sometimes have been thought heavy and strained by his contemporaries.

From among the many transitional composers who bridged the gap between Bach and Mozart, two of the sons of Bach, Carl Philip Emanuel and John Christian, emerge as figures of the first importance. C. P. E. Bach's clavier sonatas are more to the point in this respect than his concertos; yet the whole of his music may be subsumed under Burney's contemporary judgment that his music "may serve as a touchstone to the taste and discernment of a young musician." Older conservatives apparently found his work "fantastic and far-fetched," for an admirer like Burney thought it wise to caution "that the style of this author is so uncommon that a little habit is necessary for the enjoyment of it. . . ." How significantly he contributed to the future may be judged by the unreserved tribute paid him by men like Haydn and Mozart. Haydn declared categorically that "whoever knows me well will see how much I owe to Emanuel Bach, and how I have understood and thoroughly studied him." Mozart broadened the indebtedness with the flat statement that "those of us who can do what is right, learned from him; whoever will not admit it is a bad lot" (*Lump*).

C. P. E. Bach's concertos—there are fifty-two of them—in certain respects point as much to the past as to the future. In his great D minor clavier concerto, which pianists would do well to revive, the minor tonality, the sober and dramatic intensity of expression, make little concession as yet to the refined gallantries which dominate the concertos of his brother. In mood the work predicts Beethoven more typically than it does early Mozart. The formal organization of the opening allegro still revolves around the elaboration of a single subject and its related motives. Polyphonic texture, however, no longer obtains as a fundamental idiom, and whatever counterpoint there is, is calculated primarily upon a harmonic basis. Some of the finest of C. P. E. Bach's concertos are still, as are those of his father, in minor keys. His music is characteristically expressive rather than brilliant. Burney, who heard him perform in Hamburg, reported that "he possesses every style, though he chiefly confines himself to the expressive," and noted further that in slow movements "he absolutely contrived to produce from his instrument a cry of sorrow and complaint. . . ."

The concertos of John Christian Bach are opposite in temperament and closer in this respect, as well as in style and form, to early Mozart. J. C. Bach was a composer of learning and genius who stood head and shoulders above the routine epigram-makers of the period. Yet his genuine niceties of expression and his keen sense of style seem often inhibited by the fear that a phrase may appear a trifle unpolished, or a modulation into a minor key perhaps a little indiscreet. He was the darling of the London public; a worldly composer who knew how to make a living from his art. Music was meant to entertain, not to edify; a composer, if he were so minded, might venture upon deeper emotions provided he did not seriously distract or puzzle his audiences. From the viewpoint of the concerto, Haydn managed somewhat better in this respect than J. C. Bach, while Mozart was immeasurably more successful, or perhaps one should say more daring, than either. J. C. Bach was not a timid composer. He was simply sensible, for he knew his patrons and he enjoyed the wealth and fame they were willing to shower upon his decidedly superior gift for being pleasant. It is said, and we may believe it, that when his work was contrasted with that of his elder brother, Carl Philip Emanuel, he replied: "It is easily explained; he lives to compose; I compose to live." His music, incidentally, is as neatly epigrammatic, as shrewd, and as incisive as this well-turned phrase.

The main tonalities of the J. C. Bach concertos are major rather than minor, a practice which Haydn and Mozart continued. Polyphony disappeared almost completely in his concertos. His opening allegros are already cast in a clear sonata form; indeed, in a specific kind of sonata form which Mozart took over directly from him and amplified. His genius, restricted though it was by what may be called the social content of his music, had sufficient backbone and originality to exert its influence over greater masters. Mozart, who had met J. C. Bach in London during his visit there as a child prodigy, converted three of his sonatas into concertos. This was Mozart's first effort in concerto form, and it is noteworthy that it was undertaken in frank imitation of the older master. Conversely, one of the finest of J. C. Bach's concertos, the B-flat major, Op. 13, No. 4, was transcribed by Haydn for pianoforte solo. J. C. Bach's concerto output was considerable. It includes three sets of clavier concertos, six per set, published in London (Op. 1, 7 and 13), as well as a number of symphonies concertantes and a group of clavier concertos still in manuscript. The titling of the three opus groups shows the beginning of a significant change in the character of the solo instrument. Op. 1 is composed for harpsichord whereas Op. 7 and Op. 13 offer the performer the alternative of a harpsichord or a pianoforte. The stylistic change implied was hardly realized by J. C. Bach, and we shall postpone discussion of it until the maturation of the problem in the Viennese concertos of Mozart.

Haydn's main efforts centred in the symphony and the string quartet. While he was, strictly speaking, the creator of neither, the superior quality of his genius and the sheer quantity of his production (104 symphonies and 83 quartets) assert his title as "father" of the symphony and the quartet beyond any narrow chronological claim that may be made for his forebears. Haydn's concertos are, however, decidedly more limited in quantity and in quality. It must be emphasized that this is a total judgment; the sum of his concertos as against the total body of his symphonies and quartets. Individual concertos, needless to say, bear ample evidence of his particular genius. Likewise with respect to the development of the concerto, Haydn's contribution to its special problems is slight in comparison with the variety, scope, and power of Mozart's achievement. Nevertheless his concertos are a stage more advanced than those of J. C. Bach, for his technique was richer and his temperament more rugged. An example will suffice for each.

The orchestration of the J. C. Bach concertos is still in a conservative tradition. Like the clavier concertos of his father, the solo instrument is supported only by a limited body of strings. His maturest set, Op. 13, adds two oboes and two French horns *ad libitum*, but the fact that the winds may be added or subtracted at will indicates that tone colour was still a negligible factor in the classical solo concerto. This judgment is based upon his eighteen published clavier concertos; and while a manuscript concerto such as the one in E-flat major calls for flutes, clarinets, horns, and a bassoon in addition to the strings, it is an exception not in itself sufficient to alter the general picture. If we select for comparison two of Haydn's best-known concertos,[1] the ones in F

---

[1] There are several good reasons for believing that the rather popular 'cello concerto in D major, long attributed to Haydn, is not his work at all but was composed by Anton Kraft (1752–1820), one of his pupils. At the risk of being a bit obvious, one must say that the concerto is as charming as ever even if Haydn didn't write it. One can hardly do better than Tovey, who graciously gives Kraft "the credit of his very pretty work" and confidently expects his audience "not to be snobbish about it."

major and D major for harpsichord and orchestra, we find the string section amplified by a discreet wind support. The wind instruments are relegated, however, almost exclusively to the orchestral tuttis, and virtually in every instance drop out as soon as the solo enters. The rich blending of piano and wind tone was, as we shall see, an accomplishment of late Mozart. Indeed, the first great expansion of tone colour in the classical concerto is largely identified with Mozart. During his early Salzburg period his colour range was still limited, although his orchestra did include a few wind instruments. After his trip to Mannheim and Paris the question of tone colour became a discernibly conscious one, and during his last Viennese period, as we shall note, the resources of the orchestra were exploited with notable success. Haydn's contribution shows itself, therefore, as considerably less than Mozart's and somewhat more than J. C. Bach's.

Temperamentally Haydn's hearty personality asserts itself in his concertos, even though they are duly respectful to their social surroundings. This is most easily marked in the one element which is essentially ill at ease in an aristocratic drawing-room—the treatment of folk songs or folk-like melodies. The D major harpsichord concerto of Haydn, for all its elegance and glitter, breaks into a robust Hungarian rondo at the end. J. C. Bach's dabbling in folk tune is, on the contrary, prettified and quite charming in a bloodless sort of way. His B-flat concerto, Op. 13, No. 4, concludes with a series of variations on a Scotch folk tune, *The Yellow-Haired Laddie*, which are a shade too precisely polished. Even so traditional and sedate a melody as *God Save the King*, which turns up in the finale of his Op. 1, No. 6 concerto, is adorned with a curlicue or two which transform it from a rather dull hymn tune into something close to a courtly minuet.

The concertos of Mozart occupy a position of unusual importance both in the total body of his music and in the modern history of the form. Mozart has contributed to the modern concerto repertoire numerically its largest single unit of masterpieces. He has written more great concertos than any other single composer of his standing. Likewise, in relation to his other music, we find more great concertos by Mozart than symphonies of equal merit; and this is a judgment manifestly not in dispraise of one of the leading symphonists of all time, but simply an emphasis on a ratio between concerto and symphony all the more significant in that it does not obtain in Haydn or Beethoven or Brahms. In intrinsic merit the total body of the Mozart concertos stands, at very least, on a par with the total body of his symphonies; and by whatever standards greatness in music is measured, his finest concertos must be judged equal to his finest symphonies. This relationship, too, holds for Mozart alone. Generally speaking, the nine Beethoven symphonies constitute a far weightier contribution than his seven concertos; and taken individually, no one Beethoven concerto is as vital a part of his total accomplishment as is, for example, his *Eroica* symphony. In Mozart, however, there is no such choice between two piano concertos like the ones in D minor and C minor, and two such symphonies as the C major (*Jupiter*) and the G minor. These judgments are necessarily personal ones. Nevertheless, they are worth stating, for the assumption of their validity is one of the several reasons —although, in all truth, one of the less objective reasons—for the detailed discussion of the Mozart concertos to follow.

The need for a close view of the Mozart concertos rests also upon the fact that his total accomplishment cannot be given adequately in a single descriptive summary. The concerto was a form which he cultivated from his earliest boyhood until the very last months of his life. Mozart was a composer who was continually developing in response to the pressure of new ideas and new circumstances. Since his concertos cover the entire period of his creative life, the progress registered from one group of concertos to another becomes an accurate index to his total development as a man and as an artist, from period to period, often year to year, and sometimes even from month to month. An adequate study of his concertos involves, therefore, a close understanding of specific biographical and historical backgrounds. Changes in immediate background afford an indispensable insight not only into the differences between one concerto series and another, but illuminate as well very nearly all of the many phases through which his entire music passed. The concertos are unique in that they are, to the fullest extent, as great and as varied as the man who created them. A short summary will not suffice to do them justice. Furthermore, the study of specific conditions under which each of the concertos was created turns into, as we shall see, a rather complete story of how an eighteenth-century musician lived and worked. Thus they are more than the aspect of a single personality, for an account of their origins and their contemporary meaning comes rather close to being the autobiography of an age.

In the course of its development the Mozart concerto made vital contributions to several purely technical problems. The deflection of the main course of the concerto from the violin to the piano, which received its first major impetus from J. S. Bach, was given decisive momentum in the work of Mozart. The change from the harpsichord to the pianoforte, already indicated in J. C. Bach, reached a major turning-point with Mozart. Likewise the sonority and power of the concerto orchestra was expanded to a new level, and last but not least, the classical sonata-form concerto achieved its maturity.

Mozart's first concerto efforts were not original compositions but arrangements of the work of other composers, products of his boyhood composed between the ages of nine and eleven. They reflect his earliest enthusiasms and his keen ear for the music of contemporaries which he heard during his successful tour through Europe as a child prodigy. The earliest are a group of three piano concertos (K. 107) arranged from three sonatas for clavecin or piano (Op. 5) by Johann Christian Bach, whom young Mozart met during his London visit. They were composed either in the summer of 1765 toward the end of his stay in London, or in the autumn of the same year during the trip to Holland. Four other piano concertos (K. 37, 39, 40, 41) composed between April and July 1767, after the return to Salzburg, are founded mainly on sonata movements by Raupach and Honauer, two composers whom Mozart met in Paris. Movements by Schobert, Eckardt, and C. P. E. Bach were also utilized in these concertos by the boy composer. From our present perspective, none of the composers, with the exception of the two Bachs, seem worthy of Mozart's attention; yet these arrangements, however much we may attribute them to the uncritical curiosity of youth, are an early indication of his constant interest in musical practice outside the confines of his native city. He remained all his life an avid musical tourist, absorbing for his own instruction the varying styles in composition and the diverse techniques in performance in every city that he visited. His comments in his letters on matters of style and technique show a shrewd and critical intelligence. They make engaging and instructive reading, for Mozart was quick to profit from a new idea, and later on, as an eminently practical composer faced with the prime problem of making a living from his music, many of these ideas crop up in his scores composed in foreign cities and designed to please the local palate.

Mozart's first piano concerto (K. 175 in D major) was composed in December 1773 in Salzburg, during the first years of the dismal reign of Hieronymus, Count of Colloredo, who in 1772 was installed as Archbishop of Salzburg. The new Archbishop was the very prototype of a feudal monarch who regarded the population at large as a mass to be disciplined. The Mozarts were no exception, and while the young composer, remembering the admiration lavished upon him by the aristocracy of Europe, shared acutely in the general hostility toward the new despot, old Leopold Mozart went about his usual business of securing for his son whatever advantages a connection with the Archbishop might offer. Mozart, then sixteen, produced a festival opera *Il sogno di Scipione* (K. 126), for the installation ceremony, and was rewarded in August 1772 with the post of concert master at a salary of a hundred and fifty florins. Thus began a long and irritating period of servitude against which he grew ever more rebellious, finally precipitating that open break with the Archbishop which marked the turning-point of his career.

The D major (K. 175) was, during Mozart's lifetime, one of the most popular of his concertos. He performed the "old concerto" in Mannheim early in 1778 because, as he tells us, "it is such a favourite here," adding characteristically that he "also extemporized for half an hour." It was also a favourite during his performances in Vienna in 1783, especially the new rondo (K. 382) which he wrote for it in March 1782. The new rondo with variations replaced the final canonic allegro originally composed for the work, and brought sufficient applause during one concert in Vienna to warrant a repeat performance. Mozart reported that it made "a furore in Vienna," and enjoined his father "to guard it like a *jewel*—and not give it to a soul to play," for "I composed it *specially* for myself." The cadenzas which are extant for this work were subject to Mozart's penchant for improvisation, for, as he tells us in one of his letters, "whenever I play this concerto, I play whatever occurs to me at the moment."

The following year he composed the charming bassoon concerto (K. 191) for a Baron Thaddäus von Dürnitz, an amateur performer on the instrument. Like many another aristocratic dilettante who could afford the luxury, the Baron commissioned from the distinguished composers of the period compositions for his private edification. We are indebted to him for a small number of bassoon works by Mozart: a sonata for bassoon and 'cello (K. 292) and three concertos for bassoon and orchestra, two in B-flat and one in C major. Until recently only the sonata and the B-flat concerto (K. 191) were known. A second bassoon concerto in B-flat has been edited by Max Seiffert (1934), but the C major concerto is still undiscovered. Composed in June 1774 during his eighteenth year, the bassoon concerto (K. 191) stands at one of the minor crossroads of Mozart's creative career when the superficial grace and glitter known as the *"galant"* style began to encroach perceptibly upon his music. Six months earlier (the end of 1773) his music had been cast along broader and severer lines. The structural proportions of the first piano concerto in D major (K. 175), although by no means as ample as in his maturest work, are larger than in the bassoon concerto. The canonic opening of the original allegro finale in the piano concerto likewise testifies, for all its elegance and charm, to a severer turn of mind. The viola quintet (K. 174) of December 1773 shows his interest in the sober colouring achieved through the use of an extra viola, while the "little" G minor symphony (K. 183) completed toward the end of the year, is a flaming dramatic outburst which, in comparison with the violin concertos of 1775, pointedly illustrates the difference between Mozart's "grand" (or "serious") and his *"galant"* style. The bassoon concerto of 1774 stands between the fullest expression of either style and represents, in a sense, Mozart's effort to negotiate the distance between the two. The use of such terms as *"galant"* and "serious" is not wholly satisfactory, yet they suffice to indicate a valid stylistic distinction. The bassoon concerto, however artfully it sports its gallantry and suave glitter, lapses into casual counterpoints and an occasional episode in minor (as in the first movement) and is sustained throughout by an energetic orchestration reminiscent of the more "serious" productions of the previous year.

The year following the bassoon concerto Mozart undertook a determined investigation of the violin concerto. Five violin concertos (K. 207, 211, 216, 218, and 219), his most notable contribution to this specific form, were composed in 1775, his nineteenth year. Taken all in all, this series is an amazing performance. It would seem that nineteen is hardly the age for the production of earth-shaking masterpieces. In all truth, there have been greater wonders than these concertos known in the world, some of them the productions of the maturer Mozart; yet many a reputable composer thrice his age would have been only too glad of a chance to claim as his own the incredible fluency of musical speech, the richness of texture, and the sheer beauty of melodic line that pervades this music. A genius at any age, nineteen or ninety, is one of the earth's unaccountable eccentricities, and it takes a long-standing experience in believing, like the Red Queen, "six impossible things before breakfast," to credit, on the one hand, a Titian in his nineties painting with the fresh exuberance of a young man first discovering the manifold wonders of a colourful world, and, on the other, a youth of nineteen manœuvring through the infinite complexities of the sound-world with a surety and a wisdom which he lacked years enough to derive from experience. It is the surety, the conscious command of his craft, which is most astonishing. These five concertos are, as Eric Blom has noted, the earliest of his music to maintain itself permanently in the world's concert repertoire; nor are the reasons hard to find, for Mozart's style at this period is the last word in elegance and refinement. Lest these much-maligned adjectives be misconstrued, let it be understood that at no time was Mozart capable of simulating the hard elegance, the inanimate refinement of polished enamel or carved ivory. There are moments of self-conscious "gallantry" in the concertos, just as there are moments of genuine tenderness. The elegance of the concertos is at no point a factor of shallowness of feeling, but a component rather of the mobile grace, the conscious sophistication which we associate naturally with all that is youthful, living, and lovely. To be sure, the profound agitations and exalted sorrows of the G minor symphony, the D minor piano concerto, the great *Requiem*, will not be found in the five violin concertos, for such difficult emotions presuppose, in addition to a knowledge of the craft of composition, both the personal experience and the inner mastery of profound misfortune. Part of the groundwork for this was being laid in Mozart's service to the Archbishop of Salzburg, but at the moment this undercurrent of unhappiness had broken to the surface neither in his life nor in his music.

While each of the five is an entity in itself, there are a few basic resemblances in general technique which may be noted. Purely for its sheer abundance of melody this series deserves to be ranked among the richest contributions to the violinist's repertoire. Melodies of surpassing loveliness are piled thick and fast one upon the other; so much so that often Mozart bothers not even to write in a little transitional fanfare or a scale sequence to bridge the distance from one melody to another. Even for the main melodies in a sonata-form movement he does little more than spare the time and space for their repetitions in the necessary places. In the first movement of the fourth concerto in D major (K. 218), where the embarrassment of riches is especially evident, the music becomes so crowded with new ideas that the main subject of the movement is soon lost sight of completely and fails to reappear even in the final recapitulation of all leading melodies. So far as the development of themes is concerned, more often than not, in place of the extension of an already established subject we are given a group of new ideas with only a general feeling of kinship with the old. Mozart's creative genius was truly at a fever pitch. Beautiful melodies evolved with too much spontaneous rapidity for him to have been over-concerned with extracting the ultimate amount of flavour from any one of them. Structurally, if not emotionally, these concertos are rhapsodies controlled by an innate refinement of expression and an unerring sense of inner form. The counterpoints of the previous period are wholly forgotten. These works are ruled by an expansive spirit, by a continual sense of the imminent discovery of a new melodic kingdom. While in the last three concertos the orchestration is quite substantial, in the first two (K. 207, 211) the orchestral load is noticeably lightened to speed the voyage of discovery. There is little time for a tourist's meditation on the swiftly passing landscape. The time had not yet come when, as in the G minor symphony, Mozart could probe with a passionate and single-minded concentration the ultimate depths of the profoundly tender little motive which opens the work. The world, at nineteen, is too full of wonderful variety, and these concertos, for all their maturity, are an eager reflection of this world.

The concertos were designed principally for Mozart's own use, and also for Gaetano Brunetti, who served as concert master in the Salzburg court orchestra. They are undoubtedly an accurate reflection of Mozart's style of violin playing. In one of his letters he tells us that, when he performed the fourth concerto in D major (K. 218), it "went like oil," adding that "everyone praised my beautiful, pure tone." If this describes his violin technique, it also describes the quality of the concertos. They should go like oil, and a violinist needs to bring to this music not so much an extravagant virtuoso technique as a pure and beautiful tone. As a concession to Brunetti, Mozart composed two alternative movements to the concertos. One was an adagio (K. 261) to replace the slow movement of the fifth concerto in A major (K. 219). Leopold Mozart subsequently recalled it to his son's memory by describing it as the adagio "which you wrote specially for Brunetti, because he found the other one too artificial." Brunetti may have had peculiar taste; but it is interesting that Mozart did not stalk off in outraged dignity, as we are told geniuses are supposed to do when the value of their work is questioned. Music was then a commodity intended primarily for use, not for gathering dust in attics or library cellars where it might enjoy only the ceremonial obeisances of the élite. Mozart found it inconsistent neither with his integrity nor his genius to indulge the limitations of a colleague's taste. The other alternative movement composed for Brunetti is a rondo concertante (K. 269) to replace the final movement of the first concerto in B-flat major (K. 207). Both alternative movements date from 1776, the year following the composition of the concertos. The substitution of a rondo finale in the first violin concerto brings it in line with the second, third, and fourth concertos, each of which concludes with a rondo movement. The fact that Mozart used the French form of the word, *"rondeau,"* has been taken (Wyzewa-St. Foix), along with general stylistic considerations, as evidence of the influence of the French *"galant"* violin concerto upon Mozart. Be that as it may—and the point is not an unlikely one—the final movement of the fifth concerto (K. 219) is blessed by a trio middle section which is an uninhibited Hungarian rhapsody; the kind of wonderful folkish outburst one expects to find in Haydn rather than in Mozart.

The fourth violin concerto (K. 218) has a close analogue in a concerto in D major by Luigi Boccherini (1743-1805).[1] The Boccherini

---

[1] Boccherini is the composer of several lovely 'cello concertos. The best known, the 'cello concerto in B-flat, is still often heard in our concert halls. It combines a nicety and precision of detail with a type of warm Italianate melody rich in sentiment and devoid of sentimentality.

work was composed in 1768, seven years prior to the Mozart concerto, and intended for Filippino Manfredi, a noted violinist and a friend of the composer. Despite the general thematic similarity between the two works, the influence of the Boccherini concerto can easily be exaggerated. Mozart's indebtedness to Boccherini is of much the same variety as the indebtedness of a creative portrait painter to the physical features of the subject who poses for him. There is a decided resemblance in the physical outlines of the melodies, but in the spirit which animates the Mozart concerto we recognize only Mozart and positively no one else. For example, the opening theme in the second movement of the Mozart concerto is taken over verbatim from Boccherini. Yet in Boccherini this theme is merely an inner voice accompaniment taken in the tenor part of the harmony, whereas in Mozart it is elevated note for note to the position of the first theme of the movement: a pearl that Boccherini neglected and Mozart seized upon. This melody appears, incidentally, in an ingenious rhythmic disguise in the final movement of the Mozart concerto, and curiously enough in still another rhythmic variant also in the finale of a concertone in C major (K. 190) composed by Mozart in 1773. The resemblance to Boccherini in this particular case may be accidental; just as the resemblance between the opening of Mozart's fifth violin concerto in A major (K. 219) and the opening of the Vivaldi violin concerto, Op. 6, No. 4, undoubtedly is. The fourth Mozart concerto in D major (K. 218) was referred to by Mozart and his father as the "Strassburg" concerto. A theme in the final rondo is reminiscent of a Strassburg dance.

The remaining works for violin and orchestra can only be summarized here. They comprise mainly compositions whose authenticity is doubtful. The first is the famous *Adelaide* concerto, which Mozart supposedly composed at the age of ten. It is a joyously naïve little work and has been edited by Casadesus with three cadenzas by Paul Hindemith. Whether or not its creation would be beyond the capacity of a ten-year-old is an irrelevant question in Mozart's case. The concerto was supposed to have been written at Versailles for the French Princess Adelaide. A dedicatory letter from Mozart to the Princess is reputedly extant. The concertone (K. 190) for two violins and orchestra is authentic Mozart. It was composed in 1773 and bears, in its first movement, abundant evidence of the contrapuntal writing characteristic of

Mozart's "serious" style that year. It is a minor contemporary of the first piano concerto in D major (K. 175), and much smaller in stature than the violin concertos of 1775. The other violin concertos (K. 268 and 271a) have been doubtfully attributed to Mozart, although it is probable that they are in part his work. It has been suggested, for example, that the E-flat major violin concerto (K. 268) in the form in which it now survives is a re-working of Mozartean material by Johann Friedrich Eck, a Munich violinist who had heard the work performed by Mozart. The authenticity of the D major concerto (K. 271a) is likewise doubtful, although the finale contains a motive also used by Mozart in his ballet *Les petits riens*. There has been no general agreement among scholars on the two concertos as they now stand. From a musical and technical standpoint they are markedly different from the five violin concertos of 1775, although they fall comfortably enough within the general framework of what one may call a Mozartean style. While the two concertos contain much worthwhile music, they are dominated by a virtuoso spirit foreign to the five clearly authentic violin concertos. In the case of the D major concerto (K. 271a) this has been explained on the basis of Mozart's need for a display piece during his Paris visit. The enlarged proportions of the two concertos are, unlike his later piano concertos, not a result of the greater scope of his musical ideas, but principally a matter of making room for a brilliant virtuosity which is spread-eagled over the broad surface of the music. The last work for violin and orchestra is a rondo (K. 373) which Mozart composed for Brunetti in April 1781, and which also appeared in a flute transcription (K. Anh. 184).

Following the violin concertos, three piano concertos (K. 238, 242, 246) were composed during 1776. Mozart was still bogged down in the Salzburg morass, hanging on to the dreary fringes of a small-town high society which Leopold Mozart doggedly cultivated for whatever advantages it might bring his son. Two of the concertos were designed for the local aristocracy: the one in F major for three pianos (K. 242) composed for Countess Lodron and her two daughters, and the C major concerto (K. 246) written for the "high and mighty Countess Lützow" (Mozart's own description). The Countess Lodron was the sister of the Archbishop and, in Leopold Mozart's opinion, a factor in court politics, although how successfully he courted her influence is indicated by the fact that the Mozart family subsequently charged her with deceit. The ladies were rather far from being superlative performers. One of the Lodron trio must have been especially weak, for one of the three piano parts in the F major concerto (K. 242) is consistently written on a very simple technical level. The Lützow concerto (K. 246) was once attempted by the Countess herself at a private musicale, and, according to Leopold Mozart, "all told her, and she agreed, that she played it abominably." The work seems to have served Mozart as a student piece. In Mannheim he taught "the daughter of the house" where he was staying (also referred to as "the house nymph" and "my highly esteemed pupil") to "scramble through" the concerto. Mozart was apparently rather fond of the three-piano work and indeed it is excellent entertainment both for performers and audience when the requisite forces are available for its performance. Mozart composed cadenzas for this concerto and also arranged it for two pianos.

The remaining concerto of 1776, in B-flat major (K. 238), was composed before the others. It is the best of the three, and since it was earmarked for no one in particular, one may suppose that Mozart intended it for his own use. It is, on the whole, a charming little work, with an engaging tenderness of expression which crops up frequently in his less weighty compositions. All three concertos follow the practice established by the violin works of the year previous by concluding with a rondo finale.

There is no way of knowing what Mozart himself thought at the time of the Salzburg *beau monde* in which he now moved, and which replaced the solid bourgeois citizens who previously had been his chief circle of acquaintances. Mozart and his family were in Salzburg, and so there was no occasion for the letter-writing which is, apart from inferences drawn from his music, our ground source of information on his thought and feeling. If the letters of a later period mean anything, Mozart accepted the condescension of the aristocracy with more than a single grain of salt. He was too hardy an individualist to be overcome by the flattery of the privileged. He obviously did not like the "high and mighty" Lützow; and his father, who placed great stress upon aristocratic connections, felt it necessary two years later to insist to his son that "you must cultivate extreme politeness in order to ingratiate yourself with people of standing." In any case, the effect of his new milieu is evident in the two concertos composed for the Countesses Lodron and Lützow. The elegance, polish, and poise of the concertos are a reflection of the surroundings for which they were intended. The works possess an exquisite clarity and a justness of proportion in which we recognize the hand of a master, but they are limited in profundity of expression, which would have been distinctly out of place, and in virtuosity, since they were tailor-made for the capacities of limited performers. Nevertheless, there are moments, such as the restless episode in minor in the finale of the C major concerto (K. 246), which presage the profounder utterances yet to come.

The piano concerto in E-flat major (K. 271) which followed was composed in January 1777 for Mlle Jeunehomme, a celebrated French virtuoso who most probably visited Salzburg late in 1776 during a concert tour. This work marks an important advance in Mozart's concerto writing. It is his first piano concerto intended for a virtuoso performer, and the technical timidity which characterizes the Lodron and Lützow concertos is abolished at one stroke. Free from the technical and emotional limitations of the Salzburg salons, this concerto in E-flat is the first step in the direction of the great piano concertos of his Vienna period. The expansion of technique which he now was able to permit himself provided room for a deepening of musical content; and, once released from the restrictions of aristocratic dogma which regarded music as a polite social entertainment, he composed, for the first time in his concertos, a slow movement posited on the more vital assumption that music is a profound human experience. The undercurrent of deeper emotional utterance which emerges in fleeting moments in the elegant concertos of 1775-76 are the surviving tremors of that impassioned emotional earthquake which rent the calm surface of his music in the "little" G minor symphony of 1773. In the slow movement of this concerto (K. 271), composed four years later, the bars are again down, and once more Mozart's speech takes on the accents of one deeply moved. Both the symphony and the concerto serve to remind us that the language of passion was now being spoken freely in German literature. Goethe's *Werther*, which appeared in 1774 and was thus a close contemporary of Mozart's symphony and concerto, had released over Europe a flood tide of literary romanticism. The Mozart works, and also the cluster of romantic symphonies—the

Funèbre (No. 44), the *Adieux* (No. 45), the *Passione* (No. 49), and the symphony in C minor (No. 52)—composed by Haydn about 1772, indicate that both masters were consciously or otherwise in close touch with the more progressive spirit of the age.

The formal structure of the E-flat major concerto is in many respects unusual. In the first movement the piano enters in the second measure, sharing the initial statement of the main subject with the orchestra. The immediate introduction of the piano has often been described as an innovation of the fourth Beethoven piano concerto. The principle, however, is already present in this work. The slow movement is a curious and deeply felt rendition in concerto form of an operatic aria complete even to the point of recitative; while the finale is a rondo with a menuetto interpolated as a centre piece.

Toward the middle of 1777 the strained relations between the Mozarts and the Archbishop had come to a head. Mozart was getting nowhere in Salzburg, and the conviction was growing in both father and son that they would have to look elsewhere for artistic and financial recognition. In a letter to the Archbishop dated August 1, 1777, Mozart summarized an oft-repeated request for permission to travel. He reminded the Archbishop that on March 14 his father had "set forth most accurately in his humble petition " a full account "of our unhappy circumstances," and that no reply had been received. "Later my father again applied for leave of absence, which Your Grace refused to grant, though you permitted me, who am in any case only a half-time servant, to travel alone. Our situation is pressing and my father has therefore decided to let me go alone. But to this course also Your Grace has been pleased to raise certain objections." The Archbishop's position is not difficult to understand. The relations between a composer and his patron were still based on the feudal absolutism which was rapidly being undermined in Europe. but which was not to be overthrown for another two decades. Mozart placed his finger, unwittingly perhaps, on the crux of the question by the use of the word "servant." The musician was in fact nothing more than a servant, a social convenience on a slightly higher level than a butler or a coachman; his talent was taken as a matter of course (else why hire him), and his financial reward was commensurately small. From the Archbishop's point of view servants, whether they were composers or less talented individuals, simply had no business to absent themselves for a few months in order to earn a more substantial livelihood in another city. The economic merits of the Mozart case were, so far as the Archbishop was concerned, rather beside the point. And it was precisely these merits which Mozart argued firmly and clearly. "Most Gracious Prince and Lord!" he continued. "Parents endeavour to place their children in a position to earn their own bread; and in this they follow alike their own interest and that of the State. The greater the talents which children have received from God, the more they are bound to use them for the improvement of their own and their parents' circumstances, so that they may at the same time assist them and take thought for their own future progress. The Gospel teaches us to use our talents in this way. My conscience tells me that I owe it to God to be grateful to my father, who has spent his time unwearyingly upon my education, so that I may lighten his burden, look after myself and later on be able to support my sister. . . . Your Grace will therefore be so good as to allow me to ask you most humbly for my discharge. . . ." Since Mozart (or his father, who may have dictated the letter) argued on the basis of the Gospel, the Archbishop decreed, in a memorandum to the Court Chamberlain, "that in the name of the Gospel, father and son have my permission to seek their fortune elsewhere." In other words, the petition was answered by an outright dismissal.

Mozart took to the decision joyfully, for it meant release from an irritating and unprofitable servitude, and in September 1777 he set out from Salzburg in the company of his mother, seeking a brave new world to conquer. Mozart senior was, however, quite worried at being left hanging with no official court position to sustain him, and also very lonely now that the two had gone. In a letter, reporting the first lap of the journey, his son sought to amuse him with absurd stories about a lop-sided cow and about a merchant who recognized him and presented his name which, "thank heaven, I have forgotten." He urged his father "not to worry, but to laugh heartily and be merry and always remember, as we do, that our Mufti H.C. (the Archbishop Hieronymus Colloredo) is an idiot, but that God is compassionate, merciful, and loving." Leopold Mozart replied, warning his son that such levity with respect to the Archbishop was dangerous, for his letters might get lost and fall into the wrong hands; and in another letter reported that

he had been reinstated by the Archbishop, who enjoined him—a "rig-
marole of nonsense" in the elder Mozart's phrase—"to conduct himself
calmly and peaceably with the Kapellmeister and other persons
appointed to the court orchestra."

The first stop on the journey was Munich, the capital of Bavaria,
where Mozart hoped for a court appointment which would provide a
better livelihood than Salzburg. But the various persons of influence
whom he spent his time soliciting had nothing but promises to offer.
He was told that it was too soon for him to expect an appointment,
that he ought to take himself off to Italy first and make himself a
reputation. He had not enough money to stay on indefinitely at Munich waiting for something to turn up, and a scheme for sustaining him
by collecting "ten good friends, each of whom would fork out one
ducat a month" fell through. The critical interview with the Elector
ended with that dignitary walking off, mumbling apologetically:
"Yes, my dear boy, but I have no vacancy. I am sorry. If only
there were a vacancy. . . ." Whereupon Mozart commended himself to the Elector's good graces, and mother and son moved on to
Augsburg.

The stay at Augsburg was uneventful, apart from Mozart's astounding all and sundry with his piano-playing and fantastic improvisation.
As was fitting and proper for a visiting virtuoso whose success depended
in a measure upon the extent to which he ingratiated himself with the
local authorities, Mozart's first social call was upon the local magistrate,
a Von Langenmantl whose name he gleefully twisted into every
absurd variant imaginable. Mozart made the call accompanied by his
uncle and was properly indignant when that "most excellent and
lovable man . . . had the honour of waiting upstairs on the landing like
a lackey until I should come out of the Arch-Magistrate's room." The
patrician's son, in the company of several of his boon companions,
subsequently indulged in a bit of stupid baiting of Mozart who was,
after all, only a musician and therefore a social inferior. Whereupon
Mozart promptly informed him that "it would be easier for me to
obtain all the orders which it is possible for you to win than for you to
become what I am, even if you were to die twice and be born again."
By way of easing the tension, he also informed the assembled company
that they were "a lot of mean pigs," and stalked off. He found other

companions more congenial and appreciative, particularly the piano-builder Stein and a curious gentleman called Demmler, who expressed his amazement at Mozart's playing by laughing uproariously and cursing a bit on the side. After giving a concert in which he in part replenished his resources, into which travelling expenses and the stay in Munich had made inroads, Mozart and his mother journeyed on to Mannheim, their first really important stopping-place.

The Mozarts arrived in Mannheim on October 30, 1777, and spent the next four months in that flourishing musical city which boasted one of the finest orchestras and one of the most dissolute courts in Europe. In Mannheim, Mozart came into contact with a far richer orchestral practice than anything he had hitherto known, and the influence it exerted on his music is evident in the concertos composed shortly thereafter in Paris. With respect to the purpose of his journey, which his father reminded him was "either to get a good permanent appointment, or . . . to go off to some big city where large sums of money can be earned," Mannheim turned out as disappointingly as Munich. The Elector of Mannheim took his own good time making an ultimately unfavourable decision with regard to an appointment, and in the meantime Mozart waited about doing next to nothing to replenish his fast-disappearing resources. His father was soon writing letters bordering on hysteria, accusing his son of extravagance and laziness, bemoaning the sizable debt he was saddled with at home on account of the journey, and speculating darkly after the fashion of worried parents upon what would become of his daughter Nannerl after his death. Mozart himself was meditating sarcastically over a gold watch he had received in place of a much-needed money payment for one of his court performances, and was soon thinking that his "landlord would rather hear the sound of money than of music." The flautist Wendling (for a time his particular friend) had assured him that Paris was "the only place where one can still make money and a great reputation," and a trip to that city, which several of the Mannheim instrumentalists were to undertake in two months, seemed the only solution to his problem. There was still the matter of supporting himself and his mother for two months and of buttressing his finances to sustain a trip to Paris. Wendling came to his rescue with a commission secured from an amateur Dutch flautist named De Jean (or Deschamps), "a gentleman of means and a lover of all the sciences," who was willing to pay two hundred precious gulden for "three short, simple concertos and a couple of quartets for the flute."

The commission was reported by Mozart to his father in December 1777, and in February of the following year he was forced to retail the unwelcome news that De Jean had not lived up to his obligations. "M. De Jean is also leaving for Paris, tomorrow," writes Mozart, "and, because I have only finished two concertos (K. 313, 314) and three quartets (K. 285, 285a, App. 171) for him, has sent me ninety-six gulden (this is four gulden too little, evidently supposing that this was the half of two hundred); but he must pay me in full, for that was my agreement with the Wendlings, and I can send him the other pieces later. It is not surprising that I have not been able to finish them, for I never have a single quiet hour here. I can only compose at night, so that I can't get up early as well; besides, one is not always in the mood for working. I could, to be sure, scribble off things the whole day long, but a composition of this kind goes out into the world, and naturally I do not want to have cause to be ashamed of my name on the title page. Moreover, you know that I become quite powerless whenever I am obliged to write for an instrument (the flute) which I cannot bear. Hence, as a diversion, I compose something else such as duets for clavier and violin, or I work at my mass."

There is no need to divorce from its context this statement of an antipathy toward the flute, and to deduce from it that the flute concertos are necessarily of slight musical value. A simple reading of the letter shows that if the whole De Jean project failed to evoke his strongest enthusiasm—his heart was set at the moment on doing an opera, which was impractical under the circumstances—he felt, nevertheless, a keen sense of responsibility for a work bearing his name. His critical judgment was in every respect acute and his musical conscience, as we read, beyond reproach. Regardless of how he may have felt toward the instrument he was commissioned to write for, we can feel assured that his sense of responsibility was sufficient for him to pour into his flute concertos the very best music he was capable of writing at the moment. Moreover, weighed down by unaccustomed responsibilities, badgered by letters from a worried father, and depressed by his failure to find thus far an opportunity for composing the kind of music which he felt would most surely reveal his genius, Mozart's sharp expression of dislike for the flute, the instrument to which his attention was now tied, may easily have been a matter of blaming with weary irritation whatever happened to be close at hand. Certainly neither the flute concertos nor his wonderful writing for the instrument in his symphonies and operas can have been a product of intense dislike.

It has been conjectured by Dr. Einstein that the flute concerto in D major (K. 314) may have been composed in 1777 before Mozart left Salzburg. His theory is that it was originally an oboe concerto written for Giuseppe Ferlendis, an oboeist stationed in Salzburg between 1775 and 1778, and that Mozart, pressed for time, simply re-wrote it for the flute. Indeed both concertos are still in his Salzburg manner. The orchestra is still small, the exploitation of instrumental tone colour rather limited, and the main emphasis still upon clarity and elegance. The G major flute concerto (K. 313) is more expansive, and more expressive than the D major (K. 314) which, perhaps, supports the view that the D major was the earlier of the two. The G major concerto is a longer work. The development section in its opening movement falls into an extended restless minor mood punctuated by brusque commands from the orchestra, while its slow movement is in a vein of quiet melancholy composed with that rare art of understatement of which Mozart was so consummate a master. The D major concerto, while more economical in length, is more prodigal in its melodies. Its surface is smoother than the G major concerto, and an occasional highlight of orchestral colour or of contrapuntal complexity casts an immediately perceptible glow over the music. Although the flute is almost exclusively the centre of attention, every now and then Mozart permits the violins to share the limelight, sometimes, as in the second movement, playing the first violin off against the flute, sometimes, as in the final movement, developing a contrapuntal interplay between first and second violins with the flute weaving a breath-taking figuration above the polyphony. In the context of the untrammelled simplicity of this concerto, such elementary complexities come as a multiplication of beauty and with just that note of newness which is in itself a source of delight. The Andante for flute and orchestra (K. 315), composed in Mannheim early in 1778, was written, in Dr. Einstein's opinion, for De Jean as an alternate to the slow movement of the G major concerto (K. 313) which may have been beyond this amateur's capacity.

In consequence of the failure to receive full payment from De Jean for the concertos and the quartets, Mozart's sister Nannerl back in Salzburg was forced to dip into her meagre savings for an extra fifty gulden to help defray the expenses of the trip to Paris. Mozart arrived on March 23, 1778, armed with a long list of socially prominent Parisians whom his father had recommended for his particular attention, and proceeded immediately upon the usual round of social calls. The moment was not an auspicious one, for Paris was plunged head over heels in an enthusiastically acrimonious feud between the partisans of Gluck and of Piccinni. Mozart stood aloof from the controversy for reasons of diplomacy. Moreover, to offset a pale non-partisanship, he had not even a titbit of personal scandal to offer as a calling card. His bid was made on the basis of his intrinsic worth as a composer and performer. In view of the circumstances, it was a rather colourless hand to hold in that fantastic game of chance which composers before and since have had to play for a reputation and a livelihood.

His mother found the cost of living in Paris high, and soon after their arrival she reported back to Salzburg that "our capital has become very small and won't go very far." Their living quarters were small, dark, and uncomfortable. "The hall and the stairs are so narrow," she writes, "that it would be impossible to bring up a clavier. So Wolfgang can't compose at home, but has to go to the house of Monsieur Le Gros, who has one." The great lords and ladies whom Mozart visited paid more willingly in compliments than in cash. "You say that I ought to pay a good many calls," wrote Mozart to his father, "in order to make new acquaintances and revive the old ones. That, however, is out of the question. The distances are too great for walking—or the roads too muddy—for really the mud in Paris is beyond all description. To take a carriage . . . means that you have the honour of spending four to five livres a day and all for nothing. People pay plenty of compliments, it is true, but there it ends. They arrange for me to come such and such a day, I play and hear them exclaim: '*Oh, c'est un prodige, c'est inconcevable, c'est étonnant !*' and then it is—'*Adieu.*' At first I spent a lot of money driving about—often to no purpose, as the people were not at home."

Sometimes the great ladies did not even bother to be polite, and the reception was quite discouraging to a sensitive and serious musician who was justly conscious of his worth and who demanded a full measure of respect for the dignity of his profession. His account of the reception accorded him by Madame la Duchesse de Chabot is a vividly drawn picture of the regard in which a composer was held by a so-called patron of the arts.

"I had to wait," writes Mozart, "for half an hour in a large ice-cold, unheated room, which hadn't even a fireplace. At last the Duchesse de Chabot appeared. She was very polite and asked me to make the best of the clavier in the room, as none of her own were in good condition. Would I perhaps try it? I said that I should be delighted to play something, but that it was impossible at the moment, as my fingers were numb with cold; and I asked her to have me taken at least to a room where there was a fire. '*Oh, oui, Monsieur, vous avez raison*,' was all the reply I got. She then sat down and began to draw and continued to do so for a whole hour, having as company some gentlemen, who all sat in a circle around a big table, while I had the honour to wait. . . . At last, to cut my story short, I played on that miserable, wretched pianoforte. But what vexed me most of all was that Madame and all her gentlemen . never interrupted their drawing for a moment, but went on intently, so that I had to play to the chairs, tables, and walls. Under these detestable conditions I lost my patience."

A few commissions and lessons, however, were turned his way. "I think I told you in my last letter," wrote Mozart to his father, on May 14, 1778, "that the Duc de Guines, whose daughter is my pupil in composition, plays the flute extremely well, and that she plays the harp *magnifique*." The daughter was a talented performer, gifted in particular with a marvellous memory, but her talent for composition was, in Mozart's judgment, "extremely doubtful." The charming concerto in C major (K. 299) for flute and harp was composed in April 1778 for De Guines and his daughter. The content of the music tells us that it was designed primarily for pleasant entertainment. In comparison with the G major flute concerto (K. 313) composed earlier in the year, it marks an even further stage in the retreat from the high point in thought and emotion achieved by the E-flat major piano concerto (K. 271) of 1777. Episodes in minor are infrequent and one has the feeling that they were introduced as much to meet the routine need for a varied tonality as for that deepening of emotional expression which the use of a minor key usually signalizes in Mozart. The slow movement maintains a quiet, even tenor untroubled by the note of melancholy which, in the adagio of the G major flute concerto, moves just under the surface of the music. While in the first movement Mozart is apt to fall into the use of routine devices, in the last movement he recaptures that irresistible spontaneity of expression which has rescued even his slightest music from oblivion. The final rondo moves along at a brisk pace, treating a variety of lovely folk-like tunes with inexhaustible inventiveness. Mozart is an engrossing speaker, and even when his subject-matter does not engage our deeper emotions, one feels that one can go on listening for hours. This place will do as well as any to observe that the devices which one finds in a lesser Mozart concerto may also be located, as so many well-studied mannerisms, in the work of a veritable host of minor contemporaries. The difference is simply this: in Mozart they rarely appear as mannerisms or as conveniences to replace inspiration. The spontaneity with which they bubble up in his music is an exact equivalent of the wholehearted conviction with which he put them to use. The common stylistic traits of the period—and each generation has its own—served as the basic syntax of his musical speech. But at no point did Mozart indulge in the social chitchat, the casual passing of the time of day, which has doomed many a lesser contemporary to the obscurity of a period piece.

The Duc de Guines must have thought the honour of teaching his daughter and of composing a concerto for his use was ample recompense for Mozart's labour. "Just imagine," Mozart reported to his father in July, "the Duc de Guines, to whose house I have had to go daily for two hours, let me give twenty-four lessons and (although it is the custom to pay after every twelve) went off into the country and came back after ten days without letting me know a word about it, so that had I not enquired out of mere curiosity . . . I should not have known that they were here! And when I did go, the housekeeper pulled out a purse and said: 'Pray forgive me if I only pay you for twelve lessons this time, but I haven't enough money.' There's noble treatment for you!" The sum was ridiculously small and Mozart, feeling that he was being imposed upon, refused to accept it. "It amounted to this," he continued, "that the Duke wanted to pay me for one hour instead of two—and that from *égard*. For he has already had, for the last four months, a concerto of mine for flute and harp, for which he has not yet paid me. So I am only waiting until the wedding is over and then I shall go to the housekeeper and demand my money."

The one other concerto composed by Mozart in Paris is the sinfonia concertante (K. Anh. 9) for solo wind quartet and orchestra written during April 1778. In Mannheim, Mozart had heard the "excellent and very strong" orchestra which boasted some of the finest wind virtuosi in Europe, and a broader understanding of the resources of the orchestra, particularly of its wind section, was one of the most noteworthy consequences of his tour. The form itself deserves some attention, for it stands at the crossroad between the old concerto grosso and the new symphony, having "nor youth nor age, but, as it were, an after-dinner's sleep, Dreaming on both . . ." Following the great stylistic reorientation which one may date for convenience about 1750—the year in which Bach died, and in which Haydn possibly composed his first string quartets—the sinfonia concertante appeared as a kind of diehard survival of the almost obsolete concerto grosso within the framework of the rapidly evolving symphony. In its manner of orchestration —it is an orchestral work in which several instruments appear as virtuoso solos—the sinfonia concertante is tied to the old concerto grosso. In internal structure it is a derivative of the sonata-form symphony. The first movement of the Mozart work is, for example, a fully developed sonata-form movement as is usual in the symphony. In the transition from the concerto grosso to the symphony many characteristics of the former were retained by the early practitioners of the latter form. The hold of the sinfonia concertante was strongest on the Mannheim symphonists, who were, apart from Haydn, the most important of the early founders of the modern symphony. Examples of the sinfonia concertante were composed by Holzbauer and Toeschi, who were still working in Mannheim during Mozart's visit there, and especially by Karl Stamitz and Cannabich, the latter one of Mozart's particular associates during his stay in Mannheim. Apart from Mannheim, the sinfonia concertante technique never quite lost its appeal even for Haydn. It crops up, for example, in the adagio of his symphony No. 36 in E-flat major, composed before 1769, and also in so late a work as the andante of his symphony No. 96 in D major, composed in 1791 for his first trip to London. The form enjoyed particular popularity in Paris

during Mozart's sojourn in that city. As St. Foix tells us, publishers'
catalogues and concert programmes are replete with examples not only
by the Mannheimists, but also by such composers as Cambini, Davaux,
and J. C. Bach.

The Mozart sinfonia concertante (K. Anh. 9) was composed for a
quartet of Mannheim virtuosi who had turned up in Paris. The flute
part was to be taken by Wendling, the oboe by Ramm, the bassoon by
Ritter, and the horn by the distinguished horn player Johann Wenzel
Stich, also known as Giovanni Punto, for whom Beethoven later composed his Op. 17 sonata for piano and horn. The Mannheim virtuosi,
who were among the finest performers in Europe, were favourites
with the audiences of the Concerts spirituels, and a work which would
present four of them at once was calculated to meet with approval. Le
Gros was the director of this important concert organization, and
apparently friendly toward Mozart, although he seems to have been
part of the petty conspiracy which prevented the work from being
performed. Mozart's account of the affair in the letter to his father,
dated May 1, 1778, follows:

"There appears, however, to be a hitch with regard to the sinfonia
concertante, and I think that something is going on behind the scenes
and that doubtless here too I have enemies. Where, indeed, have I not
had them? But that is a good sign. I had to write the sinfonia in a great
hurry and I worked very hard at it. The four performers were and still
are quite in love with it. Le Gros kept it for four days to have it copied,
but I always found it lying in the same place. The day before yesterday
I couldn't find it—I searched carefully among the music—and discovered it hidden away. I pretended not to notice it, but said to Le Gros
'A propos. Have you given the sinfonia concertante to be copied?' 'No,'
he replied, 'I forgot all about it.' As of course I could not command him
to have it copied and performed, I said nothing; but when I went to
the concert on the two days when it should have been performed,
Ramm and Punto came up to me in the greatest rage to ask me why
my sinfonia concertante was not being played. 'I really don't know,' I
replied. 'It's the first I've heard of it. I know nothing about it.' Ramm
flew into a passion and in the music room he cursed Le Gros in French,
saying it was a dirty trick and so forth. What annoys me most in the
whole affair is that Le Gros never said a word to me about it—I alone
was to be kept in the dark."

The upshot of this miserable bit of conniving was that Paris never heard the work and Mozart ultimately sold it to Le Gros without retaining a duplicate. The version which has come down to us calls for a clarinet in place of the flute which Mozart specified in his letters. Mozart's original manuscript has never been discovered. According to Friedrich Blume, the copy in which the music is preserved shows, in its phrasing indications, its numerous accents, and in its dynamic markings, the hand of a late romantic musician. However, the solo part now assigned to the clarinet is well suited to the characteristics of the instrument.

The work is an important one in Mozart's development as a composer. It is the finest concerto he produced during the tour and, by virtue of the unique combination of four solo wind instruments with orchestra, a notable advance over his previous concertos in richness of instrumental colour and orchestral resource. In this work he made the strong and highly coloured Mannheim orchestra his own and employed it with a solidity, a deftness, and a sheer beauty of sound which none of the Mannheim symphonists could quite approach. It is the simple superiority of his genius which makes this one work the epitome of all that the Mannheim orchestrators sought to accomplish. The four Mannheim virtuosi may well have been in love with it, for it was their own kind of music only on a higher level.

The sinfonia concertante, since it was meant to be heard by a large concert audience and to be performed by expert instrumentalists, is more amply proportioned than either the flute concertos or the work for flute and harp. The themes in the first two movements have a breadth and fullness commensurate with their rich instrumental embodiment. The first movement is straightforward and unruffled; and when the opening subject returns broadly spaced out in the bass beneath the tremolo of the violins, it brings with it some of the old-world dignity of the concerto grosso. The second movement is Mozart's first large-scale slow movement scored heavily for "colour" instruments. The earlier divertimenti are engagingly experimental in the matter of tone colour, e.g. the divertimento of 1773 (K. 166) scored entirely for ten wind instruments including two English horns or the freakish little affair (K. 187) composed for two flutes, five trumpets, and four tympani; but they are slighter pieces and their slow movements by no means commensurate with the effort Mozart put forward in the sinfonia concertante. While the slow movement in this work is one of Mozart's eminently songful creations, the expressive power of the colour instruments, the winds, is still held under restraint. In this slow movement Mozart does not yet attain the warm interweaving of tone colours, the understated though deeply felt romanticism which appears three years later in the adagio of the serenade (K. 361) for thirteen wind instruments. However, this is compensated for in the development section of the first movement, which is entirely in minor, and is as sensitive and as tender a bit of colour scoring as one will find in Mozart. One thing Mozart does not attempt in this concerto, and that is to unleash the harsh dramatic impulses which the acid edge of a massed woodwind tone can set in motion, as he did later on in the powerful C minor serenade for woodwind octet (K. 388) composed in 1782. The finale of the sinfonia concertante comprises ten decorative variations upon an unassuming folk-like tune. The pattern of the variations is strict and perhaps a bit unimaginative, each variation but the tenth being rounded out with the same eight-bar refrain. In the tenth variation the refrain is replaced by an adagio interlude, leading to an allegro which concludes the work. The movement, on the whole, is a bright display piece written in that popular style which Leopold Mozart cautioned his son to adopt for Parisian audiences.

The remainder of Mozart's Paris visit and his ultimate return to Salzburg need not be followed in detail, for they have little direct bearing upon his concerto composition. His mother died in Paris. Mozart, now quite alone, grew heartily sick of trotting around being pleasant to great lords and ladies, of being victimized by all sorts of petty jealousies, and of indulging the musical taste of Paris, which he found execrable and childish. For a while he laughed at the whole mess; but it soon began to rankle. A vacancy appeared in Salzburg for the position of court organist to the Archbishop; but the prospect did not commend itself to him for a variety of reasons. First and foremost, as he wrote to his friend Bullinger in Salzburg, were the "injustices which my dear father and I have endured there." By now, Mozart was too well schooled in the ways of the world and, in particular, in the social manners of the mighty to believe that the Archbishop had had a sincere change of heart. Furthermore, as he wrote, "Salzburg is no place for my talent. In the first place professional musicians there are not held in much consideration; and, secondly, one hears nothing, there is no theatre, no opera; and even if they really wanted one, who is there to sing? For the last five or six years the Salzburg orchestra has always been rich in what is useless and superfluous, but very poor in what is necessary, and absolutely destitute of what is indispensable; and such is the case at the present moment." Leopold Mozart brought pressure to bear, speaking of his age and ill-health, and of the great debt he had run up in Salzburg to finance the journey, which could be paid off if Mozart accepted the new post, for their combined salaries would then total a thousand gulden. He offered all sorts of inducements, professional and personal: such as, that the Archbishop was anxious to have him back and had even apologized for not immediately appointing him Kapellmeister; that the Archbishop had promised to permit him to travel wherever he liked "for the purpose of composing an opera"; that there might even be an opening in Salzburg for Aloysia Weber, with whom he had fallen in love in Mannheim; and that he would be back with his father and sister again, an argument that counted heavily, for Mozart had a genuine affection for the two. In the end he capitulated; but while he was eager enough to leave Paris, he was in no great hurry to return to the endearing embraces of the Archbishop. He found excuses for stopping in the towns along the return route. In Mannheim (November 1778) he began a double concerto (K. Anh. 56) with piano and violin as the solo instruments. The one hundred and twenty measures which survive look promising and it is a pity that he lost sight of the project. After lingering on his journey long enough to drive poor Leopold wild, he arrived in Salzburg in mid-January 1779 to begin two miserable and, by his standards, relatively unproductive years as organist to the Archbishop.

His home-coming was not altogether a comfortable one. His mother had died in Paris and this was his first reunion with his bereaved family. Moreover, while the affection between father and son was as genuine as ever, their mutual trust in one another had suffered a decided setback. Mozart wanted to work on his own, free of the restrictions of the archiepiscopal court, and he soon had reason to feel that his father had trapped him back into a distasteful servitude. Two years before, when the Archbishop refused him permission to travel, the young composer had simply walked out on him; furthermore, it was the Archbishop who had had to make the first overtures in order to secure his return. That exalted dignitary was not likely to forgive him for either offence, and it was soon evident that he intended to make a point of impressing Mozart with the humble station a musician held in the world.

The concerto compositions of 1779 still bear witness to the profound impression Mannheim and Paris had made upon Mozart. Like the sinfonia concertante for winds (K. Anh. 9) and the flute and harp concerto (K. 299) composed in Paris, and the double concerto for piano and violin projected on his return through Mannheim, the concertos composed in the year of his return to Salzburg are all in a sinfonia concertante style, e.g. orchestral works with several solo instruments. One of the concertos is again called a sinfonia concertante (K. 364) and is scored for violin, viola, and orchestra. It is certainly the most significant work he produced that year; indeed, its slow movement is among his most moving creations. The concerto has a real symphonic sweep, and in his treatment of the solo instruments he has already mastered fully the most crucial aspect of the art of concerto writing, i.e. to fuse a maximum of instrumental virtuosity into a maximum of significant musical expression for the enhancement of both and the detriment of neither. The thematic material is as plentiful and varied as we will find in a Mozart concerto. The structural devices, the essential tools of the composer's trade, are employed fundamentally for their expressive rather than their formal significance. The broad, sweeping counterpoint between violin and viola just before the cadenza in the slow movement is, for example, not simply an intelligent and creative use of an academic device; it is one of the most deeply moving moments in the entire score. There is a note of unrest unmistakably sounded in this work, a sombre coloration, an impassioned brooding all too thinly disguised under a transparent cloak of conventionality and decorum. One must agree with Eric Blom that "a passion not at all suited to an archiepiscopal court, and perhaps disclosing active revolt against it, seems to smoulder under a perfectly decorous style and exquisite proportions." Knowing the circumstances in which it was created, it seems safe to regard this sinfonia concertante (K. 364) as a frank autobiographical utterance.

The other concertante work composed in 1779, the concerto in E-flat major for two pianos and orchestra (K. 365), is smaller in scope, more limited in its emotional range, but none the less a precious composition in which both performers and audiences can find unending delight. It is his only duo-piano concerto apart from the two-piano arrangement he made of the earlier concerto for three pianos (K. 242). It was probably a domestic piece intended for himself and his sister and is endowed with all of the most ingratiating characteristics of a Mozart concerto: a graciousness of melody, a lean and alert craftsmanship, solo parts which lie thankfully under the fingers, and that astoundingly casual manner of pulling beautiful little episodes seemingly out of nowhere. Another sinfonia concertante (K. Anh. 104), this time a triple concerto for violin, viola, and 'cello as the solo instruments, was begun during the summer or autumn of 1779 but never completed.

The next two years, 1780 and 1781, are devoid of concerto production with the exception of the violin concerto in E-flat major (K. 268) which may possibly date from this period and the authenticity of which is not entirely agreed upon. A rondo for violin and orchestra (K. 373) was composed in 1781 for Brunetti, and also a rondo for a horn concerto (K. 371), probably composed for Leutgeb (of whom more later). In Einstein's opinion the fragments identified in the Köchel catalogue as K. Anh. 98b, Anh. 97, and Anh. 98 belong with the rondo as part of a projected horn concerto.

In 1782, when Mozart resumed concerto writing, he had already made the most important and difficult decision of his career—an irrevocable break with the Archbishop. Not only his concerto music, but his symphonic and chamber work as well, tell us in no unmistakable terms that his entire art rested now upon a wholly new foundation. A final flare-up had long been in the making. In March 1781, Mozart was called to Vienna to join the retinue of the Archbishop. While the injustices he had to endure were by no means the uncommon experience of eighteenth-century musicians, his especial misfortune was in being attached to one of the most backward and benighted of feudal princes. In a large city like Vienna he found a more enlightened aristocracy and, moreover, the institution of the public concert—the broad expansion of which belongs to the post-Mozartean era—and from the opportunities which both afforded he was debarred by the strict command of his patron. It was not only that the atmosphere in Vienna was less onerous than Salzburg but that in his estimation Vienna offered a free artist a better livelihood. He enumerated to his father the well-rewarded private concerts, the public concert which he regarded with great enthusiasm, the many opportunities for finding pupils, the ability to publish his music with an assured subscription, all of which added up in his reckoning to a thousand gulden a year rather than the four hundred and fifty which the Archbishop paid him. Also, as a member of the Archbishop's household, his status as a servant was impressed upon him more forcibly than ever, and at a time and in a place where an alternate way of living seemed feasible. Mozart grew more rebellious, the Archbishop more tyrannical, and the matter came to a head with some insulting name-calling on the part of the Archbishop.

It is possible, indeed probable, that Mozart was a bit conceited and quick to take offence. In fact, he admits the charge to his father, qualifying it with the statement that he is so only when confronted by a studiously contemplated contempt. He was basically generous and warmhearted; also basically decent enough to resent an insult and human enough to contemplate with relish the thought of paying it back with interest. Yet if his dignity was outraged, he was neither sufficiently warped nor sufficiently vindictive (his father at worst thought him foolhardy) to make a virtue of necessity and parade a series of petty offences as an excuse for a new way of life. He reports indignantly to his father that he was compelled to eat at the servants' table, and—"the last straw"—did not know he was supposed to be a valet. There is more in the former than a bit of middle-class snobbery and more in the latter than a deliberate untruth; for he should have been well informed by now concerning the social status of a musician. Even a great and respected composer like Haydn wore servant's livery, and it is rather unlikely that Mozart was unaware of the fact. The reasons are deeper and the issue more momentous. Indeed he ultimately confessed to his father that, apart from any specific reason, he wanted to make the break. It took courage, and Leopold's wild alarm is indicative of the boldness of the step. It has been observed often enough that Mozart's position with the Archbishop was typical of the feudal patronage upon which the eighteenth-century musician subsisted. It is worth emphasizing all the more that he was the first great composer to break violently with this system of patronage, with the social dogma and the musical tradition it represented.

Nor in so doing was Mozart ahead of his time. Times were changing. Europe in 1781 was no longer quite the Europe of 1750. If such a loose phrase as "the spirit of an age" means anything at all, it means the very specific events—social, political, economic, religious, scientific, cultural, etc.—which transpire during any specific period and which give that period its character. Mozart was growing restless under a system of patronage whereby he was personally tied to a clerical aristocrat. It is worth remembering that serf labour was growing impatient with a system of feudalism whereby it was legally tied to the land and to the local nobility who owned the land; that the growing commercial and industrial classes were also clamouring for laissez-faire, a free market and a government unhindered by the dominance of a feudal nobility; and that entire nations were growing restive under the yoke of foreign rule. The progressive spirit of the age was the expansive spirit of free expression. On the whole, literature was more sensitive to it than music. By 1781 the tide of literary romanticism had already swept past such landmarks as Goethe's *Werther* (1774), Klinger's *Sturm und Drang* (1776), a play whose title served to identify a literary era, and Wieland's *Oberon* (1780). There was a conscious orientation toward folk sources, the reality of the people as against the artificiality of the reigning aristocracy, represented by writers like Herder, Pestalozzi, Bellman, and Robert Burns. It is possible that Mozart did not know these writers; it is probable that he did not consciously understand the profounder issues fought out in the American Revolution of 1776 or in preparation in the coming French Revolution of 1789; it is certain that he was unaware of the underground struggle for Polish liberation, for it did not break into open war until the year after Mozart's death. Nevertheless these were the events which in no small measure helped to determine the spirit of the age. Mozart's break with the Archbishop was a dramatic step taken in accordance with this spirit. In this personal squabble there was more at stake than an undignified kick on the behind administered to him by Count Arco, one of the Archbishop's emissaries; for the humiliated and the offended of Europe were taking much the same kind of treatment, physically and figuratively, from the privileged few, and within a decade were to visit a much more violent and far-reaching retribution upon their tormentors than Mozart wrathfully contemplated for the Count.

The most significant part of his music composed in the remaining ten years of his life is manifestly not intended to tickle an aristocratic palate. The new spirit of the age crops up more frequently, and with ever-increasing emphasis his work ceases to conform to those technical and emotional restraints deemed desirable by his aristocratic audiences. Not only did the harmonic daring of the opening of the C major quartet, for example, disturb their placid sense of harmonic propriety; but the passions, sorrows, and perturbations of such works as the piano concertos in C minor and D minor, the G minor viola quintet, the piano quartet in G minor, the string quartet in D minor, and the famous G minor symphony, may have awakened, more sharply perhaps than we are able to imagine, presentiments of the coming storm which was soon to sweep away the very foundations of their social, political, and economic security. It is in this widening of emotional horizons, in this growing feeling for dramatic emphasis, that we discover a sense, deeper than the mere appropriation of the technical attributes of musical style, in which it may be said that Beethoven continued and brought to its culmination the work Mozart had begun. "It is true," writes Fowler, who is aware of the merits of this viewpoint, "that he (Mozart) seems to live quite outside of history, and rarely to trouble himself about its making. But he unconsciously played a part, and not a contemptible part, in the movements that were going on behind the scenes. The Holy Roman Empire was tottering, and the selfish pomp and tyranny of dynasties were being displayed for almost the last time; but long before the French Revolution put a stop to them, Europe was secretly being educated for better things. Individuals were beginning to assert themselves here and there, in spite of the feudal fetters which cramped their energies, and one of them, strange to say, was the youthful genius of Salzburg."

The remaining ten years of his life Mozart spent in Vienna, and the piano concertos composed during this period are an outgrowth of the various opportunities available in the "land of the clavier" for a virtuoso to make himself known. A few of the piano concertos were designed for pupils; the majority, however, were for his own use in the many private and semi-public subscription concerts prevalent in Vienna. In May 1782 he reported to his father that he had become associated with "a certain Martin" who, during the preceding winter, had organized a series of Friday amateur concerts at an inn called the Mehlgrube. An interesting side light on the character of these semi-public concerts is contained in an announcement which offered subscribers the following inducement: "Card tables will be placed in the anterooms, and money for play provided at discretion; the company will also be provided with every kind of refreshment." It seems, however, that at the more private concerts attended by the connoisseurs of the city the fare was strictly musical. For the summer season Martin secured the permission of the Emperor for a series of twelve subscription concerts in the Augarten, a public park in one of the suburbs of Vienna. Mozart was associated with Martin in this project and he was heard frequently as a composer-performer in his own piano concertos.

Mozart resumed concerto composition in the autumn and winter of 1782, just after his marriage to Constanze Weber in August of that year. He produced a group of three piano concertos (K. 413-15) which he published for subscription, and a horn concerto in D major (K. 412), the first of a series of four for that instrument. Mozart has left us an accurate description of the three piano concertos. "These concertos," he wrote to his father on December 28, 1782, "are a happy medium between what is too easy and too difficult; they are very brilliant, pleasing to the ear, and natural, without being vapïd. There are passages here and there from which connoisseurs alone can derive satisfaction; but these passages are written in such a way that the less learned cannot fail to be pleased, though without knowing why." This is a remarkably objective judgment which even a cursory study of the concertos will verify. Indeed, there is a deceptive ease in the three concertos which has caused them to be overshadowed by his more immediately striking work. The neat contrapuntal texture and the numerous felicities of expression call even less attention.to themselves than is customarily the case in his music. However, while they are among the most modest of his concertos they are by no means the least rewarding. The F major (K. 413) is the least ambitious of the three. It bears a surface resemblance to the earlier Salzburg piano concertos in that its primary virtues are clarity, grace, and proportion; but it is evident that a maturer mind is at work juxtaposing moods and textures so that the end result, while thoroughly charming, is somewhat serious at the same time. The light and engaging quality of the first movement is punctuated at just one point by a brief dramatic stroke, sufficient to focus the entire movement into proper perspective and to prevent it from frittering itself away in a kind of inimitable Mozartean small talk. The slow movement is of the kind rarely encountered outside of Mozart. It is music that is delicate rather than fragile, tender rather than timid. It is one of his most soft-spoken concerto movements, compelling us by its unassuming sincerity, gradually imposing a hush of deepest attention over the listener, whom it casually and inexorably (contradictions exquisitely Mozartean) absorbs in the even-flowing gentleness of its movement. The finale is one of those brilliant exhibitions of sheer artistry which Mozart could carry off as perhaps no other composer. It is a polyphonic finale in the tempo of minuet, a movement which Mozart calculated to delight layman and learned alike.

The A major concerto (K. 414), probably the first of the three to be composed, is somewhat broader in its dimensions; although, like the F major, it is quiet and reserved. It is perhaps the best known or, better said, the least unknown in the series, for none of the three have been heard too frequently in the last few decades. A sensitive critic and biographer has imputed to this work a kind of "virginal good breeding." Without attempting to decide the strange question of the innocence of a man's music, it would seem that in the slow movement, for example, the piano-writing is possessed of a fullness, sonority, and warmth (Tovey aptly recalls to us that upon occasion Mozart was fond of making "the pianoforte sound like an organ") which indicates perhaps more mature and less priggish virtues.

The C major concerto (K. 415) is the largest of the series in orchestral dimension; just as the A major, in this respect, is the smallest. The A major is scored for strings, two oboes, and two horns; the F major adds two bassoons, while the C major, the most festive of the group, comes replete with string orchestra, two oboes, two bassoons, two horns, two trumpets, and two tympani. The C major is also the most consistently contrapuntal of the three. If it is not, in its every moment, as engaging as the other two concertos—the interlocking counterpoint in the development section of the first movement, for example, comes perilously close to being a device rather than an inspiration—it springs at least one marvellous surprise in the finale, quite unequalled by any other single moment in the three concertos. The finale of the C major concerto is a light, fast-moving rondo (although not called by that name) arrested at two points by an extended adagio in minor. The odd interpolation of a deeply expressive slow movement within the body of a bright and glittering fast movement is effected with rare simplicity and power.

The interest in polyphony evident frequently in this group of concertos, and more pointedly illustrated in the arrangements of a number of Bach fugues which he made about this time, reflects a new world of music in which he was at the moment absorbed. The influence may be traced directly to Baron van Swieten, whom Mozart met in Vienna. The Baron, a wealthy nobleman and a composer of sorts—Haydn characterized the Baron's symphonies as "as stiff as himself"—owned a small but well-chosen collection of the works of Bach and Handel, and also of several more contemporary North German composers, the most important of whom was Carl Philip Emanuel Bach. As the Baron explained it, "My chief comforters are Handel and the Bachs, and with them a few masters of our own day who tread firmly in the footsteps of the truly great and good. . . ." His Sunday-morning musicales, which Mozart attended regularly, were distinguished, as Mozart reported, in that "nothing is played there but Handel and Bach." The concerts and the Baron's collection of the music of the great polyphonic masters were avidly absorbed by Mozart, who was soon engaged in making a similar collection of his own. As a boy he had gone through a routine training in contrapuntal forms, and an effective use of polyphony may be found in much of his music prior to 1782. The Van Swieten collection stimulated a more mature, a more practically experienced study of the polyphonic science. The immediate results evident in the music composed during 1782-83 only begin to tap the immense resources of the idiom. A profounder and more intensely concentrated polyphony will be found in the G minor symphony, and a vaster architecture built upon polyphonic foundations in the final movement of the *Jupiter* symphony. Both symphonies date from 1788.

Since the three works just discussed (K. 413-15) open the period of Mozart's greatest piano concertos, it is worth devoting a moment to such questions as Mozart's own piano-playing, and the precise character of the instrument for which the concertos were composed. The stories of Mozart's skill as a performer have by now assumed legendary proportions. At the age of three he is reported to have amused himself for hours on end picking out thirds; and by the time he had reached the age of six he was already on tour displaying his precocious prowess before the royalty of Europe, acquiring on the way the title of *"Kleiner Hexenmeister"* ("little magician") from the Emperor of Austria. We do not know much about his piano studies beyond the fact that he worked away at compositions by Paradies, Wagenseil, Bach, and Lucchesi. He must have possessed a prodigious variety in his execution, or else, as is probably the case, his was the kind of well-rounded performance in which every listener might uncover what he most desired to find. Thus Clementi declared that no man ever played as "intellectually" as Mozart, while Haydn protested literally with tears in his eyes that Mozart's playing was unforgettable because it came "from the heart." These opinions reveal possibly more of the conflicting temperaments of Clementi and Haydn than they do of the quality of Mozart's performance. Eye- or ear-witness accounts are unavoidably prejudiced at the source and, as all the world knows, a man may be a mountain to Tom Thumb and a molehill to Gargantua.

Mozart's descriptions of the performances of others are invaluable as a source of his opinions on how the piano should be played. In brief, we learn from his comments that he valued correct fingering, smooth, flexible execution, and a quiet, steady hand. The melodic line must flow like oil, a phrase he was fond of. Technical virtuosity exalted for its own sake he thought a monstrous distortion of the nature of music. It would seem that Mozart's audiences were as susceptible to pianistic hocus-pocus as are the audiences of our own day. "It was his greatest and oft-lamented grievance," Rochlitz tells us, "that he was generally expected to perform mechanical juggling tricks and tightrope antics on the instrument, which it amused people to *see*." Playing too fast annoyed him (his epithets are wholesomely Rabelaisian on this particular point), and he has left us several deftly worded caricatures of performers who employed facial grimaces to convey to their listeners the expressiveness with which they were rendering the music. His highest praise was for the performer who could re-create the music without taking liberties unspecified by the composer; the performer who, as he expressed it, could "play in the proper tempo, give expression to every note, appoggiatura, etc., tastefully and as they are written, so as to create the impression that the player had composed the piece."

In the course of this chapter the word "piano" has been used to describe the Mozart keyboard concertos. While this is accurate enough with respect to modern practice, it is rather uncertain as a description of Mozart's intent. It is not too easy in every instance to determine which of the keyboard instruments designated by the generic term "clavier" —harpsichord, clavichord, pianoforte—Mozart had in mind in the creation of what we now call his piano concertos. Mozart's brief lifetime spans the vital period of transition in the use of these instruments. While interest in the harpsichord declined sharply, the clavichord (at least in central Europe) reached the pinnacle of its popularity, and the pianoforte had begun to emerge rapidly from a position of comparative obscurity. As early as 1752, Quantz in his flute method (*Versuch einer Anweisung die Flöte traversiere zu spielen*) recommended the pianoforte for accompaniment above all other "clavier" instruments; and a decade later C. P. E. Bach, in his famous treatise on the true art of clavier playing, echoed this sentiment specifying "the fortepiano and the clavichord" as the best support for a performance "in which the finest nuances of taste appear." While pianos were something of a rarity up to the last quarter of the eighteenth century, Mozart may have encountered them as a boy in London during his visit there in 1764–65. One of his London friends was John Christian Bach, who, two years later (1767), is credited with having given the first public piano recital in London. There is some evidence that Mozart played the piano in Munich in 1775. In 1777, during his brief stop at Augsburg, he wrote his oft-quoted account of the pianofortes which Stein was building in that city. The detailed description which he rendered in a letter to his father indicates that, at least from this point on, the instrument was well known to him. It would seem that it became his favourite among the "clavier" instruments, for he used a pianoforte for his first public concert in Vienna on April 3, 1782, and some time thereafter acquired one of his own.

Internal evidence would seem to suggest that so far as the clavier concertos are concerned the pianoforte was the instrument Mozart had in mind starting with the K. 413–15 series of 1782. The date might be pushed back to the end of 1777 with respect to the clavier sonatas and those chamber works which call for clavier participation. "By internal evidence is meant the style that results when a work is planned for the piano, as distinguished from the style of a work planned for the harpsichord. Mozart's maturest piano style, to be sure, contains many elements that started life in answer to the needs of an instrument with plucked strings; but its most characteristic elements are those called into existence by the possibilities afforded by having hammers instead of quills. Thus embellishments, being no longer needed to emphasize particular tones, tend to disappear, the melodic line acquires a more flowing, songlike character, and sustained tones appear more frequently and are used with greater effect."[1] It is altogether likely, as Broder supposes, that the liquid quality of the piano tone enabled Mozart to effect one of the most vital advances in concerto orchestration: the subtle blend of piano and wind tone which is so remarkable in his late piano concertos. The rather dry and acute edge of the plucked harpsichord tone does not melt with any especial ease into a warm and mellow horn or woodwind passage.

However, while our modern piano serves better than a harpsichord for a performance of a late Mozart clavier concerto, Mozart's piano was a far cry from our modern concert grand, and is even substantially different from the instrument for which Beethoven conceived his greatest piano music. If the kind of piano Stein built is taken as representative of the type Mozart knew and used, then the salient characteristic of the instrument for which his mature piano concertos were conceived was a smooth, singing tone, more limited in volume than our modern piano, rather less percussive and more crystal-clear in quality. Its dynamic range was sufficient to make the distinction between piano and forte, crescendo and decrescendo, expressive; but it was unsuited as yet to the explosive dynamics which form an essential part of Beethoven's writing for the instrument. The limitations of the instrument are ideally suited to the qualities of Mozart's music, for he is anything but a percussive composer, nor yet does he tinkle upon his instrument after the fashion of some of our more precious modern interpreters (fortunately growing less numerous) who are apt to mis-

---

[1] Nathan Broder: "Mozart and the 'Clavier,' " *Musical Quarterly*, Oct. 1941.

interpret Mozart's chronological status as a predecessor of Beethoven to mean that somehow his music is smaller in stature and less emotionally mature.

In 1782, besides the three piano concertos (K. 413-15), Mozart also composed two movements, an allegro and a rondo, of a horn concerto in D major. There is no slow movement for the work. Einstein has suggested that the fragment of a slow movement for horn and orchestra, identified in the Köchel catalogue as K. Anh. 98a, is the beginning of the missing movement, although like the rondo movement it may not have been written until 1787. Two other horn concertos (K. 417 and 447), both in E-flat major, were composed in 1783. The date of the third concerto (K. 447) is a matter for conjecture. It is usually given as 1783, although St. Foix has attempted to argue on the basis of internal evidence—e.g. the romantic character of the work, the substitution of two clarinets and two bassoons for the two oboes and two horns customary in the orchestral portion of the concerto, the reappearance of a theme from the slow movement in the concluding allegro—that the work could not have been written prior to 1788 or 1789. The fourth horn concerto (K. 495), also in E-flat major, was composed in 1786.

The concertos composed by Mozart for an instrument upon which he himself was not a professional executant were in every case made to the requirements of specific virtuosi. They were compositions for use designed to display the abilities, and even limited, in certain respects, by the capacities of the performers for whom they were intended. None of these virtuosi was more amply supplied with vehicles for the display of his talents than Joseph Leutgeb (or Leitgeb), a horn player in the Salzburg Court orchestra.

Leutgeb was an old friend of the family and a Salzburger like Mozart. He had some reputation as a performer and had travelled to Germany, Italy, and to France where, in 1770, he was heard at the Concerts spirituels in Paris in a concerto of his own composition. Like Mozart, he finally settled in Vienna, where, with the help of a loan from Leopold Mozart, he set up as a cheesemonger in a tiny shop "the size of a snail's shell." Leutgeb, however, continued to perform as a horn virtuoso, and it was for these appearances that Mozart obliged his friend with four horn concertos and other compositions for the instrument. Mozart had a very particular affection for his cheese-monger, an affection which he demonstrated not only by the prodigal manner (prodigal, considering the limitations of the instrument) in which he supplied Leutgeb with a horn repertory, but also in his inter-cession with his father to "have a little patience with poor Leutgeb" in the matter of the repayment of the loan. His fondness for the horn player was characterized by that peculiar species of Mozartean good-fellowship which consisted in making "poor Leutgeb" a butt for his extravagant sense of humour. One of the horn concertos (K. 417) bears an inscription to the effect that he, Mozart, composed the work out of "pity for that ass, ox, and fool of a Leutgeb." Another (K. 495) is written alternately in black, red, blue, and green ink. A final rondo is prefaced by a little scene with the horn player in which his errors and his general incompetence are mercilessly castigated. Leutgeb's loyalty to the great master lasted until the very last days of Mozart's life. He was his constant companion during the last period, particularly when Constanze was away, and Mozart, in his letters to his absent wife, makes continual reference to the horn player with whom he shared his meals, went to the opera to hear his *Magic Flute*, and at whose house, on one occasion, he put up for the night.

The horn concertos are characterized by a mixture of high good humour and a warm, quiet romanticism so appropriate to the instru-ment in its more mellow mood. The four horn concertos, the quintet for horn and string quartet (K. 407) also written for Leutgeb, taken in conjunction with the bassoon, clarinet, and flute concertos, the sin-fonia concertante for wind quartet and orchestra, the serenades for wind octet, the serenade for thirteen wind instruments, the divertimenti for strings and two horns, the divertimenti for miscellaneous wind combinations, and the quintet for piano and wind quartet, add up to the most substantial repertory for wind instruments supplied to us by a composer of Mozart's stature.

We approach now the most intensive period of concerto creation in Mozart's career. No less than six piano concertos date from 1784, three from 1785, and three more from 1786; in all twelve piano concertos composed in three years, many of them equalled but unsurpassed in the history of the form. The reason for this intensive productivity is not hard to find. The Viennese had been awakened to the wonders of

Mozart's piano-playing, and his numerous concert commitments during those three years placed an enormous, though happily accepted, tax upon his creative resources. Early in February 1784 he wrote to his father that he was putting aside a projected opera (*L'Oca del Cairo*, which he never finished), which would always bring in money, in favour of other works, the piano concertos, "which *at the moment* are bringing in money, but will not do so later." The six concertos of 1784 were therefore compositions designed for immediate use. The following month he listed in detail no fewer than twenty-two concert appearances in less than six weeks. Three were "private" concerts at six gulden the series, for which, at the time of writing, he had already secured a hundred subscribers and was confident of some thirty more; two were to be given at the theatre, and the remainder at Galitzin's, Esterhazy's, and Richter's. The first two were members of the aristocracy, and the third (Richter) a clavier virtuoso who arranged a series of subscription concerts with Mozart as a drawing card. "Well, as you may imagine," summarized Mozart, "I must play some new works, and therefore I must compose." The concerts went well and the new concertos were applauded.

The series of six concertos composed in 1784 may be regarded as a unit despite marked individual differences, for each concerto represents another phase of a complete effort to master every element of a new concerto style. All of the concertos but one (K. 449) are scored for large orchestra, a full complement of winds and strings. The richer orchestral resources, and their counterpart, a considerably amplified virtuoso technique for the solo instrument, are investigated in detail. The matter had been broached on a smaller scale in the three piano concertos (K. 413-15) of 1782. The six concertos of 1784 represent an immeasurable gain in the precision, the delicacy, and, above all, the sonority with which the new resources are handled. Moreover, since we are dealing with one of the greatest of composers, each of the attributes of an enriched technique are used to broaden, to render at once more powerful and precise, the entire gamut of emotional expression from infectious witticisms to thoughtful melancholy.

The first of the series, the concerto in E-flat (K. 449), is the most modest in orchestral dimension. In the context of the other concertos, Mozart considered it a work "of quite a peculiar kind, composed rather for a small orchestra than for a large one." Unlike the concertos to follow, the wind parts have no real independence and the colour value of the oboes and horns is, in consequence, the least vital part of the concerto's structure and content. Mozart recognized that the wind parts are in fact dispensable, and set it apart as a concerto that "can be performed *a quattro* without wind instruments,' whereas "the other three concertos (K. 450, 451, 453) all have wind-instrument accompaniment." The limitation of this concerto is restricted only to the matter of orchestral colouring, for in other more fundamental respects it is perhaps the richest of the six.

From the very outset of this work we are aware of a new trend in his concerto music. As early as the seventeenth measure the music takes an abrupt and dramatic turn into minor. In no preceding concerto does the opening ritornel betray itself so quickly. Weighty discussions have hitherto been withheld until the solo instrument has joined the bright and resourceful conclave of instruments. It is characteristic of Mozart's opening concerto movements (with the exception of the two in minor keys) that the first orchestral ritornel serves as a kind of pre-discussion period, a succinct outlining of an agenda, meaty in implication, but for the moment emotionally detached. Its paramount function is organizational rather than discursive; a preliminary marshalling of musical facts as a groundwork for subsequent interpretation. When the solo enters it always brings with it—the A major concerto (K. 488) is in a limited sense an exception—new material reflecting its own specialized interests in the proceedings. As in a round-table discussion attended by men of intelligence and genius, the elaboration of the material on hand continually broadens out into new avenues of musical thought; an unexpected turn of a phrase (and there are many in a Mozart movement) comes as an illuminating insight, and when the propitious moment is at hand the deeper implications of the musical subject-matter are stressed by all speakers, main and subsidiary. No Mozart concerto, no matter how scintillating its initial witticisms, side-steps the relevant inquiry into the profounder levels of human emotion which the musical ideas on hand are capable of illuminating. There is a basic integrity of character even in the most off-hand of his concertos which transcends a mere striving for formal perfection; for no concerto is devoid of its moment of deeply touching humanity, although no concerto prior to the bne in E-flat (K. 449) catapults the ultimate dramatic issue with so instant and impatient a manœuvre. Many another Mozart concerto opens with a widely spaced and sharply enunciated subject. But in this concerto Mozart soon makes it clear that his healthy athleticism is set to serve for a tight and swiftly executed drama. A lean and uneasy spirit dictates almost every movement of the music. The solo writing is more restless than brilliant; the harmonies darkish and often minor, with a strained way of turning in on themselves, as in the approach to the recapitulation section which is negotiated via a series of close chromatic modulations. The essential easing of tension is ensured by an alert and subtle sense of key change, and by bringing forward, in contrast, a melody of warm and subdued loveliness. The slow movement has a sober, unassuming dignity and a way of starting a melody in an easy, restful major tonality and extending it with no perceptible premeditation into a quiet, minor melancholy. In the first movement the concentrated and economical character of the music is often managed with recourse to a polyphonic idiom. Polyphony is the dominant texture of the final movement and controls rather than releases the dampened spirit of vivacity which seems to struggle for expression. The rhythm is dancelike, but the movement keeps shifting toward more sóber preoccupations.

The E-flat concerto (K. 449) was originally composed for one of his pupils, a Barbara Ployer, the daughter of the representative of the Salzburg court in Vienna. Mozart performed the work at the first of his private concerts given on March 17, 1784. "The hall was full to overflowing," he reported, "and the new concerto I played won extraordinary praise." The concerto was completed on February 9, 1784, and became the first work which Mozart entered in his own thematic catalogue of his music; a catalogue which he began on the date of the completion of this concerto and continued until his death.

The next two piano concertos in the series, the B-flat major (K. 450) and the D major (K. 451), are richer in orchestral colouring and in pianistic virtuosity, but in comparison with the foregoing concerto rather threadbare in content. We gather from his letters that Mozart composed them expressly for his subscription and theatre concerts, which may account for the fact that they are, especially the B-flat major (K. 450), the closest approximation we have in Mozart to a pure virtuoso display piece. Mozart himself characterized them both "as concertos which are bound to make the performer perspire. From the point of view of difficulty the B-flat concerto beats the one in D." Nevertheless, as in every Mozart concerto, there are redeeming features, and the virtuosity, neither empty-headed nor profound, steers a pleasant middle course. The B-flat concerto has some charming antiphonal writing between wind and string choirs. The opening theme of the first movement is the key to the character of the entire work. Its chromaticism is decorative, rather than functional, imparting at all times an easy brilliance, and at no point a strained harmony, to the movement. The slow movement is likewise essentially ornamental. It begins with a beautifully simple melody elaborately embroidered upon its every repetition. The embroidery serves to set off, instead of to alter or deflect, the external contours of the melody. The movement is a decoration pure and simple, rather like a quiet still life hung in a tasteful although ornately chiselled frame. The finale is superb light entertainment, and tricky enough even now to merit careful manual preparation. Even the easiest Mozart concerto takes attentive practice, for his pianistic figurations, while not difficult to execute technically, are rarely routine and even an innocent scale passage is liable to unwind itself in the most unexpected directions. The pianist is always kept on the alert and cannot afford to relax, as he may in a simon-pure virtuoso concerto, on the assumption that the figurations will fall into certain stereotyped patterns. Moreover, the pianistic passage work in a Mozart concerto always has a musical, as distinguished from a pyrotechnical, point to make. It is calculated with respect to its immediate orchestral surrounding and with subtle reference to what has gone before and what it is being used to lead up to; which is another way of saying that it is not routine. The finale of the B-flat concerto, however, adds to this a few purely digital complications.

Its counterpart, the D major concerto (K. 451) has a somewhat duller surface and a less graceful stride. The characterization, however, is purely comparative, for in its own right it is neither dull nor graceless. Its orchestration is larger, though not richer, than its predecessor. The B-flat concerto is scored for oboes, bassoons, and horns (all in pairs) in addition to the usual string orchestra. In the final allegro a flute is added. The D major concerto supplements this with trumpets and tympani. It has a firmness of accent which precludes an unconditional capitulation to the brilliance and the charm of the B-flat concerto, and there are a few eventful moments which do deserve attention. In the middle of the slow movement, for example, the piano engages in a dialogue with the wood winds, arousing that quiet poignancy which always trembles just beneath the surface of the music. The first movement makes an occasional stab at a syncopated restlessness, but the music on the whole is sedate rather than preoccupied.

The fourth concerto in the series is in G major (K. 453) and like the first (K. 449) was composed for Barbara Ployer. It is one of the most captivating and resourceful of his concertos; prodigal as only a Mozart concerto can be in variety of melody, mood, and workmanship. The balance of the work is amazing, not only structurally but emotionally. The spirit of high good humour which dominates the opening movement, and bids fair to engulf it completely, is gently qualified by reflective cantabile sections, and for a moment (in the development section) is wholly deflected by an earnest conversation among the members of the wood-wind choir over which the piano hovers with a cascade of illuminating commentary. It is a typical Mozartean debate with several people talking about the same thing at the same time without interrupting one another, and managing in their own mysterious fashion to clarify the unity of their viewpoint. Like every great comedy, this smiling first movement is wise enough to indicate that sometimes there are deep issues at stake. The first melody of the slow movement opens with a sensuous and appealing inflection, secured by that most elementary device of shifting the lower harmony just a hair's-breadth before the melody is ready to fall in with it. The entire movement is governed by such effective simplicities. The episodes in minor are expected, but like the profoundest of predictable events they are all the more absorbing when they come true. The one unexpected turn comes in an orchestral phrase just prior to the initial appearance of the solo. It is stated first by the strings and then by the wind choir and is compounded out of a wonderfully controlled interpenetration of major and minor harmonies. The passage is compelling for the very uncertainty in mood which obtains literally from one note to the next. The finale, like the first movement, is conceived in the spirit of high comedy and is organized as a series of variations around the little bird-like theme which opens the movement. This melody, incidentally, cost him thirty-four kreutzers, for some bird fancier had taught a starling to whistle the tune and Mozart decided he had to own the talented creature. The movement gathers momentum as it moves along, starting allegretto and winding up presto, absorbing in its stride a characteristic interlude in minor in which a wide-sweeping syncopation by the piano is enclosed by a darkly coloured counterpoint woven in the orchestra.

The fifth concerto, once again in B-flat major (K. 456), is the most determined effort in the series to put to account the colouristic possibilities of his enlarged orchestra. In addition to the strings Mozart uses a full complement of winds minus trumpets and tympani (one flute, two oboes, two bassoons, and two horns). Leopold Mozart, who had come to Vienna for a visit, heard the concerto performed by his son and was so overcome by "the great pleasure of hearing so clearly the interplay of the instruments that for sheer delight tears came into my eyes." The elder Mozart walks through music history shrouded in the legendary shadow of his great son. He is almost always cast in the role of a worried and over-cautious father, and there is sometimes a tendency to forget that he was himself a well-schooled composer, though certainly not an inspired one, that he was his son's teacher, that his violin method was one of the standard texts of the period, and that he was, all in all, one of the most distinguished of the more conservative musicians of the era. His opinions are worthy of attention, and it is significant that his entire impression of this concerto should have been crystallized in the clear and delightful interplay of instruments. Mozart's symphonies and concertos were among the strategic cornerstones of later orchestral practice, and this concerto (K. 456) is one of the first large-scale efforts to establish the colouristic interplay between piano and orchestra on a relatively modern foundation. In the context of his foregoing concertos, this concerto in B-flat is distinguished by a more sensitive and independent handling of the wind instruments, by a more delicate antiphonal juxtaposition of wind and string choirs, and by a more mature blending of piano and wind tone. In textbooks on orchestration and in surveys of music history Mozart is rarely, if ever, accorded a place among pre-eminent orchestrators, probably because, unlike Berlioz, Wagner, or Strauss, an obvious splash of tone colour will never wholly dominate the texture of his music and will never of itself wholly condition the emotional response of the listener. The total conception of a Mozart movement will always transcend the value of any of its specialized effects; yet if these colouristic effects are subordinate to the total design, they are none the less present and essential as contributors to the music as a whole. Painters are wiser in this respect than musicians, for, as a colourist, Vermeer is not neglected because of Renoir.

The slow movement is the high point of this work. It is a variation movement and a superb example of how an endless unravelling of coloratura figurations can intensify, rather than merely decorate, the deep melancholy of the music. Few composers can succeed in being so ornate and so essentially simple and moving at the same time. The principle goes back instinctively to the neglected foundations of folk expression, where an excess of passion compels the singer into long wandering coloraturas to implement the simple melancholy of his song. The concerto was initially composed for the blind Viennese pianist, Maria Theresia von Paradis, who undertook that year a concert tour of the leading capitals of Europe. Mozart also used it for his own concert appearances.

The last concerto in the series, in F major (K. 459), is, in a way, a final summary of the technical characteristics and the emotional vicissitudes of the foregoing five. Its texture, especially in the finale, is nearly as contrapuntal as the first concerto (K. 449); and it is spotted almost as richly as the fifth (K. 456) with a precise and expressive interweaving of tone colour. There is an interesting colour technique utilized often in the first movement which consists in dividing the wind and string choirs off from each other as two relatively pure masses of background colour (instead of combining them as a single thoroughly interpenetrated colour mixture) and then applying a warm glaze of piano tone over each choir in turn. This kind of differentiation also obtains frequently in the ritornel passages where the piano is absent, and is a reflection of the mature, independent treatment he had learned to accord each choir and each instrument. The most distinctive characteristic of the concerto is its remarkable translucence; for no matter what the main stress of the moment may be, the subsidiary details—whether of colour, rhythm, melody, or harmony—are kept in a bright focus, as meticulous and as limpid as that miniature world which provides the mobile setting for the quiet foreground figures in a Renaissance painting. The concerto as a whole is neither dramatic nor placid, neither melancholy nor gay, but maintains a subtle balance of all moods, shifting and combining its inner emotions as it does its surface techniques so that all fall together with the quiet inevitability of a law of nature.

Mozart's concerto art was progressing by leaps and bounds. His command of a broader symphonic sonority and his detailed application of the individual qualities of each instrument in the orchestra were inevitably balanced by a more intensive exploration of the sonorities and the tonal richnesses of the solo piano. Solo and orchestra had to balance each other, and as one expanded so did the other. His concertos from this point on are technically more difficult, and this expansion of technical limits was seized upon by Mozart to widen and deepen the mould in which to pour the tremendous passions which were now sweeping like a tidal wave over his music. His creative power was now at its height. Early in 1785, just about the time of the creation of the piano concerto in D minor (K. 466), Haydn declared to Leopold Mozart: "Before God and as an honest man I tell you that your son is the greatest composer known to me either in person or by name. He has taste and, what is more, the most profound knowledge of composition." Each of the three piano concertos composed in 1785 are among the greatest masterpieces of the form. They are, in so many words, miracles of the profoundest inspiration, worthy in every respect to be ranked with the mighty triumvirate of symphonies—the E-flat major, the G minor, and the *Jupiter*—composed three years later.

The first of the three, the piano concerto in D minor (K. 466), has been for a century and a half the only really popular Mozart concerto. And with good reason; for it is the one Mozart concerto which takes instantaneous hold upon our emotions and compels us to follow its headlong course from the first bar to the last. It was a proper favourite with nineteenth-century composers—Beethoven composed cadenzas for the first and last movements—for its turbulent romanticism is the very body and soul of nineteenth-century music. It is even now a favourite in the modern concert hall, and contemporary audiences are intuitively wiser in this respect than some of our contemporary composers would imagine, for its uninhibited agitations and its patent drama are infinitely closer than the work of our meticulous neoclassicists to the essential temper of our own time. This concerto is no inexplicable aberration, even though it impresses itself with an emotional violence unprecedented in Mozart. The dramatic and turbulent spirit of the age has already been discussed, and in this concerto Mozart embraced it with a lost passion and a sense of suffering unequalled by the most conscious and outspoken proponents of the *Sturm und Drang.* For its own time it was both a contemporary and an exceptional document; contemporary in that it was close to the spirit of its time, exceptional in that it remained for the composers of the immediate future to realize the full implications of so total a capitulation to the tragic muse. Within the next few decades the spirit in which this concerto was composed was to quicken the work of creators like Beethoven and Goya, and was to take on in these artists the volcanic urgency and grandeur needed to mirror faithfully the bitter heroisms, the passionate idealisms, and the grim disappointments of their age.

The second piano concerto of the year, in C major (K. 467), retains the symphonic grandeur of the D minor concerto, but in its two outside movements reverts to a less urgent ordering of emotions. Two trumpets and tympani, omitted in the andante, are added to the first and last movements, and contribute to the brilliant surface and pomp of the music. The two fast movements alternate between virtuoso glitter and moods of tenderness and deep feeling. The slow movement is quite another story. It moves with a sonorous and even-paced calm, seemingly detached, like the late Beethoven quartets, in the face of its own suffering; never hastening its movement or raising for a moment its low-pitched voice, even when notes of unmistakable anguish sound up from the deepest recesses of its being. The movement is full of the most heart-touching audacities; dissonant suspensions and false relations which have not lost their point even in this day and age. Throughout the movement Mozart retains an almost impossible sense of repose, "like patience on a monument smiling at grief." The audacities must have troubled his audiences and given point to the reputation his music had for being often too full-blooded and uneasy. In any case they bothered Leopold Mozart a bit, but he had sense enough to "very much doubt whether there are any mistakes . . . . Several passages simply do not harmonize unless one hears all the instruments playing together." The harmonic audacities are marshalled with superb generalship, deployed at strategic points throughout the movement, and concealed until the most telling moment for their appearance. They are verily the "stratagems which errors seem, Nor is it Homer nods, but we that dream."

In December 1785, Mozart composed the concerto in E-flat major (K. 482) for one of a series of three subscription concerts. The andante met with tremendous success, and he was called upon to repeat the movement, which, as Leopold Mozart noted, was "a rather unusual occurrence." Besides the addition of trumpets and drums, two clarinets replace the two oboes in the orchestral score. This too is a rather unusual occurrence, and lends to the music a richness of colour rare even in these mature concertos. In the two piano concertos which follow, the clarinets are retained. In the E-flat concerto, the scoring for the winds is at times sufficiently complete and independent for the concerto to switch momentarily into a delightful wind serenade. Indeed the entire work is unique in its manner of lapsing from a grand virtuoso concerto into a quiet serenade. This happens once during the course of the slow movement, the unaccompanied winds alleviating the dark colouring of the muted strings, momentarily dispelling the severe and preoccupied mood of the movement with a bit of relaxed serenade music. Contrariwise in the finale, the naïve gaiety of the movement slows into an andantino cantabile. A beautifully tender serenade follows, with the piano and certain selected members of the orchestra (the clarinet among them) dancing an intimate minuet, almost, as it were, for their own edification, before going back with a kind of innocent determination to the serious business of amusing the assembled company with more roulades, scales, and fancy figurations.

The three concertos of 1786 continue the magnificent processional inaugurated with the D minor concerto (K. 466) of 1785. The first of the new trilogy, the concerto in A major (K. 488), is in many respects unique among his last period works. Reading extra-musical significances into a Mozart concerto is a foolish sort of business, yet one cannot help but feel a profoundly human maturity in every bar of the music, a serenity and a pathos which comes from something more than long experience in putting notes on paper. Apart from the slow movement, which is a passionate siciliana totally plunged into the most heart-gripping melancholy, the mood of the concerto is difficult to define. It is neither wholly nor in part a comedy or a tragedy or something in between, a tragi-comedy like *Don Giovanni*. It does not conveniently alternate its cogitations between the troubled midnight and the noon's repose. Rather, like the late Shakespearean plays, its essence lies in an elusive series of emotional contradictions: a calm inquietude, a reflective laughter, and a strange sort of late autumn indulgence toward the gallant gestures and the elegant phraseology of his adolescence and early manhood. It is easier to describe what this concerto is not. It is not a sentimentalist's cliché done in the image of a wise old man gently reflecting on the joys and sorrows of his species; nor is it a jovial and sunny middle age grown a bit crotchety under the inevitably encroaching winter of his discontent; nor, once again, is there an ounce of that calm resignation, that hypocritical long patience which Shakespeare knew as a mask for despair. It is simply that this engaging, ingenuous, and often vivacious music discovers, every now and again, like a character in *A Winter's Tale*, that the "heart dances, but not for joy."

The next concerto in C minor (K. 491) is as magnificent and as exceptional as any of his works composed in a minor key. There are only a handful of Mozart's compositions in minor keys, and in every instance he approached the project as a solemn and intensely dramatic occasion. Since Mozart does not repeat himself, the C minor concerto is as different from the D minor (K. 466) as an heroic drama can be from a personal tragedy. The D minor concerto is the only work of Mozart for which such adjectives as "wild" and "turbulent" are appropriate. The C minor concerto, in its first movement, has a rocklike grandeur, an angular lashed agony more approximate to the C minor wind serenade (K. 388) of 1782 than to any of his concertos or symphonies. It is his one heroic concerto and in consequence, the most heavily scored of his works in this form. The preceding work in A major (K. 488) followed the E-flat concerto (K. 482) in retaining the clarinets and dispensing with the oboes. It also dropped the trumpets and tympani of the E-flat concerto. The C minor retains trumpets, tympani, clarinets, and oboes. For the first time Mozart uses a full nineteenth-century orchestra: a string section, one flute, two oboes, two clarinets, two bassoons, two horns, two trumpets, and tympani. It is more richly scored than even the G minor and *Jupiter* symphonies and purely with respect to tone mass it has a power and a sonority unequalled in his music. The slow movement is a quiet interlude, untroubled by the precipitate despair which engulfs the romance of the D minor concerto. Yet there is genuine pathos in its quick return to a minor key after the initial statements of the gentle opening melody in major. The finale is in variation form and as intensely expressive in its own way as is the first movement of the concerto. A comparison of the opening themes of both movements is sufficient to distinguish the two. The first movement begins with a sombre melody twisting up from the deepest reaches of the orchestra, its halting, angular stride compounded out of long, even, sustained notes and wide, abrupt leaps. The movement is never free of this ironbound angularity. The basic subject of the finale is clipped and less immediately compelling. Like a good preface, it is provocative but not entirely self-explanatory. We read on; and we discover that there is more in this melody than first falls upon the ear. With each successive variation it is alternately affected by a tender decorative melancholy, by a martial heroism, by a quiet homophonic serenity, and by a wide polyphonic upsurge sweeping grandly through a maze of dissonant suspensions and twisted chromaticisms. No longer is Mozart content, as in the slow movement of the B-flat concerto (K. 456), to decorate a single mood; for he has fallen upon the mysterious key to those "kingdoms naked in the trembling heart," and the colour of each country he renders once and forever with each breathing.

The A major and C minor concertos were composed in March 1786, a feat comparable to the creation of his three last and greatest symphonies in a period of six weeks. For the winter concert season he added, in December 1786, the C major concerto (K. 503), an inscrutable work which has remained the least-known of his great piano compositions. It is technically, perhaps, the most difficult of his concertos, and the only thankless one for the pianist to perform; for its virtuosity is not of the kind that will bring the house down, nor does it at first glance seem to answer the needs of a great ruling emotion. One sensitive admirer of the Mozart concertos has complained against this work that the performer is not sufficiently repaid for his effort in overcoming its difficulties. It is hard to know what sort of payment a performer has the right to expect. The work is neither frigid nor forbidding, but a bit impersonal in a towering sort of way. The first movement has a good deal of tonal pageantry, but little of the festive spirit traditionally meet for such occasions. At times the movement is shrouded in a dissonant polyphonic grandeur, with a motive boldly predicting the opening of the Beethoven fifth symphony clashing against itself in a close stretto. There are hauntingly beautiful episodes which never quite settle down. They have a worried manner of always expecting to find themselves in foreign keys. Mozart seems uncertain whether they look better in major or minor. He keeps hurrying them from one to the other, sometimes with a singular lack of consideration for the easiest and most elegant exit. Even the engaging finale is temperamental in this respect. The opening orchestra ritornel is symptomatic. It begins, as every concerto finale seems bound to begin, in a bright and vivacious manner. Sixteen measures go by in no time; suddenly Mozart whips up a gust of passion for six and a half measures, and as suddenly calls the whole thing off with an abrupt resolution into major. A few more measures of glittering figurations, and then with a rather ungracious gesture the orchestra plunks down three C major chords and turns to the pianist with a "This is where you come in." It is conceivable that the pianist has grounds for complaint, but audiences need have no partisan interest in these matters. This concerto does not speak for itself as ingratiatingly as most of his other music. This is neither a fault nor a virtue. It just happens to be the way the music is written, and its beauty, particular though it may be, is sufficiently great to make the concerto a decidedly worth-while experience.

We are now virtually at the end of Mozart's career as a concerto composer. His intensive preoccupation with the form had ceased. During 1787 he was occupied with *Don Giovanni*, but in February 1788 he produced a solitary piano concerto in D major (K. 537). The tide of passion which had engulfed the concertos of 1785-86 had now swept beyond the confines of the concerto form. The D major is a splendid and mature work but not a deeply moving one. It is planned on a grand scale, brilliant pianistically, harmonically full and solid, and studded with rich though coolly woven counterpoints. There are, as in every Mozart concerto, moments of stress and introspective tenderness, but on the whole it is the objective workmanship which most consistently engages our attention. There has been a needless tendency to decry the concerto, largely, it would seem, because it makes none of the overt dramatic gestures of its immediate predecessors. This is a completely personal matter and is determined entirely by what any particular listener believes he has a right to expect from a Mozart concerto. If our expectation is always to enjoy the particular values which Mozart chooses to stress, then the fact that this work lives on a less passionate level of emotion will not hamper our pleasure in its superb craftsmanship and in the objective nobility of its style. *Coriolanus* is less dramatically compelling than *King Lear*, yet only an insensitive reader will fail to find pleasure in the play.

Mozart's own performances of this concerto are bound up with two desperate attempts to stem the flood of financial misfortune which embittered his last years. In April 1789 he undertook a journey to Dresden, where he played the D major concerto before the Elector of Saxony. In September 1790 he went to Frankfort for the festivities attending the coronation of Leopold II. Although not a member of the official court retinue of composers and performers, he hoped that, among the festive crowds that had gathered from all Europe for the coronation, his music would find receptive ears and generous purses. In Dresden he was rewarded with "a very handsome snuffbox" and some money. In Frankfort he achieved a Pyrrhic victory with his concerto. "It was a splendid success," he wrote to his wife, "from the point of view of honour and glory, but a failure as far as money was concerned." It is this performance, nearly three years after the composition of the work, which has given it its misleading title as the *Coronation* concerto. A second piano concerto was also performed for the occasion, probably the one in F major (K. 459).

The last two concertos were composed in 1791, the last year of his life. The first of the two, the piano concerto in B-flat major (K. 595), was composed in January. It was his last piano concerto and his first great work of the year. The other, the clarinet concerto in A major (K. 622), was composed in October, a little less than two months before his death. Mozart was now plunged into the deepest poverty, relieved by an occasional loan and an occasional commission. The first few months of 1791 were spent in producing some light dance music for

the Viennese court, and a few curiosities for a mechanical organ made
to order for a Hungarian nobleman. The piano concerto was for his
own use, and it rises, not as a reaction against, but as refuge from, his
immediate surroundings. The music is neither heavy nor light, it is
spacious; and against the vast declivities of its tonal space resound
preoccupied and introspective echoes of momentary passions and quiet
gaieties. The opening movement proceeds for nearly half its length in
a calm, and at times an almost oppressively serene, manner, before it
breaks, in the development section, into overt melancholy, a mood
which it never completely loses thereafter. The andante rarely deflects
into minor keys; it is a near-grey day, yet neither a sullen nor a dramatic one. The finale is a mellow mixture of gaiety and sadness such as
Mozart favoured so often in his last movements.

The clarinet concerto (K. 622) is its antithesis in almost every respect.
The opening ritornel is quiet enough, but the clarinet brings with it
episodes of the acutest poignancy to supplement its rendition of the
main themes of the movement. Thereafter the music is fraught with
minor tonalities. The cool counterpoints contrived in the early part of
the movement grow into a sombre polyphonic passion. There are
sudden restless syncopations and abrupt leaps in clarinet register. The
colouring of the instrument is used with telling effect. Its high register
lends a lean, acid-edged brightness to the music, and it has a way of
tumbling precipitately—the "hectic beauty" that Eric Blom speaks of
—into its darkest and lowest depths. The slow movement has all the
limpid and noble romanticism of his late music; while the finale is
bittersweet with a touch of sardonic mimicry rare in his music. The
first two of the three most important subjects of the finale have all of
the bounding Mozartean humour along with a bit of robustness to
broaden a gay occasion. The third subject floods over with the most
touching pathos. It is a seizure such as we have come to expect in a
Mozart finale: Banquo's ghost troubling the festivities with a forgotten
tragedy. It runs its full course, for such deeply felt interludes are never
casual with Mozart; whereupon the orchestra comments with the
Mozartean equivalent of a loud disrespectful noise, and the clarinet
takes off on a caricature of itself, doing clownish handsprings from the
high to the low points of its compass and running off into giddy coloraturas. Mozart always has his sense of humour and nobody has to ask

him where it is; but this sort of self-mockery does not turn up often in his music.

Prior to the composition of the clarinet concerto, Mozart worked feverishly on a series of important commissions which had unexpectedly fallen his way. In July he completed *The Magic Flute* for the impresario, Schikaneder. A commission for a Requiem came from a stranger who cloaked himself in mystery, but the work was interrupted by a third commission which necessitated a trip to Prague. The coronation of Leopold II had already been effected at Frankfort, but he was now to be crowned King of Bohemia and for the occasion Mozart hastily put together his last opera, *La clemenza di Tito* (*The Clemency of Titus*). Shortly after his return from Prague in mid-September, Mozart got to work on the clarinet concerto in A major (K. 622), which he completed, at the earliest, during the first week in October. The work was composed for Anton Stadler, for whom he had already written a wonderful clarinet quintet (K. 581) two years earlier. Stadler was an excellent clarinetist and a friend of the family who helped Constanze as musical adviser after Mozart's death. Apart from a cantata (K. 623) composed in November 1791, the clarinet concerto was Mozart's last work, for the *Requiem* was left incomplete. The years of hopeless struggle against poverty, sickness, and disappointment had begun to take their toll, and during the composition of the clarinet concerto his health was failing fast. There are few episodes in music history so completely infuriating as the record of this unequal battle. Mozart was thirty-five, still a young man, when he was carried to an unknown pauper's grave. His music during the last ten years, as we have seen it reflected in his piano concertos, had grown tremendously in stature. He had learned to unleash the most powerful of human passions, to walk in the ways of serenity and grandeur; and, for all that, his latest music had never lost its youthful insouciance, its eager and innocent loveliness. The clarinet concerto is no valedictory utterance, no last will and testament. There is no trace of the calm hail and farewell composed at the final hour by one who has lived his full life and is content to depart in peace. His final concerto is aflame rather with a sombre and feverish beauty, "the glowing of such fire that on the ashes of his youth doth lie."

CHAPTER V

The Beethoven Concerto

THE century following the death of Mozart saw the creation of a concerto literature which, for better or for worse, dominates almost exclusively the repertoire of the modern virtuoso. It is a polyglot literature reflecting virtually every major tendency, movement, and direction in nineteenth-century music. No major composer thought enough of the concerto to compose, like Mozart, some fifty examples; yet no major composer of instrumental music, with the exception of Schubert, neglected to leave at least one specimen behind him. Thus the nineteenth-century concerto was not shaped by the sustained attention of a single dominating personality, as the late eighteenth-century concerto had been under Mozart's unrelenting guidance. During the nineteenth century a large number of important composers contributed a small, though typical part of their talent to the concerto, and the result of their collective labour emerges as a divided and partisan composite, each concerto or group of concertos waging sonorous and urgent warfare on behalf of the diverse and often divergent ideologies of a century of supreme individualists. Programmaticism and nationalism both found refuge in the concerto; the experimenters and the traditionalists alike sought to bend it to their purposes; the demon virtuosi used it as a favourite stamping-ground, while the least showy and most subjective of romanticists turned to it as a medium for their innermost meditations. The basic similarities which hold this heterogeneous complex together are founded on a series of interrelated developments which matured after the death of Mozart: the total emergence of the modern concert hall to a position of unchallenged dominance in musical life, the rise of the modern virtuoso, an altering of the status of the concerto with respect to other instrumental forms, the unfolding of a somewhat different relationship between composer and performer on one hand, and, on the other, the evolution of a markedly new attitude on the part of composers and performers toward their audiences.

Mozart's accomplishment forms the terminal point of the eighteenth-century concerto and the starting-point of the nineteenth-century form. In Mozart most of the basic elements which modern audiences have come to look for in a concerto are already present. Both the virtuosity of the solo instrument and the magnitude of the orchestral force are already treated from a recognizably modern point of view. Solo and orchestra join with and against each other in a manner which the nineteenth-century concerto has taught us to accept as normal. And the sonata-form structure for the opening movement is already an accomplished fact. The nineteenth century made specific innovations in each of these directions; yet from the viewpoint of modern concert-hall practice a Mozart concerto sounds less archaic than the concertos of any of his predecessors. Indeed, apart from the Bach concertos and an occasional performance of a concerto by Haydn or Boccherini, Mozart's concertos are chronologically the earliest examples still heard with considerable frequency in the modern concert hall.

However, Mozart is a terminal point in another and equally funda-mental respect. The concerto does not stand alone as an isolated musical activity, and in some measure its character is determined by its relation to the total body of instrumental music during any period. During the first half of the eighteenth century the concerto—the concerto grosso and the solo concerto—was the most important of the large-scale instrumental forms. The violin sonata and the clavier suite did not, properly speaking, offer any competition; for the concerto is primarily orchestral rather than chamber music, and no independent orchestral form challenged the concerto's supremacy. The composer-performer was the dominant phenomenon in the musical world, and the solo concerto sufficed as a vehicle to display simultaneously both aspects of his personality. Specialization of function was not yet sufficiently strong to distract his interests as a composer, as distinct from those as a virtuoso, into more altruistic forms of orchestral expression. During the latter half of the eighteenth century the symphony took over the leading position in orchestral music, a position it was to hold all through the nineteenth century. This signalized, among other things, the fact that the identity between composer and performer was no longer as compelling as it once had been.

This question of the relation between composer and performer is a confusing one, and the problem has sometimes been settled in the usual fashion of claiming for Beethoven nearly all the possible and impossible things that can be claimed for so great a composer. Beethoven's deafness undoubtedly cut short his career as a virtuoso, and it is altogether possible that but for his deafness he might have composed many more concertos than he did. The fact that as a consequence of his deafness Beethoven was compelled to concentrate more upon composition than upon performance has sometimes been taken as the accidental starting-point of modern music history, and in this fashion a vast historical and social phenomenon has been made to pivot upon a personal misfortune. "Hitherto it had been taken for granted," writes Bekker, "that composer and virtuoso should be one; evil chance now provided an example to the contrary, and proved the historic origin of the present-day distinction between productive and reproductive activity."

This viewpoint is at best naïve, for we are dealing with a tendency, not with an accident. The distinction between composer and performer was in the process of being established before Beethoven. Haydn, for example, was no virtuoso. His technique on the clavier and violin was no doubt adequate enough for most purposes, but it was not of virtuoso calibre and he never found it necessary to attempt to raise it to such a level. Haydn had already demonstrated that an instrumental composer, even one who wrote about two dozen concertos, need not be a performing virtuoso in his own right. His position was probably unique in eighteenth-century music; yet well before Beethoven he serves as an example of a great instrumental composer who worked purely as a composer.

The composer-performer relationship bore more closely upon the general status of the concerto during the latter part of the eighteenth century than it did during the nineteenth. The difference, for example, between the position of the concerto in the total work of Haydn and of Mozart may be safely reduced to the fact that Mozart made a living as a performer and Haydn did not. Haydn had no self-interest in the concerto and he turned to it only as a secondary and occasional occupation. Mozart's livelihood depended in large measure upon his appearances as a virtuoso. The concerto did not fail to interest him for its own sake, as most musical forms did; yet he composed concertos not out of curiosity, but because they served a simple economic necessity. A secondary stimulus was the wealthy amateur like Dürnitz or Deschamps who occasionally commissioned a concerto for private use, or a virtuoso like Leutgeb or Stadler whom Mozart was willing to oblige. Mozart is the last great composer to treat the concerto very nearly as the central part of his total instrumental work. In this sense he writes an end to an era in the history of the solo concerto which began early in the eighteenth century with the great succession of Italian composer-violinists. Haydn and Mozart represent two opposing views on the position of the concerto in instrumental music. From Beethoven on, composers accepted Haydn's evaluation rather than Mozart's.

The point is worth illustrating. Beethoven's symphonies and quartets are, as a whole, of greater consequence than his concertos, while the bulk of his most important piano music is contained in his thirty-two sonatas rather than in his five piano concertos. Weber wrote several concertos, but he achieved the summit of his creative power in his operas. Schubert turned toward the song, the symphony, and chamber music. Like Beethoven, Schubert's finest piano music is contained in his late sonatas, although unlike Beethoven, he neglected to compose even a single concerto. Mendelssohn composed more symphonies than he did concertos, and it is possible that the oratorio interested him more than either. Chopin composed two concertos, but he made his most vital contribution to nineteenth-century piano music in small solo forms. Even Liszt, perhaps the greatest piano virtuoso of all time, worked more often and to much better advantage in the symphonic poem than in the piano concerto. Beethoven, Schubert, Weber, Mendelssohn, Chopin, and Liszt were all superlative performers; as brilliant a galaxy of virtuosi as any eighteenth-century group of composer-violinists. The composer-virtuoso obviously did not die a sudden death with the turn of the century; but the solo concerto no longer sufficed, as it did for Vivaldi and Tartini, as the main channel for instrumental composition.

There is no single, simple, and absolutely indisputable reason for this. In part it is a reflection of an emphasis on specialization which, as the century progressed, developed in the arts and sciences and in all fields of human endeavour. The growth of the modern concert hall during the nineteenth century brought forth in every succeeding generation an ever larger number of musicians who earned their reputation and livelihood entirely as virtuosi. They gradually took possession of the performance field not so much through superior merit as by default. An excellent pianist like Brahms, for example, after an early period of concertizing, no longer chose to compete. As an unconscious tribute, perhaps, to a growing spirit of specialization, a general tendency ultimately settled into what we now mistakenly accept as a normal state of affairs: composers concentrate on composition and virtuosi on performance.

Another factor might possibly have been the fact that the solo concerto is the least disinterested of musical forms. Apart from several experimental efforts motivated by its peculiar properties, the solo concerto, throughout its entire history, has been composed for use, and frequently to order. With the liberation of the composer from the confining taste and temperament of private patronage, there emerged a vast reorientation of opinion directed against music "made to order" and toward what the whole of nineteenth-century romanticism deified as "self-expression." Bach, Haydn, and, to a lesser extent, Mozart understood no contradiction between the two. Beethoven and the composers who succeeded him did. Tschaikowsky, for example, found nothing so abhorrent as composing to order and took little pleasure in his *1812* overture largely because it was a commissioned piece. It was part of the romantic attitude to hold as worth-while only that which proceeded from disinterested inspiration. The concerto could hardly have been as attractive to such a temperament as the symphony or the symphonic poem, for under the impress of the concert hall and of the virtuoso whom no difficulty could daunt the concerto took on increasingly the character of a show-piece, often tailor-made to the requirements of a specific performer. In the concerto self-expression had formidable competition in virtuoso self-interest, in the need for making an impressive display. The concerto, therefore, was not a medium which would interest the romantic composer for its own sake, which may explain in part why he turned to it with relative infrequency.[1]

Another element which may have distracted composers away from an assiduous cultivation of the concerto was the fact that even in its own specialized domain its position as the main vehicle for virtuoso display was being strongly challenged by a host of smaller forms. Liszt's fantasias and Hungarian Rhapsodies, Chopin's études and polonaises, Schubert's impromptus and the *rondos brilliants* and caprices of dozens of other composers were becoming as serviceable for purposes of display as the solo concerto. The growth in the physical proportions of the concerto began to impose limitations on its use. The tendency toward a large orchestra already evident in many of the later Mozart piano concertos was given further impetus in the concertos of composers like Beethoven and Liszt. In external growth the concerto kept pace with the symphony. A performance of a concerto now involved a larger body of instrumentalists than could conveniently fit into the

---

[1] The romantic distinction between self-expression and music made to order occasionally also appears in music criticism, much to the detriment of the eighteenth century and the glorification of the nineteenth. It has sometimes been assumed, in face of the facts, that serious music must necessarily have been motivated only by self-expression and that mere virtuosity was the inevitable concomitant of music made to order. And once again Beethoven has been charged with establishing this dubious distinction. Paul Bekker, for example, notes that Beethoven put forth his work "on its own merits, without reference to any particular performance or to the personality of any particular interpreter"; and on this basis goes on to claim that Beethoven "established for all time the distinction between serious composition and music of mere virtuosity." It goes without saying that this distinction existed for all time, and will continue to exist for any composer intelligent enough to know the difference. If anything, as the example of the nineteenth-century virtuoso concerto shows us, more serious composers were confused on the subject after Beethoven than before him.

salons of the nobility where virtuosi were still wont to make their appearances; nor was it always feasible, even for a concert-hall recital, for a soloist to secure the services of a symphony orchestra to accompany him in a concerto. For salon appearances and, to a more limited extent, also for concert-hall recitals, straight solo pieces minus orchestral support were developed with increasing emphasis throughout the century.

The physical growth of the concerto, both with respect to a richer soloistic virtuosity and a larger orchestral complement, was stimulated by the development of the modern concert hall during the nineteenth century. The salon was an aristocratic institution and it dominated the musical world just so long as the aristocracy itself dominated society. New audiences had already appeared in the latter half of the eighteenth century, particularly in large cosmopolitan centres like Paris and Vienna; audiences that gravitated toward the concert hall for their musical entertainment. Since the question of audience and place of performance is as much a social as a musical question, the French Revolution may be taken as the basic dividing line between the old and the new. Before the Revolution the feudal aristocracy maintained, as a concomitant of its political and social power, a stranglehold on the productive energies of the composer. We have seen it operate in Mozart's case, and we have noted the effort he made to break away toward the relative freedom of the metropolitan concert hall. Following the French Revolution the balance of social forces was reversed. The commercial and industrial bourgeoisie, the professional groups, and the middle classes generally—that broad anomalous grouping that stretches between the two extremes of the social complex—poured into the concert hall. Private patronage and the closed salon were the hall-marks of an overthrown system of privilege. The composer's share in the victory over feudalism was his emergence as a free artist able to present the fruit of his labour in a theoretically free and unlimited market. The concert hall, which became for composer and performer alike the main base of operation, was a public and relatively democratic institution in that it was open to anyone with the price of admission. This reorientation was neither sudden nor complete. The public concert hall made its appearance prior to the French Revolution in response to those classes of society which were growing in strength

but had not yet achieved complete dominance. The aristocratic salon
survived the French Revolution as a vestige of the old nobility who
had been overthrown but not destroyed. In essence, however, following
the French Revolution and on through the entire nineteenth century,
the concerto—a musical form above all else acutely sensitive to audience
reaction and to the specific conditions under which it is to be heard—
was directed toward the victorious and ever-growing public concert
hall, rather than to the defeated and ever fading aristocratic salon.
During the nineteenth century the concerto became, to a greater
extent than ever before, a form of public speech. It was addressed to a
large audience; it was to be heard in a large hall. While the physical
outlines of the form were appropriately expanded, its texture enriched,
and its resources more dramatically exploited, the concerto also fell
victim to the magnitude and heterogeneity of the concert hall, just as
during the preceding century it had been afflicted with the many petty
limitations of the salon. At its best, the nineteenth-century concerto
filled its ample form with music of great power and deep feeling. All
too often, however, the orchestra underscored its statements with
broad obvious gestures meant to be seen even from the cheapest seats,
just as previously it had often tiptoed discreetly through its ritornels to
avoid offending patrons who prided themselves on their taste. The
soloist now stormed into a fantastic bravura uproar intended to
astound the multitude, just as hitherto he had spun a filigree of graces
and embellishments to amuse the initiate.

Beethoven's position as a revolutionary is assured in the history of
music; and even the exaggerated claims made for him are by way of
unnecessary tribute to his vast innovating force. A revolutionary composer or thinker is usually defined as one whose projects are necessarily
in advance of the thinking and the practical living of his age; hence as
an impractical visionary he is doomed to be misunderstood in the
present and to be honoured only by post-mortem enlightenment. Yet
the most vociferous misunderstanding derives usually from those who
out of habit or self-interest would live in the past, who would willingly,
to use a cliché, put back the clock of history. This is a familiar phenomenon in the political world, and in musical circles it is all too evident
among critics trained upon the models of the past, who listen with

strange apprehension to the language of their own contemporaries. Yet the stature of a revolutionary programme is measured not so much in its visions of the future as in the extent to which its proposals constitute effective and fundamental remedies for the immediate present. The essence of revolutionary thinking is contained in the simple and overwhelming fact that it is in step with history, and the core of Beethoven's revolutionary thought and accomplishment lies likewise in the fact that, for his age, he was the most contemporary of composers.

Beethoven was the first great composer to mature after the French Revolution; the first, that is, to embrace consciously in its broad social and political implications the fundamentally democratic and revolutionary tenets of a new way of life. Humanitarianism, democracy, and freedom were immediate realities struggling as bitterly for survival then as now. The imprint of this ideology upon Beethoven is indelible. It lives in the broad dramatic phrasing, in the eternally heroic gestures of his music. Technically his work is fraught with the spirit of liberated energy, with a feverish sense of the exploration of new harmonic, rhythmic, and structural possibilities. His symphonies and his piano music, even from a narrow technical viewpoint, are milestones in music history. The *galant* salon style is, to all intents and purposes, dead from the very outset in Beethoven's piano music; its vestigial appearances are the remnants of a heritage which he honoured by destroying. His music welcomed the wide housing of the concert hall, for it is rich in sheer sound mass, in abrupt dynamic shadings, in robust and urgent rhythms. The firebrands which Mozart set loose in the plush parlours of an aristocratic Utopia were fanned by Beethoven into a conflagration which raged with fitful violence through the music of the entire century. The path broken by Mozart in his battle against the constricted atmosphere of a feudal court had now become the main highway. The principle of free creative expression, and the concert hall where such freedom might be exercised, were both matters of accomplished fact. History was ready for Beethoven. He was not a visionary on a mountain-top proclaiming the music of the future. He was a composer of the practical present, writing music entirely coherent with a body of principles whose victorious emergence was for him a matter of present history. While a hard-headed commercial institution like the publishing house of Breitkopf & Härtel saw fit to reject the manuscript of the *Eroica* and to berate it mercilessly in the issues of its journal, it was nevertheless this "impractical" composer who lived far more in the present than the mass of his eminently practical and, at times, pathetically alarmed listeners.

Among Beethoven's contemporaries there were many no doubt who appraised his music for what it was truly worth, just as there were many who simply failed to understand and who attacked his music with a ferocity equalled only by their ignorance. Beethoven was too dramatic a phenomenon to be overlooked, and while he may not have been completely understood, he was certainly not neglected. Even the timid souls who were ill at ease in the presence of his music warned against his work, for they could not ignore it. Moscheles, for example, tells a rather naïve story of how his teacher cautioned him away from Beethoven, who, it seems, "wrote the most curious stuff in the world—a baroque type of music, contrary to all rules, which no one could play and no one could understand." Even from the outset, relatively sympathetic observers chronicled something strange and disturbing in his piano-playing and in his music. As early as 1791 a Chaplain Junker who heard him perform declared that "his playing is so utterly different from the usual methods of the pianist that he seems to be striking out on an entirely new path." And his early music, likewise, was thought advanced and modern.

There still is an uncritical tendency to estimate Beethoven's so-called first-period music as imitative of Mozart and Haydn, and present-day performances of his early music still tend to stress what is presumed to be a Mozartean graciousness and delicacy at the expense of those elements characteristically his own. An indebtedness certainly exists not only to Mozart and Haydn but to others as well; for it would be ungenerous to deny traces of his piano style, and of certain idiomatic turns of phrase which are thought to be typically Beethoven, in the music of such lesser men as Dussek and Clementi. Yet his early music is hardly an imitation of Mozart or Haydn. Beethoven, who was wiser in this respect than later historians and critics, knew that such masters were inimitable. His own contemporaries were aware of both his indebtedness and his originality; and contemporary estimates stress—sometimes with malicious displeasure—the latter at the expense of the former. An early review of his first symphony termed it "a caricature of Haydn pushed to absurdity." One may judge this a caricature of criticism pushed to inanity, yet it does serve to emphasize that the differences between early Beethoven and his predecessors were once properly understood to be more notable than the similarities.

Beethoven's first two piano concertos (Op. 15, 19),[1] composed when he was in his twenties, belong to his so-called first period and are neither as innocent nor as unenterprising as has been sometimes supposed. Tomaschek heard Beethoven perform the two concertos in 1798, and his contemporary judgment is worth noting, for he was sensitive, as we are not, to novelties in the music which seemed strained and disturbing upon first hearing. "I admired his powerful and brilliant playing, but his frequent daring deviations from one motive to another, whereby the organic connection, the gradual development of idea was put aside, did not escape me. Evils of this nature frequently weaken his greatest compositions, those which sprang from a too exuberant conception. It is not seldom that the unbiased listener is rudely awakened from his transport. The singular and original seemed to be his chief aim in composition. . . ." Tomaschek's viewpoint is rather too timid, but the modern pianist might do well to observe the emphasis on Beethoven's "exuberant conception" and rediscover if possible the freshness of those elements which are indeed "singular and original." There are many elements in the two concertos which are typically Beethoven. In the first concerto in C major, Op. 15, the very first orchestral ritornel, for example, establishes a wider harmonic framework than the opening ritornels of the Mozart concertos are apt to employ. The second subject is carried through a series of beautifully simple and effective modulations, lending to the opening ritornel a tone of discursive harmonic richness which Mozart preferred to reserve for a later portion of the proceedings. In the second concerto in B-flat, Op. 19, the first orchestral ritornel turns quickly into minor keys and assumes rather

---

[1] There are two early piano concertos which antedate these. One was composed by Beethoven at the age of twelve and consists of a complete solo part with the orchestral portion in piano reduction. The other has been dated vaguely somewhere between 1788-93, although in Thayer's opinion "perhaps before rather than after 1790." It consists of only one movement, not in Beethoven's handwriting, and was discovered in the possession of the head of an educational institution for the blind in Prague.

impatiently those urgent dramatic gestures which we associate characteristically with Beethoven. A preoccupation with dramatic issues at so
early a stage is, as has been noted in the previous chapter, an exceptional
occurrence in Mozart. On Beethoven's own evidence, the second
concerto in B-flat was the first of the two to be composed; and it is
typical of his approach that he seized upon a dramatic device, rare in
Mozart, as the starting-point for his first piano concerto.

The third piano concerto in C minor, Op. 37, constitutes a great
advance over the preceding two. Beethoven was conscious of his
progress. Once the third concerto was completed, he wrote to Breitkopf & Härtel that his two earlier efforts were no longer in his judgment his best efforts in the form. This was not meant in dispraise of his
first two concertos, for he advised the publishing house to caution its
critics that "they can be best judged if one can hear them well performed." But this was by way of notice that the first two concertos
ought not to be reviewed as the summit of his present achievement,
for he had already done better. The third concerto, however, was not
yet available, for, as he expressed it, "musical policy necessitates keeping
the best concertos to oneself for a while." This serves as a reminder that
Beethoven was a performing virtuoso so long as his hearing permitted
him to be. He exploited his own music first, before turning it over to
other virtuosi by publication.

To digress for a moment: Beethoven's dealings with his publishers
indicate that the composer had already become a business man in the
modern sense of the word. A composer's negotiations were now
increasingly with publishing houses rather than with private aristo-
crats: and Beethoven's complaints were often directed against the
shrewd commercial practices of a publisher, just as Mozart's had been
against the high-handed miserliness of a nobleman. With a kind of grim
good humour Beethoven submitted several compositions to Hof-
meister for publication with the advice that "if you are as conscientious,
my dear brother, as many other publishers who grind us poor composers to death, you will know pretty well how to derive ample profit
when the works appear." In truth, Beethoven's negotiations with his
publishers were not always as aboveboard as a self-righteous biographer
would have wanted them to be. It seems an axiom in romantic biography that a great composer must, for his own vindication, necessarily

be ignorant of how to turn his music to commercial advantage and that he appear before posterity as an innocent victim of conniving realists. Thus there has been much shaking of biographical heads over Beethoven's lapses of business morality, over his deplorable manner of promising the same work to several publishers simultaneously, delivering it to none and protesting to each that he is an honest man. Apparently on the assumption that a man who deals with eternal verities in his music can do no wrong, Ernest Newman, for one, has vindicated him on the grounds that "he did not do wrong things knowing they were wrong.... The truer explanation is that ... partly because of his almost complete failure to understand the world in which he lived what most people would call his real life, but which was actually only a dim shadow-world trailing along behind the inner musical world that was the sole true reality for him, he was incapable of seeing certain of his actions as other people saw them." It is possible that Beethoven knew more about the real world than his apologists have credited him with knowing. The business world is not the best Sunday-school example of fair dealing. Perhaps Beethoven had reason to know this. In any case, with an ungenerous lack of consideration for the embarrassment of future biographers, he resorted sometimes to unorthodox business practices which indicate, at least, that as a business man he understood, if somewhat cynically, the rules of the game.

To return: the C minor piano concerto, Op. 37, is the first in that great tetralogy (comprising the third, fourth, and fifth piano concertos and the violin concerto) which constitutes Beethoven's most familiar contribution to the modern concerto repertory. Composed in 1800 and published four years later, the C minor concerto is a milestone in Beethoven's music, a major effort in reconstituting the vocabulary and syntax of music on a more sonorous and more overtly dramatic basis. It was a token that the new century, in the very year of its birth, was fast coming of age. The first movement opens with an abrupt, commanding subject; the kind of opening that his later symphonies established as a typical Beethovian gesture. The movement is full of an impassioned and heroic oratory. It is at once a lineal descendant of Mozart's C minor piano concerto and the prototype of numerous nineteenth-century concertos which sought to strike the same attitude. The slow movement moves with a luxurious solemnity which Tovey characterized as "the climax of Beethoven's powers of solemn expression in his first period . . ."; the finale, with the robust and energetic drive which we recognize as a cardinal trait in Beethoven's music. The piano-writing is dynamic and sonorous throughout.

It has been observed (Eric Blom) that Beethoven's piano-writing was always ahead of his treatment of any other medium. Prior to 1800 he had already composed eleven piano sonatas, including the *Pathétique*, one of the foundation stones of romantic piano music, and the slow movement of the Op. 10, No. 3 sonata, one of the most powerful utterances in all of his early music. The C minor concerto is the most mature of the creations to which Beethoven put finishing touches in the year 1800. It is richer emotionally and in tonal texture than the first symphony in C major, Op. 21, and certainly more imaginative than the charming though limited septet, Op. 20. Of the works composed in 1799 and 1800, only isolated movements of the Op. 18 quartet series, such as the slow movement of the Op. 18, No. 1, and the first movement of the Op. 18, No. 4, are comparable to the third concerto in dramatic fervour and in grandeur of conception. In the total body of his music the third concerto stands as an imposing landmark on the road to the *Eroica* symphony composed a few years later. The two are in a sense analogous, for each in its own field represents Beethoven's first unqualified delineation of a vast and urgent drama. A comparison with the *Eroica*, however, shows the third concerto as a preliminary essay in the handling of those ideas and emotions to which the symphony shortly gave fullest expression.

The fourth and fifth piano concertos have both been saddled with interpretations for which we find no sanction in Beethoven: the fourth with a literary programme concerning Orpheus and the wild beasts, the fifth with a title, the *Emperor* concerto, which supposedly describes the lordly dignity of the music. More than any other composer, Beethoven enjoys the dubious distinction of bringing out the worst in a critic. Wagner runs him a close second, and the reader with a taste for such delicacies will find a substantial library of beautiful nonsense and bad prose accumulated around the two. Prose poems which do not suggest in forty pages of shameless literary effusion the mood of a Beethoven symphony nearly as well as four bars of Beethoven's own music; extravagant literary interpretations which profess to find not only the hand of fate, but the full cast of a Shakespearean drama, cavorting under the bed of a Beethoven sonata or quartet; accounts of his deafness which run for illumination to yogi and Hindu mysticism no less; sober technical analyses which profess to see in the two regularly contrasted themes of a sonata-form movement an autobiographical record of two love affairs conducted simultaneously with two different ladies; stylistic generalizations which revolve around a reverent devotion to the holy number "three," which led one of the prime creators of the delusion of Beethoven's three styles to the shrewd deduction that in his third period Beethoven used more notes because he yearned for more of the things which life was withholding from him—these have been among the notable contributions to an evaluation of Beethoven's life and work. There is little here to argue about, for there is little or nothing capable of proof or disproof. The reader is advised to believe, if it gives him any pleasure, that the slow movement of the fourth Beethoven piano concerto depicts Orpheus taming the wild beasts. However, this was not Beethoven's idea. The interpretation seems to have started with Liszt. Likewise, in the privacy of his own appreciation the listener is entitled, if he chooses, to regard the fifth piano concerto as an expression of imperial magnificence. Needless to say, Beethoven's democratic impulses were directed toward expressing nothing of the kind. The title *Emperor* was not of his choosing; likely as not, had he known of it, it would have offended rather than amused him.

The slow movement of the fourth piano concerto in G major, Op. 58, is a model of inspired simplicity. A brief account of its structure will illustrate the bare and almost elementary economy which underlies one of the noblest inspirations in our entire concerto literature. Piano and orchestra are set off against each other on the basis of a primitive concerto relationship. Each takes its turn alone, and each serves as an unequivocal contrast to the other in mood, tone colour, dynamics, and harmonic texture. The string orchestra plays forte in powerful unisons and bare octaves; the piano responds softly in full and expressive harmony. The grim alternation is alleviated by a brief solo interlude which embodies—if one cares to listen to it in such terms—a clear prediction of much that Chopin, in his finest piano music, sought to accomplish. The interlude ultimately unwinds into a miraculous sequence of descending chromaticisms. It merges into a sudden cadenza which leads to the final resumption of the stark dialogue between piano and orchestra. Such economy of means and simplification of design was the product of a rich experience in the complexities of orchestral and pianistic writing. The concerto was composed during 1805-06 and by that time, through his experience with the *Eroica*, his piano concertos and sonatas, the resources of the piano and the orchestra were known to him in all their violence and variety. Beethoven now chose to work for a moment with simple contrasts and in pure primary colours. Technically it is a rare problem, for few composers have been mature enough as artists and as human beings to risk working in so simple and profound a fashion.

The fifth piano concerto in E-flat major, Op. 73, was completed in Vienna during 1809. Napoleon's troops had entered the city, and Beethoven with the rest of Vienna's citizenry passed through the ordeals of occupation and war. "We have passed through a great deal of misery," wrote Beethoven; "I tell you that since May 4th, I have brought into the world little that is connected, only here and there a fragment. The whole course of events has affected me body and soul. ... What a disturbing wild life around me; nothing but drums, cannons, men, misery of all sorts." A military motive has inevitably been read into the concerto, and indeed the music does at times take on a martial stride. However, the concerto disassociates itself rather clearly from the witless assortment of naval battles and military concertos which the virtuosi of the period were fond of bombarding out of their pianofortes.

The fifth piano concerto, completed in Beethoven's thirty-ninth year, was the last of his concertos. The concertos as a whole present an arrested picture of Beethoven's development, for we find among them no counterpart to such masterpieces as his last three symphonies, the piano sonatas, Op. 90-111, and the string quartets, Op. 95-135, all of which were composed during the remaining eighteen years of his life. None of his concertos belong to the period of his maturest thought and feeling; and, of necessity, we find in them, wonderful as they undoubtedly are, only a limited expression of his full creative power.

Each of the last three piano concertos reveals an experimental tendency which blossomed forth fully in his *Choral Fantasia*, Op. 80, a unique work for solo piano, chorus, and orchestra. The fourth concerto opens with the solo piano, and while something of the sort had already occurred in an early Mozart concerto (K. 271), Beethoven gives the soloist's immediate intrusion more weight. The piano makes an immediate and more extended appearance also in the opening of the fifth concerto; but in this case the soloist forgoes the statement of a principal subject in favour of a ruminating introduction prior to the first orchestral statement of the themes. In both instances Beethoven took the first steps toward breaking down the system of a double exposition—the first for the orchestra exclusively and the second for the piano and orchestra combined—which had been a cardinal principle in the design of a sonata-form concerto. However, Beethoven did not follow up his own lead, and the collapsing of the two expositions into one, with the soloist figuring prominently from the outset, remained for the accomplishment of later composers. Likewise in the fifth piano concerto Beethoven merged the last two movements together through the device of previewing the opening melody of the third movement in the closing measures of the second. This too was part of the general tendency toward economy of structure and cohesion of movements which Weber, Mendelssohn, and Liszt sought to effect in the concerto. This constitutes a rather specialized problem in concerto structure and its ramifications are best reserved for an account of the experimental efforts of the later romanticists.

The third piano concerto of Beethoven, also modelled a type of sonata-form design which he elaborated in his fifth and which served the more conservative of romantic composers as a guide. Beethoven's prestige has been sufficiently great for certain textbook historians to accept his specific design as normal for the form, and the average student is likely to be more familiar with it than with the sonata-form structures of Mozart or Mendelssohn. There is nothing more contrary to fact than the notion that a musical form can be confused with a religious dogma, and that, in consequence, there is only one way of constructing a concerto in sonata form. Actually the evolution of the sonata-form concerto from J. C. Bach to the present, if it is subject to one ruling principle at all, seems governed by the maxim that anything that can happen eventually does. The notion of a duality between exception and rule is a textbook notion; and if books on music are apt to be a bit dogmatic on the subject, it should be remembered that rules are formulated long after the fact and that they are codified by theoreticians for the guidance of the beginner and not as a gospel for the mature composer. Beyond the elementary generalization that a concerto in sonata form will have an exposition, development, and recapitulation of themes, and a somewhat looser generalization concerning key relationships, rules for a sonata-form concerto have only a limited application to a single composer, or a specific group of composers, or even to a certain portion of one composer's work. Thus the first movement of Beethoven's first piano concerto is designed quite differently from the first movement of his fifth; yet both are in sonata form. Verily, in view of the dogmas that are sometimes taught so religiously in a few academic institutions, the Mozart concertos alone are as the thousand eyes which Cassandra would fill with prophetic tears. May those who know with such certainty how a sonata-form concerto should be constructed read Mozart, Beethoven, Mendelssohn, Liszt, etc., and weep.

Briefly, Beethoven's design as he amplified it in his fifth piano concerto is this. There are, to begin with, two expositions. The first, which is completely for orchestra, is in the full sense of the word the "first exposition"; for it exposes all the themes of the movement and states the principal themes—the first and second subjects, so called—in contrasted keys. The "second exposition" differs from the first chiefly in that the restatement of the themes by the piano and orchestra is now conditioned by necessary concessions to the specific nature of the solo instrument. Thus, the initial orchestral presentation of themes is, in a literal sense, a "first exposition"; for it outlines everything that is to be heard later on in the movement, presenting what the development section is to develop and the recapitulation section to recapitulate. In his third piano concerto Beethoven sought to loosen the possible rigidity of such a design by allowing the initial orchestral exposition to wander off into a strictly symphonic development of its own. But this was a distraction which he dispensed with in his subsequent concertos. In his fifth piano concerto he used the device of an extended preface for the solo instrument prior to the first orchestral exposition and re-introduced this preface by way of a transition from the development to the recapitulation. Thus a device which sounds at first like an introductory improvisation turns out later to have been calculated as part of the design.

There are no such devices in Mozart, for the sonata-form structure he employed was intrinsically more flexible than Beethoven's. This is not a value judgment, for Beethoven found Mozart's procedure serviceable in his first piano concerto and discarded it in his third. Nor is it an airtight generalization, for upon occasion, as in his A major piano concerto (K. 488), Mozart used a sonata-form design similar to Beethoven's. The difference in viewpoint between the two can hardly be illustrated better than to note that it was as exceptional for Mozart to use Beethoven's form as it was for Beethoven to use Mozart's. The sonata-form design as we find it in J. C. Bach, Mozart, and early Beethoven does not entirely accept the exposition-development-recapitulation formula in accordance with the literal meaning of the words. The first orchestral exposition in a Mozart concerto is not the full exposition for the whole concerto, because it does not necessarily state all the themes, nor even all the main themes, of the movement. Contrast in key is not emphasized, and it is not always easy to know at first hearing which of the several subsidiary melodies will eventually turn out to be the second main subject of the movement. During the "second exposition" the piano, as the leading participant, conducts in part a restatement of what has already been heard, and also introduces several new themes (usually two) on its own. In Mozart's D minor piano concerto (K. 466), for example, the piano opens the second exposition with an entirely new melody. This happens also in Beethoven's first piano concerto, Op. 15. Sometimes the new material in the second exposition is delayed until some of the melodies already heard are gone over once again. Sooner or later, however, Mozart usually has the solo instrument come forward with its own special contribution. The two expositions are therefore not specialized duplicates of each other. There is usually more thematic contrast between the two expositions in Mozart than in Beethoven. The development section likewise does not always take itself literally, for sometimes it does very little developing or expanding of themes. Often it is close to a free fantasia [1] with the solo instrument wandering off into glittering figurations only dimly related to what has gone before. This happens, for example, in the first Beethoven piano concerto, where at no point

---

[1] The terms "development" and "free fantasia" are often confused to mean the same thing; which is surely not the best way to clarify an all too ambiguous technical terminology.

during the development does the piano refer to any of the themes of the movement, although the orchestra keeps reiterating the initial phrase of the main subject by way of reassuring itself that it is still in the same concerto. Since the two expositions are different, the recapitulation can hardly be so tedious as to repeat both. Mozart's usual solution is to recapitulate the first and second main subjects, and those of the other melodies which have not been exhausted in the foregoing development. Thus in the D minor concerto Mozart takes the two new piano subjects of the second exposition, allots the first to the development section and the second to the recapitulation. Nothing is wasted, and—should we make rules about it—very little will probably occur in the precise places where we decide to look.

Of Beethoven's remaining concertos, the one in D major for violin and orchestra, Op. 61, rivals, if indeed it does not exceed, the popularity of his last three piano concertos. Like Mozart, Beethoven studied the violin when he was young, although while Mozart was able to render his own work, Beethoven's violin technique was certainly insufficient for the demands of his own concerto. However, the instrument was known to him first-hand and he seems to have been less dependent upon the advice of a professional violinist than pianists like Mendelssohn and Schumann. The nineteenth century was dominantly a piano century, just as the first half of the eighteenth had been devoted to the violin. The greatest of the nineteenth-century violin concertos— those by Beethoven, Mendelssohn, and Brahms—were written by pianists, and the concertos, for a long while after their composition, were inevitably associated with the virtuosi whom the composers had had in mind. The Beethoven concerto was composed for Franz Clement, who gave the work its first performance on December 23, 1806. Clement was celebrated among his contemporaries both for his technical skill and his exceptional memory. Spohr, in his *Autobiography*, relates that Clement, after hearing two rehearsals and one performance of his oratorio *The Last Judgment*, performed whole sections of it from memory without having seen the score. Likewise he was reputed to have made a piano score of Haydn's *Creation* with only the libretto to guide him, after having heard the work several times. It is said that Haydn thought enough of Clement's piano reduction to adopt it for publication. The première of the Beethoven concerto reveals an interesting sidelight on current conditions of musical performance. Clement split the work in two, giving the first movement in the first part of the programme, and the remaining two movements in the second part, a procedure by no means uncommon at the time. Between the two parts of the concerto Clement entertained with some circus fiddling, playing one of his own sonatas on one string with the violin turned upside down (*"mit umgekehrter Violine"*). It is difficult to imagine what the concerto sounded like at its first performance, for it seems that Clement rendered the solo part at sight without benefit of rehearsal. There is an unintentional irony in the bad pun inscribed by Beethoven on the manuscript of the concerto, asking of Clement clemency toward the poor composer (*"Concerto per Clemenza pour Clement"*). It is possible that the manner of its initial performance had something to do with the fact that, until revived by Joachim, the work was rarely performed.

Among Beethoven's sketches, notations for the violin concerto are mixed in with sketches for the fifth symphony; which serves to remind us that the violin concerto, composed in 1806, is only one of an amazing group of masterpieces—the fourth and fifth symphonies, the Rasoumowsky quartets, the fourth piano concerto—with which Beethoven was occupied during 1805-06. The evident fertility of his imagination carried over into every phrase of the concerto and the work stands, even among Beethoven's greatest masterpieces, as a model of melodic invention, spaciousness of design, sheer clarity and logic of organization. Beethoven subsequently transcribed the violin part for the piano. The transplantation is not especially successful, and as a piano concerto its value is negligible.

The triple concerto in C major for piano, violin, 'cello, and orchestra, Op. 56, which Beethoven composed during 1804-05, is one of his least known works. This is due in part to the obvious difficulty of getting three excellent soloists together on the same platform, and in part to the fact that audiences seem to expect Beethoven always to be making grandly dramatic gestures. By and large, the concerto shies away from impressive pronouncements. Much of its quiet non-declamatory charm derives from a deep and unassuming absorption in its own rather special problems. The work is deceptive in its appearance of making few demands upon the listener; for the subtleties of design, texture, and tone colour which are necessarily involved in a concerto of this kind often require greater concentration than more simple structures which impress through sheer beauty of melody and overpowering poignancy of emotion. The triple concerto is not lacking in either, although it is less rewarding in these respects than the violin concerto. The triple concerto has more than enough genuine music to rescue it from the category of composers' music (that mysterious domain with practically no real inhabitants); yet the listener must be willing to follow the composer through the beautiful solution of a somewhat precarious problem, and to take the composer's word for it that easy distractions are not advisable. The melodies of the first movement are graciously co-operative rather than distractingly self-assertive, and we do best to follow their lead. They are the essential media through which Beethoven is to effect his solutions and they have, when first sounded in the orchestra, that cool reserve of people who are ready to adapt themselves to expected emergencies. A melody that drips with personality, that is imperiously demanding of attention at first hearing, is apt to condition the future course of the music in its own terms. A melody that is prepared to accept selflessly any contingency that may arise—and it is this type of melody that Beethoven uses here—is apt to take on, at least at the outset, some of the attributes of a flexible formula. The melodies in the first movement are scarcely exciting in their own right, but our respect for their resourcefulness grows as the movement unfolds.

The concerto has suffered by inevitable comparison with Beethoven's greater music. By the standards of the two great concertos which it immediately precedes—the fourth piano concerto and the violin concerto—it seems a throwback to an earlier and less exciting style of composition. Comparisons, as several million people have said, are odious; and Tovey is probably right in thinking that if this concerto "were not by Beethoven, but by some mysterious composer who had written nothing else and who had the romantic good fortune to die before it came to performance, the very people who most blame Beethoven for writing below his full powers would be the first to acclaim it as the work of a still greater composer." The triple concerto possesses a quiet perfection of its own, and there is much that is stimulating and delightful in the tonal textures which Beethoven obtains in the interweaving of the solo trio and the orchestra. The treatment of three concertante instruments in a concerto is not unique. In Beethoven, however, it reflects a tendency particularly strong in his music about this time. In his duo-sonatas, both instruments tend to take on the proportions of a concerto soloist; that is, to play in a concertante style. For example, in his *Kreutzer* sonata for violin and piano, Op. 47, composed in 1805, he instructs that the work is "written in a very concertante style, almost that of a concerto" ("*scritto in uno stilo molto concertante, quasi come d'un concerto*"). As a matter of fact, the *Kreutzer* sonata might well be described as a double concerto without orchestra.

The last Beethoven work to concern us is the *Choral Fantasia*, Op. 80, an experimental oddity for piano, chorus, and orchestra composed in 1808 and first performed at a mammoth all-Beethoven concert (December 22, 1808) which also included the fifth and sixth symphonies, the fourth piano concerto, and a sizable portion of the C major mass. The orchestra got its signals crossed during the *Choral Fantasia* and what must have been a truly memorable evening nearly wound up as a fiasco. Eyewitness accounts vary as to who got mixed up over what; but all are agreed that after calling a halt and starting again, the performance concluded without catastrophe. The *Choral Fantasia* defies precise classification. It is in variation form with a preface for solo piano and a choral finale. While it is obviously a study for the ninth symphony, the duality between solo piano and orchestra is sufficiently essential to the total design for the work to be regarded as much a kind of concerto as anything else. Once again, as in the triple concerto, Beethoven is wrapped up in a unique problem of design, texture, tone colour, and balance of tonal masses; and once again his mood is light, clear, precise, and only at judicious moments distracted by weighty utterances. The comparison ends here; for there is little in the triple concerto that is experimental, and there is nothing in the *Choral Fantasia* that is not.

The programme for its first performance describes the work as a "Fantasia for the pianoforte which ends with the gradual entrance of the entire orchestra and the introduction of the choruses as a finale." A sketchbook of 1808, devoted entirely to the work, indicates that the opening fantasia for piano solo was not an original part of the design. It was apparently an afterthought and, as a matter of fact, the fantasia as we now have it was actually composed after the first performance

and not before. At the première Beethoven improvised the opening
fantasia himself. The version which he later wrote out for publication
probably contains a fairly accurate embodiment of his improvisational
style.

This brings us to one of the cardinal factors in Beethoven's piano
playing: his astounding genius for improvisation. As a performing
virtuoso he had to stand comparison with other leading pianists like
Wölfl and Hummel. Contemporary judgments are not always agreed
that Beethoven had no peer among pianists, yet all affirm that he was
beyond approach in extemporization. Czerny tells us that Beethoven's
improvisation "created the greatest sensation in the first years of his
sojourn in Vienna and even caused Mozart to wonder." A comparison
of Beethoven and Wölfl (a leading pianist of the day and the composer
of several piano concertos), published in the *Allgemeine musikalische
Zeitung* of April 22, 1799, reports majority opinion inclined toward
Wölfl. "Beethoven's playing is extremely brilliant but has less delicacy
and occasionally he is guilty of indistinctness. He shows himself to the
greatest advantage in improvisation, and here, indeed, it is most extraordinary with what lightness and yet firmness in the succession of ideas
Beethoven not only varies a theme given him on the spur of the
moment by figuration (with which many a virtuoso makes his fortune
—and wind) but really develops it. Since the death of Mozart, who in
this respect is for me still the *non plus ultra*, I have never enjoyed this
kind of pleasure in the degree in which it is provided by Beethoven.
In this Wölfl fails to reach him."

The tradition of great improvisation is bound up with the greatest
of composers like Bach, Handel, Mozart, and Beethoven, rather than
with those who excel simply as performers. Aptitude in improvisation
varies in direct proportion to one's ability as a composer. It is not inconceivable that another pianist might have excelled over Beethoven in
certain technical aspects of piano-playing; but none could approach him
in knowledge of composition and in creative fire. Just as London
audiences had been drawn to a Handel oratorio by the prospect of an
organ improvisation from the composer, so advance notices of Beethoven's concert appearances featured the fact that "Herr *Ludwig van
Beethoven* will improvise upon the pianoforte." Something of an improvisational style sometimes creeps into his music. In his concertos it is

evident in the introduction to the fifth piano concerto and in the opening fantasia for piano solo in the *Choral Fantasia*.

The charge of indistinctness and lack of delicacy brought against Beethoven in the above-quoted comparison with Wölfl is interesting because it was probably true. Beethoven's technique was well in advance of the capacities of the instrument. We know that he never found the piano altogether satisfactory, that he was keenly interested in an improved instrument, and that in an effort to meet his requirements Andreas Streicher undertook several experiments in piano building. Less original minds fared better with the piano, for they were willing to accept its limitations. Czerny makes this clear in his comparison between Beethoven and Hummel. Since Beethoven's "playing, like his compositions," writes Czerny, "was far ahead of his time, the pianofortes of the period (until 1810), still extremely weak and imperfect, could not endure his gigantic style of performance. Hence it was that Hummel's purling, brilliant style, well calculated to suit the manner of the time, was much more comprehensible and pleasing to the public."

It is something more than an historical curiosity that Beethoven's playing was often thought lacking "in purity and distinctness" and that "in the world at large" Hummel was "reputed the better player." It is another instance, and an important one for the development of piano-playing, illustrating the perpetual conflict between those who are compelled for their music's sake to challenge the limitations of the present, and those who honestly feel no such compulsion. The latter are the blessed among composers, for with no loss of integrity they enjoy the wealth and the fame which accrues from their adherence to accepted formulas. Hummel was no tyro in the art of music-making. As a child, his talent was extraordinary enough for Mozart to take him to live with him and give him instruction in music. Beethoven did not underestimate him. The relationship between the two was, of course, subject to Beethoven's sudden outbursts of anger and his equally sudden gestures of conciliation. But Hummel suffered from this no more, and possibly less, than Beethoven's other friends. At least two of Hummel's piano concertos, the A minor, Op. 85, and the B minor, Op. 89, are very respectable compositions. Hummel was both a pupil of Mozart and a contemporary of Beethoven, and his music appealed to his contemporaries largely because the former fact weighed more heavily with him than the latter. Beethoven's music, no less than Hummel's, was founded upon Mozart, But Hummel clung more closely to the formal appurtenances of the Mozartean tradition, and he lacked totally the bold and passionate imagination that led Beethoven into newer and richer paths. Beethoven's piano-playing was more significant for the future; Hummel's more pleasing to the present. It is a small point, but perhaps a revealing one, that in his *Piano School* (1824), a valuable extension upon previous methods of pianoforte technique, Hummel should still have retained the already outmoded stricture upon the use of the thumb upon black keys. Hummel's mentality is a typical one, and we meet with it among good composers in every age. Later in the century it cropped up in Saint-Saëns, and in our own day in Rachmaninoff. Future generations are indifferent to their loyalties and intolerant toward their lack of enterprise. The Hummel concertos, despite their genuine merit, have long been forgotten; the Saint-Saëns concertos have very nearly disappeared; and while the second Rachmaninoff piano concerto still holds its own, it is no longer the unqualified favourite it once used to be.

Beethoven's piano style was founded upon the essentially explosive nature of the instrument, and if in the last analysis he found it unsatisfactory, it was because the piano was less explosive and less dynamic than himself. The demands he made upon the instrument were the foundations of later technique. His piano music abounds in sharp dynamic shadings, sudden forte-piano juxtapositions. He explored the extreme ranges of the instrument, sought to draw from its various registers the differences in tone colour which the modern piano yields quite easily, and subjected it to tremendous bravura outbursts which were imitated by virtuosi for decades after his death. All of these things are more obvious in Liszt than in Beethoven, principally because in Liszt the virtuoso frankly dominates over the composer. In a Liszt concerto it is intended we should be aware of the gorgeous tone colouring and the astounding bravuras, that we be conscious of them as effects, and properly impressed with the difficulties involved in attaining them. We do not know them as effects in Beethoven because he was driven to them out of a need for richer means of expression. The inner logic of a movement reaches out toward these new resources and encompasses them as part of the nature of the music. This is especially true in his last piano sonatas; and even the torrential bravuras of the *Appassionata* make sound-musical sense when well played, i.e. with emphasis on the clarity of each configuration and on the distinctive tone colouring of each of the registers through which it proceeds, instead of a broad smudge of indeterminate tone colour and a riding up and down on the piano in a fit of virtuoso heroics. Our modern piano is closer to Liszt's and Chopin's instrument than it is to Beethoven's. Blom makes the worth-while observation that "the early piano was looked upon as an instrument ideally made to drive home a point. All the notes played were to be heard. The harmonic backgrounds into which they can be fused are the invention of a later day, due to the improved pedal technique of such composers as Chopin and Liszt . . . there is in Beethoven no mere pianistic background accompaniment as there is in Chopin and Liszt, much less anything of the harmonic haze which puts colour before design in the piano music of Debussy, for instance." It is good to know this, for in truth Beethoven does a good deal of hammering on his piano. He rushes off into grand virtuoso passions, and he lays his colour on with a palette knife. Yet all this is necessary to the total design, to the total conception of the work, and every note, configuration, and colour needs to be heard. Nowhere in Beethoven is it permissible to indulge in that judicious bit of smudging which is not always beside the point in the piano music of Chopin and Liszt. Whatever the conflict one may feel in his music, Beethoven is at peace with himself, in that he is one composer who says what he means and means exactly what he says, and he is very certain about this both ways.

CHAPTER VI

The Romantic Concerto

THE virtuoso is one of the essential and corroding institutions in music history. The development of the art owes much to the virtuoso; so does its debasement. Like a valuable poison he can both cure and destroy. At many a crisis in music history it was the overpowering virtuoso (like Paganini, for instance) who broke the deadly grip of standard practice which lay like a constricting disease on the body of a living and expanding art. This has not happened for a long time; and if the virtuoso is sometimes a liberating force, mostly he is a bore. The uncreative virtuoso—and there is always a part of the programme, the encore group at the end, where every performer seems willing to appear as such—is content to put his fingers to work and his musicianship to sleep. As a virtuoso per se, he and the hacks who write for him strictly in this capacity are among the more voluminous spoilers of public taste. They give us more sound than sense, more manual dexterity than emotional depth, more trickery than true technique. They are the Neros who fiddle while our patience burns.

Undoubtedly a good deal of satisfaction derives from watching a virtuoso at work. The encore groups are always well applauded; and in the opera house a few members of the audience seem always ready to run mad from a high C and hang themselves for joy. It is at least doubtful if this has anything to do with music, which does not mean that it is bad; simply irrelevant. Now virtuosity itself is hardly irrelevant, for no performer can attempt some of the finest music of the last hundred years without first attaining a high level of technical proficiency. The difference between the creative and the non-creative virtuoso, however, is simple. The former is called a musician, which means that he performs music; the latter is called a phenomenal fiddleplayer, which means literally that he plays the fiddle, not Beethoven, phenomenally. There is a story about Rossini and a famous tenor who came to visit him which runs something like this. "Ask him if he brought his high C," Rossini told the butler. The answer was, yes. "Then tell him to hang it up with his hat before he comes in." By definition, a musician is a virtuoso who successfully deludes us into believing he has left his high C hanging in his dressing-room.

The virtuoso has commanded a good deal of the composer's attention; and in the long run he is worth it, even at the expense of the few hundred concertos which have pandered shamelessly to his impossible appetite for self-display. The difficulties which the virtuoso overcomes are worth overcoming; the impossibilities which he attempts are worth making possible. He is a pioneer even if out of self-interest. The new effects which he makes available to standard practice are really valuable to the composer; providing the composer can genuinely think in terms of these new effects, providing he can discover in each effect the particular idea or emotion which it can convey better than any other, providing he does not take the easy way of letting the new effects do a new kind of stereotyped thinking for him. A lot of provisos; but Beethovens are rare and tricksters a penny a dozen. The splurge of demon virtuosity, which has expressed itself during the last hundred years primarily in the concerto, has also carried over into every other orchestral form. The orchestra, for the last century, has been a conglomeration of virtuosi; and composers have been treating it as such. Witness the concertante technique of the Strauss tone poems with the solo violin treated every now and then like a concerto soloist; or a highly competent bit of virtuoso orchestration like the Rimsky-Korsakov *Capriccio Espagnole* with concerto cadenzas thrown in for a variety of instruments. The orchestra from Berlioz to Stravinsky has been an orchestra of colours and virtuoso effects. This has stimulated the discovery of a whole realm of musical ideas ideally conveyed by these effects; sometimes even profound ideas which could not have been suggested by normal scoring procedures or normal standards of performance. It has also, no doubt, encouraged a good deal of entertaining and unimportant music; an opus served like a cocktail, a lot of orchestration and a dash of straight music.

The element of display had never really been absent from the solo concerto even from its very beginning. During the nineteenth century, however, it became one of the basic ingredients of the form. This development is associated largely with Paganini and Liszt, for with these two composer-virtuosi the violin and piano respectively reached very nearly the extreme limits of their technical capacities. They were joined in their effort by several dozen other composer-virtuosi most of whom history has honoured with her profoundest inattention. The survival of the lesser lights seems more a matter of chronology than of merit. Wieniawski's second violin concerto in D minor, Op. 22, is scarcely better than the Moscheles third piano concerto in G minor, Op. 58. However, a few names like Vieuxtemps, Wieniawski, Paderewski are still recent enough to mean something to modern audiences, while such names as Thalberg, Ernst, Lipinski, Moscheles are not. Even if we no longer treasure them especially, these men did their job well. They helped to codify standard instrumental technique on a high and exacting level of virtuosity, and no serious concerto composer worked in total ignorance of their effort. Their standards of execution were accepted by the concert artist, and every concerto became essentially a virtuoso work. That is, the virtuosity is always there even if some composers were conscientious enough to camouflage it with good music. Thus the Brahms piano concertos demand a formidable virtuoso technique of the performer, yet they offer him few obvious opportunities for its display.

As in the eighteenth century, the work of extending the technical capacities of an instrument was done by the composer-virtuoso. We have added little in the forty-odd years of our century to the accomplishments of the nineteenth-century composer-virtuoso, and that little has been the product largely of the composer per se. The composer-virtuoso still survives today, but he does little more than still survive. Specialization has overtaken music almost as completely as it has medicine. Since even a small technical advance necessitates a certain amount of creativeness, and since the modern performer has, by and large, ceased to create, advances in technique, such as they are, have become very nearly the exclusive concern of composers. Thus we look toward Stravinsky's piano-writing, not toward Horowitz's piano-playing, for a new conception of the instrument's capacities. (Stravinsky did do some piano-playing in public, but his reputation has scarcely been made on this basis.) Similarly new demands on the violinists' technique come from the Schönberg violin concerto, not from the performances and arrangements of a Heifetz or a Kreisler. The practitioner has little interest in such questions; the creator fortunately still has. The balance is less lopsided in the case of subsidiary instruments like the viola or harp. Hindemith, a decade ago, was a fine violist; but the splendid development of the instrument in our time owes nearly as much to a non-virtuoso like Bloch. In any case, creatively speaking, it owes nothing to Primrose, unless one considers the ability to play a Paganini caprice on the viola an act of creation. Primrose demonstrates the wonderful resources of the instrument; the composer, who ostensibly lives in another world, is left with the job of putting these resources to use. The balance would seem to be somewhat more proportionate with respect to the modern harp. Salzedo performs and composes; yet his composition is so many fathoms inferior to his performance that much of the point of his valuable extension of harp technique is necessarily lost.

The first to bridge the gap between the eighteenth- and nineteenth-century conceptions of violin-playing were a group of virtuosi known as the Paris school. The doyen of the group, and its finest composer, was Giovanni Battista Viotti (1753–1824), an Italian born in Piedmont, who worked in Paris and died in London. Viotti was a clean-cut, careful craftsman who knew his instrument and wrote for it superbly. His music is not devoid of an occasionally interesting idea, and a few of his twenty-nine concertos, notably the twenty-second in A minor, still enjoy a measure of popularity, especially among violin teachers. He has been called "the father of modern violin playing," and while the modern violinist would rather fancy his performances a reincarnation of Paganini's flaming virtuosities, he still turns first to Viotti's cooler and easier concertos for a substantial part of his basic training. Two of

Viotti's pupils, Rode (1774–1830) and Baillot (1771–1842), helped establish the tradition of the Paris school. Like many of the virtuosi of the period, Rode made his debut in a Viotti concerto. His own violin concertos attempt a greater warmth and richness of feeling than obtains in the work of his master, yet for all of his commendable striving for nobility of line and depth of thought, he reveals more obviously than Viotti the essential vacuity of emotion and the bloodless sort of classicism that characterize the music of this school. From his concertos, one gathers that Rode favoured a warm tone and an energetic style of playing. He was no doubt a splendid violinist; in any case, both Boccherini and Beethoven are said to have composed for him. Baillot's violin concertos are quite innocuous and have even dropped out of the student's repertoire. Mendelssohn praised his violin-playing, and his *L'Art du violon* (1834) was, at one time, a fundamental student text. The last member of the group, Rodolphe Kreutzer (1766–1831), wrote more operas than violin concertos, though he is remembered for neither. His études for solo violin are still an important part of the student's gospel, and the scholar remembers him as the violinist to whom Beethoven, after a quarrel with Bridgetower, dedicated his so-called *Kreutzer* sonata.

A judgment of the musical worth and the technical importance of this school has automatically been rendered by the fact that Viotti, Rode, and Kreutzer have descended from the concert hall into the classroom. The violin student inevitably encounters the concertos of Viotti and Rode, the Kreutzer études and the Rode caprices as part of his training; the accomplished artist inevitably disregards them as part of his concert repertoire. Kreisler has recently sought to revive a Viotti concerto in the concert hall. With all due respect to two very sincere artists, the example is scarcely worth following. There are more important violin concertos past and present worth bringing to light; and modern programme-making, already weighted down with an appreciable quantity of dead wood, can stagger along quite nicely without Viotti's honest and unassuming inability to say anything of major importance. Value judgments apart, the Viotti school laid a solid base for the work of Spohr and Paganini, the two leading violinists of the age. Paganini's indebtedness is less evident than Spohr's, for he was a supreme individualist and his technical methods were far in advance of his contemporaries, forerunners, and even his successors. His life, or at least the legends about his life, are a veritable *reductio ad absurdum* of a romanticist's career, but his violin concertos show a lean and precise classicism stylistically closer to Viotti than to such typically romantic music as the concertos of Schumann, Mendelssohn, or Brahms. Spohr, who admired Rode and looked askance at Paganini's gymnastic innovations, took over the solid, conservative technique of Viotti and Rode and grafted on to it a broad cantabile style of his own.

Spohr's memory is somewhat faded today, but in his own time he yielded to none in the public estimation either as a violinist or a conductor. As a virtuoso he was Paganini's antithesis, in that a conservative bowing technique and a singing tone were the essentials of his style. As a method, his *Violin School* (1831) gained wide currency; and as a conductor, he is credited with having been the first to use a baton, the notable event occurring at a Philharmonic concert in England on April 10, 1820. His music won wide applause, and while there are traces of radicalism in his style, his new thoughts, such as they are, were uttered with an air of disarming gentility and were too well coated with a slick and agreeable melancholy to have caused any disturbance in the well-groomed minds of his listeners. Moreover, he was fortunate in being able to present his own work, for his skill as a performer was persuasive enough to carry all doubts before it. Thus, in 1816, when Berlioz was in his 'teens and Liszt still in knee-pants, Spohr composed a one-movement violin concerto (the *Gesangsszene*, No. 8). Although the form of the work was certainly unorthodox, he was acclaimed wherever he performed it. His audiences, it seems, listened more to his violin-playing than to his music, for in his *Autobiography* he tells us that his solo passages were applauded so vociferously that the following orchestral tuttis were lost in the din.

The virtuoso attitude, as distinct from a virtuoso violin technique, conditioned Spohr's approach to composition, and even his quartets and symphonies have a way of sounding like concertos in disguise. In his concertos proper, violin and orchestra maintain between them a master-servant relationship. The orchestra is quite capable of expressing itself during its ritornels, but it keeps a respectful distance when the soloist clears his throat to speak. His "solo quartets," so called, are hardly more than chamber concertos for solo violin and string-trio accompaniment; and his double quartets are for the most part so scored that the second quartet constitutes a kind of ripieno background for the first. The double quartets are, on the whole, an interesting transplantation of the concerto grosso into chamber music. Spohr's methods are naturally different. He uses less of the schematic doubling for added strength or of the antiphonal echoing between choirs than one will find in the early eighteenth-century concerto grosso. The two quartets interweave to a degree, but there is little question as to which is the solo quartet and which the ripieno accompaniment. One of his symphonies, pontifically entitled *The Earthly and Divine in Human Life*, Op. 121, is an even more curiously experimental embodiment of the concerto grosso principle. It is scored for two orchestras: a small orchestra of eleven solo string instruments representing the divine, and a full orchestra representing the earth-bound elements in human existence. Spohr's trite and rather pompous philosophy is all too evident in his treatment of the two orchestras. The symphony, as Hadow observes, "like everything else turns to a concerto at his touch, and except for a few passages in the finale, the human orchestra has no function but that of accompanist."

Though nominally a purist and, according to his own lights, a disciple of Mozart, Spohr's penchant for programmaticism occasionally broke through in his music. Spohr was quite impressed with the calibre of his own thinking for, apart from his symphonic dissertation on heaven and earth, he composed an *Historical* symphony representing in its several movements several periods in the history of musical style. In all of the movements (the image is Schumann's) Spohr's presence is as thinly disguised as the Emperor Napoleon's at a masked ball. In the same lofty vein he composed a concertino called *Past and Present*, and a symphony modestly entitled *The Consecration of Sound*. The symphony was set to a poem by Pfeiffer which, Spohr instructed, was to be read aloud prior to the performance of the music, or else printed and distributed to the audience for the improvement, no doubt, of their immortal souls.

His *Gesangsszene* concerto in A minor, Op. 47, however, is not programme music. It is designed "In the Form of a Vocal Scene" and was part of his preparation for a trip to Italy where opera-loving audiences would take more willingly, he believed, to a kind of operatic concerto with the solo violin substituting for the voice. The Italians received the concerto enthusiastically, which, among other things, served to confirm Spohr's very good opinion of himself. It is the only one of his concertos which still remains in the active repertoire, although it has become more dated with every decade. It suffers less than his other violin concertos from the vacant nobility of style which he inherited from Viotti and Rode, or from the turgid melancholy which was already seeping into the consciousness of composers. Spohr's was a fat, romantic soul, with neither the strength nor the delicacy to bear up under an addiction to minor keys. His concertos are among the first carriers of that publc melancholia which later settled like an interesting sickness over romantic music.

The *Gesangsszene* concerto represents him at his best; that is, as a conservative with a contribution to make. The work is played continuously in one movement, although the conventional three-movement partition is still discernible. It was composed in 1816, and thus antedates by five years Weber's one-movement *Konzertstück* for piano and orchestra. Spohr went further in tying the three movements of the concerto into one than Beethoven did, and he broached this completer solution before Weber. His concerto is therefore a milestone in the evolution of the form. The concerto also demonstrates one of the most striking characteristics of his style: an incessant chromaticism which led many writers to represent him as one of the ground-breakers of musical romanticism. A cautious and routine temperament, however, inhibited him from using this chromaticism to broaden his limited vocabulary and to develop a real sense of harmonic freedom. He remained ever the man who could not abide the boldness of the Beethoven ninth symphony, the pedant who reported with surprised disapproval a passage containing consecutive fifths in a Rossini opera. The treatment of the first motive of the concerto is typical. It is taken through a promising series of chromatic evolutions from which it emerges as unscathed as if it had never entered. (As a matter of fact, a replaying of the Spohr violin concertos generally re-enforces the impression of music that never manages to get anywhere.) The influence of Spohr's chromaticism upon the harmonic idiom of the later romantics can easily be exaggerated. The chromaticism of Schumann and Wagner derives, if anything, from Bach, in that it makes the effort to become a functional bit of bone structure upon which the mood and movement of the music can take shape. Chopin's chromaticism is largely a matter of inspirational decoration, and while he knew Spohr as well as Field, Hummel, and Bach, it is unlikely that he discovered his chromaticism in any place other than his own very private and precious imagination.

As a group, the Spohr concertos are a minor reflection of some of the major issues at stake during a period of great musical change. As his dates indicate, 1784-1859, he was born early enough for Mozart's classicism to have exerted a chastening influence upon his formative musical imagination, and he died late enough to have encompassed, to have been influenced by, and even to have become, with reservations, a part of the romantic movement which achieved complete dominance in German music in his day. He was a contemporary of Beethoven and Schubert; he outlived Mendelssohn, Schumann, and Chopin although he was some twenty-five years their senior; and he died six years after Schumann had pronounced young Brahms a genius. There is nothing eternal about the Spohr concertos. They represent him in the parliament of composers as a local conservative who knew a few set speeches and delivered them well. In his own special province, the virtuoso concerto, he was challenged only by Paganini; and if his contribution to the development of violin-playing was objectively less progressive than Paganini's, the music in which he embodied his contribution was undeniably better.

"Strange, I admit, but true," confessed Berlioz in his *Memoirs*. "I came into the world quite naturally, unheralded by any signs which, in poetic ages, preceded the advent of remarkable personages." Paganini, on the contrary, took such matters seriously. On his own admission he was the fulfilment of the work of the Lord. "The Saviour," he reports, "appeared to my mother in a dream and told her that a prayer should be fulfilled to her; she requested that her son should become a great violinist and this was granted her." His career began, therefore, with a legend, and for decades after his death his memory still lay enshrouded in an aura of supernatural sensationalism. Some of the legends are recounted with a grim medieval mysticism which forms a kind of musical supplement to *The Castle of Otranto*. Imaginative wanderers out on the moors on a dark stormy night had a way of stumbling over

Paganini groaning prostrate under an overhanging crag. It was part of the etiquette of this medieval mythology never to inquire of Paganini what he was doing there, or even to come to his assistance. Sooner or later the wanderer turned up at a concert and there, lo and behold, was the moor-groaner and baleful-glancer fiddling away like the very devil himself.

His violinistic witchcraft was a revelation to his contemporaries, and gullible minds readily believed the weird rumours that purported to explain the origins of his technique. One example will suffice. Paganini was fond of performing with only one string mounted on his violin; a practice which, he declared, originated with a *Scena amorosa* improvised to amuse his mistress. The love scene was rendered on two strings, the E and G, "the fourth string representing the man (Adonis) and the treble string the woman (Venus). This was the beginning of my habit of playing on a single string...." The *Scena amorosa*, as he described it, was a "passionate dialogue" between two lovers "in which the most tender accents followed transports of jealousy...there were cries of rage and sounds of joy; sighs of pain and of happiness. The piece ended in reconciliation and the two lovers, more attached to one another than ever, executed a pas de deux which closed with a brilliant coda. This musical scene was highly successful. I will not speak of the intoxicating glances which the lady of my dreams sent in my direction." It was suggested to him by Princess Elise (Napoleon's sister) that if he could "perform the impossible on two strings," perhaps only one would be sufficient. "The idea intrigued my imagination," writes Paganini, "and some weeks later I composed a sonata entitled *Napoleon* for the fourth string only, and played it...before a crowded and brilliant court.... My predilection for the G-string dates from that evening." Paganini's own account is romantic enough. His audiences, however, were sure they knew better and the rumour was long current that the one-string technique was developed during a prison term which he served, so the story went, for having murdered one of his mistresses. The jailer of the prison, fearing that he might hang himself, allowed him to play the violin providing he used but one string.

Such stories were pure fantasy; but they did the box office no harm. People came to see as well as to hear "this ferocious man-eater, this seducer of women, this escaped convict" (the epithets are Berlioz's); and even in hard-headed London, where incensed music critics calculated that he earned twelve pounds ten shillings per second "while in certain counties a labourer gets only four shillings and sixpence per week," crowds packed their way into his concerts, and sober citizens tagged after him in the street. "Although the curiosity to see me has long been satisfied," he complained, "although I have played in public more than thirty times, and although my portrait has been published in every conceivable style and pose, I cannot leave my rooms without collecting a crowd, which is content to follow or accompany me; they walk beside me, ahead of me, they speak to me in English, of which I do not understand a word, they touch me as though to make sure I am flesh and blood."

No musician of the period was quite so much the rage as Paganini. His performances were fantastic, and the *Athenaeum* feared that his arrival in London "was enough to make the greater part of the fiddling tribe commit suicide." In Vienna where, according to the *Austrian Observer*, he "temporarily dethroned the giraffe recently sent by the Pasha of Egypt, and which heretofore had been the object of much attention, " everything from chops to billiard tables, sashes to cigars, snuff boxes to rolls shaped like violins, were subtitled "à la Paganini." A burlesque on the effect of one of his performances is recited by a character in a two-act farce, *The False Artist, or the Concerto of the G-String*, composed in his honour. "Three hundred victims are in the hospital suffering from over-enchantment; four hundred—all artists— opened their mouths and ears so wide in astonishment that they cannot close them again, and will have to be operated upon. Over forty critics are seriously affected by inflammation of the brain since writing their reports on him; in short, it is indescribable." One of the characters, a fiddler named Fiedler, is unimpressed, for, as he observes, like anyone else, Paganini plays after all on only one violin.

It was about the only thing he did do like anyone else. He played on one string instead of four; he used a bamboo cane instead of a bow. Once when an audience annoyed him he responded by drawing from his instrument the sounds of cocks crowing, hinges creaking, crickets chirping, dogs howling, and ended with a distinct heehaw which he produced by bowing vigorously behind the bridge first on the E-string and then on the G. Such stunts he could improvise whenever it amused him to do so; but there was more to his technique than this kind of trickery.

Much of his technique was not completely an innovation. He revived, for example, the ancient seventeenth-century art of the scordatura, or deliberate mistuning of the violin, which enabled him to execute normally impossible passages with little effort. Likewise, his use of a single string was not unprecedented. Leopold Mozart, in one of his letters, describes a violinist named Esser who played with remarkable facility upon the fourth string only; and there is a sonata for a single string by F. W. Rust dated 1796. However, no one either before or after Paganini ever made so much of the device. He enriched and complicated the violinist's technique tremendously in his extension of the range of single and double harmonics, in his development of a left-hand pizzicato, in his elaborate treatment of double-stopping; and once again, while double-stopping was one of the earliest discoveries of the violin virtuoso, Paganini raised it to a level of intricacy and perfection hitherto unknown. He was facilitated in this respect by the use of a bridge less convex than that of other violinists, particularly toward the highest strings, which made it somewhat easier, for example, to take three strings in the highest register. His enormous span was also a help, for by placing his thumb in the middle of the neck of the violin he could still perform easily in the first three positions without shifting. Among other things, he was, like Beethoven, a phenomenal sight reader, tossing off the greatest difficulties as if he had practised them for weeks, and even adding embellishments of his own without a moment's hesitation. He also played his music from memory, which in those days was something of a novelty although we have come to take it for granted today.

There were a few dissident voices in the universal roar of acclamation which rewarded his playing. Spohr, for example, admired his dexterity and his perfect intonation, but he found that Paganini broke too many rules. Even before hearing him play, Spohr wrote with conservative suspicion of Paganini's "series of bewildering tricks" which had been reported to him: "harmonics, variations on one string, a peculiar kind of pizzicato for the left hand, without the help of the right hand or the bow...." But the majority of responsible musicians —and this is a most important point—agreed with the English reviewer who found in this no trickery but true music. "The triumph of mechanical skill, astonishing as it is in itself, is the smallest part of the wonder. The real magic is not the novelty of the feat, but the surprising beauty of the effect...." Spohr was willing to believe that the strain of charlatanism in Paganini precluded "a tasteful cantabile style"; yet his slow movements were always a deeply moving experience, embodying, as one reviewer put it, "every shade and gradation of feeling."

Paganini's own dictum was that "to play with compelling power one must feel deeply"; and as a matter of fact, the most responsible criticism of the period stressed the terrific emotional impact of a Paganini performance, the flaming passion, and the acute sense of suffering which lived in his renditions of his own music. "Sorrow is the characteristic of his style and music," wrote one reviewer. "I have wept only three times in my life," added Rossini, "the first time when my earliest opera failed, the second time when, with a boating party, a truffled turkey fell into the water, and the third time when I first heard Paganini play." Paganini played only his own music and Schumann found it "ecstatic"; Chopin heard Paganini in Warsaw and worshipped him for ever after; and Liszt came away half hysterical over "what suffering, what misery, what tortures dwell in those four strings." And yet these are qualities which we look for in vain in the cold print of his concertos. The slow movement of the B minor violin concerto, Op. 7,[1] for example, was inspired by a tragedian's performance of a prison scene in which, with much extravagant breast-beating, horrible misfortunes were bewailed, and heaven implored for a release from a miserable existence. Today even the most sympathetic performance fails to uncover any great depth of feeling in this movement; yet Paganini convincingly conveyed to his audiences the emotional intensity of the scene that was his inspiration.

It is not at all likely that composers like Schumann, Schubert, Liszt, Chopin, and Rossini were easily misled into imagining profundities which do not exist. The score of a Paganini concerto has, as a matter of curious fact, very little to do with the concerto as he played it. Paganini was an improviser—one of the greatest the world has ever known— not a composer; and his concertos as they now stand are merely a bare outline (complete only in the orchestral parts) of the music he gave in

---

[1] This is the concerto with the *La Campanella* finale which still is, and probably always will be, a favourite virtuoso war horse. The concerto, according to Pulver, "was the first composition he played outside of Italy, the one with which he commenced his conquest of a continent."

actual performance. The modern virtuoso is quite satisfied if he can but master the dry difficulties of the solo part as they are recorded in the score; yet for Paganini the written solo part was not the final result of his inventiveness, but merely the ground plan for a musical edifice which he built up extemporaneously during actual performance. The written solo part, difficult as it is, was only a text to guide his improvisation, which, no doubt, he varied with every performance. Musicians in the orchestra often noted that what he played during a concert varied considerably from the concerto as he had rehearsed it with them. Even when sight-reading a work by another composer, he embellished, altered, and improvised upon what was written as he went along. He was one of the first concert artists to play without music; and while performers who followed his example memorized their parts, Paganini dispensed with the written music because he had no intention of following it anyway. It is easy to understand the spell he cast over genuinely creative minds, for his playing of one of his own concertos was the miracle of creation itself; he made music before the very eyes and ears of his listeners, giving free rein to the spontaneous urgency of his emotions, which stormed with hair-raising unconcern through the nightmare of technical difficulties in their path. Schubert pressed the five sorely needed florins which this "concert corsair" demanded for admission upon a friend, with the explanation, "I have heard him once already....I tell you that such a fellow will never come again." He was probably right.

There is little left in the printed score of the Paganini concerto which his contemporaries heard, beyond a few sweet, operatic melodies and the mechanism of a colossal technique. A modern performance of a Paganini concerto must necessarily stick to the music as written, so that what we hear today is a pleasant diversion rather than a creative experience. There is no remedy for the situation; and minus Paganini's creative fire, the technical difficulties of his concertos have become a kind of monstrously intricate and functionless piece of machinery producing nothing but its own motion.

Paganini's method was not unique, although no one carried it as far as he did. Composers often played the solo part in their concertos from shorthand notes which they embellished and varied during actual performance. A fairly good case can be made for traces of a shorthand notation in the piano concertos of Mozart. Hummel, for example, issued an edition of several Mozart piano concertos with the solo part heavily embellished; and Hummel, who was a pupil of Mozart, certainly knew his methods. The whole problem of extemporizing on Mozart's text still remains to be solved. In a recorded rendition of the slow movement of Mozart's *Coronation* concerto (K. 537), Wanda Landowska does venture to embellish the piano part. The results are not displeasing, although a pianist equipped with less than Landowska's considerable knowledge of the subject would do well to leave Mozart alone. Tovey's statement of the problem is as good as any, although on his own admission he is far from solving it. "Hummel's ornamentation will certainly not do," he writes, "but it should be studied, for he had the knowledge we have not, though his temperament was inflated rather than inspired. It is quite certain that the plain text of Mozart's pianoforte part is often incomplete; for instance, you find a clarinet and a bassoon varying their repetitions while the pianoforte part at the same moment has always the old bare outline. Clearly the orchestral players could not be left to extemporize variations, and the pianist could. But one is thankful to do as little as possible; for any deviation from Mozart's style, even a deviation into early Beethoven, sets one's teeth on edge."

In a very different measure this obtains also in Beethoven; that is, Beethoven played his concertos from a set of mnemonic devices rather than from a written score, but it is doubtful whether he improvised variations to the extent Mozart probably did, and when he finally put the solo part down on paper it was in complete form. Beethoven once asked Seyfried to turn pages for him during his performance of the C minor piano concerto, Op. 37, "but—heaven help me—," reports Seyfried, "that was easier said than done. I saw nothing but empty leaves; at the most on one page or the other a few Egyptian hieroglyphs wholly unintelligible to me scribbled down to serve as clues for him. . . . He gave me a secret glance whenever he was at the end of one of the invisible passages and my scarcely concealable anxiety not to miss the decisive moment amused him greatly. . . ." Ries, Beethoven's pupil, assures us, however, that Beethoven "very seldom added notes or ornaments. . . ."

Paganini's improvisational method of using the solo part as a point of departure had, therefore, some basis in traditional practice. His written scores, however, unlike those of Beethoven and Mozart, never got beyond the shorthand stage. We have only the word of trustworthy composers that Paganini's imagination decoded them into music of great beauty and power.

Like Berlioz, Paganini had the deepest admiration for Beethoven, and with a wonderful, romantic sincerity he wept bitter tears that such a man should die. Few among Beethoven's contemporaries felt his torrential dramatics and his liberating spirit so deeply as Paganini. In his own limited sphere Paganini was also a liberating force, and the influence he exerted over better composers was considerable. Schumann decided upon the career of a piano virtuoso after hearing Paganini, and Liszt's own prodigious flair for virtuosity was likewise stimulated by him. Violinists soon began to follow his lead. De Bériot, the composer of a few pleasantly unimportant violin concertos and the author of a famous *Violin Method* (1858), was one of the first to do so. One of Chopin's earliest piano compositions was a *Souvenir de Paganini;* Berlioz composed his *Harold in Italy* for him; Schumann dedicated a movement in his *Carnaval* to Paganini and also transcribed several of his violin caprices for the piano. Liszt, too, composed a series of *Studies Based on the Caprices of Paganini Transcribed for the Pianoforte.* The two sets of variations which Brahms composed on the theme from Paganini's twenty-fourth caprice do not indicate an influence so much as a substantial measure of respect for a man who would write a good melody. Rachmaninoff in his rhapsody for piano and orchestra likewise selected Paganini's twenty-fourth caprice as the theme for his variations. Paganini was not merely the first violinist to master and liberate his instrument; he was, as his dates, 1782-1840, indicate, part of the small determined band of musicians who were intent on accomplishing a complete revolution in the form, style, and temperament of music. The particular lesson he taught his contemporaries was to master the resources of instruments down to the last technical detail, and to utilize a total technique for expressive purposes. He gave profound and lasting stimulus to the romantic (and also modern) conception of musical expression based on the use of intricate instrumental effects. He was, in Schumann's splendid phrase, "the turning-point in the history of virtuosity."

Carl Maria von Weber (1786-1826) was the most lamentable casualty in an era of great change. Certainly a composer of genius, his worth-while accomplishment (apart from his last operas) is restricted to a few works such as the *Konzertstück* and the piano sonatas which still maintain a flickering existence in the modern concert repertoire. No one of his concertos, not even the *Konzertstück*, is wholly admirable in the sense that most Mozart and Beethoven concertos are, yet none are devoid of worth-while music, and some will repay occasional replaying with moments of genuine inspiration and beauty. Weber was the victim rather than, like Beethoven, the master of the contradictions of his age. He mirrored his period with greater fidelity than either Beethoven or Spohr or Paganini; for he suffered from its corrosions more deeply than Beethoven, he was a better composer than Spohr (whose vacillations are, in the long run, a matter of little moment), and his efforts were more diversified than Paganini's.

The times were too unstable for a talent less firmly directed than Beethoven's; nor, to begin with, was Weber's early training of the kind to prepare him for a disciplined application to the problems which beset him as a mature composer. His father had it prearranged with the fates that his son was going to be a genius. The prenatal conference with the Norns had apparently not been explicit, for while the boy was dragged around from city to city as a musical wonder child, he was also plied with instruction in drawing, oil painting, etching, etc., just in case his genius should break out in another direction. His musical training was not especially systematic under the circumstances, for with every change in residence came another master. The most famous names among his teachers were Michael Haydn, the brother of Joseph Haydn and a friend of Mozart, and Abt Vogler, a vain and provocative personality whom Mozart and Schubert thought a fool, though a few of his ideas were not entirely idiotic. Many years later Weber was to reflect bitterly that he had had "no happy childish days to look back upon, no free open boyhood." For a man who always professed adherence to Mozartean standards, this haphazard training was a sorry sort of equipment to bring to bear upon the technical and inspirational problems of a post-Mozartean era.

The restlessness of the period did not help toward disciplined and sustained thinking on problems of form, style, and expression. Music had, in truth, been reaching out to an ever-widening lay audience, and in metropolitan centres men like Rochlitz and the Rellstabs were already offering music criticism on a modern commercial foundation, i.e. as a middleman information and ten-commandment service conducted by professional non-composers. Musical journalism (reviews in daily newspapers) was a healthy sign of the broad growth of interest in music, and Weber was one of the first to insist that it ought not to be relegated to those who do not themselves compose. Toward the close of 1810, along with several other musicians including Meyerbeer, he projected the Harmonischer Verein, an organization whose members were required to be composers and whose purpose was "the elevation of musical criticism by musicians themselves." Like Schumann after him, Weber was concerned to make articulate and to defend his views not only by writing music but by writing about it. As with Schumann and his Davidsbund, there was a lot of romantic hocus-pocus tied up in this fundamentally serious enterprise. The existence of the society was supposed to be a secret, and each member submitted his contribution under a fanciful nom de plume. Weber's assumed name was Melos. For a period, literary work occupied much of his attention. He did the commentary for Vogler's presumptuous revisions of several Bach chorales, and he left a fragment of a musical novel, *Tonkünstler's Leben*, which is, in part, a collection of prejudices (some of them not very brilliant) written in an extravagant romantic style.

While this was all to the good, the larger audiences who were being attracted by the accessibility of the public concert hall were also being distracted by the more serious and horrible business of the Napoleonic Wars. When Weber came to Prague, full of hope for the restoration of the opera to the position it had held there in Mozart's time, he found that the wars had brought interest in music to a standstill and that discriminating appreciation was definitely on the wane. This was in 1813 and his experience for many years prior had been along the same line. During the last months of 1806 he had secured the post of music-intendant in the household of Duke Eugene of Württemberg; but the general insecurity which followed Napoleon's triumph over the Prussians in February 1807 caused the Duke to close down on expenditures for musical entertainment. With a living to be made, and a father to support, Weber brought his musical career temporarily to an end by accepting a post as private secretary to Duke Ludwig of Württemberg, brother of Duke Eugene. Since Ludwig believed in nothing so much as in having a very good time, Weber's duties were mainly to hold off the creditors, to secure, by fair means and frequently by foul, new money for the Duke's pleasure, and to accept upon his own head the violent recriminations of King Frederick, Ludwig's brother, for his employer's extravagance. Weber's temper at the time is indicated by a little scene which was enacted in the corridor outside Frederick's apartments after one of his violent sessions with the King. An old woman, asking the way to the laundress's room, was directed by Weber to the King's apartment with the information that "the royal laundress lives in there." The King promptly ordered him to be arrested, but the Duke managed to have him released. This entire period, during which he came to regard his music as nothing better than a dilettante's amusement, was brought to an end in February 1810 by his arrest in connection with a shady financial transaction of which he was subsequently proved innocent.

From this corroding, semi-feudal atmosphere Weber fled to the concert hall, where for several years he sought to turn his talents as a piano virtuoso to account. The ultimate solution of his problem came, however, with the patriotic cultural renaissance which burst forth following the defeat of Napoleon. His *Leier und Schwert* and his *Kampf und Sieg* embodied the intense patriotism that was the order of the day, and they were received and sung throughout the land with feverish enthusiasm. For the last nine years of his life Weber served as Kapellmeister of the German opera in Dresden and during this period produced *Der Freischütz*, a work which had a profound effect upon national German opera. Weber's *Konzertstück*, his most notable concerto, has been interpreted by Weitzmann as a reflection of the spirit of national liberation which arose in Germany toward the close of the Napoleonic Wars.

Weber's concertos show clearly enough the perils implicit in such a career. Court and concert hall are contradictory institutions, symbols of the opposite ideologies of two eras. Weber ran from one to the other; and, for all his genius, he avoided the pitfalls of neither. Impressed with the dignity of music as an important human activity, he let himself be misled into the least commendable practices of the two eras he sought to unite. The time was out of joint and he, cursed sprite, had neither the moral stamina nor the understanding to set it right. There are pages of splendid music in his concertos; also pages weighted with the inert virtuosity of the concert hall and with survivals of the slick dilettantism of a corrupt court. His positive accomplishment, so far as the concerto is concerned, was to have offered romantic composers in his best work, the *Konzertstück*, a solution to the concerto-form problem which carried weight throughout the entire century.

Weber's formative years fall within the last decade of the eighteenth century, while the period of his creative activity belongs wholly to the nineteenth century. This is mirrored in the contradiction between his thinking and his creating. Weber's tastes and personal allegiances were in large measure rooted in the eighteenth century. He fancied himself a Mozartean and, like Spohr, his appreciation of Beethoven was limited (with a few exceptions) to the master's "first compositions only." Yet in his music Weber belongs irrevocably to the new century; "he not only stands upon its threshhold, he opens it and is its first modern musician" (Einstein). This is abundantly evident in his *Konzertstück*, his other concertos, as well as in his piano sonatas, for in these works he tackled two of the touchstone problems of nineteenth-century music: the sonata form and a virtuoso technique.

Weber's concertos and sonatas indicate that a classical concentration and closeness of design are not among his strong points; that sentiment and a glittering technique (for good or evil two of the salient characteristics of the nineteenth-century concerto) have become primary considerations with the composer. Weber's life-span (1786–1826) falls wholly within that of Beethoven's (he was born sixteen years after Beethoven and died one year before); and his early death precedes that of his younger contemporary, Schubert, by two years. Beethoven expanded and altered the sonata form to a point where, in his last quartets, it is scarcely the same form; while Schubert often worked with a looseness of design inadmissible on the strictest classical standards. Yet Beethoven and Schubert, for all their implicitly destructive influence on the form, were the last of the tradition to explore its resources with the natural ease of Haydn and Mozart, Weber's sonata-form movements are the first signs of discomfort, the beginning of a new weakness in the fundamental grasp of the form. For with Schumann the sonata form is not flesh and blood; to Chopin it was an awkward discipline; to a revolutionary like Liszt (who thought clearly about such matters) it was an inheritance to be invested boldly in new ways of thinking and feeling; with a conservative spirit like Mendelssohn it assumed a surface correctness; and even with a traditionalist like Brahms its problems were surmounted only with a sense of strong intellectual effort. That Weber had conscious difficulty with sonata-form movements is demonstrated beyond doubt by the hesitant manner in which he essayed their composition. In his concertos and sonatas the opening sonata-form movement was rarely the first to be composed, and quite often it was the last. The other movements came easier, and the sonata-form movement often took shape only after the remainder of the concerto or sonata was substantially on the road to completion. Sometimes he omitted the sonata-form movement altogether, as in his adagio and rondo for harmonichord and orchestra (1811) and his andante and Hungarian rondo for viola and orchestra (composed in 1809 and reworked in 1813 for bassoon, Op. 35). These works are concertos minus the traditional first movement in sonata form. That Weber should have bothered with the form at all must be set down to the influence of the age. Beethoven was still living, Mozart and Haydn still of fairly recent memory, and a composer hoping to make his way in the world could hardly appear before his public without exercising himself in a traditional concerto or sonata which virtually served, both for him and for his audience, as a certification of his status. In his last concerto, the *Konzertstück*, Op. 79, composed in 1821, Weber ultimately dispensed with the traditional concerto form entirely, producing a work whose freshness and originality was an inspiration to generations of experimental concerto composers.

The *Konzertstück* is divided into four movements which are run together as one. Beethoven had already hinted at the procedure in the last two movements of his fifth piano concerto, and Spohr had already carried out this kind of continuous design in his *Gesangsszene* concerto. In the Weber work the character of the movements, and the manner in which they are run together, derive from an explicit programme to which the concerto is set. Weber's sense of form functioned particularly well when he had a text to illustrate, and in this he shows a type of musical-literary mentality often encountered later in the century. In a measure, this eager reliance on a programme was the romanticist's confession of weakness in his instinctive feeling for form, for while Weber, Berlioz, Liszt, and Tschaikowsky protested that their music was intended to make sense as music, they were relieved, nevertheless, to have a programme on hand, a set of ordered and unambiguous ideas on which to hang their sense of musical coherence. In any case, Weber worked more freely once he exchanged the abstract discipline of the sonata-form concerto for the coherence of a literary plot. His choice of material reflects, incidentally, the interest in the medieval past which was shared by romantic composers, novelists, and poets alike (Wagner, Walter Scott, etc.).

"The lady sits in her tower (this is the first movement, *Larghetto affettuoso*). She gazes sadly into the distance. Her knight has been for years in the Holy Land; will she ever see him again? Battles have been fought; but no news of him who is so dear to her. In vain have been all her prayers. A fearful vision (second movement, *Allegro passionato*) rises in her mind—her knight is lying on the battlefield deserted and alone; his heart's blood is fast ebbing away. Could she but be by his side!—could she but die with him! She falls exhausted and senseless. But hark! (third movement, *Tempo di marcia*). What is that distant sound? What glimmers in the sunlight from the wood? What are those forms approaching? Knights and squires with the Cross of the Crusaders, banners waving, acclamations of the people, and there!—it is he! She sinks into his arms. Love is triumphant (fourth movement, *Presto giocoso*). Happiness without end. The very woods and waves sing of love; a thousand voices proclaim its victory."

We can forgive Weber his programme, for he had sense enough to apologize for it and honesty enough to insist upon it, since this was the way the work was conceived and there was little point in pretending otherwise. "I am planning," he wrote to Rochlitz, "a pianoforte concerto in F minor. The choice of key seems curious—seeing that concertos in a minor key so rarely please unless some rousing idea is connected with them. A sort of story has taken hold of me; it will serve to link the movements together and determine their character in detail, as it were, dramatically. I intend to entitle them: Allegro, 'Separation'; Adagio, 'Lament'; Finale, 'Deepest grief, comfort, return and jubilation.' I find it very difficult to accustom myself to this conception, as I particularly dislike all musical pictures with specific titles; yet it forces itself irresistibly upon me and promises to prove efficacious. In any case, I do not care to put it forward for the first time in any place where I am not already well known, for fear of being misunderstood and accounted a charlatan."

The work is full of brilliant effects, some of which make fine music in themselves; but on the whole the effects are calculated for their illustrative rather than for their intrinsic merit. Apart from the famous crescendo and the glittering octave glissandos (which Tovey excuses on the ground that "they make admirable screams"), there are at least two memorable effects in the score: the pizzicato-like accompaniment for the left hand while the right hand takes a lovely sustained melody (the first piano entrance in the first movement), and the wailing bassoon notes above a tremolo shudder in the strings—presumably the lady falling senseless, but hark—which connects the second movement to the march. An evaluation of the virtues of the work is mainly a matter of taste. The grand rushing around in the finale adds up to a rather unfurious kind of rejoicing; but since Donald Tovey can still whip up some honest enthusiasm over it, its defence is gratefully turned over into his capable hands. "As to the finale," writes Tovey, "I frankly confess that it thrills me. Weber's range of harmony is hardly wider than Gluck's; but when he gets beyond tonic and dominant his changes are really as grand in effect as in intention. As for the pianoforte writing, it conclusively proves Weber to have deserved his reputation as one of the greatest players ever known on any instrument. Every detail of it must have been discovered during extemporization at full speed: there is no other means of guessing that such passages lie well for the hand at all."

The two earlier piano concertos—the first in C major, Op. 11, composed in 1810 and the second in E-flat major, Op. 32, composed in 1812 —abound in virtuoso glitter and gush, although the second, the more brilliant of the two, contains a slow movement that ranks among Weber's noteworthy piano creations. In point of piano technique the three concertos, as well as his piano sonatas, reveal Weber as a precursor of Chopin, Mendelssohn, and Schumann; and as a singularly imaginative one, since at the date of the latest of these works (the

Konzertstück of 1821) Chopin and Schumann were eleven years old and Mendelssohn only twelve. To all intents and purposes, Weber represents the first advance in piano technique after Beethoven. (Schubert's music, during his lifetime, remained hidden from his contemporaries; and, in any case, his greatest piano music—the last sonatas of 1828—were composed after Weber's death.) The phrase "after Beethoven" needs qualification, for it is intended only in the sense that in spirit Weber belonged to the post-Beethoven generation. In point of chronological fact Weber was almost Beethoven's exact contemporary. His three piano concertos were composed between 1810 and 1821, and his four piano sonatas between 1812 and 1822. Thus all date after Beethoven's last concerto (the *Emperor* of 1809), and all fall within the period of Beethoven's last series of great sonatas. In comparison, Weber's creations belong to a different, to a newer, and to an admittedly inferior world. The last sonatas of Beethoven contain some of the most profoundly searching music ever written for the instrument. The piano concertos and sonatas of Weber are patently the creations of a brilliant pianist and are already touched with what Einstein aptly calls "the fatal brilliance of the nineteenth century, which Schumann and Chopin did not overcome without difficulty and upon which Liszt continued to build." There is very little in Weber's piano work (and this may be said for many another nineteenth-century piano composer) which is not at least hinted at in Beethoven, but Weber was one of the first to polish up the brilliance of Beethoven's effects and to astound his audiences with them in an obvious and sometimes even theatrical sort of way.

Weber's concertos for wind instruments are likewise effective. There are moments of fine music in these concertos, although they are too insubstantial to warrant revival in the concert hall. All too often Weber is concerned to display his solo instrument rather than to make important music with it, and sometimes this takes the form of a trick effect in itself curious and interesting. In the concertino for horn and orchestra, for example, the player is required to blow one note and hum another, thus producing acoustically a third and even a fourth tone. When perfectly executed, the hornist finds himself playing a dominant seventh chord in four-part harmony all by himself. Besides the horn concertino, Weber composed a bassoon concerto, and a concertino and two concertos for clarinet. The Weber clarinet works, taken together with a series of clarinet concertos by Spohr, form an engaging group of satellites surrounding Mozart's magnificent concerto for the instrument.

Weber's *Konzertstück* and Spohr's *Gesangsszene* are operatic concertos which make explicit the deep-seated relationship (discussed in an earlier chapter) between the operatic aria and the solo concerto. The two works are unique only in that they carry the resemblance to a point not willingly admitted in most concertos. Spohr's concerto is operatic both in style and intention; Weber's work becomes so in the process of adapting the concerto form to an overtly dramatic purpose. The logic of the adaptation is inescapable, and the general relationship is inevitably given point by the use of several frankly operatic devices (e.g. the plaintive bassoon over a dark string tremolo, etc.). Weber's *Konzertstück* was not the first programmatic concerto, but as an example of a peculiarly romantic type of programmaticism it is matched only by Berlioz's *Harold in Italy*, Op. 16, a symphony for viola and orchestra. The Berlioz work was composed in 1834, thirteen years after the *Konzertstück*. Berlioz had an especial sympathy for Weber's music. He couples "Beethoven and Weber" so persistently in his praises, one would almost imagine there was really some comparison between the two. In all probability it was simply part of the generous supply of ecstasy which Berlioz always carried around for the men he particularly admired. Chronology and enthusiasm, however, are not much to go on in Berlioz's case, and it is a precarious sort of business tracing influences on his singular and original imagination.

Harold in Italy was composed for Paganini and thereby hangs one of Berlioz's peculiar tales. "I have a wonderful viola," Paganini said to him (this is from Berlioz's *Memoirs*), "an admirable Stradivari, and should greatly like to play it in public. But I have no music for it. Would you write me a solo? I have no confidence in anyone but you for such a work." Berlioz professed himself properly flattered, but explained tactfully that he was not a writer of solos. (One thinks of the *Tuba Mirum* of his *Requiem* with its five orchestras, and of his conversation with the King of Prussia which he reported as follows: "I understand," remarked the King, "that you are the composer who writes for five hundred musicians." "Your Majesty has been misinformed," replied Berlioz, "sometimes I write for four hundred and fifty." Debussy called him a "musical monster," and Heine came away from his music with visions of primeval creatures and fabulous empires.) Berlioz did not play the viola himself and countered with the suggestion that "composition sufficiently brilliant to suit such a virtuoso" should be written by none other than Paganini. However, Paganini was persuasive and, writes Berlioz, "in order to please the illustrious virtuoso, I endeavoured to write a solo for the viola, but so combined with the orchestra as not to diminish the importance of the latter, feeling sure that Paganini's incomparable execution would enable him to give the solo instrument all its due prominence." Paganini had a look at the work in progress and was puzzled by the rests in the viola part. "That is not what I want," he cried. "I am silent much too long. I must be playing the whole time." "That is exactly what I thought," answered Berlioz. "What you really want is a concerto for the viola, and you are the only man who can write it." However, Berlioz continued with his project, and Paganini eventually got to falling on his knees before Berlioz for it.

"Finding that the plan of my composition did not suit him," continues Berlioz, "I applied myself to carrying it out in another way, and without troubling myself any further as to how the solo part should be brought into brilliant relief. I conceived the idea of writing a series of scenes for the orchestra, in which the viola should find itself interwoven, like a person more or less in action, always preserving his own individuality. The background I formed from my recollections of my wanderings in the Abruzzi, introducing the viola as a sort of melancholy dreamer, in the style of Byron's *Childe Harold*. Hence the title of the symphony *Harold in Italy*. As in the *Symphonie fantastique*, one principal theme (the first strain of the viola) is reproduced throughout the work, but with this difference, that in the *Symphonie fantastique* the theme—the *idée fixe*—obtrudes itself obstinately like a passionately episodic figure, into scenes wholly foreign to it, whilst Harold's strain is superadded to the other orchestral strains, with which it contrasts both in movement and character, without hindering their development. Notwithstanding its complicated harmonic tissue, I took as little time to compose this symphony as I usually did to write my other works, though I employed considerable labour in retouching it. In the *Pilgrims' March*, which I improvised in a couple of hours one evening over my fire, I have been modifying the details for the past six years, and think that I have much improved it."

This clears up a few difficult points. For one thing, Berlioz conceived the work not as a virtuoso concerto but as a symphony with viola obbligato (elsewhere he referred to it as his "second symphony," the first being the *Fantastique*). More accurately it is "a series of scenes for the orchestra" with the solo viola wandering through the work "as a sort of melancholy dreamer"; for Berlioz was as incapable of writing a traditional symphony as he was of composing a traditional concerto. The stress is clearly on the orchestra and not on the soloist. Berlioz proceeded without troubling himself "as to how the solo part should be brought into brilliant relief," relying on "Paganini's incomparable execution," rather than on the character of the solo writing itself, "to give the solo instrument all its due prominence." It is this difference in viewpoint concerning the basic balance of forces, solo and orchestra, which distinguishes *Harold in Italy* from the traditional concerto. Berlioz conceived the work fundamentally in terms of the orchestra; the concerto composer works basically from the viewpoint of the soloist. Berlioz made the distinction explicit, for when Paganini sought to direct his attention to the soloist, Berlioz replied, "What you really want is a concerto for the viola," and that he had no intention of composing. In consequence, while the viola part is quite substantial, there is no virtuoso display in the work.

In other respects *Harold in Italy* has points of similarity to the traditional concerto. It is a full-scale work for solo and orchestra, and the first movement is in sonata form, although in one of Berlioz's own inimitable variety. Like Weber, once Berlioz gets past the opening sonata-form movement he breathes more easily. The first movement of *Harold in Italy*, while one of his happier treatments of the sonata-form structure, is typical of his strength and weakness in the form. It opens magnificently and closes just about as well, but somewhere in between the bottom threatens to fall out of the music. For all his admiration for Beethoven, he learned nothing from him in the way of developing a melody, and in this respect his flippancy toward the music of Haydn and Mozart was ill considered. "When I hear Mozart," he declared, "I am troubled with a slight nightmare; when I hear Haydn I am troubled with a big one." Berlioz at his best is quite an enchanting melodist, and at his worst a trivial and a boring one. However, his long paragraph style of melody, unique as it undoubtedly is, is hardly sufficient to carry him over a treacherous middle section; nor, in lieu of a sense of constructive development, is he quite able to carry off Schubert's uncanny trick of repeating a theme three or four times, cozening us out of our expectations with a miracle of sheer melody.

Harold in Italy, incidentally, contains persuasive evidence that Berlioz could upon occasion command an effective and thoroughly individual kind of counterpoint. This is no mean accomplishment and it is an aspect of his art that has been generally undervalued. A recent incensed biographer's belligerent claim that Berlioz was "one of the greatest masters" of the polyphonic science is, as an effort to balance the scales more justly in his favour, a forgivable piece of plain nonsense. That he could handle counterpoint for his own highly specialized purposes is sufficient to merit deep respect, for very few romantic imaginations were able to make this intractable discipline genuinely their own. However, it is quite unlikely that a leading master of polyphony could have listened, as Berlioz did, to a Bach concerto with such breathtaking inattention. "When I was in St. Petersburg," he reports, "they played me a triple concerto of Bach's on three pianos. I do not think they intended to annoy me."

The two middle movements are written with all his marvellous feeling for orchestral effect and are studded with some of his happiest melodic inspirations. The opening melody of the *Pilgrims' March* has a truly personal feeling for line and inflection; it is the kind of melody one does not find in another composer. The final movement, after characterizing the brigands with an *allegro frenetico* theme, proceeds with a recollection of the melodies from the preceding movements. The idea was probably suggested to him by the finale of the Beethoven ninth symphony, but the resemblance disappears as soon as we recognize it. Berlioz, whatever his faults, had an impressive way of knowing his own mind, and once he seizes upon an idea it becomes quite furiously (and quite convincingly) his own.

In Berlioz's account, given above, he also has several pertinent things to say about the programmatic character of the music. It was formed, he tells us, from his own (not Childe Harold's) wanderings in the Abruzzi, and the viola is introduced as a melancholy dreamer "in the style of Byron's *Childe Harold.*" Once in a while it helps to take Berlioz literally. He meant the style, not the content, of *Childe Harold*. Just as the viola meditatively wanders in and out of a *Pilgrims' March*, an orgy of brigands, and a serenade in the Abruzzi (none of which occur in Byron's Italian cantos) always preserving its individuality (the *idée fixe*) intact, so "Byron stood upon the Bridge of Sighs and stood in the Colosseum, and in this and that historic or picturesque spot, to meditate on history, politics, and family affairs . . ." (Tovey). It is the wandering and the meditating rather than any place wandered through, or any event meditated upon, that constitute the similarity to *Childe Harold*. If we assume anything more than this, then it must follow that Berlioz either did not read the poem, or did not know what he was doing. It is a wasted effort trying to find in *Childe Harold* anything that corresponds to Berlioz's programme. As a matter of fact his Childe Harold seems to have been an androgynous schizophrenic who began life both as Rob Roy and the last moments of Mary Stuart. Childe Harold (the viola) hangs on to his *idée fixe* as if it were the quintessence of his own very particular personality, yet the melody turned up years before as an English horn solo in Berlioz's overture to *Rob Roy*. He quotes Scott and assures us it is Byron; which is neither literary ignorance nor bad logic, for Berlioz was quoting his own conceptions of Byron and Scott and we may take his word for it that in his own musical imagination they were identical. It doesn't really matter much, because the *Gazette Musicale* of January 26, 1834, first reported the Paganini Project as "a dramatic fantasy for orchestra, chorus, and solo viola," entitled *Les Derniers Instants de Marie Stuart*. The singers apparently wandered off into the orchestra where, no doubt, they all took up playing the tympani, while the soloist lit out for warmer weather and casually changed its sex. Fortunately this is all quite irrelevant. "There is a river in Monmouth and a river in Macedon; there is a B in Byron and a B in Berlioz" (Tovey), and that is just about the size of it.

The Berlioz programme runs as follows: (1) Harold in the mountains —scenes of sadness, happiness, and joy; (2) March of the Pilgrims singing their evening prayer; (3) Serenade of a mountaineer in the Abruzzi to his mistress; (4) Orgy of the Brigands: Memories of past scenes. For the most part Berlioz is content with expressive mood painting, although we pick up a hint here and there that his programme was more specific than he admitted. The finale was apparently more than a generalized remembrance of things past in the midst of a band of cut-throats (fine place to sit and remember). Berlioz heard the movement well performed in Germany and approvingly described its content and effect in more detail. "In the finale of *Harold* . . that furious orgy where wine, blood, joy, rage, all combined, parade their intoxication—where the rhythm sometimes seems to stumble along, sometimes to rush on in fury, and the brass seem to vomit forth curses and to answer prayer with blasphemies; where they laugh, drink, fight, destroy, slay, violate, and utterly run riot; in this brigand scene the orchestra became a regular pandemonium, there was something positively super-natural and terrifying in its frantic life and spirit, and violins, basses, trombones, drums, and cymbals all sang and bounded and roared with diabolical order and concord, whilst from the solo viola, the dreamy Harold, some trembling notes of his evening hymn were still heard in the distance as he fled in terror."

Berlioz, declared Mendelssohn, "with all his efforts to go stark mad, never once succeeds"; and upon another occasion: "his orchestration is such a frightful muddle, such an incongruous mess, one ought to wash one's hands after handling one of his scores." There is much truth in the first remark and much misunderstanding in the second. Mendels-sohn, as a composer, was a rare phenomenon among the romantics, for he was a scholar and a gentleman—and the characterization is not intended in the pleasantly malicious manner in which we have come to mean it today. Also, he was a man of genius, although in this he was no rarity among the romantics. His opinions are revealing. In the first he betrays, perhaps willingly, his own wholesome sanity; and in the second, perhaps unwittingly, the enervating fastidiousness which robs his beautifully written scores of that crucial ounce of intellectual vigour and emotional drive.

Mendelssohn was literally a composer; that is, he knew how to put things together. He was resourceful and acute, and he could manage any form, small or large, with an unassuming effortlessness which mis-led Schumann into calling him "the Mozart of the nineteenth century." In the ease, clarity, and cleanliness of his writing, he alone among the romantics can be compared with Mozart and Schubert. His delicacy and refinement are indeed reminiscent of the surface sound of Mozart, but the comparison, by and large, ends there. Unlike Mozart, all his inexhaustible creativeness seldom adds up to a powerful creation. Also, unlike Mozart and Schubert, he never grew. There are several worlds of musical and human experience between Mozart's first symphony and the *Jupiter* or G minor, between his first concerto arrangements of J. C. Bach's sonatas and his last piano concertos; likewise between Schubert's first symphony and the "great" C major, between *Hagars Klage* and *Die Winterreise*. Mendelssohn composed his *Midsummer Night's Dream* at the age of seventeen, and nothing more wonderful happens in his music thereafter. The basic dissimilarity, however, is one of temperament. Mozart possessed the genuine classic spirit; a well-rounded and minutely complete acquaintance with the diversity of emotion which engages a human being in the making of great music, as well as a total technical control and a total technical daring in the projection of a varied and profound imagination. Mendelssohn had most of the control and a good deal of the daring (more than one might suspect from a casual hearing), but little of the emotional variety and the depth. He struck an attitude, like most romantics do, and he lived with it faithfully like a good citizen.

Mendelssohn was a melancholic with a craving for minor keys. (All his concertos are in minor keys; only two of Mozart's and one of Beethoven's are.) He shared in the general romantic cultivation of a self-indulgent sadness; life was *Les Préludes*, Childe Harold meditated among the cut-throats, the creative spirit lived in loneliness from its fellow men. (The latter, in truth, had already become a very sad fact.) With Mendelssohn, melancholia was part of the romantic "world outlook," for he had no disappointment, not even a lack of success, to grind an honest grudge on. His minor keys lack subjective power, although they possess much of instinctive gracefulness. He has no sense of tragedy, and even the genuine passion in his violin concerto has a way of posing inadvertently with a droop of the eyelids. He is sleek and well fed, and to his credit he does not pretend to be otherwise. It takes a rawbones like Berlioz, or stout men like Bach, Beethoven, and Brahms, to abide the beating of a scarcely controllable passion. However, if Mendelssohn spoke moderately even when deeply moved, he had also too much sound sense to be "dying all his life." Mendelssohn's minor keys are adaptable to all purposes, for genuine drama is not of their essence. The engaging brilliance and the wholly pleasurable virtuosity of his concertos (here too the soloist is asked to turn only the most tasteful handsprings) are quite undistracted by the minor tonality. If Mendelssohn proves anything at all, it is the obvious maxim that a minor key does not necessarily express sorrow, any more than a major tonality necessarily means merriment.

There is something in Mendelssohn's moderation which does not belong to the "high" romantic, just as there is a bias in his mood which shears him off from the classic. He is neither one nor the other, but a unique combination of both, when the words are used as adjectives instead of nouns. He has the romanticist's sensitivity to mood and atmosphere, combined with the classicist's cool perfection and impeccable control of form. It was a wonderful compromise because for him it was a natural one, although the results, as with most compromises, were limited. We can understand why Schumann and Berlioz admired him so much, for a little of Mendelssohn's natural ease in large forms would have saved them much suffering, although it may possibly have prevented much enduring music.

Mendelssohn was fastidious in his emotions and accurate in his technique, which is quite another thing from being a conservative. As a matter of fact his concertos, following in the path indicated by Weber and Spohr, present the first satisfactory solution to the problems of the post-classical concerto. Spohr's *Gesangsszene* and Weber's *Konzert-stück*[1] had already broached the question of absorbing the discrete movements into a continuous chain of music. Spohr's model was frankly opera, while Weber threaded his way through the new form with a programme to guide him. The question of the sonata-form movement was answered by neither, although both indicated that something had to be done in this connection. In his first piano concerto in G minor, Op. 25, produced and probably composed during a visit to Munich in 1831, Mendelssohn effected a simple condensation of the sonata form and discovered an ingenious method for binding the three movements together.

[1] Mendelssohn's rendition of the Weber work was apparently a remarkably sympathetic one. As a pianist he scored a notable success with the *Konzertstück* at a concert given in London on May 30, 1829.

Taking his cue from the fourth and fifth Beethoven piano concertos, Mendelssohn introduced the solo piano immediately, but with this difference. Beethoven still retained the double exposition of themes; the first for the orchestra, the second for the solo and orchestra combined. Mendelssohn collapsed the two expositions into one. The themes of the movement are exposed only once by piano and orchestra combined, and the division of labour between them is effected on a plan which holds for the two piano concertos but is slightly modified in the violin concerto. The first group of themes in the tonic key is disposed between orchestra and soloist (the orchestra making the first short, blunt statement, the piano immediately following), while the second main subject is initially given as a piano solo. Substituting one exposition for two provided a new and essentially simple design which many nineteenth-century concerto composers adopted with innumerable variations in detail.

In tying the movements together, Mendelssohn resorted neither to operatic models nor to programmatic guides. The G minor piano concerto uses a simple interlocking device. The first movement closes with a rhythmic fanfare on one note taken by violins, violas, and oboes. Simultaneously with the sounding of the final tonic chord, the fanfare is repeated boldly by trumpets and horns. The piano takes it over, harmonizing and extending it, until it lapses evenly into an andante, introducing the main theme of the slow movement in the violas and 'cellos. The slow movement draws to a close with a sustained pianissimo chord suddenly interrupted by the same fanfare; again in the trumpets and horns. This time it is accompanied by another motive in the strings, and a long dramatic introduction in minor is spun out leading to the finale in major.

All three of his concertos are in minor keys, and in all three the finale is in major. In each case a preface in minor is appended, and in the two piano concertos the effect is more melodramatic than genuine. The Mendelssohn concerto finales are all bright, glittering, and gay. It is the virtuoso movement and Mendelssohn casts all else aside for brilliant, light-hearted display.

The second piano concerto is a duller echo of the first. It is in D minor (Op. 40) and was composed in 1837. As in the G minor, there is only one exposition for the sonata-form first movement, with the second subject initially announced as a piano solo. Also the glittering finale in the D major is prefaced by a dramatic ritornel in G minor. The interlocking device, however, is absent. The first movement fades off in a piano solo which winds towards an arpeggiated dominant-seventh chord in the key of the next movement. The adagio ends with a sustained pianissimo chord, and the finale attacks forte with no interruption for rest or applause.

The two concertos, especially the G minor, were once favourite pianistic war horses, but they have been given a well-deserved rest for the last few decades. It is a distinct pleasure to replay them after an interval (the first more so than the second), for they are brilliant, engaging, and wholly natural. However, unlike Mendelssohn's other music in large forms, they are quite unconcerned with big ideas or mighty emotions.[1]

It is typical of Mendelssohn's incomparable facility that the G minor piano concerto, a work that so neatly solved a puzzling structural problem, was, as he described it, "a thing rapidly thrown off." Of the three men who worked towards the solution of the post-classical concerto, only Weber was driven towards a new form through a keen sense of discomfort with the old. Spohr was an opportunist and a craftsman. He worked hard; he mastered a solid trade; and when he felt the Italians would not take to the old concerto form, he promptly gave them a new one. He knew his innovation would succeed, and it did; and his casualness in turning out a new concerto design has something of a smugness that has already degenerated into a fine art. Mendelssohn's effort was neither smug nor annoyingly self-assured. With genuine modesty he took his own perfection for granted. Mendelssohn wrote to no one, as Weber did to Rochlitz, apologizing ahead of time for a new idea. It never enters anyone's head, least of all Mendelssohn's, that he can ever make a mistake. His concertos will never be a *faux pas* in anyone's private listening room. It is not conscious good taste that inhibits him, nor the fear that a *faux pas* will not be tolerated; in all innocence and sincerity, the question simply could not occur to him.

[1] On July 13, 1829, during a charity concerto in London, Mendelssohn and Moscheles performed a double concerto in E-flat major by Mendelssohn which still remains unpublished.

Hiller tells us that Mendelssohn's piano-playing "was to him what
flying is to a bird. No one wonders why a lark flies; it is inconceivable
without that power. In the same way Mendelssohn played the piano
because it was his nature." In the same way Mendelssohn wrote music
and made historic innovations; unalterable ones which his concertos
picked up almost inattentively. The concerto form was ready for a new
way of living which it achieved in Mendelssohn with an air of an
historically designed accident; just as fish, at a certain stage, develop
lungs to breathe out of water, and legs to walk on dry land. The
innovations announced themselves in his concertos with the casual
objectivity, the matter-of-fact perfection of a new law of nature. Yet
the discovery carried little of the emotion of Chapman's Homer and
Keats's "watcher of the skies"; for while it is unexpected, Mendelssohn
has a way of making it unsurprising. As with Spohr, there is no sound
of newness in Mendelssohn's innovations. His audiences absorbed
them quite readily. There is no sense of shock, as there still is in
Beethoven after a hundred years. This, however, does not diminish
their importance as innovations.

Between Beethoven and Brahms, the two mighty landmarks of the
nineteenth-century violin concerto, stands Mendelssohn's delicately
conceived and beautifully executed work. All three share a violin
technique more broad and full-sounding than that of the classic Mozart
models. As usual, Mendelssohn's moods are refined where Beethoven's
are deeply troubled; while Brahms holds fast to his rugged, unweeping
grandeur.

Mendelssohn made several attempts at a violin concerto in his youth,
but the E minor, Op. 64, was his only complete effort. The work occupied him intermittently for some six years. On July 30, 1838, he wrote
to Ferdinand David: "I should like to write a violin concerto for you
next winter. One in E minor runs in my head, the beginning of which
gives me no peace." A year later he decided the whole of the first solo
was to be on the high E-string, as indeed it is. As he described it, the
concerto was swimming about in his head in an amorphous condition,
with a genial day or two needed to shape it together. He settled down
in earnest to the work in 1844, and the completed score is dated
September 16 of that year.

The work was dedicated to Ferdinand David, whose technical advice he found invaluable. With David's help Mendelssohn forged an

eminently playable concerto, a work that, without avoiding technical difficulty, lies well on the violin and comes readily to a practised hand. Mendelssohn's correspondence with David shows him concerned to achieve precisely this effect. For example, concerning the cadenza: ". . . is it playable and correctly noted? I want the arpeggios to begin at once in strict time and in four parts up to the tutti. I hope this will not be too exacting for the performer. . . ." Again, he asks: "Is the alteration at the end of the first movement easy to play?" This matter of being easy to play was important to Mendelssohn. His reiteration of the phrase is continual. "Is the return to C major, without a flute, quite easy to play now?" he asks, and then with insistence: "Really quite easy, so that it could be executed with the greatest delicacy." And finally, to make sure that his concerto was not lacking in any violinistic accomplishment, he instructs David to "please alter the end of the first movement entirely according to your wish."

Formally, the violin concerto adopts the general plan of the two preceding piano concertos and adds a few structural inspirations of its own. Once again there is only one exposition in place of two, with the violin coming forward on the second measure with the main subject of the movement. The second principal subject, differently from the piano concertos, is not first stated by the soloist. It will hardly do to turn a serviceable device into a formula; and so the second subject now floats gently in the clarinets and flutes over a sustained open G on the lowest string of the solo violin. ("It is really a fact, dear Mendelssohn," wrote Schumann, though not about this moment in particular, "no one writes such pure harmonies, and they keep getting purer and more inspired.")

The great inspirations, however, are reserved for the cadenza and the close. The cadenza traditionally occurs at the end of the movement, where the continuity of thought and feeling is put aside for a session of functionless display. Continuity of thought from movement to movement, however, was the main point of Mendelssohn's concerto form; moreover, the shallowness of the traditional cadenza was no doubt offensive to his careful taste. In the two piano concertos he sidestepped the problem completely. He wrote in no cadenzas and left no room for the performer to hazard one of his own. Avoiding a problem does not usually eliminate it, although the solution Mendelssohn finally did offer in his violin concerto was so thoroughly a personal inspiration that no composer has successfully imitated it since. He transposed the cadenza from the close of the movement to a point two-thirds of the way through, and made it earn its own keep as a transition from the development section to the recapitulation. It is no longer a brilliant parasitic growth. It works humbly for a living, or for the greater glory of music, and if there is anything more wonderful than the way it grows out of the development section, it is the manner in which it leads imperceptibly into the recapitulation.

It is traditional in a sonata-form recapitulation for all the themes to troop in in the main key of the movement. Since the concerto is in E minor, we may expect the second main subject (originally in major) to wander in wearing sackcloth and ashes. The moment is a difficult one for a melancholy composer since, more than another, he is dependent upon a judicious change in mood. Mendelssohn pays his respects to tradition and remains true to his needs. He sounds the key of E, but in major rather than in minor. It is a small point, but a rather neat one, and the concerto abounds in such niceties. There is nothing so bad, as modern composers well know, as letting one's key sense be dictated by tradition; and nothing so banal as fulfilling expectations without surprise. The major tonality is doubly welcome, for the movement specializes in Mendelssohn's melancholy passion, rather than in Mozart's passionate melancholy. (Mozart's G minor symphony treats this very moment in a wholly traditional fashion, but Mozart, like no other composer, understood the original profundity of the device.) Mendelssohn's type of emotion wears less well and is more often in need of a change in mood; preferably, as in this case, a slightly untraditional one.

The movement ends in a high temper and with vigorous orchestral excitement. There is no break between the first and second movements; they are continuous. (This ought to be printed in large type on all concert programmes.) The full strength of the orchestra is suddenly broken, and a solitary bassoon, who has been pumping away with the rest, is left stranded with a single sustained tone. (That is, this is what happens when the audience does not interrupt this magical moment with applause, or a recording engineer with a break between record sides.) Bar by bar, instrument after instrument builds under and above it until full wood-wind and string choirs are engaged. The winds fade, the strings are left with a gently rocking figuration, and over it the solo violin emerges into the second movement.

As in the piano concertos, a preface in minor (this time an allegretto) provides the transition to the finale (allegro molto vivace), a vivacious and glittering display piece. This finale has as little substance as those of Mendelssohn's piano concertos, but it is more delicately made. The workmanship is a delight in itself, which is hardly the case in the piano concerto finales. A Mozart finale is rarely unaware of the profundity which may underlie scintillating conversation. His bons mots are worth remembering, for they contain an element of important and sometimes sorrowful truth. This Mendelssohn finale is too wrapped up in the eagerness of its own charm. It talks well and wittily, and is rather pleased with itself for doing so. However, a brilliant conversationalist, if we listen to him long enough, becomes something of a bore. Violinists are advised that the truly engaging freshness of this finale will preserve itself with a little less rehearing. All in all, this concerto is one of the justly prized possessions of the violin repertoire. It is too genuine an inspiration, too immaculately made, ever to prove less than a delight, although the inevitable fiftieth or hundredth rehearing (as concert programmes are at present constituted) will scarcely rank as a momentous occasion in any one's adult musical experience.

Despite Mendelssohn's discretion and good taste, piano music had fallen to a low level in Germany and in Europe generally. Virtuosity was worshipped for its own unworthy self and the musical market glutted with an endless stream of foolishness—operatic fantasias, potpourris, circus variations on inoffensive popular tunes—whose dullness varied in direct proportion to their surface brilliance. Against such a host of musical troubles Schumann took up arms in the pages of his *Neue Zeitschrift*, a critical journal which he founded in 1834. More so than Berlioz in France and Weber before him in Germany, Schumann's journalism was a vital factor in the development of romantic music.

The publication exerted an important influence; it was a clearinghouse for the music and opinions of modern composers, and Schumann was ever ready to greet a young man with sympathy and understanding. His appreciation was wider than Weber's, his judgment more acute; and unlike Berlioz, who had much of Debussy's critical tartness, Schumann seldom took refuge in a bon mot.

Like everything else about Schumann, this journalistic undertaking attired itself in the trappings of a grand romance. "We are now living such a romance," wrote Schumann of his periodical, "as perhaps no book contains." Serious criticism appeared in the *Neue Zeitschrift* saddled with a strange mixture of mawkish sentimentality and keen sarcasm, poetic rapture and plain farce. Fantastic nicknames decorated its pages. Mendelssohn, his boon companion in the campaign against those who treasured music only as "the good cow that provides them with butter," appeared as Felix Meritis; Clara Wieck (later his wife) became Zilia or Chiarina; and Schumann himself Florestan and Eusebius (a duality representing the vehement and gentle aspects of his character) as well as a whole "pageful of pseudonyms, some drawn from the Saxon calendar, some from the multiplication table" (Hadow). The efforts of the publication were implemented by a band of heroes who combined to do battle with the Goliaths of musical philistinism—Die Davidsbündler (The League of David), a "purely abstract and romantic society," as Schumann explained, peopled by the fantastic names of his *Zeitschrift* articles. An honorary board of directors included Berlioz, who never heard of his appointment, and Mozart, who had been dead for nearly a half-century. Schumann's *Davidsbündlertänze* purports to be a musical account of the doings of these apocryphal heroes.

Schumann's imagination was compounded in equal parts of a penchant for quaint grotesquerie and a profound understanding of serious musical issues. Foremost among his many enthusiasms were the eccentricities of Jean Paul, who delighted in such oddities as a preface in the middle of a book, or a dwarf "so short that he only reached up to his own knee, not to speak of other people's"; the nightmarish fantasies of E. T. A. Hoffmann, who was a composer as well as a writer; and the rational, majestic polyphony of Johann Sebastian Bach. Jean Paul's involved symbolism found its way into Schumann's *Abegg* variations, his *Davidsbündlertänze*, and his *Carnaval*. Hoffmann's ghostly and freakish Kapellmeister turned up in Schumann's *Kreisleriana;* while reverent obeisances were made to the lord of polyphonic creation in the six fugues (Op. 60) on the name of Bach, the four fugues

(Op. 72), the studies for pedal piano (Op. 56), and here and there throughout a good deal of his music. "I confess my sins daily to that mighty one," he wrote, "and endeavour to purify and strengthen myself through him. . . . To my mind there is no getting near Bach; he is unfathomable." On another occasion, however, he declared: "I have learned more counterpoint from Jean Paul Richter than from any music master." There is no contradiction; simply a matter of which of his pseudonyms he was wearing at the moment.

One of the great campaigns waged by Schumann in his critical writings was aimed at annihilating the "salon composers" and directing the romantic effort back into the main stream of great music which flowed from the past. Liszt and Berlioz recognized this in Schumann's piano music. "I cannot bring my letter to a close," wrote Berlioz to Schumann, "without telling you of the many pleasant hours I have lately spent in the perusal of your admirable pianoforte works; there appears to me no exaggeration whatever in their having been described to me as a logical continuation of those by Weber, Beethoven, and Schubert. Liszt, who thus described them to me, will make me know them more intimately by his incomparable execution of them. . . ." Berlioz and Liszt apparently saw the origin of Schumann's work in the late-classical, early-romantic tradition of Beethoven, Weber, and Schubert. Schumann himself was of the opinion that the mainspring of the best romantic music was Bach. "The thoughtful combinations, the poetry and humour of modern music," he wrote, "originate chiefly in Bach. Mendelssohn, Bennett, Chopin, Hiller—in fact, all the so-called romantic school (of course I am speaking of Germans)—approach Bach much more nearly in their music than Mozart ever did; indeed, all of them know Bach most thoroughly." The parenthesis is acute; clearly he was not talking of the French romantics. Berlioz' reaction to a Bach concerto has already been quoted.

Mendelssohn, too, was one of Schumann's enthusiasms. "Mendelssohn is a man," he wrote, "whom I look up to as to some lofty mountain"; and once again, "No day passes in which he does not utter at least two ideas worthy to be graven in gold." It would be unkind to cavil with so generous an appreciation. It is a manifest exaggeration rooted in warm friendship and a pathetic longing for some of Mendelssohn's composure in working through a worrying problem. Schumann's was a deeper and more troubled temperament, and his solutions less felicitous. However, in their own sometimes more awkward fashion, his concertos tap a vein of richer feeling than Mendelssohn's do; and, like his opinions, they are modest, intimate, and warm.

The Schumann piano concerto in A minor, Op. 54, is one of his most felicitous creations, as well as one of the most pleasurable experiences in the romantic concerto repertoire, for it combines the new freedom which Mendelssohn discovered in the form with a scrupulous deletion of all virtuoso effect. Only Berlioz's *Harold in Italy* vies with it as a non-virtuoso vehicle, and Schumann's accomplishment is all the more admirable in that he was frankly writing not a symphony but a concerto. The absence of obvious display and the intimate conversation between solo and orchestra are no doubt the reasons for the often-repeated description of this work as a symphonic concerto. However, it is no more symphonic than the Liszt concertos, only less concerned with display.

The piano concerto was not composed all in one piece. It was completed in 1845, but its first movement was originally an allegro for piano and orchestra written in 1841. During 1844, the year prior to the completion of the concerto, Schumann passed through a stage in that harrowing mental illness to which he ultimately succumbed. "An entire nervous prostration," he wrote to Mendelssohn after his temporary recovery, "accompanied by a host of terrible thoughts, nearly drove me to despair; but things look brighter now—music is again beginning to sound within me, and I hope soon to have quite recovered." Some of the music that once more was so gratefully sounding within him was the A minor piano concerto, and with a convalescent's quiet rejoicing he showered tenderness and warmth over every bar of the music.

In its general plan the work follows Mendelssohn. The double exposition is discarded for a joint presentation of themes by piano and orchestra, and the last two movements flow together. The cadenza occurs traditionally at the end of the first movement, but it is Schumann's own and sustains, in consequence, the particular tenor of the music. Schumann's treatment is no freer, but his feeling is more intimate and rhapsodic than Mendelssohn's. It had, at the time, a more pronounced air of modernity, and therefore was welcomed less readily. English musical criticism, for example, set Mendelssohn up as a paragon, but Clara Schumann's performances of the A minor concerto were patronizingly greeted in London as "praiseworthy efforts . . . to make her husband's curious rhapsody pass for music." The attitude extended to his piano music generally, and even Liszt discovered that the Davidsbündler had not slain very many of the Goliaths. "The repeated failure of my performances of Schumann's compositions both in private and in public," he wrote, "discouraged me from entering them on the programmes for my concerts. . . . This was an error which I afterwards recognized, and indeed regretted. . . ." Schumann did not take to lack of recognition with any conspicuous stoicism. "No encouragement, no art," he wrote in one letter; and in another he quoted Jean Paul: "Air and admiration are the only things which men can and must incessantly swallow." He did little to further his own cause, and his articles in the *Neue Zeitschrift*, so generous in their encouragement of others, rarely made mention of his own music. "The publishers won't listen to me," he complained. However, as an editor of an influential periodical, his work could not be ignored. "You can easily believe," he explained when his music was published, "that if the publishers did not fear the editor, the world would know nothing of me; perhaps it would be better for the world."

It was not alone the modernism of his music but the lack of a virtuoso complex which retarded the public recognition he felt he deserved. As a matter of fact virtuosity was, in Schumann's eyes, the most lamentable illness of the age. One of the major reasons for the foundation of the *Neue Zeitschrift*, as Schumann explained, looking back on it years later, was the fact that "Herz and Hünten were the sole lords of the piano. And yet but a few years had elapsed since Beethoven, C. M. von Weber, and Franz Schubert were with us. To be sure, Mendelssohn's star was in the ascendant; and wonderful things were reported of a Pole, Chopin by name: but they exercised no real influence till later." No one but a scholar is any longer aware that people called Herz, Hünten, or Rosellen ever wrote music. But they were the rage in the 1830's. "These three fashionable composers and their imitators," wrote Weitzmann, "first tickled the blasé palates of pianists with novel and piquant difficulties, and then contented themselves with setting the sweetest tid-bits before the musical gourmets, finally quite giving up the ghost at the birth of the Romantic school. . . . The pianoforte works published by Hünten and Rosellen . . . fellow pupils of Herz . . . sank to the merest factory work, although when issued they went off so rapidly that the publishers paid higher prices for single sheets of the same, than the complete larger works of Beethoven had brought. . . . With the great demand, the price of the article also rose; and Hünten finally received for a book of 8 or 10 printed pages the outrageous price of 1500 to 2000 francs. From 1835 he lived in Coblenz on his income, and his fellow pupil, Henri Rosellen, then continued the same lucrative business, for which, however, several competitors had come forward. . . ."[1]

Schumann's goal was simple: "to recall the old times and their works with great emphasis, thus calling attention to the fact that fresh artistic beauties can be strengthened only at such pure sources, and then to attack as inartistic the works of the present generation, since they base themselves upon the praises of superficial virtuosi. . . ." And as a final summary: "We write, not to enrich tradesmen, but to honour artists." This journalistic credo he carried into practice in his concertos. They were composed for musicians, not for tradesmen who make a living out of doing stunts on an instrument.

The 'cello concerto in A minor, Op. 129, composed in 1850, is likewise devoid of any element of display, although it is not without certain technical difficulties. More so even than the piano concerto, it is an eminently lyrical creation, and it is this intimate, all-pervasive lyricism which not only precludes virtuoso showmanship but dictates the peculiar construction of the work. The first movement follows the now familiar pattern of a single exposition of themes, and there are no breaks between movements. There is qualitative difference, however, between this and the piano concerto or the Mendelssohn models. There are no devices tying the movements to one another; they actually flow together. More so than any of the attempts of Spohr, Weber, and Mendelssohn, and only less so than Liszt's A major piano concerto, this has the quality of a one-movement concerto, a continuous chain

[1] C. F. Weitzmann: *A History of Pianoforte-Playing and Pianoforte-Literature*, pp. 152-154.

of music. Taken as a whole, the 'cello concerto is an elaborate, lyrical song form, with the slow movement functioning more as a middle section than as a movement. The vocal lyricism is accentuated by a fine episode which occurs right after the *langsam* section. The opening melody of the concerto returns, leading into a genuine bit of dramatic, vocal declamation for solo 'cello with orchestral responses; precisely the kind of recitative which in opera follows a slow aria and leads to a fast one.

Despite many beautiful moments (the opening melody is as fine as anything Schumann ever thought of), the concerto is not a wholly satisfactory accomplishment. For all his modernity, Schumann was too much rooted in the past. He clung to the sonata form less out of genuine feeling for it than out of faith in the great masters who had handled it so well. The form is essentially a dramatic one, with its sharp contrast in themes and keys; and for its development section it requires a virile sense of musical architecture, a disciplined and unsentimental mind capable of exhausting, motive by motive, the potentialities of the given material. Schumann's conception in the 'cello concerto is neither dramatic nor constructivist; it is loose and totally lyrical. His grapplings with the sonata form in the first movement are awkward and unhappy; yet he hadn't the courage to dispense with it. The lyrical first subject is not amenable to development, and so Schumann makes much of a short triplet figuration. There is much motion and little real movement; much determined building and nothing to live in comfortably. It is static, and the return of the opening melody becomes by comparison too much of a notable occasion. Brahms understood such problems, for he solved them, not instinctively, but with conscious effort. He summed up the matter generally, but he might well have been thinking of the Schumann 'cello concerto in particular. "The great romantics continued the sonata form in a lyric spirit which contradicts the inner dramatic nature of the sonata. Schumann himself shows this contradiction."

The form of the 'cello concerto, however, is unusual for Schumann, though not unexpected. He believed the breakdown of the boundaries between movements, the collapsing of all into one, an aesthetically unjustified procedure, and only in his 'cello concerto did he run directly contrary to his own thinking. In the A minor piano concerto and in the D minor violin concerto the only movements which are tied together are the last two; and in this, Schumann moves substantially no further than Beethoven did in his fifth piano concerto. The violin concerto in D minor, composed in 1853, is a throwback to a more classical sonata-form pattern. In the first movement the double exposition is resumed and the orchestral ritornel restored to its place in the sun. The concerto is a thoroughly uneven work: Schumann's most inspired failure. It seems to have been the consensus of opinion of Joachim, Brahms, Dietrich, and Clara Schumann that the work was below Schumann's usual power. It lay long dormant (not concealed or unknown as a few misguided sensationalists have charged). The infelicities in the score, the lapses in genuine inspiration, the awkwardness of the solo writing (Schumann consulted Joachim and made a few improvements), all unfortunately weigh heavily on the music. It is to be regretted that Schumann's illness, in which he was now far gone, soon put an end to any possibility of revision.

As the concerto now stands, it is a great inspiration as yet unmoulded into great music; nevertheless, there are a few moments which no one with a sensitivity for important music would willingly forego. The opening subject of the first movement, for example, bears an heroic passion unusual in his music. It is doubtful if Schumann in his happiest years could have realized the potentialities of such a subject, although if he had, the violin concerto would undoubtedly have been his greatest work. In scope and dramatic power, it is the kind of subject which Brahms alone among the romantics could have controlled without Schumann's inevitable let-down; and perhaps Beethoven alone among symphonists could have treated it as a starting-point for the evolution of even vaster ideas and emotions. The opening of the first Brahms piano concerto, Op. 15, bears a distinct kinship to the opening of the Schumann violin concerto (from Joachim we learn that Brahms sketched the work under the impress of Schumann's attempt at suicide). Brahms sustains his thought throughout his concerto better than Schumann does, although purely with respect to the initial inspiration Brahms is by no means Schumann's superior. The theme of the slow movement (which, according to report, Schumann imagined Schubert sang to him in a dream[1]) was selected by Brahms as the sub-

[1] Some accounts have it that the angels sang a theme of Schubert's to him; others that Mendelssohn and Schubert made the dream visitation. The concerto

ject for his four-hand piano variations, Op. 23. The Brahms variations conclude, appropriately enough, with a funeral march. This melody, incidentally, casts a dim but perceptible shadow over the melodies of the two other movements. A similarity in configuration, and sometimes of feeling, exists between it, the second subject of the first movement, and the first and third melodies in the finale.

Schumann's other works for solo and orchestra comprise an introduction and allegro appassionata for piano and orchestra, Op. 92; a concert allegro and introduction, Op. 134, dedicated to Brahms and also scored for piano and orchestra; a fantasy for violin with orchestra (or with piano), Op. 131, dedicated to Joachim; and a *Konzertstück* for four horns and orchestra which Schumann described as "something quite curious" and which Abert finds a wonderful resuscitation of the old concerto grosso.

It is scarcely possible without an elaborate sifting of sources to render anything better than a version of a Liszt biography. The facts of his life (colloquially as well as in the King's English) are mainly a matter of opinion; including Liszt's opinion. One knows with certainty less of what Liszt did and more of what several hundred vehement and verbose people thought he was doing. The happenings in Wagner's life are wholly a matter of Wagner's opinions, according to his autobiography; or rather the opinion Wagner would have wanted posterity to hold of these happenings. In this respect Liszt's case is both better and worse; he never wrote the story of his life because, as he once remarked, he was too busy living it. Few figures in nineteenth-century art, science, or politics have been plagued with so many biographers, memoir writers, and novelists (Balzac among the latter), each armed with an interpretation and most with a personal axe to grind. Liszt was either a saint or Satan's personal emissary on earth, depending on what

incidentally was composed several months before Schumann's dream; but his mental illness had already taken a strong hold on him, and a rational chronology is rather beside the point. Schumann's table tipping at this period awakens only our deepest sympathy; but we can do without the solemn hocus-pocus of those who have invoked a visitation from the spirit of Robert Schumann as an excuse to play this concerto, and who, instead of consulting available sources, dragged the spirit of Joachim out of the ether to guide them in finding and verifying the manuscript.

book you read; although allowance must be made for the occasional biographer who makes the intelligent point that a man is rarely one or the other his whole life through. Like most un-memoired mortals Liszt had his share of saint and Satan in him, although even in his greatest glory he was something less than either.

Liszt was a bundle of contradictions, the prize possession of an age that specialized in split personalities. During his long lifetime (1811–86) he served as both the august mentor and the servile lackey of his era. As a pianist and a conductor he forced much good music down its philistine throat; taught it to listen with respect, if not with admiration, to a neglected master like Schubert, and a forgotten one like Bach, to an esoteric like late Beethoven, and to uncomfortably modern composers like Schumann, Berlioz, and Wagner. Also, he shamelessly descended to the lowest levels of public taste; indulged in orgies of cheap display; amused the sensation seekers with operatic fantasias and exotic rhapsodies, with tricks and effects galore. Liszt was the Paganini of the piano. He did a very serious job of laying the foundations for a modern pianoforte technique; and, like the Italian, he enjoyed a fine stunt. He played always as a man of genius and sometimes as a charlatan. He had a genuinely romantic mind, although sometimes it pleased him to strike attitudes like a romantic poseur. He was a composer of tremendous originality whose ideas in time were taken over by the finest minds of the century; yet all but one of his symphonic poems have faded, for his penchant for rhetoric was greater than his feeling for true oration. His sonorities have an incurable sense of platitude, and he loaded his piano music to the point where it became a tremendous triviality in place of an important musical experience.

Part of the Liszt story deals with what the daring Victorians called "amorous adventures," and a novel by an embittered ex-mistress forms part of the Liszt bibliography. His love affairs, his children, his hairbreadth escapes from the stock-in-trade variety of romantic murders grew in geometric progression with every retelling, and Liszt (so Huneker observes), not unmindful of the value of such advertisement, let the legends grow with the years.

Liszt's personal life may have been the veritable pagan garden wherein flowered the choicest weeds from the devil's own wilderness, but his relations with his contemporaries (who were in many respects his rivals) were marked by an unfailing generosity which made his personality, as well as his music, an influence of the first importance. He often used his position as a leading conductor, and as the foremost pianist in Europe, to further another man's cause. As a teacher (Huneker's list of his pupils comes to five printed pages) he dispensed the vast knowledge at his command with a lavishness and an unfailing enthusiasm that have rarely been known. He had a quick sympathy for the problems of younger composers, and men like Grieg, Smetana, Saint-Saëns, and even Wagner (in a rare moment of self-abnegation) paid tribute to his generosity, guidance, and understanding.

Liszt, above all else, was for his time an eminently modern composer. He had an acute mind and a natural sensitivity to new ideas. He was also a more all-round person than any of his contemporaries. Music was his profession and his principal talent, but his interests wandered widely in the neighbouring arts, and his curiosity in social, political, and economic questions was always eager, his understanding sometimes deep. A galaxy of famous names appears in the pages of his music: Hugo, Tasso, Lamartine, Dante, Goethe, Lenau, Herder, Tolstoy, Raphael, Michelangelo, Heine, Schiller, Petrarch, Sainte-Beuve, and many others. He had a "great taste," as Heine tells us, "for speculative ideas"; and in his stormy and provocative improvisations Heine saw a reflection of that "restless head, driven and perplexed by all the needs and doctrines of his time; feeling compelled to trouble himself about all the necessities of humanity, and eagerly sticking his nose into all the pots in which the good God brews the future. . . ."

Liszt was not alone in his preoccupation with "the necessities of humanity." His lifetime encompassed such vital revolutionary struggles as those of 1830, 1848, 1860, and an intelligent artist was not apt to remain insensitive to such events. Byron lost his life at Missolonghi, Shelley polemicized brilliantly and bitterly against the Castlereagh regime. As a young man, before he decided to adopt the jungle laws of modern society and rule with them like a lord, Wagner made political speeches at the Vaterlandsverein and participated in the Dresden street fighting of 1848. One year later there was a warrant out for his arrest as a "politically dangerous individual." In 1830, after putting a few touches to a score, Berlioz descended into the streets armed with pistols and joined with the plain people of Paris in a battle against the royal masters.

Liszt's allegiances were haphazard and sincere, vehement at any given moment, and in the long run obscure. He started as a socialist of the Saint-Simonist variety (utopian and undisciplined) and wound up as the Abbé Liszt. Virtuosity with ideas is the least commendable quality in a political thinker. Liszt was not guilty of it, for he had neither the training nor the insincerity; but he did flit around picking up a stray allegiance here and there with the same quixotic warmth, although with less of the understanding which he brought to nearly every new piece of music that came his way. "For long he was an ardent upholder," writes Heine in 1837, "of the beautiful Saint-Simonist conception of the world. Later the spiritualistic or rather vaporous notions of Ballanche enveloped him in their midst; now he is enthusiastic over the Republican-Catholic dogmas of a Lamennais who has hoisted his Jacobin cap on the Cross. . . . Heaven knows in what mental stall he will find his next hobby horse!" The quality of Liszt's thinking was more ardent than systematic, but on one subject he wrote well: the bitter economic plight of the artist; the "hollow and sonorous phrases" of the politician who never cut the budget allowances for the people's culture "without expressing his solicitude for the fine arts"; the smug admissions of "the social necessity for art" and the "bourgeois vandalism" that dispensed with music "for economy's sake, as one would dismiss a useless servant." His article on *The Situation of Artists and Their Condition in Society* still makes pertinent reading today.

The Liszt concertos are a logical continuation of the experimental ideas first broached by Spohr and Weber, amplified by Mendelssohn, and reflected in his 'cello concerto by Schumann. Liszt carried the consequences of their thinking to a further stage (perhaps, from a formal point of view, even to its final stage), not only because he had the advantage of their examples, but because he was most closely in touch with the issue in its most fundamental form as it applied, not alone to the concerto, but to opera and the symphony as well. The collapsing of the traditional boundaries between movements was one of the prime efforts of the age. Wagner broke the hold of the set aria in opera, disposed of the hitherto simple distinction between aria and recitative, and set both orchestra and voices free to follow the dramatic impulses

and ideas which it was the point of his opera to illustrate. In his overtures (*Egmont, Coriolanus, Leonore*) Beethoven had already indicated
the value of a one-movement symphonic form which could render a
complex dramatic moment with a unity of mood and a conciseness of
structure scarcely obtainable in the spread of a traditional four-movement symphony. Mendelssohn's overtures amplified the point,
demonstrating that a delicate pictorial lyricism was well within the
province of the form.

This striving for a continuous form of symphonic music which could
combine greater variety of mood with greater cohesion in design ultimately worked a transformation within the traditional symphony
itself. The preparatory work was done in another form, the overture;
the experiences gained were then tested within the symphony, and in
its initial stages (with Berlioz and Mendelssohn) the results were not
wholly satisfactory. Berlioz's programme symphony and dramatic
symphony (the *Fantastique* and *Romeo and Juliette*) are unique and, by
their own standards, successful; but the *Fantastique*, for all of its originality, clung too closely to the divisions of a symphony, while *Romeo
and Juliette* represents a wholly new fusion of several art forms which no
composer after him found serviceable. Mendelssohn, in his *Scotch* symphony (1842), instructed that no pause was to be made between movements; but the continuous chain of music which he achieved thereby
was an artificial accomplishment, in that the traditional symphony,
however much he may have sought to avoid it, still stares one in the
face. The traditional sonata-form symphony, as Brahms noted, was
essentially a dramatic rather than a lyrical form; and the new design,
if it was to serve as a proper substitute, would have to join battle on
dramatic rather than lyrical issues. Mendelssohn's inspiration was entirely lyrical; Berlioz sought to make a wholly dramatic point. While
Mendelssohn's example was not without value, Berlioz in this instance
worked closer to the main problem.

The Liszt symphonic poem was the first wholly serviceable solution.
Its impulse was fundamentally dramatic, and for the unity of dramatic
thought Liszt evolved a one-movement symphonic form within which
sections, contrasted in tempo and mood, were bound together (as
aspects of a single idea) by a basic melody. The key melody was not an
unalterable idea (an *idée fixe*), but a flexible formula adapted to the

necessities of the several sections, reflecting the variety of their moods and ensuring that all moods were components of the same dramatic emotion. And what Liszt sought to do in the symphonic poem was, generally speaking, what he hoped to accomplish in his concertos. His impulse, then, was contrary to that of the Schumann 'cello concerto, and in his concertos Liszt also discarded the programmaticism of his symphonic poems. His conscious command of the problem was greater than Weber's, and he needed no harking heroines to guide him. The Weber example no doubt carried weight, and both Berlioz and Schumann have testified to the extraordinary power with which Liszt performed the *Konzertstück*.

The first piano concerto in E-flat (composed in 1848 and revised in 1853) still retains a fairly clear division into four movements,[1] although the thematic ties between them are closer than anything that had obtained previously in the concerto. The opening subject of the first movement—to which, according to tradition, Liszt used to sing the words *"Das versteht Ihr alle nichts"* ("This none of you understand")— occurs in subsequent portions of the work. Some of the other thematic connections are explained by Liszt in one of his letters. "The fourth movement of the concerto from the Allegro marziale corresponds with the second-movement Adagio. It is only an urgent recapitulation of the earlier subject-matter with quickened, livelier rhythm, and contains no new motive, as will be clear to you by a glance through the score. This kind of *binding together* and rounding off a whole piece at its close is somewhat my own, but it is quite maintained and justified from the standpoint of musical form. The trombones and basses take up the second part of the motive of the Adagio (B major). The pianoforte figure which follows is nothing other than a reproduction of the motive which was given in the Adagio by flute and clarinet, just as the concluding passage is a Variante and working up in major of the motive of the Scherzo, until finally the first motive on the dominant pedal B-flat, with a shake-accompaniment, comes in and concludes the whole."

---

[1] Even in this, the E-flat concerto is closer to the symphony than to the concerto, for the traditional symphonic division is into four movements while traditionally the concerto is in three.

The second piano concerto in A major, composed probably the same year as the first (1848) and revised twice (1856 and 1861), is the logical culmination of Liszt's thinking and at long last a genuine one-movement concerto without qualification or compromise. It is really a non-programmatic symphonic poem for piano and orchestra with contrasts in tempo, theme, and mood. There is an adagio, an allegro, a scherzo-like section, a march, an allegro animato for a conclusion, and various and sundry changes in and between these. In effect, more than any previous concerto of the kind, it boasts a genuinely new form. The formal design founded on the sonata-form alternation of orchestral ritornels and solo episodes is finally dispensed with, and in its place we have a curious restoration of one of the early meanings of the word "concerto": a work based on the opposition of two distinct tone masses, the battle between two contrasted forces. It is a specialized Lisztian restoration, and the A major concerto is simply a one-movement display piece for piano with and against the orchestra.[1]

The E-flat concerto is often referred to as the "*Triangle*" concerto, though we no longer intend this disparagingly as Hanslick did when he coined the phrase. (The concerto was also once dubbed "Donizetti with Orchestra," which is not altogether inept, for there are a few Italianate and several frankly operatic elements in the work.) It is strange, but the use of the triangle was something Liszt was obliged to defend. It involved in Liszt's mind the question of percussion orchestration, and he was among the first to see the value of this portion of the orchestra which modern composers have belaboured in so extraordinary and effective a fashion. "As regards the triangle," writes Liszt, "I do not deny that it may give offence, especially if struck too strongly and not precisely. A preconceived disinclination and objection to percussion instruments prevails, which is somewhat justified by the frequent misuse of them. A few conductors are circumspect enough to bring out the rhythmic element in them, without the raw addition of a coarse noisiness. . . . The dynamic and rhythmic spicing and enhancement, which can be obtained from percussion instruments, would in many cases be much more effectually produced by a careful trying out and

---

[1] Apthorp characterized the A major concerto as a "symphonic poem for piano and orchestra with the title, 'The Life and Adventures of a Melody.'"

proportioning of insertions and additions of that kind. But musicians who wish to appear serious and solid prefer to treat percussion instruments *en canaille*, which dare not make their appearance in the seemly company of a symphony. They also bitterly deplore inwardly that Beethoven allowed himself to be seduced into using the big drum and triangle in the Finale of the Ninth Symphony. Of Berlioz, Wagner and my humble self, it is no wonder that 'like draws to like,' and, as we are treated as impotent *canaille* amongst musicians, it is quite natural that we should be on good terms with the *canaille* among the instruments. Certainly here, as in all else, it is correct to seize upon the mass of harmony and hold it fast. In the face of the most wise prescription of the learned critics I shall, however, continue to make use of percussion instruments, and I think I shall yet win for them some effects that are little known."

Besides the two well-known concertos, Liszt also composed a rarely played *Concerto Pathétique* in E minor for two pianos without orchestra, to which Richard Burmeister sought to give wider currency through an arrangement for solo piano and orchestra; and an early unknown piano concerto in A minor which Moscheles reported endowed with a "chaotic beauty." The Liszt *Dance of Death*, inspired by the famous fourteenth-century fresco *The Triumph of Death* in the Campo Santo at Pisa, is a set of wild, sardonic variations for piano and orchestra upon the *Dies Irae* melody. The fresco depicts heaven and hell and the grim mortality that lies between. The righteous in attitudes of prayerful purity are being rewarded by angels, and the damned tortured upon a blazing mountain by a host of unclean creatures; the deformed and unfortunate among mortals are ignored by Death, a lurid female figure with claws and with hair flying wildly behind her; the nobility of the earth are being entertained with music amid pleasant surroundings in one part of the wall and, in another, pause during a hunting scene before open graves revealing those who were once powerful among men now in varying stages of dissolution. The macabre and grotesque were elements of the romantic temperament possessed not only by turbulent spirits like Berlioz and Liszt, but shared by gentler souls like Schumann. The *Dance of Death* is a Lisztian counterpart of the Witches' Sabbath in Berlioz's *Fantastic* symphony, and the orgy of brigands in his *Harold in Italy*. Schumann's *Kreisleriana* is a more fanciful and less gruesome kind of nightmare.

The variation form for solo and orchestra was not an innovation of Liszt's, but his *Dance of Death* is the earliest of the few famous examples which are still heard in the concert hall. The César Franck *Variations symphoniques* for piano and orchestra is one of the most notable examples of this particular form. It is a dramatic three-part fantasia composed of an introduction, a group of six variations, and a finale. The introduction and the finale are largely independent thematically of the middle variation section. The introduction embodies a rough outline of the variation theme to which it counterposes a melody of its own. The variation melody turns up as an occasional counterpoint in the finale. The gestures of the music are alternately angular and dramatic, long-flowing and lyrical; and its episodes are contrived with both the polyphonic control and the designed inadvertence in moving from one rumination to another characteristic of Franck's maturest music.

The Dohnányi *Variations on a Nursery Tune*, Op. 23, for piano and orchestra is dedicated with a disarming lack of subtlety "to the enjoyment of lovers of humour and to the annoyance of others." It is Mother Goose by Demosthenes, declaimed in waltz time, to a determined children's march, and finally with the nonsense syllables stumbling over the pebbles on their way out in a gleefully rushed fugue. The peroration is prefaced by a dark chorus that bewails itself lugubriously in the brass. Altogether an engaging work, although Dohnányi could bang us a little less pompously on the head with his humour. The Rachmaninoff *Rhapsody on a Theme of Paganini*, Op. 43, is also a set of variations for piano and orchestra. Paganini's twenty-fourth caprice is the source of the theme, which Brahms had already treated in the two sets of variations for solo piano. Rachmaninoff is not always free of a few late nineteenth-century clichés, but, all in all, he brings to the variations a commendable amount of freshness and individuality. Among other things, Rachmaninoff manages to prove that what Brahms neglected to say about this melody is not unworthy to be said. Perhaps the most familiar modern example of the form is the Richard Strauss tone poem *Don Quixote*, Op. 35 (1896), a series of *Fantastic Variations on a Theme of Knightly Character*. The solo 'cello takes the Don's part and Sancho Panza is represented mainly by a viola. As in Berlioz's *Harold in Italy*, the leading character is identified both by a characteristic theme and by a specific solo instrument. Each of the variations depicts another of the Don's adventures and a further stage in his deepening disorientation. The subject has always been an attractive one, although none among Cervantes' successors have handled it with his unique combination of intellect, irony, farce, and profound humanity. The most notable modern treatments of the story are those by Strauss and Daumier, and while the difference in media precludes a completely just comparison, it is clear that Strauss is much more the magnificent virtuoso while Daumier feels and understands more deeply. Strauss's talent for rendering psychological states is considerable, although it has been over-rated in the appreciation of this work. The tone poem is splendidly orchestrated, and the naturalistic depictions are by no means an unimaginative collection of orchestral tricks. The concerto opposition between solo and orchestra follows the necessities of the narrative. The orchestra provides the realistic background (including a naturalistic imitation of the bleating of the sheep) and against it the solo instrument conducts its quixotic battles. Other less familiar examples of the form include Joachim's architectural set of variations for violin and orchestra, and Tschaikowsky's *Variations on a Rococo Theme*, Op. 33, for 'cello and orchestra, an eminent display piece in the 'cellist's repertoire.

Schumann's piano sonata in F minor was originally published under the title of *Concert sans orchestre (Concerto without Orchestra)*. In the second edition the correct title was restored, for Schumann had conceived the work as a sonata and had yielded to the misleading concerto designation only under pressure from his publisher. When the work fell into Liszt's hands it was in its first edition and was called a concerto. Liszt found much to admire in it, but took objection to the title for formal and stylistic reasons. "In the first place," he wrote, "we consider the title illogical; since *concerto* means a reunion of concerted instruments. To call it a concerto without orchestra is almost the same as calling it a group of a single figure. . . . In the old days, a concerto was divided into three parts: the first with three solos interspersed with the orchestra; the adagio; then the rondo. Field, in his last concerto, has introduced the adagio via a second solo. Moscheles's 'concerto fantastique' united the three parts into a single one. Weber first and Mendelssohn afterwards, to say nothing of Mr. Herz in his second concerto, attempted a similar design. In fine, liberties from all sides have extended and diversified the form, which is surely progress, though not in the direction of our observations (e.g., a concerto without orchestra)." The genealogy of Liszt's thinking is thus clearly set down for us, and if Spohr was omitted, it was because Liszt was talking about the piano concerto. John Field (1782–1837) was an interesting Irish composer who has been lost sight of today. His music was much appreciated by his contemporaries, and Chopin in particular was indebted to him (Field's nocturnes antedated Chopin's). The other new name is Moscheles, and to an important degree Liszt owed more to him than to Mendelssohn (and more to himself than to either). Moscheles began as a pure virtuoso composer, turned in a more serious direction, though with little loss of virtuoso accomplishment, in his third piano concerto in G minor, Op. 58, and fulfilled himself in his sixth, seventh, and eighth piano concertos known respectively as the *Fantastique*, the *Pathétique*, and the *Pastorale*. The *Concerto Fantastique*, No. 6 (1835), to which Liszt referred, is in four movements run together as one, with the third movement a re-working of the themes from the first-movement allegro. It was the run-on form, the re-working of earlier material in a later movement, and above all Moscheles's dramatic conception which attracted Liszt. The dramatic, fantastic, and virtuoso qualities of the Moscheles work forecast, more nearly than the Mendelssohn concertos, what Liszt was to accomplish. Moscheles also carried the principle of thematic transformation into his *Concerto pathétique*, No. 7; and his *Concerto pastorale*, No. 8, which was his favourite, he described as possessing "the shorter, more modern form of three movements connected together. . . ." The ultimate in this "modern form" was achieved by Liszt in his A major piano concerto; and in this work he simplified the concerto down to what he correctly understood to be its original meaning: "a reunion of concerted instruments."

Liszt's use of thematic transformation in his two concertos is closer to Moscheles than either to the interlocking device which Mendelssohn used in his first piano concerto, or to the *idée fixe* in Berlioz's *Harold in Italy*. There is no hint of thematic transformation from movement to movement in Mendelssohn, and in *Harold in Italy* the *idée fixe* remains largely unaltered. Liszt was not concerned in his concertos to depict the unchangeable integrity of a hero's soul; moreover, even in his programmatic symphonic poems where thematic transformation (as in *Les*

o

Préludes) is carried out quite extensively, Liszt disliked to have melodies sung always in the same tone of voice or dressed, upon their every reappearance, in substantially the same suit of clothes. Berlioz's *idée fixe* is identified with the viola, and the viola in turn is identified with Childe Harold. Liszt varied the instrumentation as well as the contours of his themes more thoroughly. Liszt's method in his concertos is akin to the principles of the symphonic poem. That of Berlioz is a forecast of the practice of identifying a theme with an instrument, both of which are in turn identified with a particular character. Wagner's dragon motive, Strauss's *Don Quixote*, and Prokofieff's *Peter and the Wolf* are examples of the Berlioz technique.

Liszt's knowledge of the work of his predecessors, especially of those who hinted at ideas similar to his own, was quite thorough. His interest in Schubert's *Wanderer* fantasia, Op. 15, was wholly logical, for in this work for solo piano Schubert dealt with a form that has much in common with the Liszt symphonic poems and piano concertos. All four movements in the fantasia are tied together into a continuous chain of music, and the "Wanderer" melody runs through the work like a *leitmotif*. The basic melody is transformed in each movement, and the entire work is unified as much through these transformations as through the avoidance of a sharp boundary break between the movements. Liszt could scarcely forbear to cite Schubert as an authority for his own identical procedures, and so he arranged the fantasia for piano and orchestra. The result is better than we might expect. Fortunately, there is not too much of the pirate virtuoso in the Liszt transcription, and in this form it makes a respectable piano concerto of a unique Schubert-Liszt variety.

The first Liszt piano concerto in E-flat was dedicated to Henri Litolff (1818–91), and here we pick up another long-forgotten strand that was woven into the fabric of Liszt's thinking. Schumann, in his writings, had expressed the need for a closer union between piano and orchestra. The latter, he felt, should be "more than a mere spectator," should be permitted to bring more of its tonal wealth and instrumental variety into play. The piano concerto had become too much of a one-sided affair. "We must confidently await the genius," wrote Schumann, "who will show us in a new and brilliant fashion how to bind the orchestra and the piano together. . . ." This plea for a more symphonic concerto was in part answered by Liszt, and in this respect he turned with profit to the piano concertos of Henri Litolff, whose example he generously acknowledged in a dedication. The Litolff concertos were plainly titled *Concertos symphoniques*, and the general design was planned with emphasis on the symphony. "Already in Litolff's first concerto-symphony (1844)," writes Schering, "the orchestra is conceded an exceptional position; it has become the chief bearer of the ideas and it reserves for itself the last and most important word, while upon the piano devolves the role of an obbligato orchestral instrument, similar to the Beethoven *Choral Fantasia*, although, to be sure, with a strong virtuoso tendency. The composer no longer works with solo and tutti in a one-sided fashion, but seeks to effect externally through a four-movement design, as well as internally, a complete parallel to the symphony."

It is not alone the dedication of his first concerto to Litolff, but the title *Concerto symphonique* inscribed on his second piano concerto in A major, which points plainly the direction of Liszt's thought.[1] However, it was not the symphony but the structural principles of the symphonic poem which guided Liszt, and in this Litolff is the more conservative of the two. (The influence, incidentally, worked both ways; the opening subject of Litolff's fifth concerto is clearly taken from the first melody of the Liszt E-flat concerto which antedated it.) The Liszt concertos are symphonic in the sense of a tremendous use of orchestral colour, and because, at least in intention, the concertos are not meant as virtuoso solos with orchestral accompaniment.

This will take a bit of explaining, for Liszt's piano is not one instrument among many, nor is it merely the chief obbligato instrument as in Berlioz's *Harold in Italy* or Loeffler's *Pagan Poem* or D'Indy's *Symphony on a Mountain Air*. It is the leading instrument, equivalent in itself to the orchestra, and the two join with and against each other as contrasted equals in accordance with the simple meaning of the word "concerto." Liszt's title has more negative than positive meaning, for he is not so much asserting the orchestra as refusing to negate it. He will not allow it to be the mere spectator that Schumann spoke of. This

---

[1] The term "*concert symphonique*" had become rather popular at the time. It is used in the titles of concertos by Mayer, Dupont, Leborne, etc.

in itself means bringing the orchestra forward and using it more resourcefully than had previously been the case. Liszt's piano writing is colossal, and the orchestra has to dig deep into its resources if it is not to fall behind. To maintain a position of equality with the piano, Liszt's orchestra must expand beyond previous concerto usage, just as Liszt's piano technique expanded beyond the limits previously known and accepted for the instrument. The more detailed tone colouring which Liszt drew from the piano he matched with a more detailed use of the specific colouring of the various orchestral instruments, and the Lisztian piano sonority was answered by a more powerful massing of orchestral strength. It was a simple problem of balance, which pure virtuoso composers ignored. We have seen a similar matching of stride for stride between piano and orchestra in the last piano concertos of Mozart. Liszt was no Mozart, and no comparison beyond this one point is intended; but Liszt had read too widely in the music of the great masters to make any intentional mistake in a fundamental concerto problem such as this.

The virtuosity of the solo instrument is, therefore, not restrained for the sake of symphonic domination; on the contrary, it is given free rein. It was, in point of fact, a matter of deliberate opinion with Liszt that a concerto, as a form of public speech, demanded a certain measure of ostentation and display. He criticized Schumann's title *Concerto without Orchestra* on this ground, declaring that the absence of effect in this work was fit for a sonata but contrary to the nature of a concerto. "The title *concerto*," Liszt writes, "has always been applied exclusively to pieces intended for public performance and, for this very reason, exacts certain conditions of effect which Mr. Schumann does not seem to have considered. His work, from the shape and severity of the style, belongs rather to the class 'sonata' than to that of the concerto. In establishing this distinction, we do not intend to assign a special, invariable shape to each class of composition. . . . But in music, as in literature, there are two grand divisions—things written or composed for public representation or execution; that is, things clear in sense, brilliant in expression, and grand in style: and then secret works from mere solitary inspiration, where fancy rules, which are of a nature to be appreciated by but few. Mr. Schumann's concerto belongs wholly to this latter class. Therefore it is wrong, in our opinion, to give it a name which seems to call for a large audience, and promises a splendour which we seek in vain. But our criticism shall be confined to this German error; for the work in itself, considered as a sonata, is rich and powerful." Liszt, of course, was right according to the standards of the age, and in the second edition of the work Schumann altered *Concerto without Orchestra* to *Sonata in F minor*, by which title it is now known.

With Paganini and Liszt, the violin and piano respectively were raised to the highest level of nineteenth-century virtuoso perfection. Their determined investigation of every last intricacy in instrumental technique was all to the good, but as a result the virtuoso was established, as never before, as a necessary evil in the composition of concertos. Few concerto composers after Liszt and Paganini consciously neglected a display technique, and a veritable host of composer-virtuosi devoted themselves thereafter to very little else. With varying degrees of taste and musicianship, the leading virtuosi of the century created concertos like blank artillery pieces which they fired off to the astonishment of the assembled spectators. The fireworks were phenomenal, and audiences accepted the show in the spirit of a safe national celebration from which they were assured of emerging musically and emotionally unscathed. In Liszt's words, the concerto was not a "solitary inspiration where fancy rules," but a "public representation" which exacted "certain conditions of effect." Most of the virtuoso concertos of the period are forgotten, for little besides public entertainment (not public enlightenment, which was the aim of a Beethoven or a Bach) was sought after or achieved. If one looks closely enough at these concertos a certain amount of genuine musicianship and sound craft can be detected, as well as some feeling for mood and the talent to evolve a worth-while melody. The "conditions of effect," however, are all-pervasive, and the account of this phase of the nineteenth-century concerto may proceed without apology as a compressed catalogue of names.

Among Paganini's contemporaries, the Polish violinist Karl Lipinski (1790–1861) was one of the few whom he liked personally and respected as a musician. The Lipinski *Concerto militaire*, Op. 21, No. 2, went well with audiences who preferred to hear Napoleon's cannon pounding harmlessly on the concert stage rather than on the battlefield. It was long a favourite and is now forgotten even by violin teachers. Heinrich Ernst (1814–65) was perhaps Paganini's most formidable rival. Joachim and Schumann thought well of him, and his one-movement violin concerto, Op. 23, shows some feeling for melody in addition to a colossal technique. Ferdinand David (1810–73) was a pupil of Spohr and is now mainly remembered for his technical advice to Mendelssohn. His own concertos are not without a few pleasant accomplishments. De Bériot (1802–70) forms the connecting link between the pre- and post-Paganini eras. He was a pupil of Baillot, a representative of the Paris school, and was one of the first to absorb Paganini's technical developments into his own writing and teaching. The De Bériot concertos are pleasantly unimportant, but they reflect the elegant and tasteful triviality of the Franco-Belgian school of violin playing which he founded. Henri Vieuxtemps (1820–81) was De Bériot's pupil, and the most famous product of his school. Vieuxtemps' fourth violin concerto in D minor, Op. 31, which is still heard, conforms very nicely to Liszt's prescription, "clear in sense, brilliant in expression, and grand in style." Henri Wieniawski (1835–80), one of the most famous of nineteenth-century violinists, has composed at least one violin concerto, the second in D minor, Op. 22, which is still a favourite. A feeling for warm, sentimental melody, nationalist inflection, and an energetic bravura style combine to keep this essentially virtuoso work alive.

The great German violinist of the century, Joseph Joachim (1831–1907), is perhaps wrongfully remembered only for his friendship with and influence upon Brahms. There is an early violin concerto in G minor, Op. 3, in an interesting one-movement form, which Joachim himself later neglected in his performances; a *Hungarian* concerto, Op. 11, to which attention is sometimes paid; and a series of variations for violin and orchestra. Tovey, who knew Joachim and was more sensible of his merits than most non-German scholars, makes an interesting case for a more than casual concern with his work. (Moser, Joachim's biographer, is afflicted with a slight case of hero worship and, in consequence, is somewhat unreliable in his evaluations. To wit, concerning Joachim's *Hungarian* concerto, Moser finds it "far more a work of genius than the violin concerto and even the double concerto for violin and violoncello by Brahms.") "Joachim's violin works,"[1] writes Tovey, "are full of technical difficulties produced with unconscious

[1] Donald Tovey, *Essays in Musical Analysis*, Vol. 3, pp. 164-65.

ease by the masterly player handling his own instrument. But not a note is there for display. Joachim never wrote a bar that did not aim instinctively for clearness and completeness in the presentation of true musical ideas. . . . Joachim's early musical ideas and ideals might easily have occupied him as a composer for the rest of his life, had they not found easier and more direct expression in his playing of the classics. I once ventured to ask him how it came about that he ceased to compose, and this was substantially the explanation he gave me, adding thereto: 'and then, you see, there was Brahms.' " There was much valuable exchange of criticism and ideas between Brahms and Joachim, and at the outset, at least, "Joachim was by far the more experienced master of the two, especially in the handling of the orchestra. In spite of one or two obstinately conservative habits in the treatment of trumpets, Joachim's orchestral scores are remarkably rich and free; nor does it seem to make much difference whether the orchestra is acting as an accompaniment to his solo violin or is independent. . . . Popularity his works never sought, and virtuoso players will not find in them opportunities of display comparable to their difficulty. . . . Thus the interest of his works will grow with the passage of time; for it depends on ideas that stand on their own musical merits without regard to fashion." It is possible that Tovey's prediction may yet prove true, but at the moment violinists still permit the *Hungarian* concerto to gather dust. There is enough violin technique in this work to worry even the best performer, but below the surface it moves far beyond the limits of a virtuoso concerto. "Most violinists," so Tovey believes, "will probably agree that the *Hungarian* concerto is the most difficult work ever written for the violin. Its difficulties all have the double quality of being the work of a composer who could play them, and of being the most straightforward and economical expression of his thought."

Eugène Ysaye (1858–1931) is perhaps the last of the worthy tradition of great violin virtuosi with sufficient schooling and enough of the creative spark to venture into composition. A pupil of Massart, Wieniawski, and Vieuxtemps, Ysaye was one of the outstanding violinists of modern times, and a musician with an acute sensibility to the music of his contemporaries. He was among the first to see the merit of such men as Debussy, César Franck, Guillaume Lekeu, and for a long while almost alone in performing their music to an indifferent public. Both the Franck and the Lekeu violin sonatas were dedicated to Ysaye. He

gave the latter work its first public performance and is responsible for
much of the present popularity of the former. Debussy's nocturnes
were originally conceived for violin and orchestra, and in that form it
was Debussy's opinion that only Ysaye could play them. "If Apollo
himself were to ask me for them," declared Debussy, "I should have
to refuse him." The six Ysaye violin concertos are, as we might expect, no simple student pieces. An effort is occasionally made to revive
one of Ysaye's unaccompanied violin sonatas, but the concertos have
fallen into almost total disuse.

The nineteenth century was pre-eminently a piano century, and the
list of virtuosi who contributed to the concerto is somewhat longer.
In Beethoven's day Joseph Wölfl (1773–1812), Dussek (1760–1812),
and Daniel Steibelt (1765–1832) were well-known names. Wölfl still
crops up in a Beethoven biography as an accomplished pianistic rival.
By all accounts he had a clean and sure technique as well as a fine sensibility. Among his piano concertos there is a military concerto of the
kind that was popular during the period when wars were a matter for
everyone's common commiseration. There is nothing very heroic or
deeply felt about the military concertos that were turned out in abundance. The well-to-do audiences of the time found them quite entertaining, probably because it was not they but the less fortunate mass of
humanity (who did not as yet crowd the concert halls) who were
chiefly confronted with the grim reality.

Dussek is the type of modest minor composer who helps found important traditions. He was born in Bohemia and emigrated to Paris—
many Slavic musicians at that time left their native lands—and his
music, wholly western European in style and temperament, constitutes
one of the formative stages through which early nineteenth-century
piano music evolved. Several characteristic elements in Beethoven's
piano style appear first in Dussek. Blom, for example, notes a Dussek
sonata in C minor, composed some five years prior to the Beethoven
Pathétique, "which contains some startling likenesses to that work."
Dussek expanded the left-hand technique, the use of octave sequences,
explored the deeper register of the piano, etc.; in a word, he helped
shape the early piano style of the century. Among his piano concertos,
Schering finds the elements of this new style most explicit in his concerto for two pianos.

Steibelt deserves a word as an excellent example of the sensationalism that was already a part of the early romantic make-up. Programmatic concertos of the battle-and-tempest variety were fancied by a good portion of the public, and Steibelt turned them out for the trade. He did a military concerto for piano and two orchestras (No. 7); a hunt concerto (No. 5) which professed to use for its adagio a melody composed by Mary Stuart during her imprisonment; a tempest concerto (No. 3), the finale of which (*The Storm Preceded by a Pastoral Rondeau*) was a great success with thunder effects produced by a tremolo in the low piano register; a concerto called *Voyage to Mount St. Bernard*; as well as sundry assorted pieces called *Naval Combat, Martial sonata*, and the *Destruction of Moscow*. One of the sidelights of the search for new musical sensations was the concerto literature which developed around curious instruments like the Panmelodikon and the Physharmonika. Oddities spread even to sober instruments like the piano, and the Viennese models of the period boasted an assortment of colourful pedal effects. The eighteenth-century German piano had been built with several pedals, but a few special ones were now added. "Some Viennese pianos," reports Sachs, "had as many as six pedals, among them two characteristic new ones—the *bassoon* pedal, which pressed a strip of wood lined with tissue paper against the bass strings so that they rattled, and the *Turkish Music*, a pedal operating a triangle, cymbals and a drumstick hitting the sound-board." In small measure, these curiosities were part of the early romantic interest in new colour resources; for the most part, however, they were calculated as an oddity and an amusement.

The fifth piano concerto of John Field (1782–1837), *The Conflagration during the Storm*, is another of the tempest concertos of the period. To enhance the effect a second piano is used in the thunder and lightning sequences "since one pianoforte alone would be too weak to express the storm." In his more important music, such as his nocturnes and in some of his concertos, Field captured some of the sophisticated moonglow which with Chopin became part of romantic piano music. Schumann admired Field, and Liszt noted his contribution to the concerto form.

Ferdinand Ries (1755–1846) and Carl Czerny (1791–1857) were both pupils of Beethoven who knew how to put together a fluent piano concerto. Schumann thought that at least in his larger work Czerny sought "to accomplish something worthy," but of a concertino, Op. 650, he could only observe that "he who writes in this way may easily bring it up to Op. 1000." Ries's third piano concerto in C-sharp minor, Op. 55, still earns a measure of praise from the occasional scholar who bothers to dig it up. The work was apparently Ries's only accomplishment. "Even Napoleon lost his last battles," writes Schumann anent Ries's ninth concerto, Op. 177, "but Arcola and Wagram still shine in glory. Ries has written a C-sharp minor concerto, and may sleep in peace upon his laurels." History has rendered a pointed judgment of both by remembering Ries only for his memoirs of Beethoven, which are in many instances informative, and Czerny for his famous finger exercises over which modern virtuosi still spend a miserable childhood. Czerny studied with both Beethoven and Hummel and transmitted his piano technique, a careful composite of the best in the old and the new, to young Liszt, who studied with him. The Czerny technique is solid, rigorous, and dull, and piano teachers are still convinced that there is much value in it.

Friedrich Kalkbrenner (1788–1849), one of the most famous pianists of the period, represents perhaps the highest level of pre-Lisztian technique. He composed a sonata for the left hand and was, according to Weitzmann, "the first to write extended compositions for the left hand alone which he played with finished ease." Among his other accomplishments he "not only required thirds and sixths to be executed by the right or left hand, but added to the same the higher octave of the lower note"; also "he introduced effective double and triple trills." His concertos are elegant virtuoso pieces reflecting his command of the instrument and are put together with much of the solid, conservative craft plus the spark of the genuine feeling which many of Beethoven's minor contemporaries seem to have possessed. There are already evidences of the Lisztian glitter in his concertos, and Schering claims his D minor, Op. 61, as the model for Chopin's E minor piano concerto.

Minor composers are not unworthy to be studied, for the great creative spirits are too often absorbed in issues that go beyond matters of mere technique and are content to leave to lesser men the more simple and very fundamental problem of constructing the ground-work for what we later generalize as the style or technique of an era. Dussek no doubt clarified a few small matters for Beethoven; Kalkbrenner, Moscheles, and Litolff learned what they could from Beethoven and cleared the path for Liszt; Field, Hummel, and Kalkbrenner were all useful to Chopin; David helped Mendelssohn and Joachim Brahms; Czerny studied with Hummel and Beethoven and passed his training on to Liszt. The solitary mountain in music rises always upon a broad base of countless lesser men, who lie solid, essential, and miles deep below the surface. An excavation is historically instructive, and once in a while we stumble upon a rare gem as Schumann did upon the Schubert C major symphony, or even upon continents of forgotten gold mines in the same way that scholars for decades have been adventuring in the music of earlier centuries. More often than not the results are only instructive, helping us to appreciate what we already are appreciating, only with a little more understanding. Sometimes a lot of digging takes us little distance, for a Ferdinand Hiller (1811–85) or a Sterndale Bennett (1816–75) will turn up with a few promising concertos which start with Mendelssohn and go nowhere. The concertos are friendly, well made, and not without feeling; pleasant acquaintances easily forgotten in the course of a hectic century. Or we may unearth the concertos of an Adolph Henselt (1814–89), which contain a touch of poetry and a dash of temperament (a surprising number of the romantic virtuoso concertos do), along with a rare feeling for a well-decorated platitude and two large fistfuls of what, by all accounts, was a unique and stunning kind of pianism. Henselt's "novel . . . pianoforte effects" made quite an impression upon the critics. Lenz wrote of him with deep admiration, and Weitzmann was convinced that Henselt's F minor concerto, Op. 16 (1838), ranked among "the most valuable works of the pianoforte literature." Tastes change.

In the dispute which raged at the time over who was the greater pianist, Liszt or Thalberg, a French critic boldly decided: "It is Chopin." This was supposed to be a witticism, but it places Chopin as one of the triumvirate that ruled the pianistic world during the 1830's and 40's. By all accounts, his playing was less showy than Thalberg's and more limited than Liszt's, but it was unique, not as an oddity, but in the best sense as a new and persuasive contribution. Thalberg we can forget about. Tired of recognizing in him "a decided talent for composition that threatens to be ruined by the vanity of the executive artist," Schu-

mann reviewed his solitary virtuoso concerto, Op. 5, with the fond
hope that Thalberg would recognize his betters and stick to piano
playing. The difference between Liszt and Chopin, however, is worth
illustrating. Hearing that Liszt intended to review his concerts in a
musical periodical, Chopin remarked: "He will give me a little kingdom in his empire." The evaluation is inadvertently just, for Liszt
worked in all fields and Chopin in only one. His kingdom is a small
one, although it boasts some of the finest scenery on the earth's surface, and Chopin reigned within it unchallenged.

Chopin, like Shelley, has become a state of mind which all of us grow
into, through, and out of. Moonlight becomes him, as it should all of us
before we are forced to learn better or different. He is too much a speci-
alist on too refined a subject to constitute an adult gospel for the complexities of modern living; yet we can return to him occasionally for a
moment of rare and particularized loveliness. There are, of course,
Chopin specialists just as there are people, no doubt, who live out of
preference, and not from necessity, in the extreme arctics or tropics.
Most of us, however, are inveterate tourists; we admire the beauties,
pay our respects, and pass on—in the long run to Bach, Beethoven,
Mozart, to composers who have lived through all hours in a musical
day, all seasons in the world's weather, through all of the ordered and
capricious climates in a man's soul.

It has long been the general critical consensus that Chopin's two
piano concertos do not represent him at his best. In Liszt's words, they
show "more effort than inspiration." He was essentially an intimate
miniaturist, a composer of preludes which precede nothing in particular, of waltzes not intended for dancing. He is uncomfortable in large
forms, and it has been repeated often enough that orchestration was
one of the mysteries of which he was no master. None of the attempts,
however, to reorchestrate the Chopin concertos (Klindworth, Tausig,
Burmeister) are wholly satisfactory. Handling the orchestral mass in a
concerto is not a pure problem in orchestration but a matter rather of
adjusting the balance (really the essential disproportion) between solo
and orchestra. There is always the danger, in touching up the orchestration, that tampering with the piano part will prove necessary (Klindworth, for example, tampers a good deal), and this is something to be
risked only by a superior Chopin. The form itself was uncongenial to

him, and the two concertos are structurally conservative and imitative. While there are anticipations of Chopin in Field, Hummel, and Weber, his piano-writing was essentially revolutionary; yet his concerto form stands apart from the main tradition of post-classical experimentation which started with Spohr and Weber and culminated in Liszt. The traditional first orchestral exposition was restored, as well as the old schematic balance between ritornel and solo, and the rigid demarcation between movements. For one of his temperament, formal conservatism was a strait-jacket; and the traditional manner in which the two concertos were designed made them an easy victim for the kind of partitioning in the performance of the movements which has already been noticed with the Beethoven violin concerto. At the first performance of the F minor, Op. 21, the allegro was followed by a divertissement for the French horn composed by Görner, after which came the last two movements of the concerto. At its first performance the E minor concerto, Op. 11, was similarly partitioned, this time with an aria and chorus by Soliva in between. Such liberties could no longer be taken with the Mendelssohn or Liszt concertos. Chopin anchored his revolutionary instincts to a traditional design, but not out of veneration for the classics. However, he had little understanding of the problems of post-classical construction in large forms, and he could do nothing better than play safe. The influences that may be traced in the concertos—Hummel, whom he admired, Kalkbrenner, to whom the E minor, Op. 11, is dedicated—are all conservative although, in this respect, it is evident that he had enough personal genius to mould his models to his own will.

It is not so much the infelicities in orchestration or the unadventurous reliance on already outmoded models which inhibited Chopin, so much as a temperament that was basically unsuited to the concerto. The two Chopin works, both of which are in minor keys, are part of the melancholic tradition of the romantic concerto. "Four-fifths of the newest concertos which we are in the habit of reviewing for our readers," wrote Schumann anent a concerto by Doehler, "are in minor; one sometimes fears that the major third will disappear altogether from the tone system." And when he came to a concerto by Herz, Schumann consoled himself as follows: "'Heart, my heart, oh, why so mournful?' sang I, as I went on playing; three times in the first movement we have con dolore, while the espressivos and smorzandos are countless." All Schumann's concertos, like every one by Mendelssohn and Chopin, are in minor keys. This was part of the emotional credo of romanticism. As Liszt expressed it, it was "grief, that terrible reality which Art must strive to reconcile with Heaven." The concerto, however, by Liszt's definition was a public representation, and Chopin's sorrows were too private to parade before more than a few friends.[1] Neither Mendelssohn, Spohr, Liszt, nor Tschaikowsky minded public lamentation particularly, but Chopin's sensibilities were too fragile, and whatever it was he believed he had reason to suffer from he revealed most comfortably in a series of miniature confessions. Thus in the concertos it is the small, poetic piano interludes and the slow movements that are most convincing and were most admired. Liszt cavilled with the two outside movements, but for the slow movement of the F minor concerto he had nothing but praise. It was also one of Schumann's enthusiasms. "What are ten editorial crowns," he wrote, "compared to one such adagio as that in the second concerto!" And from Liszt we learn that the movement was also one of Chopin's particular favourites. It might well have been, for Chopin is at his best here, moulding with precision the restless improvisational contour of the music. His piano interludes are very nearly as good as anything he has done in the small forms, and the concertos are studded with many a fine melody. But the solo interludes have a way of slipping into preludes or mazurkas sufficient unto themselves; and the nocturne-like haze that floats in with the piano after a strident ritornel is scarcely a functional unit in a large form so much as a self-contained and self-satisfied digression content to exist for its own sweet sake. The initial orchestral ritornels are courageous enough, but thereafter the main interest lies in the piano's private nursing of "an internal wound" (the phrase is out of its context, and it is Liszt's) rather than in the fashioning of a public and heroic form. "All the interest," wrote Berlioz, "is concentrated in the piano part; the orchestra of his concertos is nothing but a cold and almost useless accompaniment."

[1] Concerning Chopin's playing, Berlioz wrote: "To appreciate it thoroughly I believe it is necessary to hear him at no great distance, rather in a salon than in a theatre..."

Should we want to know why Chopin bothered with an uncongenial form, the answer is that the concertos are early works, written before he came to Paris, at a period when it was necessary to his future success that he should establish himself through public concerts. The second concerto in F minor, Op. 21, was composed in 1829, at the age of nineteen, and the first in E minor, Op. 11, a year later. (The F minor, composed first, was published later than the E minor; hence it is numbered as the second.) Both were consciously designed for big concerts which he intended to give, and from the outset he voiced the deep suspicion that nobody would understand him. "The allegro of the F minor concerto (not intelligible to all)," he wrote, reviewing the reception the work was first given, "received indeed the reward of a 'Bravo,' but I believe that this was given because the public wished to show that it understands and knows how to appreciate serious music. There are people enough in all countries who like to assume the air of connoisseurs."

This mistrust of the public soon led him to give up active concertizing. He became a salon artist instead of a concert pianist, with the aristocracy now replaced by a select circle of kindred souls, mainly musicians, novelists, and poets.

> *We have been, let us say, to hear the latest Pole*
> *Transmit the Preludes, through his hair and finger-tips.*
> *"So intimate, this Chopin, that I think his soul*
> *Should be resurrected only among friends*
> *Some two or three, who will not touch the bloom*
> *That is rubbed and questioned in the concert room."*[1]

Yet even in this closed circle Chopin did not feel himself thoroughly appreciated. Liszt makes a shrewd point in showing that Chopin gained little solace in turning from the public concert hall to the closed salon. "It is to be regretted," he writes, " that the indubitable advantages for the artist resulting from the cultivation of only a select audience, should be so sensibly diminished by the rare and cold expression of its sympathies. The *glacé* which covers the grace of the *élite*, as it does the fruit of their desserts; the imperturbable

---

[1] From *Collected Poems*, T. S. Eliot. Reprinted by permission of Harcourt, Brace and Company, Inc., New York, and Faber & Faber, Ltd., London.

calm of their most earnest enthusiasm, could not be satisfactory for Chopin."

The fragility of his temperament and the cultivation of an air of isolation are borne out by what Liszt tells us of Chopin's opinions. "He loved Shakespeare only under many conditions. He thought his characters drawn too closely to the life, and spoke a language too true." Also he was dismayed by Shakespeare's "poor details of humanity." If Shakespeare's sense of reality was more than Chopin's delicate taste could tolerate, his feeling for humanity was also wider than Chopin s narrow intelligence could comprehend. Chopin had the highest admiration for Beethoven but here too with reservations. Certain portions of Beethoven's music "always seem too rudely sculptured," continues Liszt, "their structure too athletic to please him, their wrath too tempestuous, their passion too overpowering, the lion-marrow which fills every member of his phrases was matter too substantial for his taste; and the Raphaelic and Seraphic profiles which are wrought into the midst of the nervous and powerful creations of this great genius, were to him almost painful from the force of the cutting contrast in which they are frequently set." It is true that, à la Rochefoucauld, we have all of us somehow the strength to endure Chopin's particular misfortunes. Beethoven's sorrows trouble us more deeply. We are inexorably driven by his passions, and the lyricism, the "cutting contrast," that emerges out of Beethoven's tempest haunts us forever. Schubert was less of a favourite, and with even more reservations. "In spite of the charm which he acknowledged in some of the melodies of Schubert, he would not willingly listen to those in which the contours were too sharp for his ear, in which suffering lies naked, and we can almost feel the flesh palpitate, and hear the bones crack and crash under the rude embrace of sorrow." However, despite Chopin's longing for solitude, it is not to his twenty-four preludes, but to Schubert's *Die Winterreise*, that one turns for twenty-four of the profoundest variations on the theme of the man alone known in the history of the several arts. It is easy to guess the composers who did not irritate him. "Among the composers for the piano," Liszt tells us, "Hummel was one of the authors whom he re-read with the most pleasure." Small wonder that Berlioz, in a moment of inspired malice, declared Chopin "was dying all his life." (Turner, who has rushed to Berlioz's defence, fails to see this as a "famous sneer" but simply as a statement of fact; which is a fine way of adding injury to an insult.)

This was manifestly not the temperament for the kind of public posturing that was a declared ingredient of the romantic concerto. With the increase of mass concert-hall audiences, and the concomitant "conditions of effect," the romantic concerto could only follow either the epic and heroic path of a Beethoven or the knockdown, drag-out showmanship of a Liszt. Chopin had too little heart for the first and too much good taste for the second. It is he, and not Mozart or Haydn, who is small-boned and, in a precious sense, refined. Even Mendelssohn in his *Songs without Words* is not nearly as genuine a poetic miniaturist as Chopin in his concertos. Mendelssohn could accept as little as Chopin the difficult alternatives offered the romantic concerto; but Mendelssohn got by with his ease in large forms, and he could manage, moreover, a serviceable imitation of the dramatic. He was more accustomed to public speech and he steered a middle course with no sense of strain. The Chopin concertos were composed out of necessity by a young man struggling to make his way in the musical world. They are an uneasy compromise with the concert hall, an unwilling gesture towards the impersonal public he was altogether too eager to distrust. The concertos are the meeting-ground between his genius and his disinclination; a strange composite of public speech and private day-dreaming. It is a tribute to his amazing talent that they are nevertheless still worth re-hearing.

Apart from the concertos of Chopin, the main course of the romantic concerto after Beethoven ran in a clear stream of post-classical experimentation which culminated in a free, rhapsodical one-movement design such as Liszt evolved for his second piano concerto. The fluent, classical sonata-form constructions of Mozart and Beethoven had been based upon a balanced alternation of orchestral ritornels and solo episodes, upon an opening ritornel and a double exposition of themes in the first movement, and upon a sharp demarcation between the fast-slow-fast sequence of movements. From Spohr through Weber, Mendelssohn, Schumann, and Liszt, one or another of these tenets were called into question. The opening orchestral ritornel was suppressed, the two expositions condensed into one, and the boundaries between movements relaxed to the point where all flowed together into a continuous stream of music. The new design had much to commend it, and its principles may be discovered with many variations underlying such diverse concertos as those by Saint-Saëns, Rimsky-Korsakov, Glazounov, Medtner, Sibelius, and Delius.

For a variety of reasons the experimental romantic concerto was regarded with suspicion by Schumann and Brahms. Schumann possessed sufficient critical acumen to feel certain of the weaknesses of the new form, but it required a composer of Brahms's power, acuteness, and integrity to dispense with it successfully and undertake a belated restoration of the classical design. An expansive temperament counted more with the romantics than purity and clarity of structure, and while their design was more condensed than the classical Mozart model, their concertos were often more lengthy and always less economical. The romantics possessed a fatal talent for good theatre. They knew how to handle atmosphere, how to block in a colourful orchestral stage setting against which the soloist might pose in an assortment of interesting virtuoso attitudes. The emotions certainly were genuine enough, but, as in the romantic theatre, extravagant posturing was often thought the essence of a grand passion. It happened inevitably, even in the best romantic concertos, that grand attitudes (i.e. certain stereotyped musical devices) were mistaken for the great emotions they were intended to convey. Despite its obvious emotionality and a greater freedom in design, the romantic concerto developed, in consequence, certain peculiar limitations in the range of its expressive ideas. A self-indulgent melancholia, for example, fell over the form, and a rhapsodic type of emotionalism became the favourite mood in which the romantic concerto was cast. With less obvious stress on emotional surface, Mozart's range is broader. He is, by comparison, the complete classical dramatist dealing in heroism, tragedy, tenderness, high comedy, gaiety, and witticism, either as isolates or in combination, and with careful reference to the indefinable emotions which lie within and between.

As might be expected, the emotional outpourings in the romantic concerto stormed with ever-increasing indifference past the traditional disciplines of the classical masters. The occasional gestures towards an elementary kind of counterpoint, for example, demonstrate that polyphony, like Latin, was fast becoming a dead language, fit for students to sharpen their wits upon and to discard once they had progressed beyond the classroom. Virtuosity reared its alluring head, and sensationalism frankly, snobbishly, and callously calculated for the least literate of large audiences took hold of the form.

A conservative counter-attack was clearly in the making, especially since the hope for a classical restoration consistent with the romantic outlook had never really died. Schumann fought for it in his music and through the pages of his journal. Virtuosity and sensationalism were the arch-enemies of the Davidsbündler, and the "pure sources" towards which Schumann sought to redirect German music were Bach, Mozart, Beethoven, and Schubert. Schumann looked askance at the experimental concerto with its amorphous merging of movements. His own lyrical outlook led him to an awkward compromise with it in his 'cello concerto, but he had previously questioned the procedure on aesthetic grounds. He looked forward confidently to a Messiah with the courage and the discipline to dissolve the romantic dilemma, and it is a tribute to his perspicacity that he recognized him in the youthful Brahms.

Brahms's first piano concerto in D minor, Op. 15, is a declaration of his principles and a record of the labour it cost to formulate them. It took shape first as a symphony during the summer of 1854, at which time the first three movements were composed and the first completely scored. In 1855 he wrote to Clara Schumann of a dream in which he had used his "luckless symphony to make a piano concerto, and was playing it as such. It was composed of the first movement and the scherzo with the finale terribly difficult and grand. I was quite carried away." Subsequently Dietrich reported seeing the work also sketched as a sonata for two pianos. Brahms was hard at work on it during 1856; two years later the Detmold *Signale* carried a report that finishing touches were being put to a piano concerto; and on January 22, 1859, the work was premiered with Brahms at the piano and Joachim conducting. All in all, from its inception to its first performance, the concerto occupied Brahms nearly five years.

The work is a landmark in the romantic concerto, the first telling blow struck against the post-classical experimentators. The sharp boundaries between movements were restored, the classical sonata-form design again put to work, and the opening orchestral ritornel monumentally reconstructed along clear classical lines. Brahms's superior regard for the symphony as a musical form is indicated by the fact that his first attempt at a classical restoration was ultimately cast as a concerto; only many years later did he venture upon a first symphony. The first attempt in both fields are mature, complete, and successful, largely because Brahms, unlike Schumann, could handle the essentially dramatic issues involved in a classical sonata form. The first symphony harks back to Beethoven, and when the obvious resemblance was pointed out to him, he declared any man a fool who could not see it. Appropriately and tragically enough the first concerto stems from Schumann; not literally—although its opening resembles the first ritornel of the Schumann violin concerto—but in its inspiration. Schumann's tragic attempt at suicide haunted Brahms during the initial sketching of the concerto. The grim and turbulent heroism of the first movement bears the imprint of the event; and the slow movement, one of Brahms's quietest and most deeply touching creations, is an instrumental requiem which originally bore the inscription *Benedictus qui venit in nomine Domini* (Blessed is he who cometh in the name of the Lord). The stark, angular utterance which opens the concerto reveals Brahms's downright grasp of the fundamental drama of the classical form. No opening since Beethoven's ninth symphony shows so clear a conception of the correct path.

In every one of the concertos there is the same adherence to the classical design. The first piano concerto and the violin concerto utilize the classical sonata-form structure in a comparatively transparent fashion. However, it would be a basic error to construe whatever liberties Brahms took in his two other concertos as a process of dispensing with, or even calling into question, the fundamental role of the opening orchestral ritornel in a traditional sonata-form concerto. No true artist, conscious of the original radicalism of a great tradition, will treat its creative principles as tiresome, legalistic formulas. In the second piano concerto and in the double concerto, Brahms took necessary liberties in adaptation, but the essentials of the classical design remain intact. The opening orchestral ritornels in both concertos are prefaced by thematic statements involving the immediate participation of the solo instruments. Beethoven's preface in his fifth piano concerto was improvisational and non-thematic. The immediate introductions of the solo in Weber, Mendelssohn, Schumann, and Liszt were not, as we have seen, by way of a preface, but actually the first page in the first chapter of the work. In his second piano concerto in B-flat, Op. 83, Brahms opens with the first main subject previewed softly in the horn answered by a broad, rolling commentary from the solo piano. The wood-winds round out the announcement and the solo piano breaks into a vehement and abrupt declaration which sets the immediate stage for the first orchestral ritornel (or exposition of themes). The first subject to be stated by the orchestra is a matured version of the introductory horn call. Reasoning close to the main dramatic problem, Brahms transforms what just appeared as an innocent and severe-sounding motive into a strident subject endowed with true heroism and a sonorous orchestral majesty. Thus the way is prepared for the contrasting lyricism of the second subject. The thematic duality, the resultant emotional conflict determined by the form, is thus ensured. Brahms's method is a combination of controlled daring and careful observance of the essentials of the traditional design.

The preface to the opening ritornel in the double concerto for violin and 'cello in A minor, Op. 102, is even more spacious. The orchestra opens with a terse outline of what is to be the main subject of the movement. The solo 'cello, reiterating in augmented time values the last three notes of the orchestral statement, plunges into an impassioned and unaccompanied recitative. Wood-winds announce the quiet second subject, which is marked by a sequence of lyrical, falling inflections. Again the last three notes are taken as a point of departure; this time by the solo violin. The solo 'cello enters and the unaccompanied duet builds to a powerful climax ushering in the first orchestral ritornel, which now fully exposes the main themes of the movement in all their contrasted majesty. There are no such prefaces in either the first piano concerto or in the violin concerto, which shows that Brahms knew how to vary the details of his design from work to work.

Yet the concertos for all their traditional first-movement structure are aware of specifically romantic developments. Brahms was as adept a miniaturist as Chopin, and small solo forms, quasi intermezzos, and capriccios, are woven ingeniously into the structure of the classical first-movement sonata form. For example, in the D minor piano concerto, during the second exposition, the piano disposes first of its restatement of the main themes and then lapses unaccompanied into a quiet chorale-like intermezzo. And in the B-flat piano concerto, the piano breaks into a short unaccompanied capriccio which forms part of the preface to the first orchestral ritornel. Brahms at his best is never free of a certain amount of sectionalism in his structures; the design is well knit, but the seams somehow show. However, the small solo forms are absorbed as a convincing part of the concerto. Unlike Chopin, he does not turn to them as a relief from an unwilling discipline. The solo 'cello recitative in the opening of the double concerto likewise has its analogies to the recitatives in Spohr, Weber, Schumann, Liszt, and Chopin. But here it is clearly not a case of the influence of romantic models, so much as a natural device which crops up in the solo concerto at least as early as Locatelli. It is a homologue of the operatic recitative and points back to the common æsthetic impulses which underlie many of the fundamental similarities between opera and the solo concerto. There is this difference, however, between Brahms's concerto recitative and Spohr's and Weber's. Their recitative actually sounds operatic and betrays its origin quite openly; Brahms's recitative does not.

In the treatment of the solo part, the Brahms concertos are a throwback to an earlier and superior conception of virtuosity. In this case both the sinners and the saints indulged in preliminary skirmishes to prepare for the Brahmsian counter-attack. The bravura posturings of the virtuoso composers had been, on Schumann's own account, one of the principal reasons for the foundation of the *Neue Zeitschrift*; and in his piano concerto, Schumann had shown that an intimate and lyrical spirit could profitably forego the fatal histrionics of the concert hall. In this respect Liszt nominally, though not in fact, belonged among the Davidsbündler. In his concertos he was plainly guilty of virtuoso heroics, but he had too critical an intelligence to be misled by his own example. Repenting perhaps the error of his own ways, he called sincerely for a return to the high purposes of the art. "Let us renounce," he wrote, " the corrupt spirit of the time in which we live, with all that is not worthy of art, all that will not endure." And in particular he urged composers and performers to cease "labouring so constantly to attract listeners, and striving to please them at whatever sacrifice." The Brahms concertos are an answer to such pleas. The solo writing is

prodigiously difficult, since it must match a majestic orchestra and fill
an enormous design. Furthermore, Brahms could scarcely ignore the
serviceable technical advances which had been made by the virtuosi.
However, as with Beethoven, the difficulties arise out of the necessities of his conception and his design. They are at all times functional;
at no point employed for stunt flying. They are thankless to the virtuosi for they are never obvious and hence do not obviously impress.

However unforbidding the works of Brahms may appear today, in
the context of the romantic concerto they are unusually disciplined
and austere. The severity of his classical structure brought with it a re-
version to a rigorous polyphonic discipline which he invoked as often
as was consistent with the non-polyphonic nature of the solo concerto.
He suppressed obvious virtuosity and restored the concerto to its
classical status as a symphonic form for solo and orchestra, rather than
as an extended solo display piece with orchestral accompaniment.
Even his languorous slow movements, which he treated like an elaborate orchestral *lied*, are comparatively restrained when we glance at
other concertos of the period. (The andante of the B-flat piano concerto actually uses a melody almost identical with his song *Immer leiser
wird mein Schlummer*.) However, despite his choice of a classical form,
Brahms was quite thoroughly a romantic. He revelled in minor thirds
and sixths; and he enjoyed sonorous meditations spiced with a generous dash of melancholy. Yet there is seldom any mawkishness in his
slow movements, and none of the artificial moonlight that shines only
in aristocratic drawing-rooms. There is a sober integrity, a hard fibre at
the bottom of each concerto, even in its gentlest moods and in its most
brilliant soloistic moments.

The reception accorded the concertos was, as we might imagine,
mainly an uncordial one. The violin concerto, Op. 77, was called a concerto against the violin, which shows how deep a distortion the virtuoso concerto had wrought in the critical understanding of the form.
The D minor concerto, Op. 15, was a total failure. Leipzig audiences
had run mad from an overdose of Mendelssohn, and compared with
the Mendelssohnian glibness and casual grace, the Brahms concerto
seemed like "three-quarters of an hour of labouring, burrowing, strain-
ing, and struggling—a product of hopeless aridity carried to its grave."
Brahms took his defeat stoically. "At the conclusion," he wrote to

Joachim, "three pairs of hands were brought together very slowly, whereupon a perfectly distinct sound of hissing from all sides forbade any such demonstration. . . . The failure made no impression whatever upon me. After all, I am only experimenting and feeling my way." The double concerto, Op. 102, of course, laboured under the disadvantage of an unfamiliar combination and a singularly rigorous and economical structure. Even his biographers, who usually can be trusted for sympathy if not for understanding, were puzzled by the work. Specht thought it "one of Brahms's most unapproachable and joyless compositions"; and Niemann regarded it "as one of the works elaborated by strictly polyphonic methods, rather than as a record of an intense experience." For a long while Brahms was misjudged to be a strictly intellectual composer, and there were those among his contemporaries who placed an ungenerous construction upon his intensely disciplined formalism. Tschaikowsky, for example, questioned whether Brahms's aim were not to appear "incomprehensible and obscure," whether his "whirlpool of almost unmeaning harmonic progressions and modulations" were designed "only . . . to have the semblance of depth in order to mask the poverty of his imagination." Compared with the obviousness of a Tschaikowsky, Brahms could conceivably be mistaken for an esoteric.

Brahms did not help his own cause with the conspicuous self-advertisement of a Liszt or a Paganini. He was an inveterate romantic afflicted with a classicist's reticence in parading an overweening emotion. Thus, even to a close friend, he announced a new work with a sort of deprecating sarcasm which was inept as a description of the music and too heavy-handed to serve for a sense of humour. The double concerto he described as a "strange notion" and his latest "piece of folly"; the slow movement of the violin concerto as a "feeble adagio." The addition of an extra movement (the stupendous scherzo) in the B-flat piano concerto, he explained with a "well, you see, the first movement was so harmless"; and the work as a whole he passed off as "a tiny, tiny piano concerto with a tiny, tiny wisp of a scherzo."

He approached his concertos with a profound respect for the dignity of the form. He sought advice from Joachim on the violin concerto and sent him the solo part with the intention "that you should correct it, not sparing the quality of the composition and that if you thought it not worth scoring, you should say so." It is typical of Brahms that he dedicated his concerto to Joachim and took very little notice of his advice. He also had his doubts about the double concerto. "I might have left the idea," he wrote to Clara Schumann, "to someone else who understands fiddles better than I do. (Unfortunately Joachim has given up composing). It is quite a different thing writing for instruments whose character and sound one can only incidentally imagine, than for an instrument which one knows thoroughly—as I do the piano, and know exactly what I write and why I write it." His equipment and experience in handling instruments was, of course, as thorough as any composer had ever had at his disposal, for the concerto was written in 1887, after the violin concerto, the four symphonies, and two of the three violin sonatas.

In the long run his modesty derived from an honest reverence for the great men whose structures he sought to re-create. The shadow of Beethoven hung over Brahms and revealed to him, as it can to no critic, the shortcomings of his labour. "You have no conception," he said to Levi while working on his first symphony, "how the likes of us feel when we hear the tramp of a giant like him behind us." Inevitably he compared the classicism of his own concertos to that of Mozart's, and with a critical justness that detracts nothing from the value of his own accomplishment, he found himself wanting. "That people in general," he wrote, "do not understand and do not respect the greatest things, such as the Mozart concertos, helps our kind to live and acquire renown. If they would only know that what they get from us in drops, they could drink there to their hearts' content."

This summarizes acutely and honestly both what Brahms attempted in his concertos and the extent to which he succeeded. There is the famous story of Brahms's visit to Liszt, and how the latter with unfailing generosity made the young man welcome. Liszt read through some of Brahms's music, which he praised highly, and then went on to play some of his own. He turned for comment and found Brahms asleep. The fatigue of a journey suffices to explain the discourtesy; but the incident is a minor symbol, a clear prediction of Brahms's path. For all his failings, Liszt possessed a powerful revolutionary intelligence which he sought to express in his music, and Brahms was metaphorically asleep to the main progressive trends of the time. Brahms accepted the

role of Schumann's Messiah; he lived with an almost biblical consciousness of the great past, and he was doggedly intent on leading the new
music back to the ancient promised land. He sought, and he succeeded
as well as any man could, in housing the new romantic spirit in the old
classic form. Hitherto only Mendelssohn seemed able to manage the
union of the two. Brahms had a deeper understanding of the issues;
and he fought harder than Mendelssohn, casting and recasting his work
until it took acceptable shape. By and large he succeeded, but in the
long run he was too late. The powerful currents set in motion by
Wagner and Liszt governed the last tide that washed upon the modern
world. As nineteenth-century music rolled to its denouement it carried
Brahms with it as an aloof and disinterested passenger, regarded by the
respectful as a learned iconoclast and by the impatient as a bewhiskered
anachronism. The works of Brahms are the tremendous and impassioned utterances of a prophet with no future to predict, with only the
splendours of the past to re-create and humbly worship. To the end of
his days he knew, not alone from inveterate modesty, but with cold,
critical certainty, that Beethoven and Mozart were his superiors. His
concertos live not because he alone mastered the impressive classical
structures of the past, but because as a true creator he found within
them the fabled treasures of the human spirit which are common property for all men in all ages.

CHAPTER VII

The Modern Concerto

Obackward nations to a position of the struggle of subject peoples for national liberation and the emergence of backward nations to a position of world importance. Nationalism in music is no longer a dated issue, as was so smugly supposed during the 1920's and 1930's. We know today how powerfully the national struggles of oppressed peoples can act upon the hearts and minds of millions. Then as now, the cause of national liberation engaged the urgent loyalties of composers, painters, and poets who, in so vital a matter, were no more and no less human than anyone else. National consciousness became as much a part of a composer's equipment as his knowledge of counterpoint, and he reflected it either directly through his use of folk tunes, or indirectly through a general tendency toward characteristic rhythms, moods, and tonalities.

The nineteenth-century concerto is hardly the place to look for the most typical expression of national music. The romantic concerto is too much a concert-hall display piece, too completely metropolitan an accomplishment; it pares itself down only with colossal condescension to the rustic rhythms, the simple emotionalism, and the naïve coloraturas of a folk tune. Folk elements often crop up merely as exotic curios designed to amuse the urban listener. In such cases they are reserved

for the finale, after the serious business of the concerto is done, just as
Spohr, for example, used Spanish folk tunes in the last movement of
his G minor violin concerto, Op. 28. Such finales are an entertaining
spot of melodic and rhythmic colour, rather than an impulsive capitulation to a deeply rooted national consciousness. However, there
were composers like Dvořák, Tschaikowsky, and Grieg who made
little ado over the easy manner in which they reflected their national
origins in their concertos. The distinctive coloration came through
naturally, and this, as Dvořák shrewdly insisted, was something quite
apart from the calculated use of a folk tune. Brahms fared better than
most in his use of Hungarian melodies and rhythms in a concerto finale,
for he had an honest love for folk idioms, virtuoso glitter was the least
important of his preoccupations and, above all, he could genuinely feel
a spacious symphonic movement that was both lusty and naïve.

It is notable that there are only two important violin concertos—
the Joachim *Hungarian* concerto and the Lalo *Symphonie Espagnole*—
which make a deliberate point of a national orientation. The first has
all but disappeared from the active repertoire, and the second, while
thoroughly entertaining, hardly pretends to be a profound work.
Pointedly enough, despite the titles of their concertos, Joachim is
clearly associated with the German and Lalo with the French school.
The Lalo *Symphonie Espagnole* (despite its title, a five-movement violin
concerto) is an excellent example of a nationalist idiom appropriated
for its picturesque qualities. It is a bravura piece composed for a great
virtuoso (Sarasate), and the pyrotechnics plus a clever use of piquant
rhythms and a highly coloured orchestra combine to place it as a species
of exotic entertainment, rather than as an expression of the cultural
consciousness of Spain.

By and large, nationalism in music expressed itself most comfortably
in musical-literary forms like the opera or the song. A text drawn from
folk sources or from national history afforded the composer a clear
opportunity to match a literary folk idiom with a musical one, or (as
in the case of a Smetana or a Mussorgsky opera) compelled the composer to draw upon the deepest resources of his national consciousness
in rendering a dramatic event in the history of his people, or in de-
picting a characteristically national way of life. In non-vocal forms it
was the programmatic symphonic poem, like Smetana's cycle *Ma*

Vlast (*My Country*), or characteristic dance forms like the polonaise and the mazurka, the *dumky* and the *furiant*, which enabled composers to tap the rich vein of folk-like melody and rhythm which was their natural heritage. In his concertos Chopin betrays his national origin solely in the finales, and there only occasionally. Music historians still often mistake him for a French composer; but in small dance forms such as the polonaise and the mazurka there is little secret either about his origin, his temperament, or his devoted allegiance. A folk tune will go very nicely in a concerto upon its first uncomplicated statement, but once it falls victim to virtuoso ornamentation and to a ponderous orchestral ritornel, its national flavour is necessarily adulterated and becomes shortly a distinctly secondary consideration. The nineteenth-century concerto, therefore, is not one of the main avenues of national expression, and there are only a few important concertos which bear the deepest earmarks of its influence.

Two of the concertos of Antonin Dvořák (1841–1904) are among the small group of genuinely national expressions in the form. They are Slavonic concertos not out of deliberate intent, but because, as his *New World* symphony demonstrates, Dvořák could scarcely turn out any piece of music, even one founded on foreign idioms, without a distinctly Slavonic coloration. This derived from his identification with the long and bitter tradition of Bohemia's battle for political and cultural independence. Dvořák grew up in the early victories which marked the modern history of this struggle, and while European influences subsequently touched him more deeply than they did Smetana, they were not strong enough to obliterate the background of embattled patriotism against which his earliest thinking and feeling were formed.

Dvořák's work, *The Heirs of White Mountain* (1873), was his first important success, which spoke eloquently for the fact that neither he nor his audiences had forgotten their own history. In 1620, Bohemia's national independence had been bombarded out of existence at the battle of the White Mountain. Prior to this, Bohemia's contribution to the body of European culture had been a consistently vital one and her men of learning received with merited respect in all parts of the civilized world. The loss of her independence was followed by the prohibition of her language, the consequent collapse of her national literature, and the exile or servitude of her artists, scientists, and scholars. For a century and a half thereafter Bohemia's cultural history is a record of near oblivion. In the latter half of the eighteenth century Bohemian musicians who won a name for themselves lived and worked outside their native land and, as in Dussek's case, frankly adopted the coloration of the country to which they emigrated. There were plenty of Bohemian composers, but their work formed an adjunct mainly of the dominant Austrian or German schools of music. Late in the eighteenth and during the first decades of the nineteenth century, a coalition of forces moving towards freedom of national cultural expression was once again becoming evident. Folk-lore is indestructible without the annihilation of a whole people, and it was therefore to the countryside that scholars repaired to relearn a language forgotten in the metropolitan institutions of learning. Poets rediscovered the true basis for a national literature, and folk idioms served to inspire the beginnings of a national music.

The appearance of Smetana (1824–84) furnished the growing movement with a leader equipped with energy, loyalty, and genius. His effort was deflected temporarily by the abortive national revolution of 1848 to which he rendered musical tribute. The stifling atmosphere of intolerance and suspicion directed against all patriots forced Smetana to emigrate to Sweden. A series of Italian victories (1859) compelled Austria to relax her iron-handed regime, and in October 1860 Bohemia won a measure of political and cultural freedom from the Hapsburgs. It was a heavily restricted freedom to be sure, yet sufficient to make possible such important cultural developments as a national theatre with plays and operas performed in the Czech language. Smetana's national operas are closely bound up with this development, and all Dvořák's music rooted in the broad and many-sided struggle which helped bring it about.

The Dvořák violin concerto was completed in 1879 and sent to Joachim for approval. "Joachim was so kind," writes Dvořák, "as to make over the solo part." A few finishing touches were added in 1880 and the work dedicated "to the great master Joseph Joachim with deepest respect." The year prior to its composition Dvořák was deeply absorbed in a series of intensely national works. "The national character of Dvořák's music," writes Ottokar Sourek, "became strongly marked when he began to make his appeal outside his own country, and felt impelled to emphasize his national origins and characteristics. This was about the beginning of 1878." The music composed during 1878 comprises the three *Slavonic Rhapsodies*, Op. 45, and a series of *Slavonic dances* (Op. 46). The sextet in A major, Op. 48, also composed that year, uses a *dumky* (a Slavonic lament) as a slow movement, and a *furiant* (a Czech folk dance) in place of a scherzo. A *Concert piece* ("Capriccio") for violin with piano or orchestra, of which only the violin-piano version survives, also dates from 1878, and "its affinity," writes Stefan, "with the immediately preceding Slavonic dances is apparent." During 1879, the year in which the violin concerto was composed, the stream of national music continued unabated. There was a *mazurek* for violin and small orchestra, Op. 49, a suite, Op. 39, comprising a group of Czech dances, the eminently Slavonic quartet in E-flat major, Op. 51, and the violin concerto in A minor, Op. 53.

At the very outset the violin concerto reveals the intensely national spirit which pervaded Dvořák's music during 1878–79. After a few bars of orchestral introduction the violin solo announces a melody characteristically Slavonic in intonation. The slow movement is quiet and lyrical with periodic interludes whose intensity is soon dispelled. The finale moves along on the impetus given it by sharp folk rhythms, which impart a charming Slavonic dance quality to the movement. Dvořák uses folk rhythms in the concerto without descending merely to the picturesque. The Slavonic coloration, which lends a poignant melancholy to some of the melodies, is free of sophisticated concert-hall exoticism, although not always of frank sentimentality. A thin coating of corrosive virtuoso glitter sometimes appears on the surface of the music; yet, by and large, Dvořák carries the concerto clear of the most dangerous pitfalls in the path of an attempt to unite brilliant virtuoso writing with an unsophisticated folk spirit. The concerto utilizes the post-classical first-movement design with the solo instrument engaged from the outset. The first two movements are merged together and performed continuously.

The 'cello concerto in B minor, Op. 104, a very much greater work, was composed during the last year of Dvořák's second visit to America. Unlike most of his music composed in America, there is no attempt to employ new-world idioms. The 'cello concerto is clearly and wonderfully Slavonic from the first bar to the last. Very likely, as Stefan believes, the finale "definitely expresses his jubilation over the approaching return to Bohemia." The first movement follows the general design of the classical sonata-form concerto with a spacious opening ritornel for orchestra and a second exposition for the soloist's restatement of the leading themes. The subsequent details are Dvořák's own, e.g. the foreshortened development and a recapitulation which proceeds contrariwise with the second subject prior to the first. It is not on this account superior to the loose post-classical design utilized in the violin concerto; but the 'cello concerto is much more effective in its organization and it is more consistently inspired. Dvořák's methods here, as in his best music, are totally unmysterious. Nevertheless, each of the transformations and restatements ring true; the simple devices are used with conviction, and their success is attended by an air of innocent splendour. For example, one of the calculated "surprises" of the design consists in marching the rather tender second subject in out of turn. To make the point clear, somewhat after the fashion of a man who will put a bold face on a timid defiance of convention, Dvořák summons his entire orchestra to bear this little melody in majesty. The device is wonderful because it really works, and however transparent his thinking we are impressed with his triumph. Conversely, the opening subject, muscular and robust, is transformed during the development into a beautiful cantilena for the 'cello. This comes off better than the dramatic treatments accorded this theme, although the dramatic moments are more successful here than in the violin concerto. (Dvořák's minor keys are energetic and are impelled with a genuinely athletic drive. He rarely languishes in this concerto in the way that Chopin and Mendelssohn do. Yet the minor keys are not, in Beethoven's sense, dramatic.) Perhaps it is the discreet nature of the solo instrument involved, but the virtuoso element is much more to the point here than in the violin concerto. When the 'cello first enters, the virtuoso figurations with which it adorns the initial subject have a genuine folk energy which flows directly out of the music itself. Later on in the development, when the cantilena is turned over to the winds, the 'cello weaves with rare discretion a beautiful sequence of scintillating arpeggios over the main melody. The movement is one of Dvořák's masterpieces, comparable to the best in his symphonic music. The slow movement, however, barely escapes being over-long. Dvořák can write a lovely melody and he provides us generously with samples of his talent. They are just sufficient to sustain interest to the very end, for this movement is not a model of tight thinking and economical utterance. The finale opens dramatically with a march rhythm sombrely predicting the first subject. The 'cello breaks in with one of its lusty and serious folk dances in a minor key (not all the dance ceremonials of the countryside are light-headed and gay). The movement bounds off into successions of sun and shade, vigour and calm, a brilliant virtuoso epigram and a relaxed lyric. The opening subject of the first movement returns towards the close. It hovers mournfully in the clarinets, but the movement picks up speed, and the work winds up with a tremolo, a fanfare, and a flourish. There is another 'cello concerto in A major, an early work composed in 1865, and a four-movement piano concerto in G minor which dates from 1876. The early 'cello concerto is negligible. The piano concerto, imbued with a sombre national coloration, is not a wholly successful undertaking.

There are hardly two nationalist composers more unlike than Dvořák and Grieg (1843–1907). Neither bothered much with the citation of traditional folk tunes, but there is genuine folk feeling in Dvořák and perhaps only a generalized air of nationalism in Grieg. Also Dvořák had greater energy and more discipline. He could fill a strong and spacious form with wide symphonic gestures and a broad-shouldered simplicity. Dvořák wrote nine symphonies, Grieg not one; and the Grieg piano concerto is notable not for its architectural strength, but for its warmth of melody and its feeling for harmonic colour. Grieg is much more of a sophisticate than Dvořák, and sometimes a rather precious one. He specializes in national mood coloration, in the atmospheric aspects of folk-lore. He prefers the subtle nuances of nationalism, for he is an eminently poetical creature; and while he admired the poetry of the people, in his own music there is a genteel lifting of skirts over a coarse rustic couplet. Folk song interested him deeply; not the idiom, but the "inner life." Both in Grieg and in Nordraak (who first opened to Grieg the attractive vistas of a national music) there is much vague talk about Northern, Norwegian, Scandinavian, the fresh air and the mountains. When Grieg got down to cases, he discussed the concise, earnest quality of Norwegian speech, its carefully guarded manner of registering the most agitated of "the heart's emotions," its ability "to say much in few words." He found in this an index to the character of a whole people. "One can say," he continued, "that in the same fashion the folk-song mirrors musically the inner life of the people." Björnson and Ibsen had built upon the qualities of a people's speech, and "what the poets have accomplished in this connection, I aspire to accomplish in music. . . ." Whatever Grieg's intentions, it can hardly be said that his piano concerto is especially guarded in its registering of the heart's emotions; nor, whatever its virtues, does it specialize in saying much in few words. The piano concerto is conceived in an expansively romantic spirit: brilliant, colourful, and warm. Neither concise utterance nor bluntness nor classical restraint are of its essence.

The Grieg piano concerto in A minor, Op. 16, composed during the summer of 1868, has proved his most consistently popular work apart from *Peer Gynt*. By the time of its creation several important projects (including his marriage) were already behind him; chief among them the foundation, with Rikard Nordraak, of a society for the performance and propagation of Scandinavian music. Grieg was already well launched on the search for a national music, and the concerto is imbued with as much Norwegian atmosphere as he could disseminate over the area of a large orchestral form. The Copenhagen premiere of the concerto was a huge success, which must have given him much gratification, for his in-laws had been complaining that "he *is* nothing, *has* nothing, and writes music no one will listen to." As a matter of fact the critics at home were not altogether receptive to the entire notion of a national music. The Norwegian upper classes suffered, as upper classes often do, from the smug variety of a national inferiority complex. For generations they accepted the standards of judgment which obtained on the continent and especially in Germany; and Grieg, like other Norwegian boys whose parents could stand the expense, was sent to the Conservatory of Leipzig at the age of fifteen to acquire a correct musical education. No doubt it was correct enough, but it was hardly the kind to train him for his later tasks. As he expressed it, he came "like a parcel stuffed with dreams," and returned convinced that he had "learned absolutely nothing." Once firmly set on the road towards a national music, he found much unprogressive

criticism in his path. Nordraak cautioned "calm, calm and again calm . . . towards those who until now have called themselves critics, however much reason they give for fury. . . ." The circle of enlightened musicians was still small. Hence the success of the concerto in Copenhagen (it failed miserably at first in Germany) must have been a decidedly pleasant change. However, his path thereafter was by no means smooth, and there remained always the attitude of a partisan in a holy cause both in his letters and in his music. Tschaikowsky, in appraising Grieg's music, had few comments to make which may be taken out of their general context and applied as a serviceable appreciation of the A minor concerto. "Perfection of form," writes Tschaikowsky, "strict and irreproachable logic in the development of his themes are not perseveringly sought after by the celebrated Norwegian. But what charm, what inimitable and rich musical imagery! What warmth and passion in his melodic phrases, what teeming vitality in his harmony, what originality and beauty in the turn of his piquant and ingenious modulations and rhythms, and in all the rest what interest, novelty, and independence! If we add to all this that rarest of qualities, a perfect simplicity, far removed from affectation and pretence to obscurity [this, incidentally, happens to be a dig at Brahms] and far-fetched novelty, it is not surprising that everyone should delight in Grieg."

The prose style is, of course, solid Tschaikowsky, for he works up a literary appreciation much as he does one of his symphonies. He does not pose his appreciation—as Schumann once did so delightfully— "ten paces away from the man himself, lest I should praise him too warmly to his face." Tschaikowsky's close enthusiasm notwithstanding, there are a few pertinent observations which, when toned down and applied to the piano concerto, may properly read something like this. The concerto does not persevere in formal perfection or in strict structural logic. Its charm, such as it is, is inimitable. Its melodies are warm, and its harmonies and rhythms piquant and pleasantly picturesque. There is a perfect simplicity to the concerto in the sense that it is a thoroughly obvious work and quite unlikely to challenge anyone's immediate understanding. (This, of course, is not Tschaikowsky's meaning.) Add to this the fact that it is a wonderful war horse for the virtuoso, and there is little reason why, with judicious periods of quiescence, this concerto should not continue a periodic favourite with millions.

Grieg considered himself a conscious exponent of nationalism; Tschaikowsky did not. Yet there is more citation of actual folk song in Tschaikowsky than in Grieg. Tschaikowsky made no particular point of the use of folk song or of national coloration, and he had no great sympathy for "The Five" (Balakirev, Borodin, Rimsky-Korsakov, Cui, and Mussorgsky) whose aim was the constitution of a national music. Tschaikowsky was a cosmopolitan and an eclectic who drew both from Russian folk song and from the main stream of western European romanticism whose prime representative he is in Russian music.

Tschaikowsky derived much of his eclecticism and his respect for the mannerisms of western European music from his teacher Anton Rubinstein (1829–94). Rubinstein founded the Petersburg Conservatory in the hope of achieving for the Russian musician a professional and social status. "Evidently the name and estate of a musician, universally acknowledged in other lands," he wrote, "had in Russia no clearly defined meaning. Who was Glinka after all? A landowner, a nobleman in the government of Smolensk. Serov? An official in the Post Office Department. . . ." He discovered "that a man who had adopted music as his profession had no recognized position in Russia as a musician pure and simple." Feudalism survived late in Russia; thus to the aristocracy, who had appropriated music as a privileged entertainment, a musician was either a distinguished foreign prima donna or a domestic servant. Rubinstein graduated his pupils with the degree of Bachelor of Music and bestowed upon them the honourable title of Free Artist.

With regard to musical aims, Rubinstein cared little for the nationalism of Mussorgsky and the famous Five. His entire effort was to bring Russian music closer to the western European tradition, and he preached a cosmopolitanism which went well with his own European success as a virtuoso. Tschaikowsky called him the "Tsar of pianists," and Liszt, who was growing old, was his only European rival. Rubinstein's piano concertos were the first Russian concertos to win acclaim in the concert halls of Europe. They had sufficient national coloration to make them interesting and were cosmopolitan enough to prove

palatable to western European taste. Moreover Rubinstein's performances were probably magnificent enough to convince most people
that his concertos were music of the first importance. Tschaikowsky
always bore toward him something of the reverence of a pupil toward
a master. "Can I compare myself to him?" he wrote. "He is the first
pianist of our time. In Rubinstein great virtuosity is united with grea
talent for composition, and the first carries the second. I shall never in
my life achieve a tenth of what Rubinstein has achieved, because he
begins by being the greatest virtuoso of our time." His piano concertos
are evidence both of his virtuosity and of his great talent; but, as
Tschaikowsky remarks, the first carries the second, which is reason
enough for their disappearance from the active repertoire.

Tschaikowsky (1840–93) also disassociated himself from the aggres-
sive Russianism of "The Five." He disapproved of narrow nationalism and moreover, as a Rubinstein pupil, he was duly sceptical of their
lack of professional training as composers. They in turn thought him
an eclectic who had sold his birthright for a mess of pure (e.g. western
European) beauty. In truth, there is in Tschaikowsky a strong tendency toward French salon refinement which, as we learn from the
novels of Tolstoy and Turgenev, was one of the aberrations of the
Russian aristocracy. It minces prettily in the more elegant measures of
his music and parades its utterly sensitive soul in his critical appraisals.
Mussorgsky's aggravated national consciousness derived from what in
those days was a startling discovery, i.e. that the Russian peasant was a
human being and a true type of humanity. Tschaikowsky discovered
no such thing, although he was not above borrowing a beautiful folk
tune, e.g. the first movement of his first piano concerto, the finale of
his fourth symphony, the andante cantabile of his first string quartet,
his second symphony, etc. According to Tschaikowsky, Mussorgsky
"was altogether too deeply impregnated with the absurd theories of
his little circle." The "absurd theories" held that a true national music
was founded on folk song, on the life, the history and the legends of
the people. Moreover, declared Tschaikowsky, Mussorgsky "belongs
. . . to a rather low type, which loves what is coarse, unpolished, and
ugly. . . . He is in love with his own lack of culture and seems to be
proud of his ignorance." Tschaikowsky's evaluation is manifestly too
refined to permit his own variety of nationalism to be based on genuine

folk consciousness. His nationalism is not of the deliberate, manifesto-making variety. It is instinctive, part of his heritage, and it comes through sufficiently in his concertos to preclude mistaking them for anything but the work of a Russian. Neither Mussorgsky's folk nationalism nor Tschaikowsky's cultured and international eclecticism are in themselves sufficient to ensure or preclude the creation of important music. The bedrock of essential humanity can be tapped or ignored by either method. Mussorgsky dug down to it through a broad social identification with the humiliated of the earth, with the poor in purse, and the proud in spirit. "To feed upon humanity," he wrote, "as upon a healthy diet which has been neglected . . . there lies the whole problem of art." Tschaikowsky fed only upon himself, yet he reached into the recesses of his own being deeply enough to touch that modicum of common humanity which is each man's private and inalienable possession.

The Tschaikowsky concertos enjoy the particular virtues and suffer from the specific defects of his music generally. Here as elsewhere his inspiration is sometimes interrupted. "In such cases," he wrote, "I am often compelled to fall back upon cold calculation, upon technical ingenuity. Even with the greatest masters the thread of organic unity has failed them and artistic craftsmanship has been called upon to mend the seams and bind the work as a whole together. That cannot be avoided. If what is called inspiration . . . were to possess the artist's soul uninterrupted, one could not survive it even for a single day. The strings would snap and the instrument fall to pieces. It is indispensable only that the basic idea and the general outline of the work are not arrived at by searching, but appear spontaneously as the result of that unanalyzable, supernatural power called inspiration." The motivating force in the concertos is inspirational enough, but sometimes, particularly in the first movement of the violin concerto, it is evident that "the thread of organic unity has failed"; there is much mending of seams and a patchwork solution of the design. Toward the end of his life Tschaikowsky had the insight to see, and the candour to confess, that his work "has always a mountain of padding," and that he laboured under an "inability to grasp and manipulate form in music." This goes for the concertos as well as for his music generally. The criticism embodies substantial truth, and it is just as well that it was Tschaikowsky who uttered it.

Comparisons with Beethoven or with Mozart (who was his most consistent enthusiasm) are useless, for they will only reveal a weakness already admitted, and tend to obscure Tschaikowsky's profound understanding of the rarest of artistic mysteries: the secret of direct communication. There is no difficulty in following Tschaikowsky or in feeling with him. Nothing stands between his music and a listener but a matter of personal taste; hence for someone who agrees with the quality of Tschaikowsky's emotion, there will hardly be a more satisfying composer. For the last several decades audiences have been engaging in much comfortable soul searching via Tschaikowsky, although in recent years a species of sophisticate has appeared who takes on over Tschaikowsky's music as though it were intended as a personal insult. No doubt it is just as well that modern music (despite one of Stravinsky's less admirable aberrations) is, by and large, little indebted to Tschaikowsky. Soul searching is a wonderful thing, but sound craft happens to be the least dispensable basis for a vigorous tradition. Nevertheless, modern music can learn from Tschaikowsky's ability to convey without circumlocution the power of a deeply felt emotion. As a matter of fact there probably is not an honest composer who would not auction his immortal soul, or at least put it in pawn, for precisely this gift. It is a mark of fundamental genius, whatever one may think of his music; and because of it his first piano concerto is, at the moment, *the* piano concerto so far as millions of serious music lovers are concerned.

The first piano concerto in B-flat minor, Op. 23, was composed during November and December of 1874, and the orchestration completed the following February. It is among the first of Tschaikowsky's important creations, for of his compositions prior to this only the *Romeo and Juliet* overture-fantasia equals it in importance and in popularity. Between *Romeo and Juliet* and the piano concerto fall his first two string quartets, Op. 11, 22, the second symphony, and a symphonic fantasy entitled *The Tempest*. This, taken together with several early and unsuccessful operas and the rather immature first symphony, scarcely constitutes a remarkable accomplishment for a thirty-four-year-old composer, if we apply the standards of a Schubert who died at thirty-one or a Mozart who died at thirty-five. By comparison, Tschaikowsky relied much upon inspirational seizures and little on instinctive craft. His early work, in consequence, is often awkward and he achieved the full expression of his talent only after years of tortured trial and error.

The history of first impressions is a notoriously dismal one, and Tschaikowsky's first piano concerto was accorded its share of incomprehension by Nicholas Rubinstein, to whom it was first submitted. Tschaikowsky tells the story as follows:

"In December 1874 I had written a piano Concerto! Not being a pianist, I considered it necessary to consult a virtuoso as to any point in my Concerto which might be technically impracticable, unprofitable or ineffective. I had need of a severe critic, but at the same time one friendly disposed towards me. Without going into trivialities, I must admit that an inner voice protested against my selection of Rubinstein to judge the mechanical part of my work. However, he was not only the best pianist in Moscow, but undeniably a musician of great distinction, and I also felt sure that he would take offence if he should learn that I had passed him over and shown the Concerto to another pianist. Therefore I decided to ask him to hear the Concerto and make his observations concerning the solo part."

Tschaikowsky might have added that he had reason to regard Rubinstein as a firm friend. Some nine years previously, he had come to Moscow young and unknown as a teacher of harmony in Nicholas Rubinstein's newly organized conservatoire. Rubinstein was a brilliant pianist, the possessor of a family name which he, and more especially his brother Anton, had made known throughout Europe. Moreover, he was the founder of a conservatory in one of Russia's two major cities. He had received his young subordinate with a friendliness and a solicitude which caused Tschaikowsky to declare that Rubinstein had cared for him almost as a nurse. Rubinstein replenished his wardrobe, provided him with a bedroom in his own house; in short, gave every evidence of that generous concern, maintained throughout the succeeding years, upon which Tschaikowsky relied in presenting his piano concerto for inspection. To continue with Tschaikowsky's story:

"On Christmas Eve 1874 we were invited to Albrecht's, and Nikolai Gregorievich [Rubinstein] proposed before going there that we should play the Concerto through in one of the classrooms of the Conservatoire. We did so. . . .

"I played the first movement. Not a word, not an observation. If you only knew how uncomfortably foolish one feels when one places before a friend a dish one has prepared with one's own hands, and he eats thereof and—is silent. At least say something; if you like, find fault in a friendly way, but, for heaven's sake, speak—say something, no matter what! But Rubinstein said nothing; he was preparing his thunder. . . . I took patience and played the Concerto to the end. Again silence.

" 'Well?' said I, as I arose. Then sprang forth a vigorous stream of words from Rubinstein. At first he spoke quietly, but by degrees his passion rose, and finally he resembled Zeus hurling thunderbolts. It appeared that my Concerto was worthless and absolutely unplayable, that the passages were manufactured and withal so clumsy as to be beyond correction, that the composition itself was bad, trivial and commonplace, that I had stolen this point from somebody and that one from somebody else, that only two or three pages had any value, and all the rest should be either destroyed or entirely remodelled. 'For example, that! What is that, really?' (and the offending passage would be caricatured at the piano). 'And that? How is it possible?' etc., etc. I cannot reproduce what was worst, the accent or the voice with which Nikolai Gregorievich said all this. In short, an unbiased spectator of the scene could only have thought I was a stupid, untalented and conceited spoiler of music paper, who had had the impertinence to show his rubbish to a celebrated man. . . . I left the room without a word and went upstairs. I was so excited and angry that I could not speak. Soon afterwards Rubinstein came up to me, and seeing that I was very depressed, called me into another room. There he repeated that my Concerto was impossible and pointed to several places which required a thorough revision, adding that if these alterations were completed within a certain fixed time, he would play my Concerto in public. I replied that I would not alter a single note, and that I would have the Concerto printed exactly as it then stood. That is, in fact, what I have done."

Rubinstein subsequently acknowledged himself mistaken, threw himself into a careful study of the work, and became its foremost exponent throughout Russia and Europe. Rubinstein's strictures, however, may have had some effect, for despite his vow never to alter a note of the concerto, Tschaikowsky did undertake a fairly considerable revision of the piano part for the 1889 edition.

The work opens with a majestic four-bar preamble, the horns sounding the first four notes of the melody to follow. The piano enters with a series of sonorous chords while the orchestra continues with a full statement of the melody. Solo and orchestra are from the outset locked in their famous "duel." The entire opening carries the principle of concerto opposition nearly as far as a composer dare, for the piano keeps crashing away quite oblivious of the orchestra's effort to make itself heard. From the way the concerto is usually performed, the pianist apparently reasons that since he is soon to repeat the melody anyway, there is little need for the audience to hear it first in the orchestra. The conductor, however, keeps arguing that the orchestra got the melody first, and he intends to make the most of it while he can. There is a battle royal for a while; which is as it should be, for this, after all, is a concerto. However, since solo and orchestra must live together, they settle their grievances as best they can. Presumably the truce was drawn over a bottle of vodka, for when the main subject of the movement finally shows up (*allegro con spirito*), the piano prances off with it in a series of slightly intoxicated octaves. The melody is a folk tune which Tschaikowsky once heard blind beggars sing at a village fair. The second movement is a combination of a slow movement and a scherzo. It opens with one of Tschaikowsky's *dolcissimo* inspirations announced by the flute. Piano and orchestra are dutifully melancholy and meditative, although, after a while, the piano scrambles off *prestissimo* for a bit of leg-stretching. The orchestra leaves the cavorting to the piano; for itself, it is content with a pleasant song. The piano wanders unaccompanied back to its devotions, turning a final handspring, discreetly and pianissimo, on the way. Returned to its meditations, the movement lingers through a few repetitions of the opening melody, and after the piano completes a sequence of broken chords it subsides in peace. The finale opens with the orchestra throwing a challenge from the string section to the winds. The piano responds with a dynamic dance measure which it tosses off with stunning agility. The two are well matched, for the piano flaunts a brilliant virtuoso part while the orchestra counters with massed sonorities and sheer tonal power.

There are several other works by Tschaikowsky for piano and orchestra which are all but forgotten. There is a second piano concerto in G major, Op. 44, composed early in 1880 and dedicated to Nicholas

Rubinstein. It has never been performed with any notable success. The third piano concerto was originally a discarded symphony sketched in May 1892 (a year before his death). Tschaikowsky reworked only the sketches for the first movement of the symphony, and these he shaped together into the first movement of a piano concerto in E-flat major, Op. 75. After his death the unorchestrated sketches for the two remaining movements of the discarded symphony were discovered among his manuscripts. These were reworked by Taneiev for piano and orchestra and appended to the one-movement concerto in E-flat. There is, in addition, a rather effective two-movement concert fantasy, Op. 56, for piano and orchestra composed in 1884, which at one time enjoyed considerable popularity.

The violin concerto in D major, Op. 35, composed in 1878, ranks beside the first piano concerto as Tschaikowsky's most important contribution to the form. The famous canzonetta which serves for its slow movement is, of course, known to every violinist and is an excellent example of Tschaikowsky in one of his sweet and elegantly melancholy moods. The first movement stumbles somewhat over its own scaffolding but, by and large, it manages to hold together. There is not an over-supply of the grand Tschaikowskian passion in the two outside movements. There is much of his inevitable melancholia in the first movement; yet it runs not to the dejected heroisms of the *Pathétique*, but to an expensively styled and well-tailored mournfulness. The last two movements are merged together, with an orchestral preface and a solo recitative before the finale really gets under way. The finale is a brilliant and difficult virtuoso movement like the first. Apart from the canzonetta, which is straightforward lyricism, the concerto is an emotionalized display piece calculated to win the everlasting loyalties of the virtuoso who can master its particular difficulties.

The two famous Tschaikowsky concertos are neither notably traditional nor experimental in form. The first piano concerto follows the general post-classical design in eliminating the opening orchestral ritornel, while the violin concerto, on the contrary, restores it in a foreshortened form. Nothing so advanced as the merging together of all movements into a continuous unit, or the cyclical process of recollecting or progressively transforming themes from movement to movement, occurs in either concerto. In the violin concerto the canzonetta leads directly to the finale; but that procedure is as old as Beethoven.

With Rimsky-Korsakov, Glazounov, and Medtner, however, there is a noticeable attempt to do something with the concerto form. The piano concerto in C-sharp minor, Op. 30, of Rimsky-Korsakov (1844–1908)—though heavily Russian in melody, mood, and general coloration—derives from Liszt both in its structure and in its grand virtuoso style. The work is in one movement with an allegro, an allegretto quasi polacca, an andante, and a final allegro, providing a succession of sectionalized contrasts.

Alexander Glazounov (1865–1936) was a pupil of Rimsky-Korsakov and he had also met and admired Liszt. The one-movement form adopted by both appears also in Glazounov's famous violin concerto, Op. 82. The work, composed in 1904, utilizes an idiom that is conservative and palatable; and makes, once again, the Tschaikowskian point that a Russian melody can comport itself with social grace amid elegantly cosmopolitan surroundings. The concerto strikes many of the early twentieth-century attitudes which most modern composers no longer find worth-while. It deals mainly with expiring passions; and for all its glitter, it is essentially soft. Even the cadenzas languish somewhat; the violinist lingers over his double-stopping and he indulges in mysterious forebodings via the routine tremolo on the G-string. The brilliant military movement which follows the cadenza is promising, but it too softens in time. The concerto is an excellent sample of the urbane turn-of-the-century habit of crossing melancholia with virtuoso brilliance. It accomplishes its specific task with skill and with honesty, and it should always prove popular with audiences who admire the nearly defunct tradition of good manners, brilliance, and obvious poetical feeling. In his F minor piano concerto, Op. 92, Glazounov utilizes a somewhat unusual design. It is in two movements, the second a series of variations upon a quiet and pliable theme. The first variation is untitled, but from the second to the eighth they are labelled respectively *chromatica, eroica, lyrica, intermezzo, quasi una fantasia, mazurka,* and *scherzo.* The ninth variation serves as the finale and works up the variation theme in conjunction with melodies recollected from the first movement. It is not a separate movement, but it distinguishes itself from the preceding variations as a final summing up of the entire concerto. (The opening melody of the first movement is, incidentally, a sober and slightly modernized version of one of the melodies in Liszt's first piano concerto.) The Medtner piano concerto in G minor, Op. 33, was composed in 1918. The date need not be taken too seriously for Medtner is a gentle soul with a rare feeling for carefully contrived and quietly spoken consonances. The structure of the work is curious, for it is a classicist's attempt to solve a post-classical form. Brahms did not resolve the post-classical dilemma. He dismissed it and restored to his concertos the general framework of the traditional classical design. Medtner accepted the one-movement structure of Liszt's A major and Rimsky-Korsakov's C-sharp minor concertos, combined it with the variation technique of Glazounov's F minor piano concerto, and organized both experiments along the lines of a classic sonata form movement. The concerto "consists, broadly speaking," writes Medtner, "of an exposition, a series of variations [nine of them,] on the two chief themes, constituting the development, and then the recapitulation." A short piano cadenza falls between the exposition and the variation-development section. Thus we are given a classical sonata-form movement combined with an experimental one-movement design; also, a traditional three-movement division implied, but not explicitly stated, by the three main sections of a sonata-form movement (the cadenza, for example, occurs at the end of the exposition or first main section, corresponding to its usual appearance at the end of the first of the three traditional concerto movements). The structure is uniquely classical and experimental. Like a Picasso, it compresses several angles of vision at once. Unlike Picasso, its modernism is only formal and not idiomatic.

The four piano concertos of Sergei Rachmaninoff (1873–1943) are the last stages of the line of descent which runs from Anton Rubinstein through Tschaikowsky and Glazounov. The concertos of this branch of the Russian family tree are all marked by the same urbane and indelible nationalism, the same international concert-hall orientation, the same sophisticated lack of interest in a distinctively national folk spirit. Glazounov and Rachmaninoff bring this specific tradition to an end, for, the dates of their deaths notwithstanding, they belong, with Rubinstein and Tschaikowsky, to the nineteenth century. In his later music Rachmaninoff was ever so gently touched by the more

advanced idioms of the day; yet he remained wedded to accepted
and more or less familiar patterns of musical expression. His concertos
are composed with a conservatism that is intelligent and sincere. For
this precise reason the vast majority of modern listeners have accepted
him as their contemporary. Like his audiences, whose taste was also
largely formed on late nineteenth-century music, Rachmaninoff was
capable of slow growth and retarded adaptation to newer idioms. There
is a close parallel between Rachmaninoff's development as a composer
and the slow reorientation of average musical taste. Rachmaninoff was
always aware of the untraditional inflections in modern musical speech;
so were his audiences. Several decades after their first appearance, certain of the inflections began to emerge in his music; and by that time
audiences were already accustomed to them. Rachmaninoff's slow
thinking kept pace with average appreciation. He was never ahead of
the majority of his audience and rarely behind it. Thus his music was,
and still is, inevitably popular.

The process whereby popularity derives from an undesigned coin-
cidence between the progress of a composer and the progress of average taste is a profound and ever-recurring phenomenon. Advanced
composers are impatient with it, as they have a right to be, for so slow
a development retards the merited appreciation of their own music.
However, the advance guard among critics who fail to consider it a
part of the definition of such terms as "modern" and "contemporaneity" are snobbish and, in point of fact, mistaken. It is beside the
point that history, in all probability, will validate the judgment that
the Rachmaninoff concertos are dated, not only in idiom and style,
but in content and emotion. (For the future, content and emotion are
the crux of the question. It is unlikely that Rachmaninoff will ever be
rediscovered as a "modern" the way, at the moment, Gesualdo, Bach,
Mozart, and late Beethoven are.) Slang ultimately becomes the King's
English (also vice versa as, for example, several favourite Anglo-Saxon-
isms); and a standard dictionary, like a Rachmaninoff concerto, always
pays its pontifical respects a decade or more too late. It is a catching-up
with the past, and it is a contemporary phenomenon for the incon-
trovertible reason that it happens always in the present. For most
people a standard dictionary is, with reason, a contemporary document; and for most audiences, so is a Rachmaninoff concerto. Both

are useful as guides, not to experimental idioms, but to currently accepted usage. There is nothing more useless, or in its own way more charming, than an outdated dictionary or a concerto by Hummel, Bruch, Elgar, or Saint-Saëns. The dictionaries of our time, Rachmaninoff, Sibelius, and Richard Strauss, have proved instructive to millions. Like all good dictionaries, they are compendious, wordy, repetitive (a dozen excellent ways of saying the same thing), in part obsolete, and also well informed in rare and rather precious constructions. Our children will buy themselves new dictionaries, which, ironically enough, will certainly be compiled by our present specialists in untraditional speech. Many of the old usages will carry over, but the general make-up will be different enough to mark a new era, not only in verbal expression, but in ideas and emotions expressed.

Apart from the bedraggled prelude in C-sharp minor, the second piano concerto in C minor, Op. 18, is Rachmaninoff's most famous creation. The work was composed (1901) after he had emerged from an especially severe attack of the pessimism and lethargy which were much cultivated by the upper-class Russian intelligentsia about the turn of the century. The restitution of his will to compose required the services of a Dr. Dahl who managed to cure him by the use of autosuggestion. The concerto is gratefully dedicated to Dr. Dahl. The work is filled with an impassioned melancholia, a Russian coloration combined with a brilliant solo part thrown in relief against a sonorous orchestration. The first piano concerto in F-sharp minor, Rachmaninoff's official Op. 1 composed in 1890–91, was revised during the historic upheavals of October 1917. In the revision, according to Riemann, "hardly one note was left in its place. In its present form it may no longer be classed with the composer's early work, but must be placed between the Third and Fourth Piano Concertos . . . the new setting has left little more of the old Concerto than a few of the most beautiful themes, which have, however, retained all the charm and freshness of their youth." One of the unique features of the work is the cadenza which is firmly woven into the fabric of the first movement, emerging as a logical outgrowth of what has gone before. The third concerto in D minor, Op. 30, composed especially for his first American visit (1909), carries the integration of the cadenza one step further. As the cadenza unfolds, flute, oboe, clarinet, and horn each takes up a variant of the main subject. The piano goes off into typical virtuoso work, but the principle of collating solo and orchestra during a cadenza is an interesting one. The fourth concerto in G minor, Op. 40, is, like the first, a revision, although apparently not so extensive. It was originally composed in 1926 and reworked during the summer of 1941. The recasting is said to affect mainly the orchestration. As in his other concertos, Rachmaninoff uses a generously spaced style of melody, a sombre coloration, and a brilliant piano part (especially in the finale). There are several mannerisms here to be met with in the concertos as a whole, e.g. the habit of surrounding a broad melody sung in the deep, rich voices of the orchestra, by the arabesque-like caperings of the soloist. Sometimes the orchestra indulges in vague forebodings, but the piano keeps decorating every mood that comes its way.

Rachmaninoff and Paderewski (1860–1941) are the last of the great turn-of-the-century tradition of composer-pianists. The piano concerto in A minor, Op. 17, by Ignace Jan Paderewski, composed in 1888–89, is less individual in idiom than the Rachmaninoff concertos. It leans heavily upon Chopin, especially in the slow movement. There is much sophisticated nostalgia in this movement, and also an odd folkish lilt which saves it from sentimentality. The concerto, as a whole, is written with discretion and skill. The finale runs to virtuoso display, but the opening movement is earnestly national in feeling.

We turn back now to pick up the thread of those late nineteenth- and early twentieth-century concertos which fall outside the confines of specifically nationalist music. The concertos of Saint-Saëns, Chausson, Bruch, Goldmark, Elgar, etc., are too varied and personalized to form a definable school of concerto thought; yet, generally speaking, they may be grouped as a coherent bloc of cautious liberals, or of enlightened conservatives. The formal experimentations of the earlier romantics are impressed upon each with greater or lesser indelibility; yet in the style and content of their musical speech, they maintained a clear distance from the progressive and radical idioms which were already emerging in their day. Their conservatism was idiomatic rather than structural, and in this they differed from a consciously uncompromising traditionalist like Brahms. Brahms represents the apex of the classicist revival, the counter-attack from the right in its most logical form. He knew his task deliberately and in detail; he maintained a consistent effort from his first piano sonata to his last symphony and concerto; and his accomplishment was marked with true eloquence and undeniable genius. Saint-Saëns represents a counter-current of a less important and more common variety. Brahms dedicated his life to a noble undertaking. Saint-Saëns simply lived too long. This was surely not his fault, and no one would seriously begrudge him his years; but he aggravated an historical accident by a belligerent habit of poking younger men in the ribs. His conservatism was not structural or organic like Brahms's; he formed his early style among the romantic radicals and his concertos, in the main, are in the tradition of the dissident post-classical form. However, the world changed while Saint-Saëns did not; and in his later years, the one-time radical seemed more a vestigial survival than a consistent conservative such as Brahms had ever been. Saint-Saëns, incidentally, was two years younger than Brahms, and survived him by twenty-four years.

In 1835 when Saint-Saëns was born, Rossini's *William Tell* was still recent history; in 1921, when Saint-Saëns died, Stravinsky's *Sacre du Printemps* was fast becoming ancient history. Saint-Saëns remained Saint-Saëns; hence in his youth he was a radical and in his later years a bulwark of conservatism. In the 1860's Berlioz, the apostle of the romantic revolution, the anathema of musical officialdom, sanctified Saint-Saëns as "one of the greatest musicians of our time." Liszt and Von Bülow added their praises; but by 1907 times had changed, and the distinguished American critic, Henry Krehbiel, advised the musical world to hold fast to Saint-Saëns (the "old moorings") until the "turbulent and aimless wanderings of today are over." The aimless wanderers were then Richard Strauss, César Franck, and Claude Debussy, and against their musical theories and practices Saint-Saëns directed many a wrong-headed and well-written polemic. Saint-Saëns lived to see Strauss, Franck, and Debussy supplant him as the "old moorings" toward which the timid beat a terrorized retreat, when a new horde of "turbulent and aimless" wanderers—Stravinsky, Milhaud, Hindemith, Honegger, and Schönberg—descended upon the musical world.

The phrase "outlived his time" is, no doubt, a singularly inhuman and ineffectual way to pass post-mortem judgment; for it is equivalent to telling the dead composer that he might have had the decency to die sooner. There is a kinder and more generous way of saying the same thing. As Romain Rolland phrases it: "M. Saint-Saëns has had the rare honour of becoming a classic during his lifetime." It takes more courage, more artistic integrity than is at first apparent for a composer to become a classic during his own lifetime. Among other things, it means that, immune to praise or censure, he was able to evolve a musical vocabulary completely natural to him; a personal language through which he could always express himself honestly and with ease. "I take very little notice of either praise or censure," wrote Saint-Saëns, "not because I have an exalted idea of my own merits (which would be foolish), but because in doing my work, and fulfilling the function of my nature, as an apple tree grows apples, I have no need to trouble myself with other people's views." Even Debussy, who used Saint-Saëns's conservatism as a grindstone for his wit, thought such honesty worthy of a tribute. "M. Saint-Saëns," he wrote, "is uncompromising in a contrary sense. . . . Whilst others are uncompromising in order to demolish everything, he is so only in order to preserve everything. His masters bequeathed to him formulas which he considers good, and the respect he holds them in prevents him from wishing to make any change in them. I do not think he should be blamed for this. I see in it evidence of an artistic clairvoyance which is rare enough in our day when many things change their name without achieving any other appreciable result. To be conscious of one's effort is undeniable proof of artistic honesty (La Fontaine has a fable on the subject)."

The ten concertos of Saint-Saëns (five for piano, three for violin, and two for 'cello) fall between 1858 and 1902, his twenty-third and his sixty-seventh years. The first 'cello concerto in A minor, Op. 33 (1873), is designed in three contrasted movements that are run together and performed continuously as one. Both the second 'cello concerto in D minor, Op. 119 (1902), and the fourth piano concerto in C minor, Op. 44 (1875), are constructed with only one break, so that the sequence of movements falls into two main sections. Each section is a continuous unit and embodies within itself two or more well-defined quasi movements contrasted in key, tempo, and mood. In the fourth piano concerto, for example, the first main section comprises an allegro and an andante; then, following the break, the second main section resumes with an allegro vivace linked to an andante which, in turn, merges into the final allegro. Saint-Saëns uses a semicyclical method of construction to tie the main sections together. The second 'cello concerto is an especially clear example, for the finale which follows the cadenza is organized mainly as a recapitulation of the main subject of the first movement.

The first 'cello concerto still clings to the 'cellist's active repertoire somewhat more tenaciously than the third violin concerto in B minor, Op. 61 (1880), does to the violinist's, or the second, fourth, and fifth piano concertos to the pianist's current concerto programme. It is a decidedly pleasant work, although it is a moot question whether its high standing is due to the comparative paucity of important 'cello concertos or solely to its own intrinsic merit. The third violin concerto in B minor was, until recent years, a great favourite with audiences and violinists alike. The concerto is replete with all Saint-Saëns's engaging glitter, and its dramatic gestures are of an eminently unperturbing variety. The dramatic challenges in all the Saint-Saëns concertos are engrossing enough in performance, but they will scarcely haunt us thereafter. Saint-Saëns is ever a gentleman, pleasant, serious, and polite; he will insist upon a moment of our attention and not trouble us beyond the final bar. Also, like a less memorable Mark Tapley, he would be an earnest philosopher, only cheerful optimism always seems to break through. The second piano concerto in G minor, Op. 22 (1868), which Liszt enjoyed so much, still affords casual entertainment. The piano virtuosity is of a pleasantly sentimental sort. Saint-Saëns likes to languish over his runs, to splurge a bit of bravura over a melancholy tune. He postures somewhat in the middle of a grand passion, and his phrases wind up with a dying and sometimes with a drooping fall. His lighter moments are light in every sense; his gaieties manufactured out of a few vigorous orchestral accents, a sustained rhythm, and a shower of bright, soloistic figurations. The C minor piano concerto has several pleasantly pathetic melodies and much scintillating small talk. However, his sentiment is sometimes sticky and the fancy virtuoso ornamentations often in bad taste. The Saint-Saëns concertos are all well dressed and rather expensively bespangled, but this concerto seems to have been in a hurry to get to the concert hall and a cheap variety of rhinestone was apparently picked up in haste. It is rather a pity, for the orchestra's first stated intentions are commendably high-minded. However, as the work proceeds the inevitable, optimistic lilt and the cheap pianistic finery combine to defeat the orchestra. The orchestra is an easy prey to soloistic machinations, for the Saint-Saëns piano concertos are mainly fluent solo pieces artfully posed against an orchestral background.

Ernest Chausson (1853–99) is another non-classicist conservative content to talk quietly about a bold and free concerto form. Chausson was a pupil of César Franck and he learned, as all Franck pupils, to work both with freedom and with care. Chausson's creative activity falls within a difficult period in French music. Schumann was only a remembered enthusiasm among the French, and Debussy had not yet arrived. In the interim Saint-Saëns provided sustenance too insubstantial for an alert mind; and from both the teachings of César Franck and the Wagnerian tide which washed over French music, Chausson shaped the elements of his timid and highly personal style. The Chausson *Poème*, Op. 25, for violin and orchestra, an extended one-movement work, is his best-known composition. It is not free of stylistic clichés, but it boasts a rhapsodical lyricism that is deeply felt and distinctly his own. The concerto in D major for violin, piano, and string quartet, Op. 21 (1890–91), has the Chausson mixture of the traditional and the unique. As a piece of chamber music (a sextet), it exhibits the customary four-movement form. Chausson's inspiration is entirely lyrical and his gestures always restrained. A tender *sicilienne*, for example, serves in place of a scherzo. The slow movement (the third) is the finest of the four. It opens with a sober chromatic passage in the low register of the piano over which the violin begins a quiet and impassioned song. The chromatic motive is heard again at the close, where its solemn descent through the registers of the piano provides a simple and effective contrast to a sequence of sustained harmonies in the strings. The solo violin and piano are given more prominence than the individual members of the quartet; but there is no virtuoso work, and even in the finale the animated figurations are motivated by an un-concerto-like reserve. However, the division between two disproportionate bodies, a solo duo and a quartet, is sufficient to establish the original and fundamental conception of a concerto. Chausson's non-dramatic lyricism counsels him to forego head-on clashes between the two, and also to surrender the soloists' prerogatives to display. Even when the two soloists perform apart from the quartet, their conversation is in the nature of a double sonata rather than in the style of a solo interlude in a double concerto. In short, the work is a chamber sextet organized upon the ancient and essential concerto principle of the coalescing of two unequal and contrasted bodies of tone. During the nineteenth century the word "concerto" came to mean a specific form of inequality and contrast, i.e. between solo and orchestra; as well as a specific kind of soloistic display, i.e. directed towards large audiences in large places. Chausson simply cut away the superstructure of nineteenth-century meaning and founded his design upon first principles.

There are few things so radical as reviving the forgotten meaning of a word, and thus the Chausson concerto is unique amid its surroundings. It is unnecessary to suppose that Chausson came upon the form out of a passion for experimentation or a compelling need to stand alone. He used the form because it suited the lyricism and the modesty of his temperament, and he called it a concerto because he knew the essential meaning of the word. His idiom is likewise modest, although it is much less original. Chausson was largely content with the vocabulary of his contemporaries, and he shunned those modernisms which only the next generation might completely comprehend. However, within the general confines of accepted musical speech, he discovered fine nuances of meaning. His subtle and personalized inflections were sharp enough to disconcert the most grimly conservative ears of the period, but they were hardly striking enough to command the attention of the Debussyist generation to follow. Debussy wrought a major revolution in French music, and some two or three decades ago French critics felt the need to apologize for still finding pleasure in Chausson. His music has been overtaken by the fate which afflicts all timid and sincere creations. He was a composer of distinction who spoke with tenderness, clarity, and quiet eloquence. Apart from the *Poème*, Op. 25, the concerto, Op. 21, and the symphony in B-flat, Op. 20, his music is all but forgotten.

The violin concertos of Carl Goldmark (1830–1915) and Max Bruch (1835–1920) are among the most ingratiating of the conservative concertos in the current repertoire. Despite their hardy survival well into the present era, both men are incorruptibly nineteenth-century, and their concertos have begun to date rather rapidly in recent years. However, the concertos are much too grateful to the violinist to be relinquished, although at the moment they are housed more comfortably in the conservatoire than in the concert hall. In the narrowest formal sense neither Goldmark nor Bruch failed to make a mildly curious and untraditional point. The most famous of the Bruch violin concertos, the first in G minor, Op. 26, utilizes, in place of a sonata-form construction, a first-movement prelude based on solo recitative and romantically dramatic encounters between the soloist and the orchestra. The Goldmark violin concerto in A minor, Op. 28, is planned in the traditional first-movement sonata form, though there is a neat juxtaposition of leading melodies which caused critics several decades ago to disagree amiably (there are no great issues at stake in the work) over the identification of the principal subjects. In each case the idiom is too engagingly fervent and lyrical (with a virtuoso finale thrown in), and the workmanship too easy, for a disagreement ever to turn into a dispute. The two concertos represent the least objectionable variety of unadventurous musical experience; for they are period pieces, not museum pieces, and the distinction denotes that modicum of inspiration which is the difference between the dated and the dead.

Edward Elgar (1857–1934) is one of the choice spirits among those who are aristocratically indifferent to the passage of time. He had certainly the craft to command the newer idioms which were appearing in music, and whenever he referred to them in passing (e.g. an acute moment or two in the finale of the violin concerto) it was with calculation and surety. In his large symphonic works Elgar was no trifler, even when he dealt with new and disreputable ideas. Elgar was a gentleman and a conservative both by choice and by training, and the relatively modern harmonies which crop up ever so rarely in his concertos are the carefully inspected acquaintances to whom he nodded upon occasion, but for whom he felt no confirmed friendship. The violin concerto in B minor, Op. 61, is in the high romantic tradition; broad, impassioned music that can truly trust itself to talk only from the heart. The luscious emotional outpourings are not pointed up with the cheaper variety of romantic extravagance. In this concerto Elgar is very much the heroic aristocrat who entertains always the noblest even if the most unoriginal ideas. The 'cello concerto in E minor, Op. 85, a later work, is as largely planned and as spaciously scored as the violin concerto. Yet there is a greater reserve which affects not only the quality of emotion but the sound of the orchestra; the former is more lyrical and the latter paradoxically rather more austere. The Elgarian exultations lie more firmly below the surface, yet not too deep to take much rehearing before they are fully ferreted out. It is a just companion piece to the violin concerto. Both are highly individual variations upon the same theme by the same composer. The differences between the two concertos were apparently more striking to their first audiences than they are today. The 'cello concerto failed to please at first, for audiences who had admired the fullness of the violin concerto found the 'cello work rather frugal fare. The violin concerto is spread over a spacious classical sonata-form structure, replete with an amply proportioned opening ritornel. The softer-spoken 'cello concerto dispenses with monumental forms. In place of the traditional first-movement sonata form it builds up "a simple lyric design with a middle section in 12/8 time" (Tovey).

The concertos of Frederick Delius (1863–1934) hold themselves preciously apart from pretentious dramatics or public showmanship. Delius confines his utterances to elegiac intimacies, and he walks with an air of untouchable ecstasy. Orchestral colour and atmosphere are as basic to his total design as the ordered recurrence of melodies and motives. The soloist is above all a lyricist. In his violin concerto the soloist is absorbed in decorative meditations, soaring out of the orchestra just as a leading soprano voice emerges out of a group of sympathetic choristers. The C minor piano concerto (1897) was, according to Percy Grainger, conceived in Florida, where as a young man Delius had gone to manage his father's plantation, "and where the untutored singing of the Negro workers so captivated his imagination that he resolved to become a composer. . . . Out of these promptings the concerto was born. Negro feeling is especially noticeable in the slow movements. . . ." The concerto is performed continuously although there are three main tempo divisions—moderato, largo, and vivace—which partition the work. The 'cello concerto (1921) is reported to be a springtime piece although there is little stretching of youthful legs or spirited gambolling about. The concerto is one of Delius's tranquil rhapsodies,

unhurried, carefully coloured, and reflective; attributes well suited to
the pace and the temperament of the 'cello as a solo instrument. Like
the piano concerto, it is in a continuous one-movement form. Delius
also composed a double concerto for violin, 'cello, and orchestra which
is likewise lyrical in feeling.

The solitary violin concerto, Op. 47, by Jean Sibelius (b. 1865),
composed in 1903 and revised in 1905, is a comparatively early work,
and in many respects adheres strongly to the late romantic conceptions of the form. Its violin technique, for example, is largely drawn
from the standard equipment which served the later nineteenth-century concerto composer so well. Sibelius still believes in sudden emotional seizures rendered through routine double-stoppings, the soloist
posing figuratively with chin up, eyes down, and one hand over his
heart. There are the customary high-register trills with dramatic
double-stoppings breaking in on the lower strings; and the operatic
leap from one extreme in register to another—a traditional concerto
mannerism which occurs even in Mozart—is usually executed by
violinists trained in the late romantic virtuoso tradition with a slight
and somewhat sentimental glissando. Too much, perhaps, has been
made of Sibelius's unconventional first-movement design. The movement is fashioned in a loose sonata form, and by classical standards it
is indeed peculiar and original. However, it has been the point of the
foregoing chapter to show that a free and experimental opening sonata-
form movement has been, since Mendelssohn's day, the rule rather
than the unconventional exception. Sibelius's unorthodoxies are within
a venerable and nearly defunct tradition, for he does not venture, as
many modern composers do, beyond the general confines of the
sonata form.

The popularity of this violin concerto is surely in part due to the
routine violin technique which audiences are pleased to recognize and
applaud. In larger measure, however, its appeal derives from the great
melodic beauty which enlivens many of its pages. The opening of the
concerto is certainly magnificent lyricism, and throughout one hears
the rough, curt folk melodies and rhythms which Sibelius handles
with such fondness and assurance. The concerto has its share of romantic melodramatics, and at one point the slow movement suggests
that the *Valse Triste* mood was not a temporary one with Sibelius.

His celebrated feeling for wide open spaces is generously evident in this concerto, and, in truth, a vast quantity of space, even when it happens to be empty, is quite impressive. It has been the fashion among sympathetic commentators to brood over this dark Sibeliusian void, and a rich critical mythology has already been hatched, dealing with ancient bardic songs and pagan torches glowing in the forest primeval. It is possible that this has something to do with the violin concerto; yet there are rational musical reasons—a conventional virtuoso technique, an idiom at once traditional and particular, and a genius for melody—which suffice to explain the enjoyment it currently offers to so many listeners.

While the composers just discussed belong chronologically to the present century, one feels a certain hesitation in comprising their work under the heading of "The Modern Concerto." The word "modern," whenever it has been used in music history, has raised problems. Opinions and definitions differ to the point of utter confusion, and any chance assortment of composers, critics, and music lovers will probably volunteer a variety of unsorted and incongruous meanings for the word. Chronology, temperament, and idiom are among the most relevant factors, yet no single one suffices for a complete criterion. The youngest radical needs to be told, perhaps even more than Sibelius, that there is nothing essentially modern about being alive. Stray Victorians are still conducting courses in musical etiquette; and conversely, the youngest generation is not necessarily the most modern. It so happens that, at the moment, younger composers are apt to be more cautious, technically and idiomatically, than the elderly deities who splurged so magnificently during the 1920's. Likewise, technical daring and idiomatic novelty are hardly in themselves the essentials of modernism. It is possible, no doubt, to restrict the word "modern" only to music which embodies the most advanced methods in the technique of musical composition. However, we have no Cassandras among our critics able to foretell which of a variety of new methods will bear fruit fifty years hence. An advanced technique or principle of composition must, by definition, advance to something beyond itself. If future composers find it worthless, it is not an advance but an idiosyncrasy. For all practical critical purposes this meaning of the word comfortably leaves the decision to the future; for, as the experimentation of the last few decades has taught us, the definition, recognition, and acceptance of an "advanced" principle has been more a matter of personal loyalties and prejudices than a question of simple musical logic or an articulate and rational aesthetic. Moreover, while Schönberg's *Pierrot Lunaire* is still idiomatically "advanced" and as emotionally convincing as ever, its decadence is a relic of a lost generation, a near-forgotten and (as we hope) a never-to-be-repeated era in human dejection, hysteria, and escapism. Temperamentally, it represents a mood history at the moment has no public use for. And this finally brings up the notion that a work is "modern" if, for one vaguely formulated reason or another, it is thought to reflect the emotional quality, the temperament, and tempo of contemporary life. Yet by such a standard, vital as it is, the heroisms of a nineteenth-century Beethoven or the nervous and impatient chromaticisms of a sixteenth-century Gesualdo are closer to these difficult times than, for example, the complacent atmosphericism of the early twentieth-century impressionists. A precise weighing of chronology, temperament, idiom, and technique will offer a serviceable definition of modernism to anyone who wants one badly enough. It is not the point of this chapter to offer infallible definitions. Since the account here is chronological (and not too argumentative) the word "modern" will be used rather generally to refer to all twentieth-century composers whose concertos are not too closely identified with late romantic idioms and procedures.

Since the turn of the century the concerto, through all its evolutions, has remained an integral part of the music of our time, sharing the stylistic vicissitudes and motivated by the same impulses evident in the general body of present-day music. Thus there are neoclassical, neoromantic, atonal, and quarter-tone concertos. The twentieth-century concerto has known the experimentation, the lean orchestration, the upsurge of polyphony, and the reversal of the techniques of the preromantic past which characterized the modernist's general disgust with the lushness and looseness of late nineteenth-century music. It has known also the conventionally effulgent virtuoso pieces by older composers solidly rooted in the moods and methods of the last century. Nationalism is still a factor in the modern concerto as it is in modern music generally. This is a nineteenth-century inheritance adapted to contemporary requirements; and like the romantic composer, the modernist has also by-passed the solo concerto as the major vehicle of symphonic expression. The multiplicity of forms, styles, and techniques in the modern concerto needs no apology. Put it down at best to the complexities of modern life and to the inventiveness of modern composers; at worst, to the frantic trial-and-error system of living which was Europe's misfortune between two wars. From a strictly musical point of view it will be shown later in this chapter that this apparent complexity and confusion rests upon the simplest and most fundamental notions of concerto construction. And again from a narrow musical standpoint, it is no longer necessary to argue that there is, in general, direction and intelligence in modern music. Our composers, in the largest majority, are extremely competent; many of them are truly inspired. By and large, they know what they want, and a sizable number are even clear on why they want it. This is not an arbitrary judgment; it is a matter of fact, and it stands quite apart from anyone's private misgivings concerning the lasting importance of the direction followed in modern music and by the modern concerto.

The concerto is not an atrophied form, nor is it likely to become one so long as there are virtuosi and a curious public. Show pieces for the trade, however, are fast disappearing, and student concertos for various levels of accomplishment are a thing of the past. The modern student confines himself, even more than the virtuoso, to the safe romantic war horses. A critic is not apt to shrug his shoulders over a dull contemporary concerto and commend it to the student, as Schumann did a Herz or Thalberg concerto, as an acceptable finger exercise. Schumann once listed a new concertino as a piece "effective on the birthdays of pleased fathers of untalented daughters." Today, a considerate daughter is not likely to walk in on father's birthday with the latest concerto under her arm. However, while publishers and composers have fortunately forgotten the untalented-daughter market, other avenues of concerto consumption have not been remarkably active. Some composers still produce concertos for their own use. Hindemith, for example, composed *Der Schwanendreher* because, among other reasons, "I played too many times my two other viola concertos"; and Stravinsky explained his *Capriccio* on the grounds that he had played his piano concerto so often "that I thought it was time to give the public another work for piano and orchestra." Yet while the composer-performer still exists, he is no longer a flourishing institution. A few composers are fortunate enough to secure commissions for concertos; most write in the hope that somebody will play their work, and sometimes somebody does. Perhaps a sense of isolation from living audiences, and the feeling that one may as well go the whole hog in experimenting as one pleases, constitutes one of the minor reasons for the eccentricities which clutter the concertos of the last several decades. The modern concerto is certainly not lacking in novelty or variety, and while this scarcely compensates for the paucity of memorable musical ideàs, it is a point of definite and genuine interest. Few modern concertos are remarkably great music; but it is just as relevant to observe that few are unentertaining.

Principally, however, the experimental drive in modern music derived from a reaction to the music of the late nineteenth century; a reaction (or a revulsion) which consisted, generally speaking, in negating the principles, the practices, and even the moralities of late romantic music and enthroning their opposites. For a decade or two experimentation was the norm whereby the calibre of a composer's musical mentality was measured. The reasons for this are profound enough to reach out beyond musical aesthetics into the real world in which music is only one of the many preoccupations of mankind. The unsettling cynicism and disorientation with respect to the accepted verities which corroded the heart and mind of the post-war world is one of the many cogent extra-musical explanations. The First World War was followed by a great calling-into-question era, and matters more important than the accepted ways of constructing a concerto were up for revision. For many creative minds experimentation was an inner necessity, and the results achieved were not only technically valuable, but the music itself still retains, after much rehearing, the power of the initial emotional compulsion. With the majority, however, novelty was the latest cliché, the fashionable attitude, momentarily the most compelling social convention in the mores of the profession. A young man without a musical idiosyncrasy and an esoteric system of aesthetics was fit only for organ-playing in the Bible belt. The modern concerto shared in this development, devouring with uncritical objectivity the idioms, techniques, inspirations, and mannerisms thrown its way. The general lines of experimental thought need not be stressed since they affected all forms alike and were not peculiar to the concerto. They are of interest here only in that, when applied to the particular problems of concerto composition, they produced definable mutations in the concerto form and in concerto technique.

A composer tackling the composition of a concerto is faced with a series of specific problems, e.g. the degree of prominence to be accorded the soloist in relation to the orchestra, the technique of the solo instrument, the traditional first-movement sonata form, the balance between solo and orchestra with respect to tone colour and sound mass, the elevation of neglected instruments to the rank of concerto soloists, etc. As indicated in preceding chapters, many of these problems were posed sharply during every major period of musical reorientation, and the precise character of the concerto during such a period has been determined by the kind of solutions composers have effected. The cleavage between the romantic and modern solutions is rather sharp, for many modern composers have made a deliberate point of dispensing with nineteenth-century procedures.

With the development of the modern orchestra to a point where very nearly each instrument is called upon to perform a virtuoso part, instruments like the piano, hitherto reserved only for solo concertos, have been absorbed into the orchestra as part of a multicoloured fabric. There would be little point in introducing the instrument unless its full range and resources were put to use. Thus in many symphonic works the piano is active from start to finish, and even emerges as the dominating tone colour in the general mass; but it is not segregated from the rest of the orchestra, and it does not function as a concerto soloist. The difficulty of the piano-writing may require the services of a virtuoso, but it is not the composer's intention to confuse a prominent or even a leading part with a solo part. He is careful to offer the pianist no excuse for what has aptly been called an attack of "glass chandelier hysterics," and he takes the elementary precaution of not calling such a work a concerto. There is a leading piano part of major dimensions and virtuoso difficulty in Loeffler's *Pagan Poem*, in D'Indy's *Symphony on a French Mountain Air*, and in Manuel de Falla's *Nights in the Gardens of Spain*; yet none are called concertos. In the Falla work, for example, the virtuoso writing derives from the nature of the subject-matter. The coloratura passages for the piano in the third nocturne are based upon

the type of ornamental figurations characteristic of the popular Andalusian melodies upon which Falla modelled this portion of the
music. They do not serve for the arbitrary instrumental showmanship which is an inevitable part of the typical nineteenth-century
concerto.

This indicates that even among composers whose music is not remarkable for its advanced thinking there is a tendency to break with
the romantic conception of the soloist's paramount position. This has
been carried over to a large number of modern works called concertos,
and it is noticeable that a substantial number of modern concerto composers are remarkably unimpressed with the soloist's conventional
claims for attention. The pure virtuoso concerto has shown encouraging signs of disappearing. There is less soloistic splurging for its own
sake; fewer obviously grateful opportunities for the virtuoso to ride
his instrument like a wild charger or to belabour it as though it were
his favourite foe. The soloist is less often the unbridled commander
roaming with romantic heroism a league ahead of his orchestral regi-
ment; more often he is simply a participant in the general musical
manœuvres. There is, of course, no absolute unanimity of opinion on
this point. Ravel, for one, still held the nineteenth-century notion that
the proper function of a concerto was to offer the virtuoso a platform
for public display. His piano concerto, for all its idiomatic modernity,
is closer in conception therefore to the typical romantic concerto than
it is to the typically modern. It does not follow that the solo part in a
modern concerto is any less difficult than in the romantic concerto.
Technical difficulty is not always equivalent to virtuoso showmanship.
The essential point is that the spectacle of a soloist overcoming monumental technical obstacles is rarely the cardinal point of interest in the
modern concerto.

Much of the difficulty in a modern concerto is likely to derive from
the performer's lack of proper adjustment to new ways of writing for
his instrument. The modern composer turned his critical intelligence
upon all phases of his romantic inheritance, and in so doing evolved
for himself a new set of ideas and emotions, new formal structures to
house them in, new harmonies to convey their meaning, and new instrumental techniques to render them articulate. The performer who
approaches the Schönberg violin concerto in the hope of handling his

instrument as he would in a Bruch or Tschaikowsky concerto is invit-
ing as much disaster as if he were to approach the Tschaikowsky concerto for the first time with a violin technique founded solely on
Mozart.

The modern composer is even apt to claim ignorance of traditional instrumental technique as a virtue. The following passage in
Stravinsky's *Autobiography* concerning the composition of his violin
concerto is pertinent. As Stravinsky explains, he "was not a complete
novice in handling the violin. Apart from my pieces for the string
quartet and numerous passages in *Pulcinella*, I had had occasion, particularly in the *Histoire d'un soldat*, to tackle the technique of the violin
as a solo instrument. But a concerto certainly offered a far vaster field
of experience. To know the technical possibilities of an instrument
without being able to play it is one thing; to have that technique at
one's fingertips is quite another. I realized the difference, and before
beginning the work I consulted Hindemith, who is a perfect violinist.
I asked him whether the fact that I did not play the violin would make
itself felt in my composition. Not only did he allay my doubts, but he
went further and told me that it would be a very good thing, as it
would make me avoid a routine technique, and would give rise to ideas
which would not be suggested by the familiar movement of the
fingers." The violinist should know beforehand that "a routine technique" and "the familiar movement of the fingers" will not help him
much in performing this work.

With instruments so well explored and so firmly established in the
concerto repertoire as the violin and the piano, the novelty in the style
of modern composers has been largely a matter of emphasis on specialized phases of a total technique. Both the romantics and the moderns
knew the capacities of the piano thoroughly, but they chose to focus
attention upon different aspects of the instrument's resources. In the
piano concertos of Stravinsky, Honegger, Shostakovitch, Bartók, etc.,
the lingering pedal technique and the thick, juicy sonorities of romantic piano-writing were replaced by a clipped and percussive treatment
of the instrument. Sharp rhythmic impact was stressed more than sustained cantabile tone. For a while the poetical sweet singers were van-
quished and the drum beaters took power in the piano concerto. The
limited amount of truly radical pianistic experimentation in the

modern concerto has not widely affected either the instrument's technique or the concerto form. The tone-cluster system of Henry Cowell calling for the use of fist and forearm (exemplified in his piano concerto) remains, for example, a curiosity rather than an accepted contribution. So basic a revision of performance method derives logically from a very specialized system of harmony which few composers besides Cowell seem willing to accept. However, Cowell's system need not be adopted in its entirety; there is no reason why occasional use cannot be made of the tone cluster as a specialized effect, and the appropriate performance method absorbed as one more element in our present-day piano technique.

A much more notable advance in solo technique, however, was registered with instruments like the viola and harp which had hitherto received scant attention from concerto composers. The viola concertos of Hindemith, for example, explore the range and variety of the instrument with remarkable effectiveness, and the suite for viola and orchestra by Ernest Bloch calls for such standard violinistic accomplishments as the col legno, the ponticello, and harmonics. Harp technique is carried well beyond nineteenth-century norms in *The Enchanted Isle*, a symphonic poem for harp and orchestra by Carlos Salzedo. "In this work," writes Salzedo, "the harp is treated in an unexpected, unaccustomed fashion by taking advantage of the unlimited tone colours of the instrument, thirty-seven in number. The conception and execution of these effects have been made possible only by the recent perfection of the instrument."

Interest spread, from secondary concerto instruments, to instruments whose potentialities for concerto work had never been suspected. Percussion, voice, and quarter-tone instruments, for example, were allotted the role of concerto soloists. The Milhaud concerto for percussion instruments is designed, as the composer describes it, "for a solo player of the instruments of percussion, accompanied by a small orchestra of strings and wind." The percussion group which constitutes the solo comprises tympani, snare drum, tenor drum, bass drum, tambourine, tambourin de Provence, cymbals, ruthe, castanets, triangle, rattle, metal block, wood block, and tam-tam. Hans Barth requires a specially constructed instrument for his concerto for quarter-tone strings and quarter-tone piano, while a revision of normal technique is necessarily demanded in the concerto by the Mexican theorist, Julian Carillo, for violin, viola, 'cello, French horn, harp octavino, and guitar, based on quarter, eighth, and sixteenth tones with accompaniment of a symphony orchestra. John Hausserman, an American, and Reinhold Glière, a Russian, have both experimented with a concerto for voice and orchestra. The saxophone does not really fit into this category, for at this late date there can be little argument over its capacities for solo work, and a concerto for the instrument is scarcely a far-fetched undertaking. However, the saxophone still lacks the concerto repertoire it merits. Debussy's rhapsody for saxophone and orchestra was a casual beginning. Jacques Ibert has composed a *Concertino da camera* for saxophone and orchestra, and Glière a saxophone concerto.

The revival of ancient instruments in the modern solo concerto is definitely an experimental undertaking, for, curiously enough, this specific aspect of their modern use is not explicitly tied up with the attempt to recover the styles and forms of the past. The most notable concertos of this kind are not imitative of eighteenth-century methods or idioms, for the modern composer is wise enough to know that the value of a harpsichord or a viola d'amore as a concerto solo will depend on how well it can be adapted to typically modern idioms, how coherent a place it can find for itself in the modern orchestra. The harpsichord concerto by Manuel de Falla, for example, is essentially an example of modern national Spanish music, e.g. modern in idiom and in coloration often distinctly national. Out of deference to the harpsichord, however, Falla restricts his supporting ensemble to a flute, oboe, clarinet, violin, and 'cello. The balance is, for the most part, delicate and subtle, although he does secure sequences of gorgeous sonority when he so desires. Perhaps the most ambitious undertaking with ancient instruments in concerto form is the *Quintuple Concerto*, Op. 31, by Arthur Cohn, scored for five ancient solo instruments and a huge modern orchestra. The solo instruments are the pardessus de viole, the viola d'amore, the viola da gamba, the basse de viole, and the harpsichord. The orchestra against which these supposedly delicate instruments are set off comprises no less than two flutes and piccolo, two oboes and English horn, two clarinets and bass clarinet, two bassoons and double bassoon, four horns, three trumpets, two tenor trombones, a bass trombone, and a contrabass tuba; also sixteen percussion instruments (requiring six players) including glockenspiel, ratchet, wood blocks, anvil, four assorted drums, two kinds of gong, harp, celeste, and finally a full string orchestra. There is obviously no question here of an eighteenth-century concerto, and in order that so complicated an ensemble should remain coherent, the ancient instruments are made to sound as no eighteenth-century composer thought possible or even, from his point of view, desirable. The work is consistently modern in harmony and form, and the intricate orchestration proceeds with a nervous stride and an elastic sense of balance temperamentally so typical of a good deal of modern music.

The motivations for the use of ancient instruments in the concerto vary widely from case to case. Falla composed his work for the famous harpsichordist Wanda Landowska; Cohn wrote his for the American Society of Ancient Instruments. Loeffler's *La Mort de Tintagiles* for viole d'amour and grand orchestra, Op. 6 (revised 1900), is, as the title describes it, a "dramatic poem based on a play by M. Maeterlinck." In this case, the choice of a viole d'amour was determined by the nature of the subject matter. Maeterlinck's little marionette play deals, after his favourite fashion, with an ancient and jealous queen living in a nameless and unknown land where the seas howl and the trees groan, and Tintagiles awakens and suffers and knows not wherefore or why. Loeffler wanted a solo instrument that would convey the discreet nuances of a delicate and unexplainable sorrow; an instrument which for centuries had lain imprisoned like Tintagiles in an anonymous and forgotten kingdom. Loeffler explained that he wanted his music "pervaded by the sadness and inevitableness of the play," and he chose the viole d'amour "as the only instrument capable of expressing the spirit and the mood of the doomed."

The orchestral portion in the concerto has also been subject to experimentation, and in the search for new expressive resources interesting colouristic combinations of solo and orchestra were evolved.[1]

---

[1] The Busoni piano concerto, Op. 39, is not precisely a case in point, but it is interesting in this connection because of its choral finale in which a six-part male chorus is added to the orchestra and solo piano.

New emphasis was placed on wind instruments as the complement to a piano or string solo. In his *Autobiography*, Stravinsky traced his interest in wind instruments from his *Symphonies à la mémoire de Debussy*, through *Mavra*, the *Octuor*, and finally to the piano concerto "which, as regards colour, is yet another combination—that of piano with a wind orchestra reinforced by double basses and timbals." The Ibert 'cello concerto utilizes an orchestra composed solely of wood-wind and brass; Salzedo has written a concerto for harp and seven winds; and in the *Kammerkonzert* (chamber concerto) by Alban Berg the piano and violin are set off against an ensemble of thirteen woodwinds. Apart from four 'cellos and three double basses, Hindemith's viola concerto, *Der Schwanendreher*, employs a wood-wind and brass orchestra supported by a harp and two tympani.

This has been motivated not only by an increasingly general interest in the expressive power of wind instruments but by a desire to accentuate the colouristic distinction between solo and tutti. Colour contrast has always been implicit in the fundamental meaning of a concerto as a work founded upon the conflict of two clearly distinguishable forces. Modern concerto composers, however, have often concentrated upon colour contrast as the essential defining element in the concerto opposition. Hence the clear duality between a string or piano solo and a wind orchestra. Hence also the effort some composers have made to avoid any possible confusion between, for example, the tone colour of a solo string instrument and the tone colour of the orchestral string mass. Previously, concerto composers had been content to rely on the obvious difference in weight or sound mass between a solo violin and the two violin sections of the orchestra. The modern composer tends to stress not the distinction in mass but the distinction in colour. Thus in writing a violin concerto he is liable to eliminate all violins from the orchestra and confine the tuttis only to the lower strings. In the Roger Sessions violin concerto, for example, there are no violins in the orchestra; in the Berezowsky 'cello concerto (*Concerto Lirico*) there are likewise no orchestral 'cellos; and in Hindemith's *Der Schwanendreher*, where the solo instrument is a viola, the orchestral violins and violas are both eliminated. The clear distinction in colour is entirely intentional, for Hindemith explains that it was his purpose "to keep the soloist separated from the orchestra, therefore no higher strings than 'cellos." The procedure is not totally modern (Mozart, for example, omitted the clarinets from his orchestra in his clarinet concerto); but the modern concerto composer tends to emphasize it more than did his predecessors.

The modern concerto orchestra is a much more elastic instrument than its romantic precursor, for it has suffered the extremes of contraction and expansion and in neither case has it proved too slight or too cumbersome. The process of contraction is apparent in such titles as Roussel's *Concert pour petit orchestre*, Op. 34, Miaskowsky's *Lyric concertino* for small orchestra, Op. 32, No. 3, Ibert's *Concertino da camera*[1] for alto saxophone and eleven instruments, Hanson's *Concerto da camera* for piano and string quartet, Alban Berg's *Kammerkonzert* scored for a total of fifteen instruments, George Antheil's chamber concerto for eight instruments, Hindemith's *Der Schwanendreher*, subtitled a "Concerto for viola and small orchestra," and his *Kammermusik* (chamber music), a series of chamber concertos, the second and third of which are, for example, for solo piano and solo 'cello respectively with an orchestral complement not exceeding a dozen instruments, while the fifth is a viola concerto supported by a large chamber orchestra.

To some extent the elasticity of the concerto orchestra developed in connection with the return to early eighteenth-century principles of concerto composition. Both the romantics and the moderns sought inspirational sustenance in the cultures of the past. However, while the nineteenth-century composer was apt to steep himself in medieval romance (witness Weber's programme for his *Konzertstück*), the modern mind found points of valuable kinship in the music of the pre-romantics. The modernist revolution was in part directed towards tightening up the flabby emotionalism of romantic music and clearing away the dead wood that cluttered up the romantic orchestra. In the effort toward functionalism, clarity, and economy, composers could hope for no better guidance than that provided in the early concerto. Thus polyphony was once again restored to its high place, and such

---

[1] The reader will remember that, as indicated in the first chapter, the title *Concerto da camera* (German, *Kammerkonzert*) refers to an early concerto form, small in orchestral dimension and intimate in approach, to be performed in a room (*camera*) in distinction to concertos designed for church use (*da chiesa*).

titles as "concerto grosso," "concerto da camera," "symphonie concertante," etc., began to reappear with increasing frequency. A polyphonic concerto grosso style, modern in idiom but traditional in its structural principles, is the basis of many modern concertos. The two major varieties of concerto grosso writing were both revived, e.g. the alternation of predetermined concertino and grosso blocs, and the obbligato style with individual instruments stepping out of the orchestra for brief solos. In the concerto grosso for piano and strings by Ernest Bloch, the piano is used as an obbligato instrument although, because of its range, it virtually constitutes a concertino group in itself. Gustave Holst in his fugal concerto, Op. 40, No. 2, employs a string orchestra grosso with flute and oboe operating as obbligato solos; in Pizzetti's *Concerto dell'Estate* various solo instruments come forward from time to time; and Hindemith's *Kammermusik* has been described (Einstein) as a group of works organized in the classic manner of a concerto grosso with obbligato solos.

The severer concerto grosso style based upon predetermined concertino and grosso units has served as a method of expanding the concerto orchestra. Thus the solo concertino group has varied from a string quartet to a small dance band, while the grosso has been provided by a full modern symphony orchestra. The Van Vactor concerto grosso is scored for a concertino of three flutes and harp. Berezowsky's toccata, variations, and finale, Op. 23, is a concerto grosso utilizing a solo string quartet as the concertino unit and a symphony orchestra for the grosso. The two units are used as indivisible blocs and are played off against each other in the traditional Corellian concerto grosso fashion. There is a certain lack of elasticity in this routine application of the concerto grosso pattern to an expanded modern orchestra. This is even more marked in Robert Russell Bennett's concerto grosso for dance band and orchestra. The concertino bloc is a dance band comprising two alto saxophones, one tenor saxophone, two trumpets, one trombone, a guitar, and a piano, while a regular symphony orchestra supplies the grosso. The work is really a concerto for two orchestras, one small and the other large. The undertaking is a provocative one, but the execution extremely routine. A strict alternation technique is employed—first dance band then symphony orchestra. The two rarely merge, and their isolation with respect to each other reduces what might have been an interesting venture in modern orchestration to a mere formula. There is no vital juxtaposition of choirs, no real playing off of one against the other. The two orchestras simply take turns in an orderly rotation pattern that continues unvaried for five movements.[1]

The concerto grosso by Heinrich Kaminski further illustrates the expanded application of an eighteenth-century method. It is scored for two orchestras, each containing its own concertino and grosso groups, with a piano pivoting between the two orchestras. A string trio forms the concertino in each orchestra, and both grosso groups, except for a slight variation in the percussion, are scored alike. Kaminski not only doubles up on an eighteenth-century principle of orchestral balance, but he utilizes an austere, modern polyphony which looks directly to Bach for its inspiration.

Max Reger has often been cited as the patron saint of the reorientation in modern German music towards Bach and the methods of the eighteenth-century polyphonic masters. Reger is an excellently obvious composer, erudite, enterprising, and not wholly unoriginal. He knew how to order the intricacies of a ponderous polyphonic apparatus, and his predilection for strict Bachian forms no doubt exercised a valuably corrective influence upon early modern German music. Inspiration is not always lacking in his music, nor is it always evident; and far from deserving the title of the deadest of dead composers, Reger is, on the whole, only a trifle tedious. However, his *Konzert im alten Stil*, despite its title, scarcely qualifies as a revival of early concerto methods. The work is, as Tovey observes, "a somewhat vague imitation of an eighteenth-century concerto grosso, but it does not achieve much more of an 'ancient style' than an impression of remoteness, and it makes no attempt to use the real forms of the old concertos."

The revival of early concerto technique represents only a limited although much publicized aspect of the modern effort to create a non-

---

[1] The *Quintuple Concerto* by Arthur Cohn is, as the title states, a concerto for five solo instruments. It is not a concerto grosso, for the five instruments are independent and do not group themselves into a concertino unit against an orchestral grosso. The soloists are also provided with a series of cadenzas, single, double, triple, quadruple, and quintuple, to meet all emergencies. The scoring of the work, which has already been given, is an extreme example of the expansion process at work in the modern concerto orchestra.

romantic concerto. For approximately one hundred and fifty years after the death of J. S. Bach (1750) the first-movement sonata form has been the backbone of the concerto structure. Post-classical experimentation was conducted primarily within the confines of the sonata form, and the sum total of romantic ingenuity succeeded only in prying loose certain of the classical formalities and imposing new ones in their place. Sceptical modern opinion held, with some justification, that the romantics had managed only to batter an economical structure out of shape and to inflate a looser design with virtuoso trickery and obvious emotionalism. The sonata form seemed just about used up, and while it still has its vigorous champions (e.g. Prokofieff, Piston, etc.), the list of concerto composers who have turned elsewhere for their structural models is remarkably large.

The variety of forms that have replaced the sonata-form concerto is momentarily bewildering, until one realizes that modern composers have not been seeking any one substitute but have simply recovered the original concept of the word "concerto." Originally the concerto presupposes only that two sharply contrasted tonal forces be opposed to each other. It makes no stipulation concerning the specific form in which this opposition is to be patterned out, nor does it specify what the dimensions of the instrumental apparatus shall be. The moderns have simply refused to abide by any classical or romantic limitation in the specific form to be evolved out of this general definition. Thus a modern concerto may be either a chamber quintet or a work for double orchestra, it may be cast in sonata form or in any other mould the composer may desire. Bloch's *Schelomo* is titled "a rhapsody for 'cello and orchestra." Pick-Mangiagalli's *Sortilegi* (*Sorcery*) for piano and orchestra, and Salzedo's *The Enchanted Isle* for harp and orchestra are both called symphonic poems. Casella composed a partita, Bartók a rhapsody, D. G. Mason a prelude and fugue, Busoni a three-movement *Indianische Fantasie* (*Indian Fantasy*), and Stravinsky a three-movement *Capriccio*, all for piano and orchestra. In place of the conventional sonata form, the first movement in the Stravinsky violin concerto and in the Berezowsky quartet concerto is a toccata. Add this to the concerto grosso of Bloch, the *concertino da camera* (chamber concerto) of Ibert, the *Concerto Sacro* (sacred concerto) by Werner Josten, the *Three Psalms* (a 'cello concerto) by Frederick Jacobi, the symphonie concertante of Karol Szymanowski, and it is clear that the modern concerto may be shaped in any form, style, and dimension provided it remains true to the generalized but fundamental definition of a concerto.

The bewildering confusion in forms and methods turns out, therefore, to be a relatively clear matter of working freely with the simplest and most essential concerto principles. The modern composer tends to think with both greater formal freedom and greater stylistic discipline than the romantic. He desires a free hand in working out his musical design and he is prone to capricious juxtaposing of ideas; yet fugato episodes and often even a thoroughly rigorous polyphonic technique are apt to be among the essentials of his musical speech. Stravinsky's *Capriccio* for piano and orchestra illustrates rather neatly this curious and effective contradiction. "I had in mind," he writes, "the definition of a *capriccio* given by Praetorius. . . . He regarded it as a synonym of the *fantasia*, which was a free form made up of *fugato* passages. This form enabled me to develop my music by the juxtaposition of episodes of various kinds which follow one another and by their very nature give the piece that aspect of caprice from which it takes its name."

It is worth making the very special point that the modern composer, far from encouraging anarchy in music, strives for the maximum of discipline and clarity. The multiplicity of movements and trends indicates a disagreement in method rather than in fundamental intention, and it is notorious in fields other than music that quarrels over procedure are often more acrimonious than disputes over first principles. Like every truly great radical, Schönberg is the most disciplined and careful of composers, and his twelve-tone system requires not only a formidable proficiency in polyphonic methods but a strict accounting of every element in the total ensemble. The violin concertos of Arnold Schönberg and Alban Berg illustrate the range and variety of dodecaphonic concerto technique, as well as the peculiar disparity between tremendous intellectual control and the projection of an overpowering emotionalism. Despite the coolness and precision with which the intricacies move on paper, Schönberg's music is an extreme form of romantic hysteria. Schönberg himself discounts the so-called mathematics of his music and insists upon a credo which is singularly conventional and romantic. "If a composer," he declares, "does not write from the heart, he simply cannot produce good music. I have never had a theory in my life. . . . I write what I feel in my heart—and what finally comes on paper is what first coursed through every fibre of my body."

Of the two, Berg is more the forthright romanticist less concerned to contract and armour-plate the urgency of his emotions, although he is just as concerned to control them. Even upon first hearing, his violin concerto is obviously warm, human, and romantic in feeling. Bach is the chosen deity of many tone-row disciplinarians, and into the second movement of his violin concerto Berg has woven a simple and deeply touching chorale from a Bach cantata. The inspiration for the work is a throwback to the high romance of the Weber, Schubert, Schumann tradition. It is a requiem concerto dedicated to the memory of a young girl and presumably depicts, in its first movement, the maiden's angelic nature and, in the second, her tragic death and deliverance.

Both composers write on a level of nervous excitement where the peaks of ecstasy are just a hairbreadth removed from complete nervous collapse. Like men with vertigo they teeter on the mythical mountain-tops of hysteria, frantically desirous of plunging over into the dark and comforting abyss. Such music, for its own preservation, demands a bitterly premeditated control even over the moment of wildest abandon, an impersonal sanity guiding each turn of so unpredictable and precarious a road. In brief, Berg and Schönberg are disciplined romanticists who have learned from the excesses of their chosen tradition; to paraphrase an excellent line, they bind bones and veins in their music before fastening to it flesh. In this connection, it is symptomatic that Křenek, upon his own admission, came to Schönberg's twelve-tone technique through a "concentration, condensation, sophistication of the Schubert style" which had just previously engrossed him. His second piano concerto shows the extreme contrapuntal logic, the building from germinal ideas, which characterize the twelve-tone system. His temperament is less frenetic than either Berg's or Schönberg's, less romantic than the former and less austere than the latter.

Older modernists who have never quite taken to tone-row writing have been singing requiems over it long before its demise. Typically enough, Respighi rejected the sophisticated logic of tone rows for his own notions of clarity. "Atonality? Thank Heaven that's done for! . . . I mean it is so far as modern Italian musicians are concerned. . . . The Italian genius is for melody and clarity. Today there is a noticeable return to the less sophisticated music of the past—in harmony to the church modes and in form to the suite of dances and other charming forms." The forms of the past are evident enough in his symphonic suite arrangements of sixteenth- and seventeenth-century airs and dances, while the return "in harmony to the church modes" is shown clearly in his concertos; e.g. the concerto in the Mixolydian mode for piano and orchestra, and the *Concerto Gregoriano* for violin and orchestra. The mode of the piano concerto is specified in the title, and the work concludes, incidentally, with a rare example of a concerto passacaglia. The violin concerto uses the Aeolian and Dorian modes and is partly based upon citations of medieval plain chant. The *Victimae Paschali* appears in the second movement, while the finale (an alleluia) employs the *Beatus Vir Qui Timet Dominum.*

Modal harmony appears often enough in modern music, and Vaughan Williams, for example, makes use of it in his *Concerto Accademico* in D minor for violin and string orchestra. Vaughan Williams utilizes a small orchestra as do many modern composers, but he restricts it to the traditional strings instead of experimenting with winds or percussion. The concerto is trimly titled "D minor," and until recently, when something of an about-face has been brewing in this direction, few modern composers would suffer a single main tonality to be hung plainly over a piece of their music. Also his idiom, his manner of musical speech, is perhaps more readily comprehensible to the average listener than are other idioms in modern music. However, Vaughan Williams is too sturdy an individual to write a routine concerto, and the title's disarming admission of malice aforethought does much to dispel the suspicion that the work is academic in any derogatory sense of the word.

Perhaps the true academicians in modern music are the self-conscious neoclassicists who are still politely beating their miniature tom-toms against the excesses of the last century. The neoclassicist notion of clarity is directed as much against the multiplicity of experimental trends in modern music, which it terms confusion, as against a ponderous technique of any sort, whether it be the bloated orchestrations of the romantics or the complicated conventions of a strict twelve-tone system. Neoclassicism is a form of musical calisthenics designed to cultivate lean muscularity of movement and an instinctive agility in the execution of a precisely premeditated manœuvre. It is for the limber and small-boned athlete whose stamina is sufficient only for a short relay. It is the most unencumbered style in modern music and its productions are weighed down by excesses neither of foolishness nor profundity. As an articulate movement its chastening influence has been all to the good, and with justice Slonimsky has commended a neo-classicist like Walter Piston as the builder of a future academic style. The components of a neoclassical style are varied enough. Counterpoint is very nearly a basic technique; the harmonic structure is simplified down towards recognizable tonal centres, and clear diatonic melody is apt to prevail. Rhythmic patterns are precise, whether modelled after eighteenth-century configurations or after modern jazz. Classical forms such as the sonata-allegro or the rondo are once again deemed useful, and early concerto forms such as the concerto grosso (Piston) and the chamber concerto (Casella) are regarded with affection. The idiom of the neoclassical composer is likely to be highly personal. Piston carries a hangover from an impressionist youth, while Casella sustains the ancient Italian tradition of limpid melody and solid design. The more obvious expressions of nationalism are not apt to interest the neoclassicist. He is primarily a polylinguist, or rather (despite possible protestations to the contrary) an advocate of an international Esperanto which the sophisticated of all nations can comprehend. Characteristically enough, Piston, for example, believes that self-conscious nationalism only hinders the development of a sound school of American music.

The importance of neoclassicism lies not so much in the music of its most consistent exponents as in the fact that it has in some measure touched the work of virtually every modern composer. Eclecticism, as a matter of fact, is more typical of the modern composer than allegiance to any one school. Even Stravinsky, who has been charged with the parentage of this anti-romantic movement, cannot keep the sources of his inspiration straight. The *Capriccio* for piano and orchestra has been regarded validly enough as an example of a neoclassical concerto. There is a strong eighteenth-century flavour to the slow movement, but it is curious that, on Stravinsky's own account, the period during which the *Capriccio* was composed was "dominated by that prince of music," the inveterately romantic Carl Maria von Weber. There are elements of neoclassicism in the concertos of Honegger and Bartók, but Honegger's intense emotionality and Bartók's incorrigible nationalism jut too emphatically for concealment. Besides, they are notoriously impolite composers; they take whatever they need wherever they can find it and they use it only according to the dictates of their own conscience. Milhaud's eclecticism is of another variety. He is a musical gadfly pestering every idiom he can alight upon. "What I cannot tolerate," he writes, "is the slavish adherence to any one system." Such broadmindedness is perhaps commendable, and in any case it suits Milhaud's type of creative talent. He is a voluminous composer; one of the uncritical naturals who has signed his name to music of extraordinary merit as well as to a good deal of unexplainable trash. His concertos for violin and for piano are lightweight pieces, inevitably entertaining (which is a great virtue) and quite unmomentous.

A movement so self-consciously sophisticated as neoclassicism was bound, sooner or later, to overstate its case and to provoke composers into a return to the very principles it held most abhorrent. In recent years romanticism (neoromanticism as it is sometimes labelled) has reappeared with a vengeance. It is fashionable, at the moment, to deride neoclassicism as something grown stale and flat; but it is often forgotten that it was once necessary for modern music to blow its nose, so to speak, and to breathe clean, fresh air again. The two already famous examples of the new romantic upsurge are the violin concertos by Sergei Prokofieff (No. 2, in G minor) and William Walton. Walton's progress from a dissonant modernist much approved of by the International Society for Contemporary Music to a kind of unofficial English composer laureate, is illustrated in the difference between his *Façade* for declamation and orchestra set to a series of satirical poems by Edith Sitwell, and his *Crown Imperial* written for the coronation of George VI. There was something deliberate about Walton's youthful modernism, and the consciousness that he was an advanced composer showed rather plainly in his scores. The viola concerto marks a significant turn towards patent lyricism and strong, uninhibited emotion. It is safe from any serious charge of sentimentality but is certainly not unromantic. The violin concerto, however, is romantic without reservations and has already won a warm place for itself in the modern virtuoso's repertoire.

Prokofieff is a kind of modern Mendelssohn, facile and by no means inconsequential. Like Mendelssohn he talks well and upon every conceivable subject. In its day romanticism was also a revolutionary ideal, and Mendelssohn served it with a naturalness and a gift for immediate persuasion which was the despair of less articulate composers. Every once in a long while, when a performer recaptures this quality in Mendelssohn, the stale truisms are suddenly infused with meaning and the music transformed into an unadulterated delight. Prokofieff likewise possesses the precious gift of naturalness. His music is modern without being deliberately modernistic, and this despite the fact that he handles, whenever he so desires, the most advanced or the most conservative of contemporary techniques. There is scarcely an infelicitous phrase or an unclear construction in his music, and the unconscious ease with which he delivers himself of whatever he has to say is a virtue which no amount of critical carping can devalue. Much of his music is merely pretty, some of it smart; but a residue remains which is worth careful attention. The first violin concerto, a relatively early work, is brittle and succinct. There is something of Prokofieff's early street-gamin irreverence in the first violin concerto and in the five piano concertos. He has a gift for deliberate dryness which is a mockery of all that is pretentious and obscure. Nevertheless, a strong vein of traditionalism runs through the first violin concerto; and while the piano concertos are percussive and clearly modern, they hold fast to warm and simple cantabile melodies.

Prokofieff left Russia in 1918, wandered about a good deal, going first to America via Japan and then establishing headquarters in Paris. In 1934 he returned to his native soil, and since that date his music has undergone a marked change. As Slonimsky observes: "In his works of the Soviet period there is a notable renascence of the lyrical quality, together with a decrease in the element of pure grotesque." The renascence of lyricism, warm melody, and simple emotionality is the essence of the second violin concerto. It too, like the Walton concerto, has been rapidly gaining in popularity. No doubt this is due to the average listener's preference for the familiar romantic temperament and for music in which warm melodiousness is valued above an erudite witticism. Whatever the explanation, popularity is not in itself any reason to distrust the music.

The concertos of Walton and Prokofieff, like the fifth, sixth, and seventh symphonies of Shostakovitch, raise issues far more momentous than the intrinsic merit of these particular compositions. It would be ungenerous to suppose that such responsible composers have been motivated by a cheap desire for popularity. For several decades now composers have been hammering out and refining new idioms and new techniques. Recently some composers have begun to feel that modern music has matured beyond disputations over technique. Prokofieff, for example, is of the opinion that "we have gone as far as we are likely to go in the direction of size or dissonance, or complexity in music." He is ready now, as he expresses it, "for greater simplicity and more melody," and with regard to experimentation in form he openly sounds a retreat: "I want nothing better, nothing more flexible or more complete than the sonata form, which contains everything necessary to my structural purpose." Walton's formulation is more impersonal and more fundamental: "We welcome all experiment that enriches the vocabulary and idiom of music; and we hail as the great ones of the earth those who use these newly-won symbols significantly in an act of lyrical creation." This is the most valid basis for the new romanticism in modern music. Neither Prokofieff nor Walton will be mistaken for anything but moderns; but they passed from primary concern over originality of idiom to primary concern in utilizing these idioms for the "act of lyrical creation." The violin concertos of Prokofieff and Walton merit close attention, for they are illustrations of the growing tendency to revert to those vastly simple and universally intelligible emotions and ideas which are the foundations of the profoundest and most enduring works of art. Regardless of one's private opinion of the ultimate worth of these concertos, it would be well to preserve a measure of respect towards so ambitious an undertaking.

It remains to note the effect of nationalism upon the modern concerto. The vigorous scepticism which followed the First World War looked askance at anything so nineteenth-century as an interest in national idioms. For the post-war intelligentsia, noble and altruistic undertakings, such as the glorification of one's native culture, were definitely passé. Experimentalism and originality were all that mattered. The true individualist was advised to forget his derivations and strike out on his own. Such iconoclasm could scarcely survive in a world where the loneliest mountain top has been charted, and the composer who repairs to it is likely to find a group of ordinary tourists with whom he must live on terms of common sociability. Even those who can afford it economically no longer, for their own preservation, live apart from the rest of humanity. The world has grown close around us; and the composer—an ordinary citizen in every respect other than his musical talent—finds himself sharing the common fears and aspirations of his people. So long as the right of nations and peoples to self-determination remains in question, so long will national consciousness remain an acute phenomenon, felt deeply by millions and reflected in the work of their musical spokesmen. In this sense musical nationalism goes beyond the mere use of a folk tune and becomes a part of contemporary history. Martinu's double concerto, for example, was composed, as Paul Nettl tells us, "during the tragic fate of his people following the Munich Pact of 1938." A type of "mourning melody" is evident, and the concerto "is, in fact, an elegy which strikes the heart of the hearer deeply—a cry of despair."

The surface manifestations of nationalism are, however, the characteristic rhythms and melodies of a people. Earlier in this chapter it has been indicated that the concerto is not the best place to look for the most characteristic use of a local dialect. Nevertheless a number of modern concertos bear the imprint of national idioms. Prokofieff's second violin concerto opens with a melody in minor recognizably Russian in feeling. Bartók's second piano concerto is orientated towards Hungarian songs and dances. In Szymanowski's symphonie concertante and in his second violin concerto "a thematic type derived from peasant music predominates, as well as rhythmic features borrowed from Slavonic dances and then made his own with the utmost skill" (Stuckenschmidt). Hindemith's *Der Schwanendreher* is based upon fifteenth- and sixteenth-century German folk songs. It was his intention, Hindemith explains, "to try how the old German folk songs could be adapted for today's concert work, e.g. with a modern arrangement and even in the spirit of the originals." Manuel de Falla reverted to a sixteenth-century Spanish *villancico* in the opening movement of his harpsichord concerto, and in his *Nights in the Gardens of Spain* he employed a variety of popular Andalusian melody known as the *cante hondo*. The Spanish element in Ravel's music, as well as his aristocratic refinement, are both evident in the concerto for the left hand which he composed for the one-armed pianist, Paul Wittgenstein.

The musical renaissance in Latin and South America has brought forward a group of strongly national composers. While concerto scores are not available in any quantity, the few on hand indicate that national idioms play a notable part. The *Concierto Sinfónico* for violin and orchestra by the Chilean composer, Pedro Humberto Allende, is a rather conservative work not too deeply touched by either nationalism or modernity. However, the first violin concerto in A major by the Brazilian, Oscar Lorenzo Fernandez, is based on popular idioms, while the 2nd *Phantasia Brasiliera* by his compatriot, Francisco Mignone, as its title implies, is a completely nationalist creation. Mignone adds a dash of American jazz and a dose of terrific virtuosity to his score. Another concerto whose title indicates its national orientation is the *Concierto Argentino* for piano and orchestra by the Argentine composer Alberto E. Ginastera. A concerto for four horns by Carlos Chavez, Mexico's most famous composer, has been described by Aaron Copland as "superbly Mexican in quality . . . but Mexican Indian—stoic, stark, and sombre as an Orozco drawing."

Although composers have long been aware of the need for a distinctive idiom, nationalism in American music is still something difficult to define. A few early composers turned towards extra-musical subject-matter, e.g. the peculiarities of national history which, they believed, were worth celebrating. The concerto form is not especially fit for a patriotic occasion, but Anton Philip Heinrich (1781–1861), one of the first to concern himself with the question of a national music, did venture a work elaborately entitled *The Treaty of William Penn with the Indians—Concerto Grosso—An American national dramatic divertissement, for a full orchestra, comprising six different characteristic movements united in one*. In the closing decades of the last century the recipe for a national music called for Negro and Indian folk material as the basic ingredients. Dvořák in his *New World* symphony and in his chamber music composed in America, and MacDowell in his *Indian*

Sketches, directed considerable attention towards these neglected and indigenous sources. But it is notable that neither the Dvořák 'cello concerto written in America nor MacDowell's two piano concertos are examples of this variety of nationalism. The Dvořák concerto is entirely Slavonic, while the MacDowell concertos—No. 1 in A minor, Op. 15 (1884), and No. 2 in D minor, Op. 23 (1890)—are essentially in the then dominant tradition of European romanticism.

The modern American concerto wisely restricts itself to no pre-conceived formulas, although native idioms like jazz make themselves strongly felt. Without any condescending gestures, several composers have recognized jazz as an accepted and even a dated phenomenon in American musical life. Copland, for example, was willing to predict some time ago that American music would eventually yield evidence of its influence. "Since jazz is not exotic here but indigenous," he wrote, "since it is the music an American has heard as a child, it will be traceable more and more frequently in his symphonies and concertos."

The concerto grosso by Robert Russell Bennett for dance band and symphony orchestra qualifies as an obvious type of national concerto. Its idiom is jazz, its medium in part the characteristically American dance band, and its intention is to offer a series of *Sketches from an American Theatre*, e.g. the five movements are (1) Praeludium (opening chorus, *vigoroso*), (2) Dialogue, ingenue and juvenile, (3) Theme song, (4) Comedy scene and blackout, (5) Marcia—Finale with flags. The Copland piano concerto is one of the most frequently cited examples of the use of jazz in a large symphonic form. It is an excellent if somewhat mannered work, unusually thick in scoring for those who know Copland as an angular and economical composer. George Gershwin once expressed the belief that jazz could "be made the basis of serious symphonic works of lasting value, in the hands of a composer with talent for both jazz and symphonic music." Copland certainly possesses this dual talent, and as a serious symphonic work based upon jazz his concerto acquits itself creditably enough. However, symphonic music founded on jazz is quite different from the music of a small jazz ensemble, and neither the enlargement of the symphonic apparatus nor the sanctity of the concerto form are in themselves sufficient to ensure that the former is the superior variety. As a matter of fact, while Copland lacks neither vitality nor sensitivity, his concerto is less spontaneously exuberant, less earthy in its melancholia, less subtle in its rhythmic variations than the music of our finest "popular" jazz composers.

However, it is to Copland's credit that he recognized the value of the idiom and sought to make it socially acceptable. Not so very long ago jazz was still a controversial subject and most composers were walking around it, in Damrosch's phrase, "like a cat around a plate of hot soup waiting for it to cool off. . . ." By now jazz is an established international idiom, and composers of all countries have found it emotionally refreshing and technically suggestive. Křenek, a German, used it in his opera *Jonny spielt auf*; Milhaud, a Frenchman, in his beautiful *Création du monde*; Honegger, a Swiss, in a wholly delightful concertino for piano and orchestra; and Stravinsky, a Russian, in the finale of his *Capriccio* for piano and orchestra.

While jazz remains, nevertheless, primarily an American manner of speech, it scarcely constitutes a complete folk music. Gershwin was responsible for stimulating a good deal of interest in symphonic jazz, and his *Rhapsody in Blue* and the concerto in F, both for piano and orchestra, are both engagingly melodious contributions to music of this type. Yet, while it was his chosen medium of expression, Gershwin did not claim jazz as the sole element of nationalism in American music. "It is not always recognized," he wrote, "that America has folk music; yet it really has not only one but many different folk musics. It is a vast land, and different sorts of folk music have sprung up in different parts, all having validity, and all being a possible foundation for development into an art music. For this reason, I believe that it is possible for a number of distinctive styles to develop in America, all legitimately born of folk songs from different localities. Jazz, ragtime, Negro spirituals and blues, southern mountain songs, country fiddling and cowboy songs can all be employed in the creation of American art music, and are actually used by many composers now . . ." The most that Gershwin claimed for jazz was that it was a "powerful" source of folk music, "probably in the blood and feeling of the American people more than any other style of folk music."

It would be well to extend the boundaries of even so broad a conception. Americans are the possessors of a heterogeneous cultural heritage in which every national, racial, and religious component shares alike the capacity to contribute something of permanent value. The vast resources of this assemblage of heritages are just beginning to be realized. Copland and Gershwin turn to jazz; Harl McDonald, in his concerto for two pianos and orchestra, to what he calls a Hispanic-American style; while the well-established tradition of American Hebraic music now stretches through the composers of four decades (Bloch, Jacobi, Copland, and Arthur Cohn). Bloch's *Schelomo* for 'cello and orchestra, Copland's *Vitebsk* trio, Jacobi's rhapsody for harp and strings, and the *Kaddish* in Cohn's flute concerto are all Hebraic in inspiration.

Multiplicity of idiom does not signalize a lack of national consciousness; neither does the failure of American composers to achieve, or to seek for, a uniformity in style and content. The jazz concerto, secular in intent and inspiration, finds its counterpart in works like Jacobi's 'cello concerto based upon the 90th, 91st, and 92nd Psalms, and Werner Josten's *Concerto Sacro* which, like Hindemith's *Matthis der Maler*, is inspired by Grünewald's famous triptych for the Isenheim Altar at Colmar. The cool neoclassicism of a Piston concerto is countered by the sober, purple-toned romanticism of the Hanson organ concerto. The jazz concerto dispenses with erudition and austerity, but jazz is not the ultimate symbol of the American temperament. The Sowerby organ concerto is written with much musical learning while the Sessions violin concerto abounds in subtleties. Neither work will instantly amuse or entertain after the fashion of a jazz concerto, but each has its compensations. Sessions, in particular, is sober, clean-cut, and austere, and his lyricism has that warm-hearted reticence which we associate with profound integrity of emotion.

American music is compounded, then, out of Negro, Indian, Hebrew, Spanish, jazz, and a hundred other idioms. Temperamentally it is both popular and austere, classical and romantic, experimental and conservative, unsophisticated and erudite. It is important to assemble this diversity of idioms, moods, and temperaments and to accept this diversity as characteristic. There is an essential democracy in the act of creation which supposes that each composer will express himself as he feels he must. In a nation so vast and so various it is possible only to uphold the principle of free creative expression and, regardless of national, racial, or religious derivation, honour each man's insight into that universal humanity which is the generalized content of all enduring art.

INDEX OF COMPOSERS

Certain more detailed studies of composers are indicated by heavy type.

INDEX OF COMPOSITIONS

GENERAL INDEX

A CATALOGUE OF SELECTED DOVER BOOKS
IN ALL FIELDS OF INTEREST

A CATALOGUE OF SELECTED DOVER BOOKS
IN ALL FIELDS OF INTEREST

THE DEVIL'S DICTIONARY, Ambrose Bierce. Barbed, bitter, brilliant witticisms in the form of a dictionary. Best, most ferocious satire America has produced. 145pp. 20487-1 Pa. $1.50

ABSOLUTELY MAD INVENTIONS, A.E. Brown, H.A. Jeffcott. Hilarious, useless, or merely absurd inventions all granted patents by the U.S. Patent Office. Edible tie pin, mechanical hat tipper, etc. 57 illustrations. 125pp. 22596-8 Pa. $1.50

AMERICAN WILD FLOWERS COLORING BOOK, Paul Kennedy. Planned coverage of 48 most important wildflowers, from Rickett's collection; instructive as well as entertaining. Color versions on covers. 48pp. 8¼ x 11. 20095-7 Pa. $1.35

BIRDS OF AMERICA COLORING BOOK, John James Audubon. Rendered for coloring by Paul Kennedy. 46 of Audubon's noted illustrations: red-winged blackbird, cardinal, purple finch, towhee, etc. Original plates reproduced in full color on the covers. 48pp. 8¼ x 11. 23049-X Pa. $1.35

NORTH AMERICAN INDIAN DESIGN COLORING BOOK, Paul Kennedy. The finest examples from Indian masks, beadwork, pottery, etc. — selected and redrawn for coloring (with identifications) by well-known illustrator Paul Kennedy. 48pp. 8¼ x 11. 21125-8 Pa. $1.35

UNIFORMS OF THE AMERICAN REVOLUTION COLORING BOOK, Peter Copeland. 31 lively drawings reproduce whole panorama of military attire; each uniform has complete instructions for accurate coloring. (Not in the Pictorial Archives Series). 64pp. 8¼ x 11. 21850-3 Pa. $1.50

THE WONDERFUL WIZARD OF OZ COLORING BOOK, L. Frank Baum. Color the Yellow Brick Road and much more in 61 drawings adapted from W.W. Denslow's originals, accompanied by abridged version of text. Dorothy, Toto, Oz and the Emerald City. 61 illustrations. 64pp. 8¼ x 11. 20452-9 Pa. $1.50

CUT AND COLOR PAPER MASKS, Michael Grater. Clowns, animals, funny faces . . . simply color them in, cut them out, and put them together, and you have 9 paper masks to play with and enjoy. Complete instructions. Assembled masks shown in full color on the covers. 32pp. 8¼ x 11. 23171-2 Pa. $1.50

STAINED GLASS CHRISTMAS ORNAMENT COLORING BOOK, Carol Belanger Grafton. Brighten your Christmas season with over 100 Christmas ornaments done in a stained glass effect on translucent paper. Color them in and then hang at windows, from lights, anywhere. 32pp. 8¼ x 11. 20707-2 Pa. $1.75

AUSTRIAN COOKING AND BAKING, Gretel Beer. Authentic thick soups, wiener schnitzel, veal goulash, more, plus dumplings, puff pastries, nut cakes, sacher tortes, other great Austrian desserts. 224pp. USO 23220-4 Pa. $2.50

CHEESES OF THE WORLD, U.S.D.A. Dictionary of cheeses containing descriptions of over 400 varieties of cheese from common Cheddar to exotic Surati. Up to two pages are given to important cheeses like Camembert, Cottage, Edam, etc. 151pp. 22831-2 Pa. $1.50

TRITTON'S GUIDE TO BETTER WINE AND BEER MAKING FOR BEGINNERS, S.M. Tritton. All you need to know to make family-sized quantities of over 100 types of grape, fruit, herb, vegetable wines; plus beers, mead, cider, more. 11 illustrations. 157pp. USO 22528-3 Pa. $2.00

DECORATIVE LABELS FOR HOME CANNING, PRESERVING, AND OTHER HOUSEHOLD AND GIFT USES, Theodore Menten. 128 gummed, perforated labels, beautifully printed in 2 colors. 12 versions in traditional, Art Nouveau, Art Deco styles. Adhere to metal, glass, wood, most plastics. 24pp. 8¼ x 11. 23219-0 Pa. $2.00

FIVE ACRES AND INDEPENDENCE, Maurice G. Kains. Great back-to-the-land classic explains basics of self-sufficient farming: economics, plants, crops, animals, orchards, soils, land selection, host of other necessary things. Do not confuse with skimpy faddist literature; Kains was one of America's greatest agriculturalists. 95 illustrations. 397pp. 20974-1 Pa. $2.95

GROWING VEGETABLES IN THE HOME GARDEN, U.S. Dept. of Agriculture. Basic information on site, soil conditions, selection of vegetables, planting, cultivation, gathering. Up-to-date, concise, authoritative. Covers 60 vegetables. 30 illustrations. 123pp. 23167-4 Pa. $1.35

FRUITS FOR THE HOME GARDEN, Dr. U.P. Hedrick. A chapter covering each type of garden fruit, advice on plant care, soils, grafting, pruning, sprays, transplanting, and much more! Very full. 53 illustrations. 175pp. 22944-0 Pa. $2.50

GARDENING ON SANDY SOIL IN NORTH TEMPERATE AREAS, Christine Kelway. Is your soil too light, too sandy? Improve your soil, select plants that survive under such conditions. Both vegetables and flowers. 42 photos. 148pp. USO 23199-2 Pa. $2.50

THE FRAGRANT GARDEN: A BOOK ABOUT SWEET SCENTED FLOWERS AND LEAVES, Louise Beebe Wilder. Fullest, best book on growing plants for their fragrances. Descriptions of hundreds of plants, both well-known and overlooked. 407pp. 23071-6 Pa. $3.50

EASY GARDENING WITH DROUGHT-RESISTANT PLANTS, Arno and Irene Nehrling. Authoritative guide to gardening with plants that require a minimum of water: seashore, desert, and rock gardens; house plants; annuals and perennials; much more. 190 illustrations. 320pp. 23230-1 Pa. $3.50

CONSTRUCTION OF AMERICAN FURNITURE TREASURES, Lester Margon. 344 detail drawings, complete text on constructing exact reproductions of 38 early American masterpieces: Hepplewhite sideboard, Duncan Phyfe drop-leaf table, mantel clock, gate-leg dining table, Pa. German cupboard, more. 38 plates. 54 photographs. 168pp. 8⅜ x 11¼. 23056-2 Pa. $4.00

JEWELRY MAKING AND DESIGN, Augustus F. Rose, Antonio Cirino. Professional secrets revealed in thorough, practical guide: tools, materials, processes; rings, brooches, chains, cast pieces, enamelling, setting stones, etc. Do not confuse with skimpy introductions: beginner can use, professional can learn from it. Over 200 illustrations. 306pp. 21750-7 Pa. $3.00

METALWORK AND ENAMELLING, Herbert Maryon. Generally coneeded best all-around book. Countless trade secrets: materials, tools, soldering, filigree, setting, inlay, niello, repoussé, casting, polishing, etc. For beginner or expert. Author was foremost British expert. 330 illustrations. 335pp. 22702-2 Pa. $3.50

WEAVING WITH FOOT-POWER LOOMS, Edward F. Worst. Setting up a loom, beginning to weave, constructing equipment, using dyes, more, plus over 285 drafts of traditional patterns including Colonial and Swedish weaves. More than 200 other figures. For beginning and advanced. 275pp. 8¾ x 6⅜. 23064-3 Pa. $4.00

WEAVING A NAVAJO BLANKET, Gladys A. Reichard. Foremost anthropologist studied under Navajo women, reveals every step in process from wool, dyeing, spinning, setting up loom, designing, weaving. Much history, symbolism. With this book you could make one yourself. 97 illustrations. 222pp. 22992-0 Pa. $3.00

NATURAL DYES AND HOME DYEING, Rita J. Adrosko. Use natural ingredients: bark, flowers, leaves, lichens, insects etc. Over 135 specific recipes from historical sources for cotton, wool, other fabrics. Genuine premodern handicrafts. 12 illustrations. 160pp. 22688-3 Pa. $2.00

THE HAND DECORATION OF FABRICS, Francis J. Kafka. Outstanding, profusely illustrated guide to stenciling, batik, block printing, tie dyeing, freehand painting, silk screen printing, and novelty decoration. 356 illustrations. 198pp. 6 x 9. 21401-X Pa. $3.00

THOMAS NAST: CARTOONS AND ILLUSTRATIONS, with text by Thomas Nast St. Hill. Father of American political cartooning. Cartoons that destroyed Tweed Ring; inflation, free love, church and state; original Republican elephant and Democratic donkey; Santa Claus; more. 117 illustrations. 146pp. 9 x 12. 22983-1 Pa. $4.00
23067-8 Clothbd. $8.50

FREDERIC REMINGTON: 173 DRAWINGS AND ILLUSTRATIONS. Most famous of the Western artists, most responsible for our myths about the American West in its untamed days. Complete reprinting of *Drawings of Frederic Remington* (1897), plus other selections. 4 additional drawings in color on covers. 140pp. 9 x 12. 20714-5 Pa. $3.95

CREATIVE LITHOGRAPHY AND HOW TO DO IT, Grant Arnold. Lithography as art form: working directly on stone, transfer of drawings, lithotint, mezzotint, color printing; also metal plates. Detailed, thorough. 27 illustrations. 214pp.
21208-4 Pa. $3.00

DESIGN MOTIFS OF ANCIENT MEXICO, Jorge Enciso. Vigorous, powerful ceramic stamp impressions — Maya, Aztec, Toltec, Olmec. Serpents, gods, priests, dancers, etc. 153pp. 6⅛ x 9¼. 20084-1 Pa. $2.50

AMERICAN INDIAN DESIGN AND DECORATION, Leroy Appleton. Full text, plus more than 700 precise drawings of Inca, Maya, Aztec, Pueblo, Plains, NW Coast basketry, sculpture, painting, pottery, sand paintings, metal, etc. 4 plates in color. 279pp. 8⅜ x 11¼. 22704-9 Pa. $4.50

CHINESE LATTICE DESIGNS, Daniel S. Dye. Incredibly beautiful geometric designs: circles, voluted, simple dissections, etc. Inexhaustible source of ideas, motifs. 1239 illustrations. 469pp. 6⅛ x 9¼. 23096-1 Pa. $5.00

JAPANESE DESIGN MOTIFS, Matsuya Co. Mon, or heraldic designs. Over 4000 typical, beautiful designs: birds, animals, flowers, swords, fans, geometric; all beautifully stylized. 213pp. 11⅜ x 8¼. 22874-6 Pa. $4.95

PERSPECTIVE, Jan Vredeman de Vries. 73 perspective plates from 1604 edition; buildings, townscapes, stairways, fantastic scenes. Remarkable for beauty, surrealistic atmosphere; real eye-catchers. Introduction by Adolf Placzek. 74pp. 11⅜ x 8¼. 20186-4 Pa. $2.75

EARLY AMERICAN DESIGN MOTIFS, Suzanne E. Chapman. 497 motifs, designs, from painting on wood, ceramics, appliqué, glassware, samplers, metal work, etc. Florals, landscapes, birds and animals, geometrics, letters, etc. Inexhaustible. Enlarged edition. 138pp. 8⅜ x 11¼. 22985-8 Pa. $3.50
23084-8 Clothbd. $7.95

VICTORIAN STENCILS FOR DESIGN AND DECORATION, edited by E.V. Gillon, Jr. 113 wonderful ornate Victorian pieces from German sources; florals, geometrics; borders, corner pieces; bird motifs, etc. 64pp. 9⅜ x 12¼. 21995-X Pa. $2.50

ART NOUVEAU: AN ANTHOLOGY OF DESIGN AND ILLUSTRATION FROM THE STUDIO, edited by E.V. Gillon, Jr. Graphic arts: book jackets, posters, engravings, illustrations, decorations; Crane, Beardsley, Bradley and many others. Inexhaustible. 92pp. 8⅛ x 11. 22388-4 Pa. $2.50

ORIGINAL ART DECO DESIGNS, William Rowe. First-rate, highly imaginative modern Art Deco frames, borders, compositions, alphabets, florals, insectals, Wurlitzer-types, etc. Much finest modern Art Deco. 80 plates, 8 in color. 8⅜ x 11¼. 22567-4 Pa. $3.00

HANDBOOK OF DESIGNS AND DEVICES, Clarence P. Hornung. Over 1800 basic geometric designs based on circle, triangle, square, scroll, cross, etc. Largest such collection in existence. 261pp. 20125-2 Pa. $2.50

CATALOGUE OF DOVER BOOKS

DRIED FLOWERS, Sarah Whitlock and Martha Rankin. Concise, clear, practical guide to dehydration, glycerinizing, pressing plant material, and more. Covers use of silica gel. 12 drawings. Originally titled "New Techniques with Dried Flowers." 32pp. 21802-3 Pa. $1.00

ABC OF POULTRY RAISING, J.H. Florea. Poultry expert, editor tells how to raise chickens on home or small business basis. Breeds, feeding, housing, laying, etc. Very concrete, practical. 50 illustrations. 256pp. 23201-8 Pa. $3.00

HOW INDIANS USE WILD PLANTS FOR FOOD, MEDICINE & CRAFTS, Frances Densmore. Smithsonian, Bureau of American Ethnology report presents wealth of material on nearly 200 plants used by Chippewas of Minnesota and Wisconsin. 33 plates plus 122pp. of text. 6⅛ x 9¼. 23019-8 Pa. $2.50

THE HERBAL OR GENERAL HISTORY OF PLANTS, John Gerard. The 1633 edition revised and enlarged by Thomas Johnson. Containing almost 2850 plant descriptions and 2705 superb illustrations, Gerard's Herbal is a monumental work, the book all modern English herbals are derived from, and the one herbal every serious enthusiast should have in its entirety. Original editions are worth perhaps $750. 1678pp. 8½ x 12¼. 23147-X Clothbd. $50.00

A MODERN HERBAL, Margaret Grieve. Much the fullest, most exact, most useful compilation of herbal material. Gigantic alphabetical encyclopedia, from aconite to zedoary, gives botanical information, medical properties, folklore, economic uses, and much else. Indispensable to serious reader. 161 illustrations. 888pp. 6½ x 9¼. USO 22798-7, 22799-5 Pa., Two vol. set $10.00

HOW TO KNOW THE FERNS, Frances T. Parsons. Delightful classic. Identification, fern lore, for Eastern and Central U.S.A. Has introduced thousands to interesting life form. 99 illustrations. 215pp. 20740-4 Pa. $2.50

THE MUSHROOM HANDBOOK, Louis C.C. Krieger. Still the best popular handbook. Full descriptions of 259 species, extremely thorough text, habitats, luminescence, poisons, folklore, etc. 32 color plates; 126 other illustrations. 560pp. 21861-9 Pa. $4.50

HOW TO KNOW THE WILD FRUITS, Maude G. Peterson. Classic guide covers nearly 200 trees, shrubs, smaller plants of the U.S. arranged by color of fruit and then by family. Full text provides names, descriptions, edibility, uses. 80 illustrations. 400pp. 22943-2 Pa. $3.00

COMMON WEEDS OF THE UNITED STATES, U.S. Department of Agriculture. Covers 220 important weeds with illustration, maps, botanical information, plant lore for each. Over 225 illustrations. 463pp. 6⅛ x 9¼. 20504-5 Pa. $4.50

HOW TO KNOW THE WILD FLOWERS, Mrs. William S. Dana. Still best popular book for East and Central USA. Over 500 plants easily identified, with plant lore; arranged according to color and flowering time. 174 plates. 459pp. 20332-8 Pa. $3.50

HOUDINI ON MAGIC, Harold Houdini. Edited by Walter Gibson, Morris N. Young. How he escaped; exposés of fake spiritualists; instructions for eye-catching tricks; other fascinating material by and about greatest magician. 155 illustrations. 280pp. 20384-0 Pa. $2.50

HANDBOOK OF THE NUTRITIONAL CONTENTS OF FOOD, U.S. Dept. of Agriculture. Largest, most detailed source of food nutrition information ever prepared. Two mammoth tables: one measuring nutrients in 100 grams of edible portion; the other, in edible portion of 1 pound as purchased. Originally titled Composition of Foods. 190pp. 9 x 12. 21342-0 Pa. $4.00

COMPLETE GUIDE TO HOME CANNING, PRESERVING AND FREEZING, U.S. Dept. of Agriculture. Seven basic manuals with full instructions for jams and jellies; pickles and relishes; canning fruits, vegetables, meat; freezing anything. Really good recipes, exact instructions for optimal results. Save a fortune in food. 156 illustrations. 214pp. 6$\frac{1}{8}$ x 9$\frac{1}{4}$. 22911-4 Pa. $2.50

THE BREAD TRAY, Louis P. De Gouy. Nearly every bread the cook could buy or make: bread sticks of Italy, fruit breads of Greece, glazed rolls of Vienna, everything from corn pone to croissants. Over 500 recipes altogether. including buns, rolls, muffins, scones, and more. 463pp. 23000-7 Pa. $3.50

CREATIVE HAMBURGER COOKERY, Louis P. De Gouy. 182 unusual recipes for casseroles, meat loaves and hamburgers that turn inexpensive ground meat into memorable main dishes: Arizona chili burgers, burger tamale pie, burger stew, burger corn loaf, burger wine loaf, and more. 120pp. 23001-5 Pa. $1.75

LONG ISLAND SEAFOOD COOKBOOK, J. George Frederick and Jean Joyce. Probably the best American seafood cookbook. Hundreds of recipes. 40 gourmet sauces, 123 recipes using oysters alone! All varieties of fish and seafood amply represented. 324pp. 22677-8 Pa. $3.00

THE EPICUREAN: A COMPLETE TREATISE OF ANALYTICAL AND PRACTICAL STUDIES IN THE CULINARY ART, Charles Ranhofer. Great modern classic. 3,500 recipes from master chef of Delmonico's, turn-of-the-century America's best restaurant. Also explained, many techniques known only to professional chefs. 775 illustrations. 1183pp. 6$\frac{5}{8}$ x 10. 22680-8 Clothbd. $17.50

THE AMERICAN WINE COOK BOOK, Ted Hatch. Over 700 recipes: old favorites livened up with wine plus many more: Czech fish soup, quince soup, sauce Perigueux, shrimp shortcake, filets Stroganoff, cordon bleu goulash, jambonneau, wine fruit cake, more. 314pp. 22796-0 Pa. $2.50

DELICIOUS VEGETARIAN COOKING, Ivan Baker. Close to 500 delicious and varied recipes: soups, main course dishes (pea, bean, lentil, cheese, vegetable, pasta, and egg dishes), savories, stews, whole-wheat breads and cakes, more. 168pp. USO 22834-7 Pa. $1.75

CATALOGUE OF DOVER BOOKS

How to Solve Chess Problems, Kenneth S. Howard. Practical suggestions on problem solving for very beginners. 58 two-move problems, 46 3-movers, 8 4-movers for practice, plus hints. 171pp. 20748-X Pa. $2.00

A Guide to Fairy Chess, Anthony Dickins. 3-D chess, 4-D chess, chess on a cylindrical board, reflecting pieces that bounce off edges, cooperative chess, retrograde chess, maximummers, much more. Most based on work of great Dawson. Full handbook, 100 problems. 66pp. 7⅞ x 10¾. 22687-5 Pa. $2.00

Win at Backgammon, Millard Hopper. Best opening moves, running game, blocking game, back game, tables of odds, etc. Hopper makes the game clear enough for anyone to play, and win. 43 diagrams. 111pp. 22894-0 Pa. $1.50

Bidding a Bridge Hand, Terence Reese. Master player "thinks out loud" the binding of 75 hands that defy point count systems. Organized by bidding problem—no-fit situations, overbidding, underbidding, cueing your defense, etc. 254pp. EBE 22830-4 Pa. $2.50

The Precision Bidding System in Bridge, C.C. Wei, edited by Alan Truscott. Inventor of precision bidding presents average hands and hands from actual play, including games from 1969 Bermuda Bowl where system emerged. 114 exercises. 116pp. 21171-1 Pa. $1.75

Learn Magic, Henry Hay. 20 simple, easy-to-follow lessons on magic for the new magician: illusions, card tricks, silks, sleights of hand, coin manipulations, escapes, and more —all with a minimum amount of equipment. Final chapter explains the great stage illusions. 92 illustrations. 285pp. 21238-6 Pa. $2.95

The New Magician's Manual, Walter B. Gibson. Step-by-step instructions and clear illustrations guide the novice in mastering 36 tricks; much equipment supplied on 16 pages of cut-out materials. 36 additional tricks. 64 illustrations. 159pp. 6⅝ x 10. 23113-5 Pa. $3.00

Professional Magic for Amateurs, Walter B. Gibson. 50 easy, effective tricks used by professionals —cards, string, tumblers, handkerchiefs, mental magic, etc. 63 illustrations. 223pp. 23012-0 Pa. $2.50

Card Manipulations, Jean Hugard. Very rich collection of manipulations; has taught thousands of fine magicians tricks that are really workable, eye-catching. Easily followed, serious work. Over 200 illustrations. 163pp. 20539-8 Pa. $2.00

Abbott's Encyclopedia of Rope Tricks for Magicians, Stewart James. Complete reference book for amateur and professional magicians containing more than 150 tricks involving knots, penetrations, cut and restored rope, etc. 510 illustrations. Reprint of 3rd edition. 400pp. 23206-9 Pa. $3.50

The Secrets of Houdini, J.C. Cannell. Classic study of Houdini's incredible magic, exposing closely-kept professional secrets and revealing, in general terms, the whole art of stage magic. 67 illustrations. 279pp. 22913-0 Pa. $2.50

CATALOGUE OF DOVER BOOKS

INCIDENTS OF TRAVEL IN YUCATAN, John L. Stephens. Classic (1843) exploration of jungles of Yucatan, looking for evidences of Maya civilization. Travel adventures, Mexican and Indian culture, etc. Total of 669pp.
20926-1, 20927-X Pa., Two vol. set $5.50

LIVING MY LIFE, Emma Goldman. Candid, no holds barred account by foremost American anarchist: her own life, anarchist movement, famous contemporaries, ideas and their impact. Struggles and confrontations in America, plus deportation to U.S.S.R. Shocking inside account of persecution of anarchists under Lenin. 13 plates. Total of 944pp.
22543-7, 22544-5 Pa., Two vol. set $9.00

AMERICAN INDIANS, George Catlin. Classic account of life among Plains Indians: ceremonies, hunt, warfare, etc. Dover edition reproduces for first time all original paintings. 312 plates. 572pp. of text. 6⅛ x 9¼.
22118-0, 22119-9 Pa., Two vol. set $8.00
22140-7, 22144-X Clothbd., Two vol. set $16.00

THE INDIANS' BOOK, Natalie Curtis. Lore, music, narratives, drawings by Indians, collected from cultures of U.S.A. 149 songs in full notation. 45 illustrations. 583pp. 6⅝ x 9⅜.
21939-9 Pa. $5.00

INDIAN BLANKETS AND THEIR MAKERS, George Wharton James. History, old style wool blankets, changes brought about by traders, symbolism of design and color, a Navajo weaver at work, outline blanket, Kachina blankets, more. Emphasis on Navajo. 130 illustrations, 32 in color. 230pp. 6⅛ x 9¼.
22996-3 Pa. $5.00
23068-6 Clothbd. $10.00

AN INTRODUCTION TO THE STUDY OF THE MAYA HIEROGLYPHS, Sylvanus Griswold Morley. Classic study by one of the truly great figures in hieroglyph research. Still the best introduction for the student for reading Maya hieroglyphs. New introduction by J. Eric S. Thompson. 117 illustrations. 284pp.
23108-9 Pa. $4.00

THE ANALECTS OF CONFUCIUS, THE GREAT LEARNING, DOCTRINE OF THE MEAN, Confucius. Edited by James Legge. Full Chinese text, standard English translation on same page, Chinese commentators, editor's annotations; dictionary of characters at rear, plus grammatical comment. Finest edition anywhere of one of world's greatest thinkers. 503pp.
22746-4 Pa. $4.50

THE I CHING (THE BOOK OF CHANGES), translated by James Legge. Complete translation of basic text plus appendices by Confucius, and Chinese commentary of most penetrating divination manual ever prepared. Indispensable to study of early Oriental civilizations, to modern inquiring reader. 448pp.
21062-6 Pa. $3.50

THE EGYPTIAN BOOK OF THE DEAD, E.A. Wallis Budge. Complete reproduction of Ani's papyrus, finest ever found. Full hieroglyphic text, interlinear transliteration, word for word translation, smooth translation. Basic work, for Egyptology, for modern study of psychic matters. Total of 533pp. 6½ x 9¼.
EBE 21866-X Pa. $4.95

JEWISH GREETING CARDS, Ed Sibbett, Jr. 16 cards to cut and color. Three say "Happy Chanukah," one "Happy New Year," others have no message, show stars of David, Torahs, wine cups, other traditional themes. 16 envelopes. 8¼ x 11.
23225-5 Pa. $2.00

AUBREY BEARDSLEY GREETING CARD BOOK, Aubrey Beardsley. Edited by Theodore Menten. 16 elegant yet inexpensive greeting cards let you combine your own sentiments with subtle Art Nouveau lines. 16 different Aubrey Beardsley designs that you can color or not, as you wish. 16 envelopes. 64pp. 8¼ x 11.
23173-9 Pa. $2.00

RECREATIONS IN THE THEORY OF NUMBERS, Albert Beiler. Number theory, an inexhaustible source of puzzles, recreations, for beginners and advanced. Divisors, perfect numbers. scales of notation, etc. 349pp.
21096-0 Pa. $2.50

AMUSEMENTS IN MATHEMATICS, Henry E. Dudeney. One of largest puzzle collections, based on algebra, arithmetic, permutations, probability, plane figure dissection, properties of numbers, by one of world's foremost puzzlists. Solutions. 450 illustrations. 258pp.
20473-1 Pa. $2.75

MATHEMATICS, MAGIC AND MYSTERY, Martin Gardner. Puzzle editor for Scientific American explains math behind: card tricks, stage mind reading, coin and match tricks, counting out games, geometric dissections. Probability, sets, theory of numbers, clearly explained. Plus more than 400 tricks, guaranteed to work. 135 illustrations. 176pp.
20335-2 Pa. $2.00

BEST MATHEMATICAL PUZZLES OF SAM LOYD, edited by Martin Gardner. Bizarre, original, whimsical puzzles by America's greatest puzzler. From fabulously rare Cyclopedia, including famous 14-15 puzzles, the Horse of a Different Color, 115 more. Elementary math. 150 illustrations. 167pp.
20498-7 Pa. $2.00

MATHEMATICAL PUZZLES FOR BEGINNERS AND ENTHUSIASTS, Geoffrey Mott-Smith. 189 puzzles from easy to difficult involving arithmetic, logic, algebra, properties of digits, probability. Explanation of math behind puzzles. 135 illustrations. 248pp.
20198-8 Pa. $2.00

BIG BOOK OF MAZES AND LABYRINTHS, Walter Shepherd. Classical, solid, and ripple mazes; short path and avoidance labyrinths; more — 50 mazes and labyrinths in all. 12 other figures. Full solutions. 112pp. 8⅛ x 11.
22951-3 Pa. $2.00

COIN GAMES AND PUZZLES, Maxey Brooke. 60 puzzles, games and stunts — from Japan, Korea, Africa and the ancient world, by Dudeney and the other great puzzlers, as well as Maxey Brooke's own creations. Full solutions. 67 illustrations. 94pp.
22893-2 Pa. $1.25

HAND SHADOWS TO BE THROWN UPON THE WALL, Henry Bursill. Wonderful Victorian novelty tells how to make flying birds, dog, goose, deer, and 14 others. 32pp. 6½ x 9¼.
21779-5 Pa. $1.00

MANUAL OF THE TREES OF NORTH AMERICA, Charles S. Sargent. The basic survey of every native tree and tree-like shrub, 717 species in all. Extremely full descriptions, information on habitat, growth, locales, economics, etc. Necessary to every serious tree lover. Over 100 finding keys. 783 illustrations. Total of 986pp.
20277-1, 20278-X Pa., Two vol. set $8.00

BIRDS OF THE NEW YORK AREA, John Bull. Indispensable guide to more than 400 species within a hundred-mile radius of Manhattan. Information on range, status, breeding, migration, distribution trends, etc. Foreword by Roger Tory Peterson. 17 drawings; maps. 540pp.
23222-0 Pa. $6.00

THE SEA-BEACH AT EBB-TIDE, Augusta Foote Arnold. Identify hundreds of marine plants and animals: algae, seaweeds, squids, crabs, corals, etc. Descriptions cover food, life cycle, size, shape, habitat. Over 600 drawings. 490pp.
21949-6 Pa. $4.00

THE MOTH BOOK, William J. Holland. Identify more than 2,000 moths of North America. General information, precise species descriptions. 623 illustrations plus 48 color plates show almost all species, full size. 1968 edition. Still the basic book. Total of 551pp. 6½ x 9¼.
21948-8 Pa. $6.00

AN INTRODUCTION TO THE REPTILES AND AMPHIBIANS OF THE UNITED STATES, Percy A. Morris. All lizards, crocodiles, turtles, snakes, toads, frogs; life history, identification, habits, suitability as pets, etc. Non-technical, but sound and broad. 130 photos. 253pp.
22982-3 Pa. $3.00

OLD NEW YORK IN EARLY PHOTOGRAPHS, edited by Mary Black. Your only chance to see New York City as it was 1853-1906, through 196 wonderful photographs from N.Y. Historical Society. Great Blizzard, Lincoln's funeral procession, great buildings. 228pp. 9 x 12.
22907-6 Pa. $6.00

THE AMERICAN REVOLUTION, A PICTURE SOURCEBOOK, John Grafton. Wonderful Bicentennial picture source, with 411 illustrations (contemporary and 19th century) showing battles, personalities, maps, events, flags, posters, soldier's life, ships, etc. all captioned and explained. A wonderful browsing book, supplement to other historical reading. 160pp. 9 x 12.
23226-3 Pa. $4.00

PERSONAL NARRATIVE OF A PILGRIMAGE TO AL-MADINAH AND MECCAH, Richard Burton. Great travel classic by remarkably colorful personality. Burton, disguised as a Moroccan, visited sacred shrines of Islam, narrowly escaping death. Wonderful observations of Islamic life, customs, personalities. 47 illustrations. Total of 959pp.
21217-3, 21218-1 Pa., Two vol. set $7.00

INCIDENTS OF TRAVEL IN CENTRAL AMERICA, CHIAPAS, AND YUCATAN, John L. Stephens. Almost single-handed discovery of Maya culture; exploration of ruined cities, monuments, temples; customs of Indians. 115 drawings. 892pp.
22404-X, 22405-8 Pa., Two vol. set $8.00

MODERN CHESS STRATEGY, Ludek Pachman. The use of the queen, the active king, exchanges, pawn play, the center, weak squares, etc. Section on rook alone worth price of the book. Stress on the moderns. Often considered the most important book on strategy. 314pp. 20290-9 Pa. $3.00

CHESS STRATEGY, Edward Lasker. One of half-dozen great theoretical works in chess, shows principles of action above and beyond moves. Acclaimed by Capablanca, Keres, etc. 282pp. USO 20528-2 Pa. $2.50

CHESS PRAXIS, THE PRAXIS OF MY SYSTEM, Aron Nimzovich. Founder of hyper-modern chess explains his profound, influential theories that have dominated much of 20th century chess. 109 illustrative games. 369pp. 20296-8 Pa. $3.50

HOW TO PLAY THE CHESS OPENINGS, Eugene Znosko-Borovsky. Clear, profound ex-aminations of just what each opening is intended to do and how opponent can counter. Many sample games, questions and answers. 147pp. 22795-2 Pa. $2.00

THE ART OF CHESS COMBINATION, Eugene Znosko-Borovsky. Modern explanation of principles, varieties, techniques and ideas behind them, illustrated with many examples from great players. 212pp. 20583-5 Pa. $2.00

COMBINATIONS: THE HEART OF CHESS, Irving Chernev. Step-by-step explanation of intricacies of combinative play. 356 combinations by Tarrasch, Botvinnik, Keres, Steinitz, Anderssen, Morphy, Marshall, Capablanca, others, all annotated. 245 pp. 21744-2 Pa. $2.50

HOW TO PLAY CHESS ENDINGS, Eugene Znosko-Borovsky. Thorough instruction manual by fine teacher analyzes each piece individually; many common endgame situations. Examines games by Steinitz, Alekhine, Lasker, others. Emphasis on understanding. 288pp. 21170-3 Pa. $2.75

MORPHY'S GAMES OF CHESS, Philip W. Sergeant. Romantic history, 54 games of greatest player of all time against Anderssen, Bird, Paulsen, Harrwitz; 52 games at odds; 52 blindfold; 100 consultation, informal, other games. Analyses by An-derssen, Steinitz, Morphy himself. 352pp. 20386-7 Pa. $2.75

500 MASTER GAMES OF CHESS, S. Tartakower, J. du Mont. Vast collection of great chess games from 1798-1938, with much material nowhere else readily available. Fully annotated, arranged by opening for easier study. 665pp. 23208-5 Pa. $6.00

THE SOVIET SCHOOL OF CHESS, Alexander Kotov and M. Yudovich. Authoritative work on modern Russian chess. History, conceptual background. 128 fully anno-tated games (most unavailable elsewhere) by Botvinnik, Keres, Smyslov, Tal, Petrosian, Spassky, more. 390pp. 20026-4 Pa. $3.95

WONDERS AND CURIOSITIES OF CHESS, Irving Chernev. A lifetime's accumulation of such wonders and curiosities as the longest won game, shortest game, chess problem with mate in 1220 moves, and much more unusual material — 356 items in all, over 160 complete games. 146 diagrams. 203pp. 23007-4 Pa. $3.50

MOTHER GOOSE'S MELODIES. Facsimile of fabulously rare Munroe and Francis "copyright 1833" Boston edition. Familiar and unusual rhymes, wonderful old woodcut illustrations. Edited by E.F. Bleiler. 128pp. 4½ x 6⅜. 22577-1 Pa. $1.00

MOTHER GOOSE IN HIEROGLYPHICS. Favorite nursery rhymes presented in rebus form for children. Fascinating 1849 edition reproduced in toto, with key. Introduction by E.F. Bleiler. About 400 woodcuts. 64pp. 6⅞ x 5¼. 20745-5 Pa. $1.00

PETER PIPER'S PRACTICAL PRINCIPLES OF PLAIN & PERFECT PRONUNCIATION. Alliterative jingles and tongue-twisters. Reproduction in full of 1830 first American edition. 25 spirited woodcuts. 32pp. 4½ x 6⅜. 22560-7 Pa. $1.00

MARMADUKE MULTIPLY'S MERRY METHOD OF MAKING MINOR MATHEMATICIANS. Fellow to Peter Piper, it teaches multiplication table by catchy rhymes and woodcuts. 1841 Munroe & Francis edition. Edited by E.F. Bleiler. 103pp. 4⅝ x 6.
22773-1 Pa. $1.25
20171-6 Clothbd. $3.00

THE NIGHT BEFORE CHRISTMAS, Clement Moore. Full text, and woodcuts from original 1848 book. Also critical, historical material. 19 illustrations. 40pp. 4⅝ x 6. 22797-9 Pa. $1.00

THE KING OF THE GOLDEN RIVER, John Ruskin. Victorian children's classic of three brothers, their attempts to reach the Golden River, what becomes of them. Facsimile of original 1889 edition. 22 illustrations. 56pp. 4⅝ x 6⅜.
20066-3 Pa. $1.25

DREAMS OF THE RAREBIT FIEND, Winsor McCay. Pioneer cartoon strip, unexcelled for beauty, imagination, in 60 full sequences. Incredible technical virtuosity, wonderful visual wit. Historical introduction. 62pp. 8⅜ x 11¼. 21347-1 Pa. $2.00

THE KATZENJAMMER KIDS, Rudolf Dirks. In full color, 14 strips from 1906-7; full of imagination, characteristic humor. Classic of great historical importance. Introduction by August Derleth. 32pp. 9¼ x 12¼. 23005-8 Pa. $2.00

LITTLE ORPHAN ANNIE AND LITTLE ORPHAN ANNIE IN COSMIC CITY, Harold Gray. Two great sequences from the early strips: our curly-haired heroine defends the Warbucks' financial empire and, then, takes on meanie Phineas P. Pinchpenny. Leapin' lizards! 178pp. 6⅛ x 8⅜. 23107-0 Pa. $2.00

WHEN A FELLER NEEDS A FRIEND, Clare Briggs. 122 cartoons by one of the greatest newspaper cartoonists of the early 20th century — about growing up, making a living, family life, daily frustrations and occasional triumphs. 121pp. 8½ x 9½.
23148-8 Pa. $2.50

THE BEST OF GLUYAS WILLIAMS. 100 drawings by one of America's finest cartoonists: The Day a Cake of Ivory Soap Sank at Proctor & Gamble's, At the Life Insurance Agents' Banquet, and many other gems from the 20's and 30's. 118pp. 8⅜ x 11¼. 22737-5 Pa. $2.50

SLEEPING BEAUTY, illustrated by Arthur Rackham. Perhaps the fullest, most delightful version ever, told by C.S. Evans. Rackham's best work. 49 illustrations. 110pp. 7⅞ x 10¾. 22756-1 Pa. $2.00

THE WONDERFUL WIZARD OF OZ, L. Frank Baum. Facsimile in full color of America's finest children's classic. Introduction by Martin Gardner. 143 illustrations by W.W. Denslow. 267pp. 20691-2 Pa. $2.50

GOOPS AND HOW TO BE THEM, Gelett Burgess. Classic tongue-in-cheek masquerading as etiquette book. 87 verses, 170 cartoons as Goops demonstrate virtues of table manners, neatness, courtesy, more. 88pp. 6½ x 9¼. 22233-0 Pa. $1.50

THE BROWNIES, THEIR BOOK, Palmer Cox. Small as mice, cunning as foxes, exuberant, mischievous, Brownies go to zoo, toy shop, seashore, circus, more. 24 verse adventures. 266 illustrations. 144pp. 6⅝ x 9¼. 21265-3 Pa. $1.75

BILLY WHISKERS: THE AUTOBIOGRAPHY OF A GOAT, Frances Trego Montgomery. Escapades of that rambunctious goat. Favorite from turn of the century America. 24 illustrations. 259pp. 22345-0 Pa. $2.75

THE ROCKET BOOK, Peter Newell. Fritz, janitor's kid, sets off rocket in basement of apartment house; an ingenious hole punched through every page traces course of rocket. 22 duotone drawings, verses. 48pp. 6⅞ x 8⅜. 22044-3 Pa. $1.50

PECK'S BAD BOY AND HIS PA, George W. Peck. Complete double-volume of great American childhood classic. Hennery's ingenious pranks against outraged pomposity of pa and the grocery man. 97 illustrations. Introduction by E.F. Bleiler. 347pp. 20497-9 Pa. $2.50

THE TALE OF PETER RABBIT, Beatrix Potter. The inimitable Peter's terrifying adventure in Mr. McGregor's garden, with all 27 wonderful, full-color Potter illustrations. 55pp. 4¼ x 5½. USO 22827-4 Pa. $1.00

THE TALE OF MRS. TIGGY-WINKLE, Beatrix Potter. Your child will love this story about a very special hedgehog and all 27 wonderful, full-color Potter illustrations. 57pp. 4¼ x 5½. USO 20546-0 Pa. $1.00

THE TALE OF BENJAMIN BUNNY, Beatrix Potter. Peter Rabbit's cousin coaxes him back into Mr. McGregor's garden for a whole new set of adventures. A favorite with children. All 27 full-color illustrations. 59pp. 4¼ x 5½. USO 21102-9 Pa. $1.00

THE MERRY ADVENTURES OF ROBIN HOOD, Howard Pyle. Facsimile of original (1883) edition, finest modern version of English outlaw's adventures. 23 illustrations by Pyle. 296pp. 6½ x 9¼. 22043-5 Pa. $2.75

TWO LITTLE SAVAGES, Ernest Thompson Seton. Adventures of two boys who lived as Indians; explaining Indian ways, woodlore, pioneer methods. 293 illustrations. 286pp. 20985-7 Pa. $3.00

THE ART DECO STYLE, ed. by Theodore Menten. Furniture, jewelry, metalwork, ceramics, fabrics, lighting fixtures, interior decors, exteriors, graphics from pure French sources. Best sampling around. Over 400 photographs. 183pp. 8⅜ x 11¼.
22824-X Pa. $4.00

THE GENTLEMAN AND CABINET MAKER'S DIRECTOR, Thomas Chippendale. Full reprint, 1762 style book, most influential of all time; chairs, tables, sofas, mirrors, cabinets, etc. 200 plates, plus 24 photographs of surviving pieces. 249pp. 9⅞ x 12¾.
21601-2 Pa. $5.00

PINE FURNITURE OF EARLY NEW ENGLAND, Russell H. Kettell. Basic book. Thorough historical text, plus 200 illustrations of boxes, highboys, candlesticks, desks, etc. 477pp. 7⅞ x 10¾.
20145-7 Clothbd. $12.50

ORIENTAL RUGS, ANTIQUE AND MODERN, Walter A. Hawley. Persia, Turkey, Caucasus, Central Asia, China, other traditions. Best general survey of all aspects: styles and periods, manufacture, uses, symbols and their interpretation, and identification. 96 illustrations, 11 in color. 320pp. 6⅛ x 9¼.
22366-3 Pa. $5.00

DECORATIVE ANTIQUE IRONWORK, Henry R. d'Allemagne. Photographs of 4500 iron artifacts from world's finest collection, Rouen. Hinges, locks, candelabra, weapons, lighting devices, clocks, tools, from Roman times to mid-19th century. Nothing else comparable to it. 420pp. 9 x 12.
22082-6 Pa. $8.50

THE COMPLETE BOOK OF DOLL MAKING AND COLLECTING, Catherine Christopher. Instructions, patterns for dozens of dolls, from rag doll on up to elaborate, historically accurate figures. Mould faces, sew clothing, make doll houses, etc. Also collecting information. Many illustrations. 288pp. 6 x 9. 22066-4 Pa. $3.00

ANTIQUE PAPER DOLLS: 1915-1920, edited by Arnold Arnold. 7 antique cut-out dolls and 24 costumes from 1915-1920, selected by Arnold Arnold from his collection of rare children's books and entertainments, all in full color. 32pp. 9¼ x 12¼.
23176-3 Pa. $2.00

ANTIQUE PAPER DOLLS: THE EDWARDIAN ERA, Epinal. Full-color reproductions of two historic series of paper dolls that show clothing styles in 1908 and at the beginning of the First World War. 8 two-sided, stand-up dolls and 32 complete, two-sided costumes. Full instructions for assembling included. 32pp. 9¼ x 12¼.
23175-5 Pa. $2.00

A HISTORY OF COSTUME, Carl Köhler, Emma von Sichardt. Egypt, Babylon, Greece up through 19th century Europe; based on surviving pieces, art works, etc. Full text and 595 illustrations, including many clear, measured patterns for reproducing historic costume. Practical. 464pp. 21030-8 Pa. $4.00

EARLY AMERICAN LOCOMOTIVES, John H. White, Jr. Finest locomotive engravings from late 19th century: historical (1804-1874), main-line (after 1870), special, foreign, etc. 147 plates. 200pp. 11⅜ x 8¼.
22772-3 Pa. $3.50

THE BEST DR. THORNDYKE DETECTIVE STORIES, R. Austin Freeman. The Case of Oscar Brodski, The Moabite Cipher, and 5 other favorites featuring the great scientific detective, plus his long-believed-lost first adventure — 31 New Inn — reprinted here for the first time. Edited by E.F. Bleiler. USO 20388-3 Pa. $3.00

BEST "THINKING MACHINE" DETECTIVE STORIES, Jacques Futrelle. The Problem of Cell 13 and 11 other stories about Prof. Augustus S.F.X. Van Dusen, including two "lost" stories. First reprinting of several. Edited by E.F. Bleiler. 241pp.
20537-1 Pa. $3.00

UNCLE SILAS, J. Sheridan LeFanu. Victorian Gothic mystery novel, considered by many best of period, even better than Collins or Dickens. Wonderful psychological terror. Introduction by Frederick Shroyer. 436pp. 21715-9 Pa. $4.00

BEST DR. POGGIOLI DETECTIVE STORIES, T.S. Stribling. 15 best stories from EQMM and The Saint offer new adventures in Mexico, Florida, Tennessee hills as Poggioli unravels mysteries and combats Count Jalacki. 217pp. 23227-1 Pa. $3.00

EIGHT DIME NOVELS, selected with an introduction by E.F. Bleiler. Adventures of Old King Brady, Frank James, Nick Carter, Deadwood Dick, Buffalo Bill, The Steam Man, Frank Merriwell, and Horatio Alger — 1877 to 1905. Important, entertaining popular literature in facsimile reprint, with original covers. 190pp. 9 x 12. 22975-0 Pa. $3.50

ALICE'S ADVENTURES UNDER GROUND, Lewis Carroll. Facsimile of ms. Carroll gave Alice Liddell in 1864. Different in many ways from final Alice. Handlettered, illustrated by Carroll. Introduction by Martin Gardner. 128pp. 21482-6 Pa. $1.50

ALICE IN WONDERLAND COLORING BOOK, Lewis Carroll. Pictures by John Tenniel. Large-size versions of the famous illustrations of Alice, Cheshire Cat, Mad Hatter and all the others, waiting for your crayons. Abridged text. 36 illustrations. 64pp. 8¼ x 11. 22853-3 Pa. $1.50

AVENTURES D'ALICE AU PAYS DES MERVEILLES, Lewis Carroll. Bué's translation of "Alice" into French, supervised by Carroll himself. Novel way to learn language. (No English text.) 42 Tenniel illustrations. 196pp. 22836-3 Pa. $2.00

MYTHS AND FOLK TALES OF IRELAND, Jeremiah Curtin. 11 stories that are Irish versions of European fairy tales and 9 stories from the Fenian cycle — 20 tales of legend and magic that comprise an essential work in the history of folklore. 256pp. 22430-9 Pa. $3.00

EAST O' THE SUN AND WEST O' THE MOON, George W. Dasent. Only full edition of favorite, wonderful Norwegian fairytales — Why the Sea is Salt, Boots and the Troll, etc. — with 77 illustrations by Kittelsen & Werenskiöld. 418pp.
22521-6 Pa. $3.50

PERRAULT'S FAIRY TALES, Charles Perrault and Gustave Doré. Original versions of Cinderella, Sleeping Beauty, Little Red Riding Hood, etc. in best translation, with 34 wonderful illustrations by Gustave Doré. 117pp. 8⅛ x 11. 22311-6 Pa. $2.50

THE FITZWILLIAM VIRGINAL BOOK, edited by J. Fuller Maitland, W.B. Squire. Famous early 17th century collection of keyboard music, 300 works by Morley, Byrd, Bull, Gibbons, etc. Modern notation. Total of 938pp. 8⅜ x 11.

ECE 21068-5, 21069-3 Pa., Two vol. set $12.00

COMPLETE STRING QUARTETS, Wolfgang A. Mozart. Breitkopf and Härtel edition. All 23 string quartets plus alternate slow movement to K156. Study score. 277pp. 9⅜ x 12¼. 22372-8 Pa. $6.00

COMPLETE SONG CYCLES, Franz Schubert. Complete piano, vocal music of Die Schöne Müllerin, Die Winterreise, Schwanengesang. Also Drinker English singing translations. Breitkopf and Härtel edition. 217pp. 9⅜ x 12¼.

22649-2 Pa. $4.00

THE COMPLETE PRELUDES AND ETUDES FOR PIANOFORTE SOLO, Alexander Scriabin. All the preludes and etudes including many perfectly spun miniatures. Edited by K.N. Igumnov and Y.I. Mil'shteyn. 250pp. 9 x 12. 22919-X Pa. $5.00

TRISTAN UND ISOLDE, Richard Wagner. Full orchestral score with complete instrumentation. Do not confuse with piano reduction. Commentary by Felix Mottl, great Wagnerian conductor and scholar. Study score. 655pp. 8⅛ x 11.

22915-7 Pa. $10.00

FAVORITE SONGS OF THE NINETIES, ed. Robert Fremont. Full reproduction, including covers, of 88 favorites: Ta-Ra-Ra-Boom-De-Aye, The Band Played On, Bird in a Gilded Cage, Under the Bamboo Tree, After the Ball, etc. 401pp. 9 x 12.

EBE 21536-9 Pa. $6.95

SOUSA'S GREAT MARCHES IN PIANO TRANSCRIPTION: ORIGINAL SHEET MUSIC OF 23 WORKS, John Philip Sousa. Selected by Lester S. Levy. Playing edition includes: The Stars and Stripes Forever, The Thunderer, The Gladiator, King Cotton, Washington Post, much more. 24 illustrations. 111pp. 9 x 12.

USO 23132-1 Pa. $3.50

CLASSIC PIANO RAGS, selected with an introduction by Rudi Blesh. Best ragtime music (1897-1922) by Scott Joplin, James Scott, Joseph F. Lamb, Tom Turpin, 9 others. Printed from best original sheet music, plus covers. 364pp. 9 x 12.

EBE 20469-3 Pa. $6.95

ANALYSIS OF CHINESE CHARACTERS, C.D. Wilder, J.H. Ingram. 1000 most important characters analyzed according to primitives, phonetics, historical development. Traditional method offers mnemonic aid to beginner, intermediate student of Chinese, Japanese. 365pp. 23045-7 Pa. $4.00

MODERN CHINESE: A BASIC COURSE, Faculty of Peking University. Self study, classroom course in modern Mandarin. Records contain phonetics, vocabulary, sentences, lessons. 249 page book contains all recorded text, translations, grammar, vocabulary, exercises. Best course on market. 3 12" 33⅓ monaural records, book, album. 98832-5 Set $12.50

THE MAGIC MOVING PICTURE BOOK, Bliss, Sands & Co. The pictures in this book move! Volcanoes erupt, a house burns, a serpentine dancer wiggles her way through a number. By using a specially ruled acetate screen provided, you can obtain these and 15 other startling effects. Originally "The Motograph Moving Picture Book." 32pp. 8¼ x 11.   23224-7 Pa. $1.75

STRING FIGURES AND HOW TO MAKE THEM, Caroline F. Jayne. Fullest, clearest instructions on string figures from around world: Eskimo, Navajo, Lapp, Europe, more. Cats cradle, moving spear, lightning, stars. Introduction by A.C. Haddon. 950 illustrations. 407pp.   20152-X Pa. $3.00

PAPER FOLDING FOR BEGINNERS, William D. Murray and Francis J. Rigney. Clearest book on market for making origami sail boats, roosters, frogs that move legs, cups, bonbon boxes. 40 projects. More than 275 illustrations. Photographs. 94pp.
20713-7 Pa. $1.25

INDIAN SIGN LANGUAGE, William Tomkins. Over 525 signs developed by Sioux, Blackfoot, Cheyenne, Arapahoe and other tribes. Written instructions and diagrams: how to make words, construct sentences. Also 290 pictographs of Sioux and Ojibway tribes. 111pp. 6⅛ x 9¼.   22029-X Pa. $1.50

BOOMERANGS: HOW TO MAKE AND THROW THEM, Bernard S. Mason. Easy to make and throw, dozens of designs: cross-stick, pinwheel, boomabird, tumblestick, Australian curved stick boomerang. Complete throwing instructions. All safe. 99pp.   23028-7 Pa. $1.50

25 KITES THAT FLY, Leslie Hunt. Full, easy to follow instructions for kites made from inexpensive materials. Many novelties. Reeling, raising, designing your own. 70 illustrations. 110pp.   22550-X Pa. $1.25

TRICKS AND GAMES ON THE POOL TABLE, Fred Herrmann. 79 tricks and games, some solitaires, some for 2 or more players, some competitive; mystifying shots and throws, unusual carom, tricks involving cork, coins, a hat, more. 77 figures. 95pp.   21814-7 Pa. $1.25

WOODCRAFT AND CAMPING, Bernard S. Mason. How to make a quick emergency shelter, select woods that will burn immediately, make do with limited supplies, etc. Also making many things out of wood, rawhide, bark, at camp. Formerly titled Woodcraft. 295 illustrations. 580pp.   21951-8 Pa. $4.00

AN INTRODUCTION TO CHESS MOVES AND TACTICS SIMPLY EXPLAINED, Leonard Barden. Informal intermediate introduction: reasons for moves, tactics, openings, traps, positional play, endgame. Isolates patterns. 102pp. USO 21210-6 Pa. $1.35

LASKER'S MANUAL OF CHESS, Dr. Emanuel Lasker. Great world champion offers very thorough coverage of all aspects of chess. Combinations, position play, openings, endgame, aesthetics of chess, philosophy of struggle, much more. Filled with analyzed games. 390pp.   20640-8 Pa. $3.50

THE STYLE OF PALESTRINA AND THE DISSONANCE, Knud Jeppesen. Standard analysis of rhythm, line, harmony, accented and unaccented dissonances. Also pre-Palestrina dissonances. 306pp. 22386-8 Pa. $3.00

DOVER OPERA GUIDE AND LIBRETTO SERIES prepared by Ellen H. Bleiler. Each volume contains everything needed for background, complete enjoyment: complete libretto, new English translation with all repeats, biography of composer and librettist, early performance history, musical lore, much else. All volumes lavishly illustrated with performance photos, portraits, similar material. Do not confuse with skimpy performance booklets.

CARMEN, Georges Bizet. 66 illustrations. 222pp. 22111-3 Pa. $2.00
DON GIOVANNI, Wolfgang A. Mozart. 92 illustrations. 209pp. 21134-7 Pa. $2.50
LA BOHÈME, Giacomo Puccini. 73 illustrations. 124pp. USO 20404-9 Pa. $1.75
ÄIDA, Giuseppe Verdi. 76 illustrations. 181pp. 20405-7 Pa. $2.00
LUCIA DI LAMMERMOOR, Gaetano Donizetti. 44 illustrations. 186pp.
22110-5 Pa. $2.00

ANTONIO STRADIVARI: HIS LIFE AND WORK, W. H. Hill, et al. Great work of musicology. Construction methods, woods, varnishes, known instruments, types of instruments, life, special features. Introduction by Sydney Beck. 98 illustrations, plus 4 color plates. 315pp. 20425-1 Pa. $3.00

MUSIC FOR THE PIANO, James Friskin, Irwin Freundlich. Both famous, little-known compositions; 1500 to 1950's. Listing, description, classification, technical aspects for student, teacher, performer. Indispensable for enlarging repertory. 448pp.
22918-1 Pa. $4.00

PIANOS AND THEIR MAKERS, Alfred Dolge. Leading inventor offers full history of piano technology, earliest models to 1910. Types, makers, components, mechanisms, musical aspects. Very strong on offtrail models, inventions; also player pianos. 300 illustrations. 581pp. 22856-8 Pa. $5.00

KEYBOARD MUSIC, J.S. Bach. Bach-Gesellschaft edition. For harpsichord, piano, other keyboard instruments. English Suites, French Suites, Six Partitas, Goldberg Variations, Two-Part Inventions, Three-Part Sinfonias. 312pp. 8⅛ x 11.
22360-4 Pa. $5.00

COMPLETE STRING QUARTETS, Ludwig van Beethoven. Breitkopf and Härtel edition. 6 quartets of Opus 18; 3 quartets of Opus 59; Opera 74, 95, 127, 130, 131, 132, 135 and Grosse Fuge. Study score. 434pp. 9⅜ x 12¼. 22361-2 Pa. $7.95

COMPLETE PIANO SONATAS AND VARIATIONS FOR SOLO PIANO, Johannes Brahms. All sonatas, five variations on themes from Schumann, Paganini, Handel, etc. Vienna Gesellschaft der Musikfreunde edition. 178pp. 9 x 12. 22650-6 Pa. $4.00

PIANO MUSIC 1888-1905, Claude Debussy. Deux Arabesques, Suite Bergamasque, Masques, 1st series of Images, etc. 9 others, in corrected editions. 175pp. 9⅜ x 12¼. 22771-5 Pa. $4.00

150 MASTERPIECES OF DRAWING, edited by Anthony Toney. 150 plates, early 15th century to end of 18th century; Rembrandt, Michelangelo, Dürer, Fragonard, Watteau, Wouwerman, many others. 150pp. 8⅜ x 11¼.　　21032-4 Pa. $3.50

THE GOLDEN AGE OF THE POSTER, Hayward and Blanche Cirker. 70 extraordinary posters in full colors, from Maîtres de l'Affiche, Mucha, Lautrec, Bradley, Cheret, Beardsley, many others. 9⅜ x 12¼.　　22753-7 Pa. $4.95
21718-3 Clothbd. $7.95

SIMPLICISSIMUS, selection, translations and text by Stanley Appelbaum. 180 satirical drawings, 16 in full color, from the famous German weekly magazine in the years 1896 to 1926. 24 artists included: Grosz, Kley, Pascin, Kubin, Kollwitz, plus Heine, Thöny, Bruno Paul, others. 172pp. 8½ x 12¼.　　23098-8 Pa. $5.00
23099-6 Clothbd. $10.00

THE EARLY WORK OF AUBREY BEARDSLEY, Aubrey Beardsley. 157 plates, 2 in color: Manon Lescaut, Madame Bovary, Morte d'Arthur, Salome, other. Introduction by H. Marillier. 175pp. 8½ x 11.　　21816-3 Pa. $3.50

THE LATER WORK OF AUBREY BEARDSLEY, Aubrey Beardsley. Exotic masterpieces of full maturity: Venus and Tannhäuser, Lysistrata, Rape of the Lock, Volpone, Savoy material, etc. 174 plates, 2 in color. 176pp. 8½ x 11. 21817-1 Pa. $3.75

DRAWINGS OF WILLIAM BLAKE, William Blake. 92 plates from Book of Job, Divine Comedy, Paradise Lost, visionary heads, mythological figures, Laocoön, etc. Selection, introduction, commentary by Sir Geoffrey Keynes. 178pp. 8½ x 11.
22303-5 Pa. $3.50

LONDON: A PILGRIMAGE, Gustave Doré, Blanchard Jerrold. Squalor, riches, misery, beauty of mid-Victorian metropolis; 55 wonderful plates, 125 other illustrations, full social, cultural text by Jerrold. 191pp. of text. 8⅛ x 11.
22306-X Pa. $5.00

THE COMPLETE WOODCUTS OF ALBRECHT DÜRER, edited by Dr. W. Kurth. 346 in all: Old Testament, St. Jerome, Passion, Life of Virgin, Apocalypse, many others. Introduction by Campbell Dodgson. 285pp. 8½ x 12¼.　　21097-9 Pa. $6.00

THE DISASTERS OF WAR, Francisco Goya. 83 etchings record horrors of Napoleonic wars in Spain and war in general. Reprint of 1st edition, plus 3 additional plates. Introduction by Philip Hofer. 97pp. 9⅜ x 8¼.　　21872-4 Pa. $2.50

ENGRAVINGS OF HOGARTH, William Hogarth. 101 of Hogarth's greatest works: Rake's Progress, Harlot's Progress, Illustrations for Hudibras, Midnight Modern Conversation, Before and After, Beer Street and Gin Lane, many more. Full commentary. 256pp. 11 x 14.　　22479-1 Pa. $6.00
23023-6 Clothbd. $13.50

PRIMITIVE ART, Franz Boas. Great anthropologist on ceramics, textiles, wood, stone, metal, etc.; patterns, technology, symbols, styles. All areas, but fullest on Northwest Coast Indians. 350 illustrations. 378pp.　　20025-6 Pa. $3.50

EGYPTIAN MAGIC, E.A. Wallis Budge. Foremost Egyptologist, curator at British Museum, on charms, curses, amulets, doll magic, transformations, control of demons, deific appearances, feats of great magicians. Many texts cited. 19 illustrations. 234pp. USO 22681-6 Pa. $2.50

THE LEYDEN PAPYRUS: AN EGYPTIAN MAGICAL BOOK, edited by F. Ll. Griffith, Herbert Thompson. Egyptian sorcerer's manual contains scores of spells: sex magic of various sorts, occult information, evoking visions, removing evil magic, etc. Transliteration faces translation. 207pp. 22994-7 Pa. $2.50

THE MALLEUS MALEFICARUM OF KRAMER AND SPRENGER, translated, edited by Montague Summers. Full text of most important witchhunter's "Bible," used by both Catholics and Protestants. Theory of witches, manifestations, remedies, etc. Indispensable to serious student. 278pp. $6^{5}/_{8}$ x 10. USO 22802-9 Pa. $3.95

LOST CONTINENTS, L. Sprague de Camp. Great science-fiction author, finest, fullest study: Atlantis, Lemuria, Mu, Hyperborea, etc. Lost Tribes, Irish in pre-Columbian America, root races; in history, literature, art, occultism. Necessary to everyone concerned with theme. 17 illustrations. 348pp. 22668-9 Pa. $3.50

THE COMPLETE BOOKS OF CHARLES FORT, Charles Fort. Book of the Damned, Lo!, Wild Talents, New Lands. Greatest compilation of data: celestial appearances, flying saucers, falls of frogs, strange disappearances, inexplicable data not recognized by science. Inexhaustible, painstakingly documented. Do not confuse with modern charlatanry. Introduction by Damon Knight. Total of 1126pp.
23094-5 Clothbd. $15.00

FADS AND FALLACIES IN THE NAME OF SCIENCE, Martin Gardner. Fair, witty appraisal of cranks and quacks of science: Atlantis, Lemuria, flat earth, Velikovsky, orgone energy, Bridey Murphy, medical fads, etc. 373pp. 20394-8 Pa. $3.00

HOAXES, Curtis D. MacDougall. Unbelievably rich account of great hoaxes: Locke's moon hoax, Shakespearean forgeries, Loch Ness monster, Disumbrationist school of art, dozens more; also psychology of hoaxing. 54 illustrations. 338pp. 20465-0 Pa. $3.50

THE GENTLE ART OF MAKING ENEMIES, James A.M. Whistler. Greatest wit of his day deflates Wilde, Ruskin, Swinburne; strikes back at inane critics, exhibitions. Highly readable classic of impressionist revolution by great painter. Introduction by Alfred Werner. 334pp. 21875-9 Pa. $4.00

THE BOOK OF TEA, Kakuzo Okakura. Minor classic of the Orient: entertaining, charming explanation, interpretation of traditional Japanese culture in terms of tea ceremony. Edited by E.F. Bleiler. Total of 94pp. 20070-1 Pa. $1.25